JOHN BUNYAN

JOHN BUNYAN
From the drawing by Robert White in the British Museum

John Bunyan

THE MAN AND HIS WORKS

BY

HENRI TALON

PROFESSOR OF ENGLISH LITERATURE
AT THE UNIVERSITY OF DIJON

ROCKLIFF
SALISBURY SQUARE
LONDON

FOR
PROFESSOR HENRI PEYRE

First published in Paris by EDITIÓNS " JE SERS " 1948
under the title *John Bunyan–l'homme et l'oeuvre*

English translation by Barbara Wall

*Printed in Great Britain by Richard Clay and Company, Ltd.,
Bungay, Suffolk*

Preface to the English Edition

THE warm welcome accorded by the English critics to the French edition of this book has given me the greatest pleasure. In the first place, it is to them that I owe its appearance in an English version; and secondly, since Bunyan's works are justly considered a specifically English domain which any foreigner enters at his peril, I was happy to find that my judges thought I had succeeded in understanding the works and the man who wrote them.

It is true that in France Bunyan is hardly more than a name. Even among students of English he is treated with a polite discretion which suggests that though they may have read him as a duty, they have not enjoyed him. The fact that I was addressing myself in the first place to this Continental public explains certain characteristics of the work. If I had written directly in English for British and American readers I should have stressed points differently and some of the appendices would have been unnecessary. However, I did not feel that I could, or should, change anything in its arrangement, for a book should present a considered and coherent whole, and the modification of a few details may alter its entire aspect.

As I have tried to show my fellow-countrymen, to understand Bunyan is to penetrate the spiritual significance of Puritanism, which has had a profound influence on the Anglo-Saxon mind. Its virile and impassioned faith, its Biblical literalism, its stern moral demands—all these sources of inspiration in the Puritan life of the seventeenth century are so foreign to most of our contemporaries that it is difficult for them to sympathise with the apostles and soldiers of this historic movement, or even to imagine the atmosphere of their day. Indeed, Professor Perry Miller goes so far as to assert that only a Puritan who is also a dramatic artist can present an adequate picture of Puritanism, and that Bunyan alone fulfils both conditions.

This representative function of Bunyan is so important that it has determined one of the features of my study: an attempt to put the man in his right setting and show that his genius was nourished by the feelings and the thought of a whole nation. This is the reason for the numerous comparisons made between the author of *The Pilgrim's Progress* and his brother-Puritans, known and unknown, and this is I think the justification for the detailed analysis of books like *The Life and Death of Mr. Badman* and *The Holy War*, which are of considerable historic value, and for the place given to the study of Bunyan's religious, moral and social thought as it appears after an examination of the whole of his work.

The nature of past studies of Bunyan accounts for another feature of this book. It would have been unpardonable to write a new *Life* when there are already so many! They are largely useless, only reproducing the material provided by John Brown in an excellent biography (re-edited, with the addition of some new facts, by Frank Mott Harrison in 1928). I have confined myself to a simple sketch of the tinker's material existence, noting only those points which are essential to an understanding of his inner life. The introduction contains nothing new; its only aim is to give a clear statement of the facts.

On the other hand, I have analysed Bunyan's spiritual life at great length. In this inner biography I have not slavishly followed the course of the confessions of *Grace Abounding* in the orthodox manner, yet I have been constantly advised by great prudence and deep respect. Not forgetting that the current of the autobiography, with its turbulence, its leaps forward and its sudden returns, is the very image of life, and that a knowledge of this work is essential to good understanding of Bunyan, I have tried to discover a profound orderliness in the apparent disorder, a fundamental harmony in the tumult. Sometimes a comparative study of his books has helped to bring certain features into relief; sometimes a comparison of the author with other Christian figures. Above all, I have tried to show that this man, unstable for so long, in the end became to some extent the architect of his own fate. By heroic devotion to a cause, by preaching, by books every one of which is an act, he gave his life a firm direction and a meaning that went beyond it. So the study of his writings is presented at first as a continuation of the study of the man.

But his works have literary merits which have not yet been fully

PREFACE

appreciated. English and American critics have analysed *The Pilgrim's Progress* with penetration, but perhaps they have not given to *Grace Abounding* all the attention it deserves. Sometimes the admiration lavished on Bunyan on the other side of the Channel and of the Atlantic is rather given out of habit : for the praises bestowed on books like *Mr. Badman* and *The Holy War* testify to the generosity of the readers rather than to their critical faculty; there is a neglect of the *literary* study of the controversial and theological works where, on the contrary, I have traced Bunyan's apprenticeship to the art of writing. Finally, in spite of a strong liking for the tinker, I have tried to remain impartial. My constant effort to read the author of *The Pilgrim's Progress* with a fresh mind has not led me to ignore the scholarly researches and the shrewd analyses that already exist, and I have always emphasised my debt towards them.

In the first edition I performed the pleasant duty of thanking all those who have been kind enough to interest themselves in my work; but I wish here to express my gratitude to Mrs. Bernard Wall, my translator, who has accomplished a difficult task with great talent, and with whom it has been a pleasure to collaborate.

H. T.

Faculté des Lettres, Dijon,
June 1950.

Contents

CONTENTS

Illustrations

ILLUSTRATIONS

The Outward Man [1]

Brief Sketch of an Existence

JOHN BUNYAN was born in the village of Elstow, near Bedford, in 1628.[2] His father was an artisan, and the Bunyans lived humbly —though they were probably not so poor as their son would have us believe. When, after a careful study of Bunyan's works, we re-read the opening paragraphs of *Grace Abounding*, in which he stresses the lowliness of his parentage, we wonder whether he is not merely giving way to the temptation of pride which so often assailed him. Such self-abasement betrays a secret self-satisfaction; for the more he exaggerates the meanness of his origins, the better he can exalt the exceptional character of his destiny. And Bunyan gives himself away when he writes: " Wherefore I have not here, as others, to boast of noble Blood, or of a high-born State according to the Flesh; though, all things considered, I magnify the heavenly Majesty, for that by this door he brought me into the world, to partake of the Grace and Life that is in Christ by the Gospel." [3]

In fact Bunyan belonged to a very old family, established in the county of Bedford since 1199.[4] His ancestors were probably of Norman origin. The name Bunyan—spelt in twenty different

---

[1] Bunyan, like St. Paul (cf. II Cor. IV, 16), frequently uses and contrasts the terms ' outward man ' and ' inward man '.

[2] The exact date is unknown. " John, the sonne of Thomas Bonnion, junr. baptized the 30th novemb. 1628."—that is all the information we are given by the Transcript Registers of the Archdeaconry, in the absence of the Elstow parish registers, which have been lost up to 1641. See F. M. Harrison, *John Bunyan, A Record of Recent Research*, manuscript in the Bedford Library, 1940, p. 2.

[3] *Grace Abounding*, par. 2.

[4] Concerning all this see John Brown, *John Bunyan, his Life, Times and Work* (London, 1885).

I

ways—is merely the English form of the old French word ' buignon ' (fritter). The Bunyans had been landowners, but had lost both their fortune and their social rank. In his will John's father describes himself as a ' braseyer ' and his grandfather as a ' pettie chapman '. But however humble these trades could be, they did not justify the Bunyans' classing themselves—whatever John may say—among " the meanest and most despised of all the Families in the Land ".[5] After all, they had owned their cottage and outhouses at Elstow for generations; and do the really poor ever make wills ?

Similarly we may doubt whether a child endowed with such a remarkable memory as John could have forgotten, shortly after leaving school, the rudimentary learning he had been given there.[6] Probably the schools of Bedford at that time were not good. The townspeople complained of the masters' neglect and even of their drunkenness and brutality.[7] But if he had lost the art of reading, how could the young John have passed such happy hours in the company of the adventure-stories to which he was so frivolously devoted ?[8] Yet we can agree, since he insists on it, that the development of his genius owed very little to books, and that what was most fruitful in his learning was given him by life in one of the most troubled periods of English history.

[5] *G. A.*, par. 2. There is no doubt, however, that the ' tinker ' was generally relegated to the lowest rung of the social ladder. Let us recall Sir Thomas Overbury's lively character-sketch : " Note that where the best ale is, there stands his music most upon crotchets. The companion of his travels is some foul, sunburnt quean. . . . He observes truly the statutes, and therefore, had rather steal than beg, in which he is irremovably constant, in spite of whips or imprisonment." P. 90 in *The Miscellaneous Works in Prose and Verse*, ed. by Edward F. Rimbault. (London, 1856.)
    Could one say that there was a difference between a ' tinker ' and a ' brazier ' ? In a village of sixty-nine houses such as Elstow the social status of the ' brazier ' could not have been very different from that of a ' tinker '.
[6] *G. A.*, par. 3.
[7] John Brown, *op. cit.*, chap. 3. If, as Frank Mott Harrison says in his manuscript work in the Bedford Library—*John Bunyan, A Record of Recent Research*, 1940—Bunyan was a pupil at Houghton Conquest, he could have had no better master. On this point see chap. 3 of John Brown's biography. Richard Baxter brings important evidence to bear on the provincial schools of the period, see *Autobiography* (ed. by J. M. Thomas, 1925), p. 4.
[8] *A Few Sighs*, vol. III, p. 711. " Give me a ballad, a news-book, George on horseback or Bevis of Southampton."

It would be outside the scope of this introduction to trace the development of the political and religious conflicts from Queen Elizabeth's reign up to 1628, when Bunyan was born.[9]   It is enough to remember that for over half a century numbers of Englishmen wanted to 'purify' the Established Church, which was Calvinist in its dogma but almost Catholic in its rites.   Persecuted by the power of the Monarchy, these Puritans believed political liberty to be essential to religious liberty.   " I shall call that my country," said John Winthrop, " where I may most glorify God." [10]   They did their utmost, then, to win political liberty, and the result is the story of a long struggle in which Bunyan was inevitably involved.

When the Civil War broke out in 1642 he was fourteen years old.   In 1644 he was called under arms by consequence of an order of Parliament demanding that " the county of Bedford, within fourteen days, shall send to the garrison of Newport Pagnell 225 able and armed men for soldiers ".[11]   John stayed in that town until March 22, under the command of Sir Samuel Luke.   On this date he could have been discharged, but he preferred to enlist in Lieutenant-Colonel Charles O'Hara's regiment, which was bound for Ireland. Whether his motive here was political conviction or simply a thirst for adventure, it seems apparent that young Bunyan liked the army. Indeed, we shall have to try to disentangle the hidden influence, diffused throughout his work, that his commanders and comrades-in-arms exercised over this thought.

He was finally freed on July 21, 1647, and arrived back in Elstow without having landed in Ireland or participated in a single armed combat throughout his military career.   Sir Charles Firth, historian of the Cromwellian army, has shown [12] that no important battle took

[9] But there is a brief outline in Appendix A.

[10] See J. R. Green, *A Short History of the English People* (London, 1889), p. 508.

[11] Cf. John Brown, *op. cit.*, p. 49. Bunyan's biographers have long disputed as to whether Bunyan served in the Parliamentary or the King's army. Macaulay upholds the former, J. A. Froude the latter (cf. bibliography); John Brown brought the weight of his arguments in favour of Macaulay. To-day the debate is over. In 1896 Ernest G. Atkinson discovered, among hitherto unexplored documents, two pages of the roll of the Newport garrison on which appears the name of John Bunyan.

[12] Cf. John Brown, *John Bunyan* (ed. by Frank Mott Harrison, London, 1928), *addenda*, chap. 3, pp. 46 and 59.

place near Newport between November 1644 and March 1645, and that there is no proof of Bunyan's presence at the siege of Leicester. Nor does Bunyan claim to have fought. In his autobiography he merely notes: "When I was a soldier, I, with others, were drawn out to go to such a place to besiege it; but when I was just ready to go, one of the Company desired to go in my Room: to which, when I had consented, he took my Place; and coming to the Siege, as he stood Sentinel, he was shot into the head with a Musket bullet and died." [13]

Once more a civilian, Bunyan led the life of an artisan in the relatively closed world of his village and the small neighbouring town [14] without taking part in political frictions. We find in his work the echo, rather than the story, of public strife. He lived his own drama withdrawn from the national one, yet linked to it by currents of thought and feeling that we will try to bring out.

In 1648 or 1649 he married. We know little about his wife—not even her name. The marriage is not entered in the Elstow registers and Bunyan tells us little about it. He probably looked on it as an accident of his ' outward ' existence. Yet we consider this union as a turning-point in his spiritual life, for it marks, as we shall see, the real beginning of his inner conflicts.

Few external signs betray the painful tension of a soul at war with itself: the neighbours see the impious man going to church,[15] they notice that he no longer swears,[16] that he starts reading the Bible with a kind of fury,[17] that he abandons gaming and dancing,[18] makes friends with poor and pious women [19] and then with the pastor John Gifford who, in 1653, baptises him in the Ouse, the river of Bedford.[20] Bunyan was now twenty-five.

In 1655 his co-religionists invited him to preach at their meetings, first privately, then in public. And this was another major event in his formation, since it was by action, as we shall see, that he was

---

[13] G. A., par. 13. [14] John Brown, op. cit. (1885), p. 97.
[15] G. A., par. 16. [16] G. A., par. 28.
[17] G. A., par. 29. [18] G. A., par. 35.
[19] G. A., par. 41.
[20] G. A., par. 253. There was so much discussion and disagreement on the subject of the methods of immersion that baptism usually took place in a river. Cf. E. Whiting : Studies in English Puritanism, 1660–1688 (London, 1931), p. 93.

released from the demons that had beset him from his childhood. The converted tinker burned to spread his faith. A soldier of Christ, as his friends Ebenezer Chandler and John Wilson so rightly called him,[21] he desired to fight heresy wherever it reared its head.

In 1656 he attacked the Quakers with a violence that testified to his fervour. If he struck hard it was because the whole Kingdom of God seemed to him to be threatened. The time for moderation and a more discriminating charity had not yet come. He had to have free play for his vigour; he had to slake his thirst for conversion; moreover, his persuasive force had to reach as far as possible, and thus he wrote down the points of his controversy with the great Quaker preacher, Edward Burrough.[22]

Each year henceforward saw the publication of a new book—*Sighs from Hell* in 1658, *The Doctrine of the Law and of Grace* in 1659. But the Puritans' rule came to an end in 1660, and Charles II ascended the throne of his fathers. Charles was intelligent and libertine and would probably have been willing to show toleration and stand by his promises made while in exile. But some of his followers, and, shortly afterwards, the Cavalier Parliament, composed of young men more episcopalian if not more royalist than the King, voted a whole series of repressive measures.

By the Act of Uniformity in 1662 a new ritual was imposed which stressed the Catholic character of the Church and forced 2,000 pastors to give up their livings. Then in 1663 Edward Hyde, Earl of Clarendon, put his relentless religious policy into practice. Clarendon was disliked by the King because of his strictness, and detested by many members of Parliament, and thus he could retain his position only by getting the support of the bishops.[23] He therefore consented to the tyrannical code of laws that bears his name. In 1664 the Conventicle Act forbade all religious meetings of more than five people. The Five-Mile Act in 1665 sent away from the towns

[21] *The Works of that Eminent Servant of Christ Mr. John Bunyan* (folio 1692). 'Epistle to the serious, judicious and impartial reader' by Eben. Chandler and John Wilson: "He behaved himself like Christ's soldier," A 2.

[22] Cf. *infra*, Part II, 'The Preacher and the Controversialist'.

[23] David Ogg, *England in the Reign of Charles II* (Oxford, 1934, 2 vols.), vol. I, p. 206.

the clerks who refused to take the oath. The Puritans again had to face hard times.

Bunyan was one of the first victims. In October 1660 the magistrates of Bedfordshire gave the order to reinstate the Anglican liturgy.[24] One month later, on November 10, the tinker was arrested while preaching in a hamlet. The judge, Wingate, who signed the warrant for arrest, must have been an enemy of Dissenters in general, if not of Bunyan in particular, since—the Act of Uniformity not having yet been passed—he had to fall back on a statute of Queen Elizabeth's reign.

As Bunyan had been warned by friends, he could have fled, but he refused to do so. When Wingate offered him his liberty on condition he made certain pledges,[25] he again refused. He let himself be thrown into prison rather than renounce what he believed to be his duty—the spreading of the word of Christ.[26]

[24] On all this see John Brown, *op. cit.* (1885), pp. 135 *et seq.*
[25] *A Relation of the Imprisonment of Mr. John Bunyan*, p. 408.
[26] Where was Bunyan imprisoned? For a long time it was thought that he was twelve years in the gaol on Bedford bridge. The thought of such a damp and narrow cell made the tinker's martyrdom more moving. A careful reading of the texts should have been enough to dispose of this legend. The anonymous friend who made a biographical sketch of Bunyan in 1700 says that when he visited him he found more than sixty Dissenters in the prison. To discredit further the traditional belief, there are the arguments of a local archæologist, James Wyatt: Bunyan, having violated the law within the county's, but not the city's, limit, was naturally thrown into the county gaol (in the centre of the town). In addition, a document in the archives shows that in 1671 the prison on the river was practically demolished by a flood and could take in no prisoners. Nevertheless in his masterly work John Brown holds that during his second imprisonment of 1675 Bunyan really was consigned to the ' den ' on the bridge. And since then all the biographers have reiterated, but with less art, what the scholarly pastor believed. (See John Brown, *op. cit.*, pp. 160 *et seq.*)
But the work of W. T. Whitley (' Bunyan's Imprisonments ', in *Transact. of the Bapt. Hist. Society*, vi, 1–24; 1918–1919), and above all of Miss Joyce Godber, the Bedfordshire County Archivist (' The Imprisonments of John Bunyan ', in *Transact. of the Congreg. Hist. Society*, xvi, No. 1, April, 1949), have thrown a new light on the problem. The question cannot be adequately dealt with in a footnote, and Miss Godber's article is so important that it calls for a close examination by all Bunyan specialists. Suffice it to say here that Bunyan was excommunicated some time before 1674, that he was probably not imprisoned before the end of 1676, the prison being again the county gaol at the corner of High Street and Silver Street.
Miss Godber's hypothesis as to the date of Bunyan's second imprisonment

Three months passed. In January 1661 Bunyan appeared before the Assizes. He was indicted for "devilishly and perniciously abstaining from coming to church to hear Divine service, for being a common upholder of several unlawful meetings and conventicles, to the great disturbance and distraction of the good subjects of this kingdom ".[27]

'To the disturbance and distraction of the good subjects of this kingdom'! Yet the constable detailed to arrest Bunyan had found only a small group of men and women, their Bibles in their hands. But, as Daniel Neal points out in his *History of the Puritans*,[28] it was not possible to hunt down non-conformists solely on account of their religion: the violation of Charles' promises at Breda would have been too flagrant. They always had to be accused of being a cause of disturbance to the State.

The chairman of the Sessions was a certain Sir John Keeling (whom Bunyan was to recall in his portrait of Lord Hate-Good in *The Pilgrim's Progress*). The tinker could find no grace before this hard man, whom, were it not for Clarendon's testimony, one would believe to be both stupid and ignorant.[29] At the moment when Bunyan began to set forth his objections to the Anglican ritual, a judge cried out: "Let him speak no further; he will do harm." But Keeling answered: "No, no, never fear him . . . he can do no harm; we know the Common Prayer Book hath been ever since the Apostles' time." [30] His partisan passion ran so high that it led him to utter such absurdities!

After a vain dispute Bunyan was condemned to three months'

---

rests both on an archival document and on tradition. The document is a cautionary bond presented to Bishop Barlow in favour of Bunyan, and dated 21st June, 1677, which can be seen in Aylesbury Museum. As for tradition, the general belief is that Bunyan's second imprisonment lasted only six months.

[27] *A Relation of the Imprisonment of Mr. John Bunyan*, p. 410.

[28] Daniel Neal, *The History of the Puritans, or Protestant Non-conformists, from the Reformation in 1517 to the Revolution in 1688* (London, 1837, 3 vols.), III, p. 83.

[29] Clarendon describes Keeling as " a person of eminent learning ". It was he who prepared the Act of Uniformity. See E. A. Knox, *John Bunyan in Relation to His Times* (London, 1928), p. 74.

[30] *A Relation of the Imprisonment of Mr. John Bunyan*, pp. 413-414.

imprisonment with the threat of banishment if, at the end of the three months, he refused to attend the parish church to hear Divine Service and refused to stop preaching. It was then that he proudly said: "If I were out of prison today I would preach the gospel again tomorrow, by the help of God." [31]

At the end of some twelve weeks the clerk of the peace, Cobb, went to visit the prisoner in the hope of obtaining his submission. He pointed out [32] that since Bunyan was a good and loyal subject of His Majesty, he must obey his laws. Did not St. Paul say that all authority came from God? Bunyan agreed, but said that Paul, while acknowledging the authorities of his time, was none the less frequently imprisoned. He said that there were two ways of being obedient to the law—actively, when conscience allowed, or passively and resigned to every kind of suffering when the first way was unacceptable. And Bunyan added, quoting Wycliffe, that he who discontinues preaching and hearing the word of God for fear of the excommunication of man, was already excommunicated of God. [33]

If Bunyan was determined to remain the master of his religious convictions, if he refused to buy liberty of the body at the price of slavery of the soul, he certainly did not deliberately seek out martyrdom. "I am not for running myself into sufferings," he wrote, [34] "but if godliness will expose me to them, the Lord God make me more godly still!" An amnesty was promised for the coronation of Charles II on April 23, 1661. Bunyan would have liked to benefit from this, but his hopes were frustrated. His second wife, Elizabeth, tried several times to intercede on her husband's behalf, and approached a sympathetic judge, Sir Matthew Hale. [35] But he could not take a decision by himself. His colleague, Twisden, refused to be melted

---

[31] *A Relation of the Imprisonment of Mr. John Bunyan*, p. 416.

[32] *Ibid.*, pp. 418–419.

[33] *Ibid.*, p. 420.

[34] *Seasonable Counsel*, vol. II, p. 694.

[35] Richard Baxter's eulogy of Sir Matthew is worth quoting here: "The last year of my abode at Acton, I had the happiness of a neighbour whom I cannot easily praise above his worth, which was Sir Matthew Hale . . . whom all the judges and lawyers of England admired for his skill in law and for his learning, and I highly valued for his sincerity, mortification, self-denial, humility, conscientiousness, and his close fidelity in friendship." Richard Baxter, *op. cit.*, p. 205.

by the courageous woman's entreaties. She implored him to free her husband. " My Lord, I have four small children that cannot help themselves, of which one is blind, and have nothing to live upon, but the charity of good people . . . it is because he is a Tinker, and a poor man, therefore he is despised and cannot have justice." And when Twisden said her husband preached the doctrine of the Devil, she said: " God hath owned him . . . and when the righteous Judge shall appear, it will be known that his doctrine is not the doctrine of the Devil! " [36]

Elizabeth Bunyan admits: " Though I was somewhat timorous at my first entrance into the chamber, yet before I went out I could not but break forth into tears, not so much because [the judges] were so hard-hearted against me and my husband, but to think what a sad account such poor creatures will have to give at the coming of the Lord." [37]

Some of Bunyan's admirers, rightly moved by his sufferings,[38] drew a picture of his captivity so highly coloured by their imaginations that a reaction set in. J. A. Froude, for example, in a book more brilliant than accurate,[39] contrived to make the tinker's trials appear slight. But Bunyan did suffer; in his body and in his heart. If he never complained, it was because of his spiritual strength and because God showered consolations upon him in his distress.[40] In the seventeenth century prisons were foul.[41] Bedford gaol—and it was not the worst—had no fireplaces and the prisoners slept on straw. Epidemics of deadly fever broke out.

At the beginning, between the Autumn Assizes of 1661 and the Spring Assizes of 1662, a friendly gaoler granted Bunyan certain liberties.[42] But his enemies raised a protest, the gaoler was given a warning, and Bunyan knew imprisonment at its strictest up to 1668. This period was followed by a less rigorous régime up to 1672.

[36] *A Relation of the Imprisonment of Mr. John Bunyan*, pp. 426–427.
[37] *Ibid.*, p. 427.
[38] For example, William Parry in his little work on the *Religious Tests* (1790).
[39] J. A. Froude, *John Bunyan* (London, 1880), pp. 68 *et seq.*
[40] *G. A.*, par. 339.
[41] Cf. John Brown, *op. cit.*, p. 166. See also John Howard, *State of the Prisons in England and Wales* (Everyman ed.), p. 198.
[42] *A Relation of the Imprisonment of Mr. John Bunyan*, p. 428.

In order to support his dependants, Bunyan spent his time making
" many hundred grosse of long-tagged thread laces ". [43]   During his
leisure hours he instructed his fellow-prisoners, gave counsel to people
who came to him for advice,[44] and managed, though far from the
faithful of his church, to maintain a spiritual authority over them.
And he was sometimes able to preach long sermons, such as the *Holy
City*,[45] which was spoken and then written down as the result of a divine
illumination.   " . . . *geschrieben nach göttlicher Erleuchtung* . . ."
Boehme's phrase exactly describes what Bunyan experienced on the
day when he saw the jasper light of the Celestial City!

Other works took the inspired tinker's message beyond the prison
walls—a treatise on prayer, *I will Pray with the Spirit*;   a manual on
morals, *Christian Behaviour*;   some poems ; [46] and above all a spiritual
autobiography, *Grace Abounding*.

In 1666, if we are to believe his first biographer, Bunyan was
released for a while " by the intercession of some in trust and power ".[47]
Of these influential friends we know nothing, but their intervention
did not bring Bunyan much respite, for when free he again preached,
and again he was imprisoned—this time until 1672.

[43] " Nor did he, while he was in prison, spend his time in a supine and careless manner, or eat the bread of idleness, for there I have been witness that his
own hands have ministered to his and to his family's necessities, by making
many hundred grosse of long-tagged thread laces." P. 26 in *A New and
Authentic Account of the Life and Death of Mr. John Bunyan, Late Minister
of the Gospel at Bedford, Written by a Friend to the Cause of True
Religion* (London, printed for Alex. Hogg at the King's Arms, Paternoster
Row).

[44] Such as the woman about whom he writes in *The Life and Death of Mr.
Badman* (vol. III, p. 610), who confesses to having robbed her employer
and asks how she can make amends.

[45] Vol. III, p. 397.   'The Epistle to four sorts of readers.'   " I felt
myself, it being my turn to speak, so empty, spiritless and barren . . . but
at last . . . I cast mine eye upon the 11th verse of the one and twentieth
chapter of this prophecy : upon which, when I had considered a while, methought I perceived something of that jasper in whose light you there find
this holy city is said to come and descend; wherefore having got in my eye
some dim glimmerings thereof and finding also in my heart a desire to see
farther thereinto, I with a few groans did carry my meditations to the Lord
Jesus for a blessing which he did forthwith grant."

[46] *Profitable Meditations* (1661), *Prison Meditations* (1665), *Ebal and Gerizim*
(1665), *One Thing is Needful* (1665).

[47] Ed. Offor, vol. I, p. 64.

These last six years do not seem to have been so spiritually fruitful. Whereas between 1658 and 1666 he had published nine books, between 1666 and 1672 he wrote only two, his *Confession of Faith* and his *A Defence of the Doctrine of Justification by Faith.*

In March 1672, before the appearance of this latter book, Charles II had signed his Declaration of Indulgence, which encouraged Bunyan and one or two other prisoners of Bedford to beg for royal mercy. This was officially granted on September 13, but it is probable that Bunyan had been set free in May, as it was in that month that he was licensed as a preacher. Ever since 1668, as the mention of his name in church registers shows,[48] he had occasionally been allowed to assist at the meetings of his co-religionists. In all probability he had been allowed yet greater liberty in 1671, for on January 21, 1672, his ' brethren ', having solemnly besought God to guide their choice, elected him their pastor.[49]

So it was with heightened authority that Bunyan again embarked on his fight as a soldier of Christ, going to preach in neighbouring towns and even as far as Reading and London. According to his friend Charles Doe,[50] his success was so great that the London public, warned of his coming the day before, flocked to the meeting-hall, and about 1,200 people were there—and this at seven o'clock in the morning of a working winter day. On Sundays there were 3,000 people hurrying to hear the man who was called derisively by his enemies ' Bishop Bunyan '.

But their jealousy was not always confined to such harmless banter. Behind his back they accused our author of being " a witch, a Jesuit, a highwayman ",[51] of having mistresses, bastards, and even two wives at the same time!

In 1674 [52] he narrowly escaped being victimised by the gossip of a clergyman and a lawyer. The former hinted that Bunyan had a young village girl, Agnes Beaumont, as his mistress; the latter, with the spite of a rejected suitor, announced that this girl had poisoned

[48] Cf. *The Church-Book of Bunyan Meeting* (fac-simile, 1928), and John Brown, *op. cit.*, p. 168.

[49] *The Church-Book of Bunyan Meeting*, ff. 50–51.

[50] *The Struggler*, ed. Offor, vol. III, p. 766.

[51] *G. A.*, par. 307.

[52] Cf. *The Narrative of the Persecution of Agnes Beaumont in 1674* (ed. G. B. Harrison, 1929), and John Brown, *op. cit.*, pp. 242–243.

her father, John Beaumont. It is true that the facts lent themselves to a slanderous interpretation. Agnes, against her father's wishes, belonged to the Baptist chapel of a neighbouring village. One day in February the friend who was supposed to take her to her meeting failed to turn up. Before she had got over her disappointment, the preacher himself, John Bunyan, appeared on the road. Agnes's brother entreated him to take Agnes up behind him on his horse. Bunyan did not want to do this, as he knew that John Beaumont disapproved of him; however, he finally consented. John Beaumont happened to see them as they started off, and was so angry that on her return he refused his daughter entry into the house unless she promised to leave the Baptist chapel. Then, two days after Agnes's re-admission to her father's house, the old man died. Public malice immediately raised a scandal; but fortunately an official investigation was able to establish that John Beaumont's death, though sudden, was none the less natural.

But there were many further trials in store for Bunyan. In 1673 Charles was forced by the House of Commons to repeal his Declaration of Indulgence: Parliament did not allow ecclesiastical laws to be abolished without its consent, nor, as Macaulay says,[53] " an act so liberal [to be] done in a manner so despotic ". Even the Puritan dissenters who benefited by the royal clemency refused an ' indulgence ' by which the Catholics, as well as themselves, profited. To the Catholics the Test Act struck a sharp blow: not only did every civil or military servant of the State have to take the oath of allegiance, but also declare himself against the doctrine of transubstantiation and receive the sacraments according to the Anglican rite.[54]

Charles acquiesced. Too intelligent not to admit the failure of his policy favouring the Catholics, he decided to win back the support of a Parliament still dominated by royalists of the High Church Party. He appealed to the Earl of Danby, who hated equally the Protestant non-conformists and the papists, and he revived more or less Clarendon's policy. Religious persecution was resumed. The licences hitherto granted to Puritan or Quaker preachers were withdrawn. Bunyan was arrested again on March 4, 1675. He spent

[53] Macaulay, *op. cit.*, vol. I, p. 220.
[54] On all this see, for example, *Cambridge Modern History*, ' The Policy of Charles II and James II (1667–1687),' vol. I, pp. 198 *et seq.*

another six months in prison, during which he began *The Pilgrim's Progress*.[55]

With this new book his notoriety became a sort of glory. In ten years, from 1678 until his death in 1688, twelve editions of it were published. The work was as popular in Scotland, Ireland and the American colonies as in England itself. Before the second part of *The Pilgrim's Progress* appeared in 1684, Bunyan had had the happiness of seeing his book translated into French and Dutch.[56]

His last—extremely fertile—years were marked by several major publications: *The Life and Death of Mr. Badman* in 1680, *The Holy War* in 1682, the second part of the *Pilgrim* in 1684, not to mention some fourteen other books. ' Bishop Bunyan ' was now a man to be reckoned with by the powers-that-be; and when, in 1687, James II tried to rally the non-conformists to a policy condemned by the Anglicans, he offered Bunyan "a place of public trust".[57] But Bunyan was not taken in by this gesture of royal favour. According to his biographer of 1692,[58] he guessed that the sudden toleration of a monarch who was, in fact, more intolerant than any other, had but one purpose—to serve the Catholics. He believed the Puritans would reap but one advantage from this royal mercy—the one that Polyphemus wanted to bestow on Ulysses: the privilege of being eaten last. He even refused to receive James' emissary.

This is the explanation given by his biographer and friend; but Bunyan's motives were subtler and suppler than his contemporary imagined. If he was not prepared to uphold the royal policy personally, he asked no better than to obtain every possible indirect benefit from it. Thus, while refusing a post for himself, he allowed six or seven members of his church to sit on the Bedford Municipal Council reorganised by James II.[59]

Even if Bunyan had accepted James' offer he would not have benefited by it for long. In August 1688 he offered to go to Reading

[55] The new dates suggested by Miss Godber for Bunyan's second imprisonment (see her article in *Transact. of the Congreg. Hist. Society*, XVI, No. 1, April, 1949) may call for a new hypothesis as to the period of the composition of *The Pilgrim's Progress*. (See Appendix B.)

[56] Cf. John Brown, *op. cit.*, Appendix, pp. 483–484.

[57] Ed. Offor, vol. I, p. 63.

[58] *Ibid.*

[59] John Brown, *op. cit.*, p. 367.

to make the peace between a father and son. His mission was successful, but on the way home he covered about forty miles on horseback [60] in pouring rain. He arrived soaked through at the London house of his friend, John Strudwick. On Sunday, August 19, he preached a sermon, the text of which has been preserved for us by a listener; but on the following Tuesday he had to take to his bed. Although he was only sixty, Bunyan was worn out by a life of work and suffering. A malignant fever took hold of him which he endured courageously. " I desire nothing more," he said, " than to be dissolved and to be with Christ." [61] His wish was granted, and on August 31 he died.[62] He was buried in the Bunhill Fields cemetery, called by Southey " the *campo santo* of dissenters ".

Thus one last act of love and charity put an end to a life almost entirely devoted to the good of others. For, if this sketch of an existence seen from the outside does not give a true impression of the greatness of Bunyan's soul and the strength of his genius, at least it may have revealed a little of that love for God and men which gave his life its purpose and direction.

[60] To take the coach was considered, in the 17th century, as a ' symptom of an effeminate nature ' (cf. David Ogg, *op. cit.*, vol. I, 102). The virile Bunyan always seems to have travelled on foot or on horseback.

[61] Ed. Offor, vol. I, p. 64. ". . . and expressed himself as if he desired nothing more than to be dissolved, and to be with Christ, in that case esteeming death as gain, and life only a tedious delaying of felicity expected."

[62] *The Church-Book of Bunyan Meeting*, f. 73.

PART I

THE INWARD MAN

. . . The inward man is renewed day by day.

1

The Biographical Value of
Grace Abounding

OUR principal source of information concerning Bunyan's spiritual life is his autobiography. It is therefore important to discover how much faith we can put in the author's self-revelation. Must we, like many of his admirers, believe unquestioningly all that he writes, or may we, like others,[1] read *Grace Abounding* with certain reservations?

To begin with we must define the character of the book. The *Confessions* of St. Augustine are often mentioned in connection with Bunyan's autobiography, but the comparison is usually left vague, and is therefore valueless, whereas if it were pushed further it might be fruitful. In fact it is by comparing the two books that we see that *Grace Abounding*—though in lower relief—has that double character that is so apparent in Augustine's work. The two books are, in the first place, the confession of past sins and the painful narration of a spiritual struggle: in the second place they tell the story of the love

[1] Without even mentioning the very first biographers and editors who were absolutely convinced of the authenticity of Bunyan's story, we must note that nearly all the critics of the 19th and 20th centuries believed in Bunyan's sincerity. The most eminent Bunyan specialists—John Brown and Frank Mott Harrison—accept his confessions without reserve. An American commentator to whom we are indebted for an edition of the text writes : " We are above all impressed by Bunyan's sincerity." (Edward Chauncey Baldwin, Ginn and Co., Boston, 1909.) And the most recent biographer, Mr. P. Willcocks, holds that Bunyan takes a place, by reason of his sincerity, " among the first of the moderns ". (*Bunyan Calling*, London, 1943, p. 125.) But this is not the opinion of the American psychologist James Bissett Pratt : " One cannot read an account of a conversion of the Bunyan–Brainerd type without seeing that its whole course runs along conventional lines predetermined by an unquestioned and accepted theology." (*The Religious Consciousness*, New York, 1921, p. 149.) Mr. York Tindall, whose thesis we shall examine, is equally sceptical.

of God for the author.[2] " For love of Thy love I do it; reviewing my most wicked ways in the very bitterness of my remembrance, that Thou mayest grow sweet unto me," [3] writes Augustine; and Bunyan: " It is something a Relation of the Work of God upon my own soul." [4] From this come their great fervour and tone of religious exaltation. Indeed, if these two works are not one long prayer, they often have the accents of prayer, the ardour of a dialogue with God, and the tremor of love.   Augustine and Bunyan wish to tell mankind—like David in a psalm that Bunyan loved—what Our Lord has worked on their souls.[5] " To whom tell I this? " asks St. Augustine; " not to Thee, my God; but before Thee to mine own kind." [6] And Bunyan in his turn says: " Thou shalt remember all the way which the Lord thy God led thee. . . . Wherefore this I have endeavoured to do; and not only so, but to publish it also; that if God will, others may be put in remembrance of what he hath done for their souls, by reading his Work upon me." [7]

Now, is this frame of mind conducive to accurate self-observation? Does not such living fervour vitiate the truthfulness of the story? It is so easy to twist the truth!   There is no need to tamper with the facts—they can be shaded or picked out by the tone of the confession: the tone can modulate their colour and alter their spirit.   And again, are we ever capable of recapturing our past in its immediate truth, when it was the present, holding only the seeds of the future?   Will not Bunyan shut his eyes to the thousand potentialities of the past and attribute to events an inevitableness that they never in fact had? Instead of reconstructing for us the fluctuating uncertainty of life, will he not, by the very order of his narrative, introduce into it a note of fatalism?

[2] Cf. Jean Guitton, *Le temps et l'éternité chez Plotin et Saint Augustin* (Paris, 1933), p. 26.

[3] " *Amore amoris tui facio istud, recolens vias meas nequissimas in amaritudine recogitationis meae ut tu dulcescas mihi.*" *Confessions*, II, chap. 1, 1.

[4] *Grace Abounding*, preface, p. 294. A translation of the *Confessions* appeared in 1660, but it is unlikely that Bunyan was able to read it. His model was rather St. Paul.

[5] Cf. *Doctrine of the Law and Grace*, I, p. 548.

[6] " *Cui narro haec?   Neque enim tibi, Deus meus : sed apud te narro haec generi meo, generi humano.*" *Confessions*, II, chap. 3, 5.

[7] *G. A.*, preface, p. 294.

Let us take an example. God, writes Bunyan in *Grace Abounding*,[8] did not utterly leave him, but followed him still—even in his worst moments of confusion. God miraculously snatched him from death several times: the day he fell into the sea, the day he fell out of a boat into the Bedford river, the time he put his fingers into the mouth of the adder he had just stunned, and finally when one of his comrades-in-arms took his place at the siege of a town and was killed.

Bunyan's devout admirers never fail to be impressed by these manifestations of divine favour, and believe that these miracles deepened his religious sentiment.[9] We, however, think otherwise. We do not consider that, at the time, Bunyan attributed to these incidents the providential significance that he gave them later. Paragraphs 12 and 13 of *Grace Abounding* are not to be found in the first edition of the work. They were added later [10] during one of those meditations on the past that were for Bunyan a spiritual exercise and a source of joy. But would he have omitted to mention these signal marks of grace if he had thought of them as such when they happened? No; but later, when convinced that one of the ' elect ' would not die before his conversion, he recalled these banal accidents

[8] Pars. 12 and 13.

[9] Cf. Edmund Venables : " This undercurrent of religious feeling was deepened by providential escapes." *Life of John Bunyan* (London, 1888), p. 24. See also the intro. to his ed. of the *Pilgrim* (1896), p. ix.

[10] Pars. 12 and 13 are given in the 3rd ed., of which the Pierpont Morgan Library possesses the only known copy. This 3rd ed. is not dated but is listed in the official catalogue of 1679 (Trinity Term) under the heading ' reprinted '. What does this mean? Does it refer to a new ed. or only to a new impression of the 2nd ed. of which there exists no known copy and of which we do not know even the date, since the official Catalogue of the books does not begin before 1668 ? One piece of exact data : pars. 310–317 are not to be found in the copy of the 3rd ed., the American library informs me, thereby clarifying a rather confused article by Frank Mott Harrison (' Notes on the early editions of *Grace Abounding* ', *The Baptist Quarterly*, 1943, vol. XI). As these paragraphs allude to incidents in 1674 (the affair of Agnes Beaumont, cf. *supra*, p. 11) one can conclude by their absence from the 1679 ed. that this is merely a re-impression of the second. This is also the opinion of F. M. Harrison, article quoted p. 161.

The 2nd ed. was published between 1666 (1st ed.) and 1668 (when the Catalogue of books started). Pars. 12–13 (and certain others that we will examine later, pars. 29, 34, 35, 115 : see *infra*, p. 25 footnote) can have been added one or two years after the compilation of the first text.

of his adolescence and read a hidden meaning into them. This is made plainer when we look at another of his books in which, behind the didactic generalisations of the pastor, we find the personal confession of the tinker, but enriched by a theological commentary [11] which gives meaning to these additions in *Grace Abounding*. " How many deaths have some been delivered from and saved out of before conversion," he writes. " Some have fallen into rivers, some into wells, some into the sea, some into the hands of men; yea they have been justly arraigned and condemned, as the thief upon the cross, but must not die before they have been converted." [12]

The example we chose above illustrates another aspect of the same risk of inaccuracy on the author's part. His story reflects religious convictions, and takes place within the framework of ideas and doctrines, which the author had not yet embraced when he was actually living the moments he describes. Metaphysics falsify psychology. *A priori* one might even suspect that the Calvinist Bunyan, believing that his destiny was predetermined, was sometimes inclined to bind together the facts of his existence with a logic seldom experienced in real life. Since God had chosen him for a high mission—" designed me for better things " [13]—must He not have arranged the smallest details of this human life to His eternal designs? Should not an ' accident ' be excluded from such a life which can only be ruled by " an awful necessity " ?

We are now at the heart of this psychological problem, and a new difficulty presents itself.

Can we believe Bunyan when he describes himself as the greatest of sinners, the leader of a vicious band of young men, experiencing a sort of demoniacal joy in evil-doing ? " It was my delight to be taken captive by the Devil." [14] There are some who do. Others, such as Macaulay or J. A. Froude, [15] are sceptical about Bunyan's

[11] See for example : " As we may be said to be saved in the purpose of God before the foundation of the world, so we may be said to be saved before we are converted, or called to Christ." *Saved by Grace*, 1675, vol. I, p. 338.

[12] *Saved by Grace*, p. 338.

[13] *G. A.*, par. 45. See too *The Doctrine of the Law and Grace Unfolded*, I, p. 549 : " I have set thee down on purpose, for I have something more than ordinary for thee to do." [14] *G. A.*, par. 4.

[15] T. B. Macaulay, essay on Bunyan (1831) in *Essays* (Nelson, 1925). J. A. Froude, *op. cit.*, p. 63.

CHRISTIAN AND EVANGELIST

This cut was introduced after the Tenth Edition. From the Thirteenth Edition of 1692

THE PILGRIMS ARE BORNE UP TO THE HOLY CITY

Eighth Edition 1682

Frontispiece from the Palmer Nash copy of the First Edition. This portrait is found in no other edition earlier than the Third, 1679

CHRISTIAN MET BY LIONS ON THE WAY TO PALAC
BEAUTIFUL

Engraving by Sturt, from the 1743 edition

confessions and believe him to have been a highly virtuous young man. Each person judges according to his temperament and his particular conception of evil. An impartial critic could not be satisfied with such personal judgments. He knows that there is no common measure for sins and that the gravity of the fault is relative to the sensibility of the person. The intensity of remorse varies according to the quality of the man and the fervour of his soul. Bunyan, searching for an impossible perfection, was always dissatisfied. " I know not anything that ever I did in my life," he wrote, " but it had a flaw, or wrinkle, or spot, or some such thing in it. Mine eyes have seen vileness in the best of my doings." [16] There are torments undreamed of by those of common clay. And has it not been said that everyone receives the share of tragedy he deserves ?

For Bunyan there was no such thing as a little sin. " There is no little sin." [17] Because the least fault offends against God's majesty and every backward step of a soul striving towards good marks the victory of Satan over Jesus. Most people believe, with Mr. Badman, that swearing, far from being serious, is a sign of virility,[18] but Bunyan saw it as an affront to the Creator,[19] and he knew that the Bible classes this sin with murder and adultery.[20]

If sin is relative to man's sensibility, it is also, obviously, relative to his theology. If man is totally corrupt,[21] if the newly-born child is already soiled, then a schoolboy's prank assumes the magnitude of an angel's sin.[22] Augustine judged his childhood thus: " *Tantillus puer et tantus peccator !* " [23] And it was the same with Bunyan. One observes oneself to be a sinner in proportion as one believes oneself to be a sinner—as is so well illustrated by paragraph 77 of

[16] *The Work of Jesus Christ as an Advocate*, vol. I, p. 175.
[17] *The Jerusalem Sinner Saved*, vol. I, p. 94.
[18] *The Life and Death of Mr. Badman*, III, 601, 602.
[19] *Ibid.*
[20] *Ibid.*
[21] Following the Bible, Luther reiterates : " For the law saith thou art a corrupt tree (Matt. vii, 17), thou canst not bring forth good fruit." *A Commentary on St. Paul's Epistle to the Galatians* (trans. Erasmus Middleton, ed. by John Prince Fellowes, London, 1940).
[22] See the penetrating analysis of the development of the consciousness of sin in St. Augustine in Jean Guitton's thesis, *Le temps et l'éternité chez Plotin et Saint Augustin* (Paris, 1933), pp. 238 *et seq.*
[23] *Confessions*, I, xii, 19.

Grace Abounding. From the day that Bunyan started visiting the pastor John Gifford and his friends, where he became familiar with Puritan theology, he discovered all his faults.[24] The state of soul was born in him in which—according to another Puritan, William Perkins—one feels the need to " suspect oneself of unknown sins ". [25] Bunyan was a reader of Luther, and believed himself to be a sinner rotten to the core, like a decayed tree.   It was God who revealed this to him.   Without divine grace the fleshly man would not even know his sinfulness.   Thus the greater the grace, the deeper the sense of sin and the more desperate the ' peccavi '.[26]   Whence the confessions of which St. Paul and Luther give us examples: " I am the chief of sinners." [27]

Bunyan, then, followed in a literary and religious tradition, and this again compromises the sincerity of his autobiographical evidence. Mr. York Tindall has shown, in a remarkable thesis,[28] that *Grace Abounding* resembles many other confessions ascribed to these ' mechanic ' preachers—so numerous in England under the Stuarts and during Cromwell's government.   But, by his constant irony, the American professor insinuates that Bunyan, loyal to this tradition, was a clever writer rather than a sincere autobiographer.   " The delicate surgery of soul for which Bunyan is known was the monotonous exercise of his contemporaries; but what the Spirit was content to inspire, it was unwilling to preserve, and of these almost identical autobiographies *Grace Abounding* alone has survived." [29]   And he

[24] " But he [Mr. Gifford] invited me to his house where I should hear him confer with others about the dealings of God with their souls, from all which I still received more conviction, and from that time began to see something of the vanity and inward wretchedness of my wicked heart, for as yet I knew no great matter therein."   Par. 77.

[25] William Perkins, *Works* (3 vols., London, 1616–1618), I, 364.   Quoted by M. Knappen, *op. cit.*, p. 344.

[26] Cf. Luther.   " *Deus non facit salvos ficte peccatores.*"   Quoted by Lucien Febvre, *Un destin, Martin Luther* (Paris, 1928), p. 158.   And especially : " All our effort should tend to exalt, to aggravate our faults," quoted by Imbart de la Tour, ' Luther ' in the *Revue des Deux Mondes*, Sept. 15, 1912.

[27] St. Paul, I Timothy, I, 16.   Compare Cromwell's letter to Madame Saint John in 1638 : " Oh, I lived in darkness and hated light.   I was the chief of sinners."

[28] William York Tindall, *John Bunyan, Mechanick Preacher* (Columbia Univ. Press, 1934), chap. 2.

[29] W. York Tindall, *op. cit.*, p. 22.

establishes curious similarities with Arise Evans, the tailor,[30] John
Crook, Quaker of Bedfordshire,[31] or Anna Trapnel, who belonged
to a London church well known to Bunyan.[32] "The details of Bunyan's conversion", he goes on with the same amused scepticism,
" could be supplied by a diligent anthologist from the autobiographies
of other preachers. Even the words ' My grace is sufficient for
thee ' which the Lord Jesus condescended to direct through the tiles to
the ears of John Bunyan and by which the salvation of that saint
was finally consummated, were the instrument of the orthodox re-
generation." [33]

In our opinion Mr. York Tindall's ' diligent anthologist' would
not achieve the triumph he anticipates. To begin with, caught in
the toils of his task, he would overlook the fact that Bunyan could not
possibly have been familiar with the hundreds of ' tracts' since discovered by librarians. In his excellent chapter on ' The State of
England in 1685 ', Macaulay draws attention to the scarcity of books.
" An esquire ", he writes, " passed among his neighbours for a great
scholar, if *Hudibras* and *Baker's Chronicle*, *Tarlton's Jests* and the

[30] Arise Evans, *An Eccho to the Voice from Heaven or a Narration of the Life
and Manner of the Special Calling and Visions of Arise Evans* (1652).

[31] John Crook, *A Short History of the Life of John Crook, Containing some
of his Spiritual Travels and Breathings after God, in his Young and Tender
Years : Also an Account of Various Temptations Wherewith he was Exercised,
and the Means by which he Came to the Knowledge of the Truth* (London,
1706), published posthumously.

[32] Anna Trapnel, *A Legacy for Saints ; Being Several Experiences of the
Dealings of God With Anna Trapnel, in, and After her Conversion (written
Some Years since with her own hand)* (London, 1654). *The Cry of a Stone*
(1654).

Concerning all the ' mechanick' and other prophets, consult : W. T.
Whitley, *A History of British Baptists* (2nd ed. revised 1932). A very clear
work.

C. E. Whiting, *Studies in English Puritanism from the Restoration to the
Revolution (1660–1688)* (London, 1931), where there are some excellent
accounts of the Baptists and the ' minor sects '.

And always Robert Barclay, *The Inner Life of the Religious Societies of the
Commonwealth* (3rd. ed. 1879).

[33] York Tindall, *op. cit.*, pp. 33–34. For our part we recommend for whoever is interested in this question a study in the *Christian Directory* by Richard
Baxter. The author points out some of the characteristics of the religious
life of the Puritan ' enthusiasts '. We will quote them in footnotes as occasion
arises.

Seven Champions of Christendom lay in his hall window." [34]   A contemporary who visited Bunyan in prison saw only two books there—the Bible and John Foxe's *Book of Martyrs*; [35] and the archæologist Thomas Hearne writes in his private journal: " I heard Mr. Bagford, some time before he died, say that he walked once into the country on purpose to see the study of John Bunyan . . . but his study consisted only of a Bible and a parcel of books, the *Pilgrim's Progress* chiefly, written by himself, all lying on a shelf." [36]

We must not, however, jump to the conclusion that Bunyan was an isolated genius who owed nothing to anyone.   Such simple admiration as that is no longer possible since the works of James Blanton Wharey, [37] Harold Golder [38] and York Tindall.   And even the quotations and allusions in Bunyan's own work [39] should have checked the growth of a belief in his intellectual virginity.   Bunyan had not read only the Bible and John Foxe: like many of his contemporaries, he had inherited a rich popular culture acquired chiefly by oral tradition, and he remembered perhaps the remarks of his fellow-soldiers, of an army chaplain, of all his lay and clerical friends.

[34] T. B. Macaulay, *op. cit.* (ed. 1852), vol. I, chap. 3, especially pp. 391-392.

[35] *A New and Authentic Account of the Life and Death of Mr. John Bunyan, Written by a Friend to the Cause of True Religion* (ed. annotated by W. Mason), p. 27.

[36] John Brown, *op. cit.*, p. 372.

[37] James Blanton Wharey, *A Study of the Sources of Bunyan's Allegories—with Special Reference to Deguileville's Pilgrimage of Man* (Baltimore, 1904).

[38] Harold Golder : see in the bibliography the list of his various articles.

[39] Mr. York Tindall, in his thesis which we consider the most important contribution to Bunyan studies since John Brown, has drawn up a list of the names quoted by our author : " The spiritual integrity of his sixty works could not be injured, however, by the casual mention of a dozen men, John Foxe, Luther, Tindall, Campion, Ainsworth, Owen, Baxter, Jessey, Dent, Bayly, Samuel Clarke, and the author of *Francis Spira*; nor even by more casual references, apparently at second hand, to Machiavelli, Origen, Cranmer and the Koran ; nor by the detestable names of his controversial enemies . . . That Bunyan was also acquainted with Hobbes's *Leviathan* is apparent from a hitherto unnoticed allusion to that book etc." *Op. cit.*, p. 193.   Let us point out that the English author of *Francis Spira* is Nath. Bacon, *A Relation of the Fearful Estate of Francis Spira in the Year 1548, Compiled by Nath. Bacon esq.* (London, 1653).   The allusion to the *Leviathan* is in *Justification by Faith*, II, 319.   Edward Fowler pointed it out in *Dirt Wip't Off* (1672), p. 70.

Moreover, like many men of his time, he was stamped with the theology then in vogue.

With this in view, we must again turn our attention to the significance of the ' additions ' made in the third edition of *Grace Abounding*. The enrichment of the text is so peculiarly characteristic that it is strange that no one should have examined its psychological import.[40]

We have already shown that paragraphs 12 and 13 call for reservations—not as to Bunyan's sincerity but as to the evidential value of the events he relates. But we are equally surprised that, in the first edition, he should have omitted to mention the delight he derived from ringing the bells at Elstow, and the morbid fears that tortured him if he gave way to this innocent pleasure.[41] We are surprised, too, that in 1666 he refrained from giving us an account of his meeting with the ' Ranters ' whose Antinomianism so dangerously titivated all that was riotous and sensual in him.[42] And finally we are surprised that he left it so late to pay Luther the debt of gratitude which was apparently very great.[43]

All these additional touches were probably due to contemporary influences—but these influences, in our opinion, did not play quite the part that Mr. York Tindall seems to think, or at any rate hints at.

We do not for a moment doubt the accuracy of the facts themselves. We have no difficulty whatever in believing that Bunyan repented of his frivolity in going to ring the bells for service, or in simply watching the ringers—the Puritans had protested [44] against the

[40] Cf. *supra*, p. 19.   [41] *G.A.*, pars. 33–34.
[42] *G.A.*, pars. 43–45.   [43] *G.A.*, pars. 129–131.
[44] Daniel Neal, *op. cit.*, II, 180–181, records that from 1571 the pastors of Northampton forbade the ' excessive ringing of bells ' on Sundays. We emphasise the omission of pars. 33–34 (' bell-ringing ') because it seems to us the most significant as regards the value of Bunyan's own evidence. On the other hand it seems quite natural that our author should have at first omitted to mention his reading of the *Commentary on the Epistle to the Galatians*; for it is only by meditating for a long time on the past that he can measure the deep influence of this book on his spiritual development.

As for the pars. on the English Antinomians, or ' Ranters ', we are tempted to believe that Bunyan inserted them either in answer to accusations of Antinomianism levelled against himself, or else to prove that the doctrine of election by grace does not lead the faithful into anarchy. In recalling this incident of his youth, he clearly indicated that he had seen the danger and had been able to escape it.

It is also to answer accusations (the Beaumont affair, 1674, cf. pp. 11–12,

excess of chimes for so long that poor John could not fail to see sin in them.   But it is none the less tenable that his remorse as a young man was not so dramatic as he imagined thirteen years later.   We believe that his retrospective vision was coloured by the fashion of the day, by the accounts everyone was writing of the horrors of the inherited customs of the papists, and finally by the wave of repentance and confession that took so many good people on its tide.

This is an essential point.   The similarities which can be observed in the different works of the period are not deliberate plagiarism. Imitation of one author by another plays its part in literary creation, but it is secondary and often fortuitous; whereas it is of primary importance in the formation of a mind.   It is not books that copy books, but souls that copy souls.[45]   If all the biographies that ' the diligent anthologist' examines resemble each other, it is first and fore-most because all the Puritans lived in the same *milieux*, passed through the same psychological experiences and belonged to the same spiritual family.   The observation once made by Charles du Bos about the great French Christian writers of the seventeenth century can be

---

Intro.) that he wrote pars. 306–317, which are in the 5th ed. (1680) and were perhaps in the 4th, of which no copy has been found.

It remains to explain another important omission, that of par. 174, in which Bunyan recounts that when he was near fainting with fear and grief " there was, as if there had rushed in at the Window, the Noise of wind upon me, but very pleasant, and as if I heard a voice speaking : *Did'st thou ever refuse to be justified by the blood of Christ?*   And, withal my whole life and profession past was, in a moment, opened to me, wherein I was made to see that designedly I had not : so my heart answered groaningly, *No.*   Then fell, with power, that word of God upon me, *See that ye refuse not Him that speaketh.*   This made a strange seizure upon my spirit ; it brought light with it, and commanded a silence in my heart of all those tumultuous thoughts that before did use, like masterless Hell-hounds, to roar and bellow and make an hideous noise within me."   How could he have omitted so ' miraculous ' an incident ?   In our opinion quite simply by a reticence characteristic of his solid good sense.   " But as to my determining about this strange dispensation, what it was I knew not ; or from whence it came, I know not ; I have not yet, in 20 years' time, been able to make a judgment of it ; I thought then what here I shall be loth to speak.   But verily, that sudden rushing of wind was as if an angel had come upon me."

[45] We will allow ourselves to reverse and adapt Joubert's remark about Racine and Boileau, ' Jugements littéraires ', *Pensées*, p. 378 of Didier's ed. (Paris, 1864).

adapted to describe these Puritan preachers: "*Un Bérulle, un Pascal, un Bossuet, ne se rencontrent point parce qu'ils s'imitent, dans l'acception littérale et tâtillonne où l'imaginent trop de nos universitaires ; ils se rencontrent parce qu'ils sont tous participants de la même vérité chrétienne.*" [46] Bunyan and all his brother preachers were participators in the same Puritan faith. All, therefore, can use the same terms and yet each remain deeply sincere.[47] *Grace Abounding* in our opinion presents problems not so much of source and literary originality as of psychology and tactical approach—and it is with these that we are trying to deal here.

In calling oneself ' the greatest of sinners ', for example, one is not imitating this or that person, but trying to convince oneself that one is saved. It is not mere rhetoric, but the anxious questioning of a soul. " For he who looks on the foulness of his face by the *halves*, will wash by the halves; " Bunyan wrote, " even so he who looks on his sins by the halves, will seek for Christ by the halves. Reckon thyself, therefore, I say, the biggest sinner in the world." [48] And we cannot fail to share the shudder of anguish implicit in this categorical assertion: " I am sure the greatest sins have been committed by the biggest saints." [49] No, Bunyan was not sure, but, with all his straining will, he desired to be. His logic is not school logic but the passionate logic of an unquiet heart.

Yet another characteristic of *Grace Abounding* slightly blurs the true ring of the work. Bunyan wants to bring comfort to scrupulous souls, and therefore says to them: " If you have sinned against Light, if you are tempted to blaspheme; if you are down in despair, if you think God fights against you, or if heaven is hid from your eyes, remember it was thus with your father; *but out of them all the Lord*

---

[46] Charles du Bos, *Approximations*, 6th series (Paris, 1934), p. 201.

[47] Judging from a more spiritual point of view than ours, a fervent Christian would bring to our thesis this kind of argument : " For all that comes from the living God, and is worked out by living souls, is ever living and enlivening : there is no such thing as mere repetition, or differentiation by mere number, place and time, in this Kingdom of Life, either as to God's actions or the soul's." Friedrich von Hügel, *The Mystical Element of Religion as Studied in Saint Catherine of Genoa and her Friends* (2 vols., 2nd ed., London, 1909), I, 73.

[48] *The Doctrine of the Law and Grace*, vol. I, p. 494.

[49] *The Work of Jesus Christ as an Advocate*, vol. I, p. 171.

delivered me." [50] And in *The Jerusalem Sinner Saved* Bunyan makes his desire to edify, console and convert still plainer. Jesus Christ first wanted to show His mercy to the greatest of sinners, he wrote, so that the others, seeing this grace and this salvation, should be the more encouraged to come and seek life in Him. [51]

To this proselytism we fear is due an over-dramatic presentation of the actual facts. For a ' prophet ' is listened to, surely, in proportion as the path he has trodden is long and painful; his ' sanctity ' is all the more manifest the greater the anguish of its birth. Moreover, Bunyan could, in all piety, have changed the character of certain events, for he had read Luther's *Commentary on the Epistle to the Galatians* and the latter's explanation of how he had come to admire in St. Paul that pride of vocation that had first shocked him. In dealing with the first verse of the Epistle with its trumpet-blast: " Paul, an apostle, not of men, neither by man, but by Jesus Christ and God the Father . . .", Luther remarks that when he boasts like that he is not glorying in himself " but in the King who has sent him, whose authority he desires to be revered and held sacred." [52]

While reading the narrative, then, we must try to hear those overtones produced by the didactic intentions of the repentant sinner combined with the preconceived ideas of the theologian. Nor must we forget that each of us notices only the things we are prepared to see; that, to a certain extent, the glance creates the thing seen, and that introspection, like the vision of the external world, involves an unconscious choice.

On every page, then, we are aware that *Grace Abounding* is a work of art. [53] But we know that the artist transposes everyday reality, strips it of its coverings, so as to reach its soul. We know that there is in art a kind of lie, but that this lie is the necessary con-

---

[50] *G. A.*, preface, p. 295.

[51] *The Jerusalem Sinner Saved*, vol. I, p. 76.

[52] Luther : *A Commentary on St. Paul's Epistle to the Galatians* (London, 1940), chap. I, p. 3.

[53] This is denied by John Livingstone Lowes in an excellent article : " It is molten stuff which is not yet moulded—a profoundly significant human document, but not a work of art. It is intensely personal, but it is not universal." ' *The Pilgrim's Progress*, a study in immortality.' *Of Reading Books* (London, 1930), p. 17. For a study of *Grace Abounding* as a work of art see below, Part II, chap. 2.

dition for a higher truth. And therefore, in spite of all our reservations, we can look on the evidence of Bunyan's confession as revealing.

Bunyan wants to tell the truth. " I protest before God, I lie not." [54] He achieves sincerity in so far as it is compatible with human forces. And although his beliefs are the cause of a slight distorting of his book, they nevertheless guarantee its veracity. A man of his stamp, so rich in faith, does not treat serious things lightly. He himself tells us that God was not playing when He convinced him of his sins; nor was the devil playing when he tempted him; and he himself was not playing when he slid into a bottomless pit and endured the sufferings of hell. Thus, he says, he cannot play in recounting these things.[55]

And there are other guarantees. First, as Mr. Jack Lindsay [56] has pointed out, Grace Abounding was written when the people who had known Bunyan personally as a young man were still alive. No one doubted the truth of the book. Furthermore, Bunyan wrote about himself and his conversion in several other works [57] and never contradicted himself. Finally and above all, the work carries with it the mark of authenticity—not only in its tone but in the very ordering of its narrative. It hardly ever suffers from the stiffness of line and rigidity of logic that we had feared a priori, nor is the unfolding of events governed by an implacable determinism. Reading the book dispels most of our apprehensions. We feel in touch with the currents of life. Analysis shows that Bunyan has been able to avoid the pitfalls of such converts as Miss Baker, who says: " I tend to write as though my religious evolution was a constant progress; actually that was not at all the case." [58]

There is no trace of 'constant progress' in Grace Abounding. Indeed, the superficial reader might well be upset by the irregularity of its rhythm, by the contrary waves that sweep the author's spirit, by the fear that he is never going to make any headway! Yet there

---

[54] G. A., par. 24.   [55] G. A., par. 24.

[56] Jack Lindsay, John Bunyan, Maker of Myths (London, 1937), p. 12.

[57] See for example A Few Sighs from Hell, III, p. 711, and indirect allusions pp. 719–722. The Doctrine of the Law and Grace, I, p. 548, and there are many indirect allusions. The Jerusalem Sinner Saved, I, p. 79.

[58] Quoted by Th. Mainage, Introduction à la psychologie des convertis (Paris, 1913), p. 66.

is an advance, though the goal is never reached, for, as Bunyan says in his allegory, conversion is a 'progress' which has no end on earth. *Grace Abounding* admirably illustrates this perpetual becoming, precisely because its author is faithful to the truth of life.

So we end this study of the biographical value of these confessions, feeling assured of their exceptional interest and confident that they will reveal new depths not only in the man, but in the spiritual life itself.

2
The Awakening and First Formation of a Personality

FOR the critic, the most important period in the life of the man whose secrets he wants to lay bare is undoubtedly childhood. According to James Bissett Pratt [1] the drama of a man's maturity is played out against a backcloth designed by his social heredity and his first experiences. If this is true, Bunyan's silence about his childhood and, by and large, about all his material existence, is a matter for deep regret. Of the 339 paragraphs of his autobiography only fourteen are concerned with his first nineteen years; and his native village, where he spent over a third of his life, is referred to only once, and that in passing. [2] The explanation is that a mystic's happiness lies in those moments when his soul is in a state of recollection, and thus he tends to ignore the influences from the outside world. [3]

Bunyan has told us that his home was poor. But what sort of education did his parents give him? How tenderly did his mother love him? Which precepts did she especially teach him? Was the Elstow cottage governed by peace and devotion, or did young John have the unhappiness of witnessing parental strife? We would like to know all these things, and it is precisely these things that Bunyan does not tell us.

It is only by guesswork that we can establish the hypothesis that his father was irreligious, [4] that he was an Anglican in the same way

[1] James Bissett Pratt, *op cit.*, p. 61.
[2] *G. A.*, par. 51.
[3] Cf. F. von Hügel, *op. cit.*, II, 284.
[4] Gwilym O. Griffith, who has written a good study of Bunyan, believes on the other hand that his parents were devout; but his theory rests on a slender hypothesis, since he states without proof (*a*) that Badman in his youth represents Bunyan before his conversion, and (*b*) that therefore the

as he was a tinker—because fortune had ordained it.[5]   All this is
pure conjecture, and the stones we build with are never quite secure.
But it is certainly difficult not to hear a personal note in the prayer in
Christian Behaviour written at a time when we know the author's
father was still alive.[6]   " The Lord, if it be his will, convert our
poor parents, that they, with us, may be the children of God." [7]
And more still in: " Oh, how happy a thing would it be, if God
should use a child to beget his father to the faith ! " [8]

The autobiography provides us with two other stones to prop up
our hypothesis.   When, in paragraph 15, Bunyan draws attention to
the piety and holiness of his father-in-law's life, we cannot help
noticing the absence of praise for his own father.   And when, in
paragraph 27, we read: " I wished with all my Heart that I might be
a little child again, that my Father might learn me to speak without
this wicked way of swearing," we seem to feel his regret at not having
been born into a really Christian home, a home in which God could
have sought out his heart immediately.

A believer would, of course, say that God had already sought the
child out without his knowing it.

But even if his parents were not devout, it is certain that friends,
neighbours and most of the villagers were.   The child could hardly
have failed to be aware of the supreme importance of religion when he
saw so many people going to church, heard them talking about
theology at all hours, and discussing, as was the custom of the day,
their spiritual development.   When the pastor, Henry Jessey, went
for long journeys " he laid down rules to regulate the conversation for his fellow-travellers. . . . He was so great a Scripturist
that if one began to rehearse any passage, he could go on with

religious home in which Badman grew up must be similar to that of the
Elstow cottage. *John Bunyan* (London, 1927), pp. 46 *et seq.*

For the sources of *The Life and Death of Mr. Badman*, see *infra*, Part II,
chap. 4.

[5] " His father . . . vulgarly a tinker, and of the national religion, as
commonly men of that trade are." Charles Doe, *The Struggler* (1692), re-
edited by G. Offor, vol. III, p. 760.

[6] *Christian Behaviour* was published in 1663. Bunyan's father died in
1676. (Brown, *op. cit.*, p. 301.)

[7] *Christian Behaviour*, vol. II, p. 564.

[8] *Ibid.*

it ".[9] Bunyan himself, in many dialogues in the *Pilgrim*,[10] has given us a model of the art of this kind of religious interchange.

The influence over him of his native village and the small neighbouring town [11] cannot well be exaggerated; and, next to reading the seventeenth-century historians, nothing can make us appreciate this more than a visit to Elstow. A timeless atmosphere reigns there, a tranquillity to which we are unaccustomed nowadays, as if for three hundred years the village had forgotten to grow. It is a charming anachronism in our toppling world.

The framework within which medieval civilisation had flourished —the village and the borough [12]—had for some time been bursting its bonds. But still this little world where religion was fashionable— as indeed it was everywhere in England at that time [13]—had left its mark on Bunyan. " Theology rules there," said Grotius, just two years after the death of Queen Elizabeth.[14] Twenty years later he would have seen a still greater enthusiasm, which has led Mr. Arthur Bryant rightly to observe: " For one without faith, it is difficult to understand seventeenth-century England. For faith was part of the air the men of that day breathed." [15]

On the other hand, false charity and the back-biting of busybodies have altered so little that it is easy for us to imagine the social

---

[9] Daniel Neal, *op. cit.*, vol. III, p. 140.

[10] For example : " Come, how do you ? How stands it between God and your soul now ? " etc.

[11] An American Puritan, Jonathan Edward, who distinguished himself at the time of the ' great revival ' of 1740, bears witness to the influence of environment on all the child's spiritual development when he says that he ' played at ' religion in his childhood as naturally as he played at ball. See the quotation in Herbert Wallace Schneider, *The Puritan Mind* (London, 1931), p. 42.

[12] See among others Richard Tawney : " Inelastic in its external, Europe was hardly more flexible in its internal relations. Its primary unit had been the village . . . beyond the village lay the greater, more privileged village called the borough. . . . Above both were the slowly waking nations. . . . This narrow framework had been a home. In the 15th century it was felt to be a prison. Expanding energies pressed against the walls." *Op. cit.*, p. 62.

[13] " Religion, which had been in vogue . . ." wrote Daniel Neal (*op. cit.*, vol. III, p. 107) which actually refers here to the ' interregnum '.

[14] J. R. Green, *op. cit.*, p. 462.

[15] Arthur Bryant, *The England of Charles II* (London, 1934), p. 76.

pressures in a village where everyone spied on everyone else so as to enforce a proper respect for the orthodoxy of time and place. The account that Agnes Beaumont—an admirer of Bunyan in all honour and good faith—has left of her 'persecution' in 1674 admirably suggests the atmosphere of hamlets at that time.[16] Students of the humbler aspects of social history report that in a certain village a man was brought to justice for listening under other people's windows, and a woman for having been suspected of roasting chickens in her house at improper and unlawful hours.[17]

And Puritanism was very strong in Bedfordshire. The county had imbibed the new Protestant ideas on a large scale.[18] As a well-known stronghold of religious liberty it had given refuge to Huguenots from Alençon and Valenciennes since 1658.[19] The records of the ancient Archdeacons' Courts give us some idea of the Puritanism of the people of these parts. There were those who refused to carry the Cross in procession and others who obstinately lowered their heads at the Elevation instead of raising their eyes to the elevated Host. Others washed their hands in the baptismal fonts, refused to keep feast-days and—what was even more characteristic—read heretical works during Mass.[20]

The many pastors who were themselves Puritans refused to wear surplices and did not make the sign of the Cross when they administered baptism. In 1633, when Bunyan was five, the Bishop of Lincoln drew Laud's attention to the Puritanism of his diocese.[21] Some years later [22] the vicar of St. Paul's in Bedford was cited before the High Commission Court for consenting to give Communion to people who refused to come up to the altar-rails. Three parishioners

[16] See G. B. Harrison's ed. (London, 1929).

[17] Quoted by M. P. Willcocks, *Bunyan Calling, a Voice from the Seventeenth Century* (London, 1943), p. 24.
'Unlawful hours' meant after 9 o'clock in the evening. "No feasts and banquets were to be given after 9 o'clock at night." Cf. Eleanor Trotter, *Seventeenth-Century Life in the Country Parish* (Cambridge, 1919), p. 178.

[18] On the interrelation of geography and history see David Ogg, *op. cit.*, vol. I, p. 38. "Thus it is noteworthy that most of the movements now considered comparatively progressive succeeded best in the English plain."

[19] John Brown, *op. cit.*, p. 5. On all matters concerning the social, religious and political life of Bedfordshire, John Brown's biography is very valuable.

[20] *Ibid.*, pp. 4–5.   [21] *Ibid.*, p. 9.   [22] Oct., 1640.

defended him—John Eston, John Grewe and Anthony Harrington, men who later helped to found the Gifford–Bunyan church.[23] Finally, in 1641 Sir John Burgoyne, with 2,000 followers—"the high sheriff, knights, esquires, gentlemen, ministers, freeholders and other inhabitants of the county of Bedford"—went to London to congratulate Parliament on the work it had accomplished and to beg it to continue even more vigorously.[24]

Over this plain, then, there hung a Calvinist atmosphere that Bunyan breathed and by which was nourished. The *milieu* in which he lived was already shaping his heart and modelling his ideas, imposing its own categories, prejudices, sentiments and beliefs. For Puritanism flourished particularly among the 'people'. An inquiry made in 1669 by order of Archbishop Sheldon showed that in one conventicle at Bedford there were thirty attendants and all of " quality, the meanest sort ": [25] two hatters, one cobbler, one heel-maker, and others of the same kind.

So the *milieu* in which Puritanism was most vigorous and in which Bunyan grew up resembled that of the French pre-Reformation, in which ' mechanick ' men met in conventicle to discuss the Scriptures. At Meaux artisans such as ' carders ', ' wool-combers ' and ' fullers ' were to be seen working with their hands and conferring on the word of God.[26] At Amiens sagathee-weavers of the Somme region were denounced as heretics. At Langres, among the evangelicals pursued in 1548, were a cobbler, a pewterer, a sword-cuttler, a barber and a builder.[27]

The Calvinist atmosphere was at once terrifying and fascinating for a sensitive and imaginative child. For Puritans believed in pre-destination—*decretum quidem horribile fateor*, as Calvin himself called it. For them Paradise was Paradise, and Hell, Hell. Their God was not a carpenter whose severity was tempered with a certain tenderness, so much as a Jehovah (the *Shaddai* of *The Holy War*) whose justice knew nothing of forgiveness.

[23] John Brown, *op. cit.*, p. 14.
[24] *Ibid.*, pp. 15–16. [25] *Ibid.*, p. 216.
[26] F. Buisson, " Note additionnelle sur la Réforme française ", *Revue de Métaphysique et de Morale*, special number on the Reformation, 1918.
[27] Imbart de la Tour, *Calvin et l'Institution chrétienne* (Paris, 1935), pp. 225 *et seq.*, and, by the same author, *Evangélisme*, 1521–1538 (Paris, 1914), p. 180.

They preferred the terrifying passages of the Bible, the constant threatenings of which Bunyan speaks in one of his books.[28] If for Protestants the Bible contained the whole of their religion, upon Puritans it imposed itself with a unique rigour. For them every word of the Bible was of equal significance. " All our words are truth, one of as much force as another." [29] It never occurred to them that divine revelation could be progressive, or proportionate to the capacity for understanding of its recipients; nor that a distinction could be made between ' the substance of the Bible's data ' and ' the mentality of those who expounded it '.[30] They thought and fought in the spirit of the Old Testament.

It was in vain that Richard Hooker tried to make them see that nothing is valid unless it can adapt itself to all the contingencies of life; in vain that he pointed out that as " the Puritans rightly maintain that God must be glorified in all things, that the actions of men cannot tend unto his glory unless they be framed after his law; so it is their error to think that the only law which God hath appointed unto men in that behalf is the Sacred Scripture." [31] In vain Jeremy Taylor

[28] " There are but few places in the Bible, but there are threatenings against one sinner or other." *A Few Sighs*, vol. III, p. 712.

[29] *G. A.*, par. 209. Thomas Cartwright held too " that all Scripture is equally binding and that therefore the death penalties announced in the Old Testament for blasphemy, murder, adultery and heresy are valid still and ought to be put into force ". Cf. Scott Pearson, *Thomas Cartwright and Elizabethan Puritans* (Cambridge, 1925), p. 90. This doctrine of the equal authority of the whole Bible was in the main held in theory. In practice the most enlightened Puritans were led to make distinctions and certain passages were looked on as the norm by which to judge the others. On this subject see, for example, M. Knappen, *op. cit.*, chap. 18. ' The Puritan Doctrine of Authority ' and in particular pp. 359–360. " As history the entire book remained divine and inerrant, but only a part was subjected to further historical treatment ", p. 360.

Those who know about recent work and research on Puritanism cannot make a picture of it in black and white, with no half-tones ; but if the picture thereby loses in relief, how much does it gain in subtlety and life ! And Bunyan, as we shall see, preached Christ and love as much as Jehovah and the Law.

[30] Jean Guitton, *Portrait de Monsieur Pouget* (Paris, 1941), p. 107.

[31] *The Laws of Ecclesiastical Polity*, Book I, p. 280. *The Works of Mr. Richard Hooker*, edited by John Keble, 7th ed. revised by R. W. Church and F. Paget (Clarendon Press, Oxford).

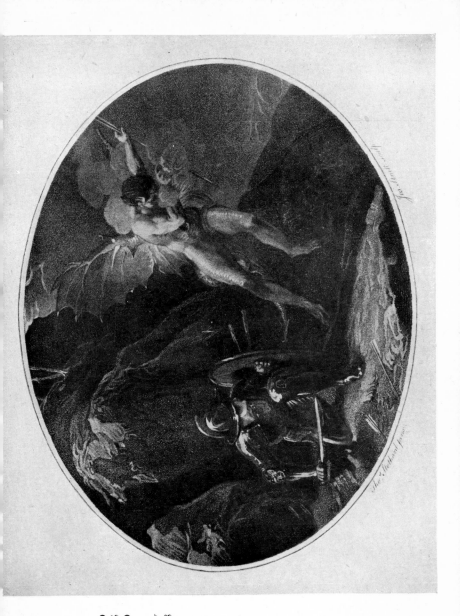

"APOLLYON SPREAD FORTH HIS DRAGON'S WINGS AND SPED HIM AWAY"

Engraved from a drawing by Thomas Stothard from the 1788 edition

CHRISTIAN READING IN HIS BOOK
From William Blake's series of water-colours, now in the Frick Collection

developed Richard Hooker's theme with eloquent variations of his own in his *Ductor Dubitantium* (1659).[32]

For the Puritans Holy Scripture represented all knowledge [33]— as Bunyan, echoing Calvin, was to say later.[34] They believed with Thomas Cartwright,[35] that the Bible was not only the sum of Christian doctrine, but a model of discipline and government too. Pym, Cromwell, and all the great Dissenters, with the exception of Milton, believed that the Church should be closely united with the State.[36] Like their master, Calvin, they dreamed of a society that would recognise God's sovereignty over the temporal as well as the spiritual order. "*Ut omnia subjaceant Deo.*"[37] In *The Holy War* Bunyan described such a society animated by the spirit of God. But no one in England has expounded this theocratic conception of the State more clearly and vigorously than Richard Baxter. "The world then is a Kingdom whereof God is the King.[38] . . . A Commonwealth properly so called . . . is the Government of a Society of God's subjects by a sovereign subordinate to God, for the common good, and the glory, and pleasing of God.[39] The more theocratic, or truly divine, a government is, the better it is."[40]

Their moral conceptions were no less severe than their religious doctrines. If the old Puritanism which fulminated against the wearing of a surplice and all that recalled the Church of Rome still survived, another Puritanism had been born which fought, above all, against

---

[32] For an excellent *exposé* of Jeremy Taylor's ideas, see Perry Miller and Thomas H. Johnson, *The Puritans* (New York, 1938), an anthology of texts with 79 pages of remarkably comprehensive introduction.

[33] "*Eschole de toute sagesse, pasture unique de nos âmes.*" *Inst. Chrét.* 1560, I, 7, 1.

[34] Cf. *A Few Sighs*, p. 718.

[35] Cf. Daniel Neal, *op. cit.*, vol. II, p. 193.

[36] J. S. Flynn, *op. cit.*, p. 35.

[37] Cf. Jacques Chevalier, "Les Deux Reformes : le Luthéranisme en Allemagne, le Calvinisme dans les pays de langue anglaise ", No. *cit.* of the *Revue de Métaphysique et de Morale*.

Cf. Carlyle, *Cromwell* (Tauchnitz ed., p. 79). "Our ancient Puritan reformers were . . . inspired by a heavenly purpose. To see God's own law made good in this world . . . that England should all become a Church."

[38] Richard Baxter, *A Holy Commonwealth* (1659), thesis 24.

[39] *Ibid.*, thesis 46.

[40] *Ibid.*, thesis 192.

sin.[41] For, as Calvin had already pointed out, there is no religion without a moral code.

It must not be thought, however, that a pervasive dreariness had chased joy out of life, nor that ' monastic gloom '—to use Macaulay's words [42]—had descended over the whole country. A picture of the face of Puritan England painted in such mournful colours is deceptive, and the best historians have tried to show it in its true light. "Zealous as were the leaders of the Commonwealth in the suppression of vice," S. R. Gardiner wrote, " they displayed little of that sour austerity with which they have been credited." [43] " In all ages ' Merry England ' has been both a living reality and a nostalgic fiction." [44] And G. G. Coulton in his *Medieval Studies* points out that the Puritans seemed almost frivolous compared with the Franciscans and Dominicans of the Middle Ages, whom he calls their ' high ancestors '.[45] " The Puritanism of the Reformation ", he wrote, " was simply the strictest and most logical attempt yet made to realise certain thoroughly medieval ideals." Let us add, moreover, that the moral standpoint of the Puritans was no different from that of other fervent Christians of the period, as modern historical works have shown and as we shall often be able to point out in the course of this study.[46]

If they condemned the excesses which debase man to the level of beasts, the Puritans were quite willing to allow healthy pleasures. " Drink ", said one of them, " is in itself a good creature of God, and to be received with thankfulness, but the abuse of drink is from

[41] S. R. Gardiner, *op. cit.*, vol. III, p. 239.

[42] T. B. Macaulay, *op. cit.*, I, p. 81, " rules such as these . . . threw over all life a more than monastic gloom."

[43] Quoted by Percy A. Scholes, *The Puritans and Music* (Oxford, 1934), p. 328. An excellent book.

[44] Douglas Bush, *English Literature in the Earlier Seventeenth Century* (Oxford, 1945), p. 3.

[45] G. G. Coulton, *Ten Medieval Studies, with Four Appendices* (Cambridge, 1930). See pp. 48 *et seq.*, the essay entitled ' The High Ancestry of Puritanism '.

[46] Perry Miller and Thomas H. Johnson, *The Puritans* (New York, 1938), Intro., p. 7. " . . . its culture was simply the culture of England at that moment. . . . Most accounts of Puritanism, emphasising the controversial tenets, attribute everything that Puritans said or did to the fact that they were Puritans ; their attitudes towards all sorts of things were pounced upon and exhibited as peculiarities of their sect, when, as a matter of fact, they were normal attitudes for the time."

Satan. The wine is from God; but the Drunkard is from the Devil." [47] Cromwell drank wine and beer, and called anyone ridiculous who wanted to prohibit all drink so as to be sure that no one would ever get drunk.[48]

We will discuss music, games and dancing when we deal with the extreme asceticism which marked the beginnings of Bunyan's conversion. It is enough now to deplore the error often committed regarding Puritan fashions. The perusual of contemporary documents makes it clear that their clothes were of all the colours of the rainbow.[49] And General Harrison appeared during the Protectorate " dressed in scarlet under golden lace ".[50]

It is certainly true, however, that the bulk of the Puritans did not allow themselves to dress up to the dignity of their leaders. Most of them were discreetly clad, without ribbons or love-locks; but it is nevertheless true that the legendary ' Roundheads ' were not numerous. Not only did Cromwell, Milton, Ireton, Harrison and Hampton [51] wear long hair, but also our tinker himself.

It is therefore fallacious to think that the Puritan could never forget his theology and enjoy himself, but it is correct to suppose that he lived his faith with an intensity almost unknown in our day. Constant battle was waged against licence, and life was a much more serious matter. In some extremist *milieux* mysticism flourished. The faith of each was fostered by the dreams and exaltation of all.

How could the young John, sensitive and imaginative, have failed to respond to this gust of collective fervour, or to be influenced by this sometimes inordinate enthusiasm ? As it happened, the flight of his imagination took a morbid turn and his nerves were deranged. To the already terrible theological discussions were added the tales of strange superstitions, of those ' judgments of God ' which Bunyan records in *The Life and Death of Mr. Badman*. For example, the

---

[47] Increase Mather, *Wo to Drunkards* (Cambridge, 1673), quoted by Perry Miller and T. H. Johnson, *op. cit.*, p. 2.

[48] C. H. Firth, *Oliver Cromwell* (ed. *cit.*), p. 353.

[49] Perry Miller and T. H. Johnson, *op. cit.*, p. 2.

[50] Quoted by Percy A. Scholes, *The Puritans and Music* (Oxford, 1934), p. 106, from F. M. Kely and R. Schwabe, *Historic Costume, a Chronicle of Fashion in Western Europe, 1490–1790* (2nd ed., London, 1929).

[51] Percy A. Scholes, *op. cit.*, p. 106.

story of Dorothy Mately, who worked in a lead mine—a woman who was "a great swearer, curser, liar, and thief", and whose "usual way of asserting things was with these kind of imprecations: I would I might sink into the earth if it be not so." One day—on March 23, 1660, as the scrupulous and credulous Bunyan noted— while she was washing ore on top of a steep hill near Ashover "she was taxed by a lad for taking two single pence out of his pocket, for he had laid his breeches by." Dorothy denied it, supporting her denial with her favourite imprecation. Immediately she went hurtling into the air with her tub and sieve and was buried in the earth beneath. A stone afterwards fell on her and broke her skull.[52]

Belief in the indwelling justice of God, belief in demons, in innumerable spirits that haunt the earth, in witches [53]—such was the constant state of fear in which rural England lived. The night especially was fraught with fears. Alone at the farm where her father lay dying, Agnes Beaumont did not dare to go and fetch her brother. And when at last, having summoned up her strength and faced the dark, she knocked at her brother's door, the fright of his servants, in their turn, was so great that they could hardly dress themselves with their trembling hands. "Soe frighted yt they could scarse put on their clothes." [54]

It was in this world, peopled by mysterious and invisible presences and resounding with the echoes of the struggle between God and Satan, that Bunyan grew up. An enchanted circle of malevolence enclosed his first horizons. He hurled himself against them, like many another, notably Luther.[55] Like Luther, he never really recovered from his childhood; so it can be said that, like Luther, he lived in the theological epoch of Auguste Comte.[56]

[52] *Mr. Badman*, III, p. 604.

[53] We know that Sir Thomas Browne links belief in witches and spirits with religion : "For my part I have ever believed, and do now, that there are witches : they that doubt of these do not only deny them, but Spirits ; and are obliquely and upon consequence a sort not of infidels but atheists." *Religio Medici*, I, sect. 30.

[54] *The Narrative of the Persecution of Agnes Beaumont*, p. 61.

[55] Luther's mother was tormented, in particular, by the diabolic enchantments of a neighbour. She and her children lived in terror (cf. Felix Kuhn, *Luther, sa vie et ses oeuvres* (Paris, 1894), I, p. 26).

[56] David Masson, *The Three Devils : Luther's, Milton's and Goethe's* (London, 1874), p. 50.

He was, he says, " greatly afflicted and troubled with the thoughts of the Day of Judgment" and trembled "night and day at the thoughts of the fearful Torments of Hell Fire ".[57]   His sleep was troubled by nightmares and evil spirits that "laboured to draw him away ".[58]   So great was his despair that he sometimes longed to be in Hell—but as a tormentor rather than a victim.

Probably he had heard some neighbour or the curate of the village [59] inveighing against Sunday games, for when he was only nine or ten, while in the middle of playing with his ' vain companions ', he sometimes felt himself crushed under the weight of sin.

There are no shades in children's judgments.   The slightest violation of the rules of morality they have just learned appears as a crime to the most sensitive and nervous among them.   Hence the curious inhibitions felt by Bunyan later, in his manhood.   " But all this while as to the act of sinning, I never was more tender than now. I durst not take a pin or a stick, though but so big as a straw, for my conscience now was sore, and would smart at every touch; I could not now tell how to speak my words, for fear I should misplace them. Oh how gingerly did I then go in all I did or said!   I found myself as on a miry Bog that shook if I did but stir." [60]

---

[57] *G. A.*, par. 6.
Compare that great admirer of Bunyan, R. L. Stevenson's, description of a tormented childhood : " The two chief troubles of his very narrow existence —the practical and everyday trouble of school tasks and the ultimate and airy one of hell and judgment—were often confounded together into one appalling nightmare.   He seemed to himself to stand before the Great White Throne ; he was called on, poor little devil, to recite some form of words, on which his destiny depended ; his tongue stuck, his memory was blank, hell gasped for him ; and he would awake, clinging to the curtain-rod with his knees to his chin." ' A Chapter on Dreams,' vol. I, *Miscellanies*, p. 319 of the 1895 Edinburgh ed., complete works.

[58] *G. A.*, par. 5.

[59] Christopher Hall, curate of Elstow, preached later on this subject (par. 20) but he did not come to the village until 1639 when Bunyan was eleven, and not nine or ten as he inaccurately says in par. 7.   In any case respect for the Sabbath was enforced by law at Bedford : " Within the year 1610–1611 Oliver Lenton and Walter Lewin of Barford were punished for looking on football players on Sunday ; John Hawkes of Renhold, for playing at nineholes ; and William Shellie of Bedford, for playing at tables on that day." John Brown, *op. cit.*, p. 6.

[60] *G. A.*, par. 82, one of the most interesting of the autobiography.

In 1644, before Bunyan was yet sixteen, his mother died. Bunyan is as mute about her death as he is about her life. We regret but are not surprised by this. We have already commented on the fact that he says nothing about his love for his first wife and mentions his second and his children only in giving the account of his imprisonment. It is not that he was unaware of the soul's complexity but rather that he did not know about all the shades of association and the interplay of thought with feeling. He did not hear the murmur of certain underground currents nor sufficiently grasp the influence of the affective life over the spiritual. Whence comes his silence regarding his domestic griefs and joys.[61]

Although actual proof is lacking, we nevertheless suspect that his mother's death was a grievous shock to Bunyan. Those who are convinced of this base their opinions on the following facts: Bunyan's mother died in the month of June; his father married again in September; John entered the army in November. Should we not interpret the boy's haste to leave home as evidence of a doubly-wounded sensibility—by the death of a dearly-loved being and by the unseemly haste of the father? And should we not also interpret it as proof of tension with the father?

This thesis [62] would hold water if it could be established that Bunyan enlisted voluntarily. To leave the family home so young—five months after his mother's death—and to enlist with the Parliamentarians when his father was a Royalist [63] would certainly help to

[61] For Bunyan's indifference (or should we say blindness?) to the relationship between the actions of others and, in general, all material contingencies, and his own interior life we can perhaps find another cause, that which F. von Hügel mentions in this passage of his large work: "The mystic finds his joy in the recollective movements and moments of the soul; and hence ever tends *qua* mystic to ignore and neglect, or to over-minimise, the absolutely necessary contact of the mind and will with the things of sense." *Op. cit.*, II, 284. The import of this quotation goes beyond its present application, but it includes it in its richness. For a discussion of Bunyan's mysticism cf. *infra, Conclusion.*

[62] It is Mr. Jack Lindsay's (*op. cit.*). The supposed tension between father and son gave the material for the psychological study of Bunyan that this ingenious commentator has attempted. His intelligent book fascinates but does not convince, as solid proofs are lacking.

[63] He made so little concealment of his royalist sympathies that on May 30, 1645, he had one of his children baptised and called him Charles. John Brown, *op. cit.*, p. 42.

prove the existence of a grave difference between father and son. But, as we have seen, John was conscripted.[64]

Thus it seems to us impossible to believe with conviction in a family quarrel; yet the impression remains with us that Bunyan had the pain of such a quarrel in his heart. Where we should bring proof we can offer only personal impressions.

These impressions are perhaps born of the passages in Bunyan's work in which he uses the word ' father '; sometimes trembling with fear, sometimes vibrating with fervent love. Is the fear real and the fervour a dream? God coming to overwhelm the man whose child's heart, weaned too soon from maternal love, had never known the warmth of a father's love? " Oh how great a task it is ", writes Bunyan, " for a poor soul that becomes sensible of sin and the wrath of God, to say in faith but this one word: ' Father! ' " [65] And again: " I myself have often found that when I can say but this word ' Father,' it doth me me more good than when I call him by any other Scripture name." [66]

These are the faint signs and fragile props of an impression that is nevertheless as tenacious as it is vague.

Whatever were the emotions in Bunyan's heart when he left home, whether he went with regret or with hatred for his family, the fact remains that he was obliged to leave so as to serve with the Parliament forces.

He was sixteen. An age when one is still malleable and sensitive to influences, and yet at the same time so generous and rich in enthusiasms and dreams! And he found himself in an army where every leader and nearly every soldier was at the same time a preacher and a theologian; where respite from fighting was talking; where the Bible was the source from which new strength was drawn; where the realisation of God's Kingdom on earth was the common dream. " Equally well founded ", wrote Sir Charles Firth in his *Cromwell's Army*, " is the popular view that a good deal of the preaching done in the Cromwellian army was done by the soldiers themselves." [67]

[64] Cf. *supra*, p. 3.
[65] *I Will Pray with the Spirit*, II, p. 629.
[66] *Come and Welcome*, I, 224.
[67] C. H. Firth, *Cromwell's Army, the History of the English Soldier from 1642–1660* (2nd ed., London, 1912), p. 334.
Chillingworth has left this interesting piece of evidence about the parlia-

And this same historian has shown that visionaries abounded in the regiments,[68] that a battle was often preluded by a religious service, and that after battle prayers of thanksgiving were offered up, sometimes on the field, sometimes the next day.[69]   And finally let us note that Sir Samuel Luke, who was in command at Newport Pagnell, was by no means the hypocritical and peevish glutton described by Butler in *Hudibras*: one is sometimes too ready to take satire for history.   Sir Samuel's letters, as John Brown has pointed out,[70] show us a man of keen penetration and undeniable courage, leading a saintly life, and capable of having a great influence over his soldiers.

At Newport, then, as at Elstow, there was Puritanism in the very air Bunyan breathed.   Thus the influences of to-day reinforced those of yesterday.   And in the privacy of his heart the leaven of to-morrow's feelings and beliefs was already rising.

As soon as he was back in civil life, John married, as we have already seen.   When a man realises that he is not made for chastity [71] it is better to follow St. Paul's advice and not burn.   His young wife, whom we imagine to have been gentle, loving and pious, told him about her father, who was a religious man.   And she introduced him to two books whose influence over him will be obvious when we analyse Bunyan's work.   One was *The Plaine-Mans Path-Way to Heaven*,[72] and the other *The Practice of Piety*,[73] which is an " en-

---

mentary army : " I observed a great deal of piety in the commanders and soldiers of the Parliament's army.   I confess their discourse and behaviour do speak them Christians, but I can find little of God or godliness in our men."   Quoted by Robert Barclay, *The Inner Life of the Religious Societies of the Commonwealth* (3rd ed., London, 1879).   An indispensable book for those who want to try and capture the spirit of the Puritanism of this really epic period of English history.

[68] C. H. Firth, *op. cit.*, p. 318.   [69] *Ibid.*, p. 321.

[70] Egerton MSS., 785, 786, 787.   Ashburnham MSS., Stowe Collection, 229, and John Brown, *op. cit.*, p. 45.

[71] The admission is implicit.   *G. A.*, par. 45, for example : " Oh these temptations were suitable to my flesh, I being but a young man, and my nature in its prime."

[72] *The Plaine-Mans Path-Way to Heaven.   Wherein Every Man may Clearly see Whether he shall be Saved or Damned*, by Arthur Dent, preacher of the word of God at South-Shoobery in Essex—the ed. used was the 21st (1631), of which there is a copy in the Bodleian Library.

[73] *The Practice of Piety directing a Christian how to walk that he may please God*, by Lewis Bayly, Bishop of Bangor (ed. Grace Webster, 1842).

deavour to extract out of the chaos of endless controversies the old practice of true piety, which flourished before these controversies were hatched ".[74]

And so the memories of his childhood rose up and awoke feelings that Bunyan believed to be dead. His wife was a model woman, and the faith from which she drew her inspiration made a direct call to Bunyan's soul. She brought him a tender love, but it only awakened his thirst for higher joys. The devotion she poured into his heart carved out the ' larger capacities ' [75] that God alone can fill.

So started the slow conversion that had been secretly at work in the depths of his being ever since childhood; only from now onwards it developed within the interplay of the light and shadow of his psychological consciousness. If Bunyan's marriage was not a starting-point, at least it was the cause of the gushing-forth of hidden founts. But he was hardly aware of this.[76]

It can be appropriately discussed at this point whether Bunyan's spiritual life and religious thought had or had not been influenced since childhood by a sense of the inferiority of his social condition and a hatred of the privileged classes. No one nowadays denies [77] that the Dissenting movement had a social significance and that the Puritan faith—anyway that of the poor—stood for aspirations other than the salvation of the soul. According to Mr. York Tindall, " The religious man may remain only half aware, or . . . quite unaware of the social and economic motives which determine his sectarian adherence. In the seventeenth century religion at once gave the masses a voice and obscured their vision." [78] The word ' economic ' seems perhaps a sort of literary anachronism here, yet nevertheless the realities it covers certainly existed.

[74] Lewis Bayly, *op. cit.*, The Epistle dedicatory, p. xxxiii.

[75] Cf. Letter of Elisabeth of the Trinity quoted by Pierre Messiaen in an article of the *Bulletin Joseph Lotte*, Jan., 1940.

[76] Par. 15, *G. A.*, is significant.

[77] " Conservatives, satisfied with things as they were, saw in Puritan radicalism a serious threat to the vested interests, those dissatisfied with the *status quo* welcomed for social as well as for religious reasons the Puritan condemnation of the episcopal hierarchy with its wealth, its monopoly of advantages, and its alliance with the court and aristocracy. Political passions and economic grievances increased the tension." Perry Miller and T. H. Johnson, *The Puritans* (New York, 1938), intro., p. 45.

[78] York Tindall, *op. cit.*, p. 94.

Bunyan's ' school of politics ' had of course been the army. Though the army's political history did not really begin until 1647,[79] and though it was not until October (Bunyan had been demobilised in July) that democratic agitation [80] really manifested itself, it is obvious that the ideas then proclaimed in the full light of day by word and deed (" The Agreement of the People ") had been simmering for some time.[81] And it is also certain that the soldiers were familiar with all these problems and had " no idea of keeping their religion and their politics in water-tight compartments ".[82] This political orientation towards greater civic and social equality was given its impetus by Lieutenant-Colonel John Lilburne, who carried the army forward in advance of the nation. Not that the ' Levellers ' grouped around him were all communists before their time! [83] Those who pushed their ideas to that extreme were a small minority, and when, in 1649, twenty or thirty enlightened men went off to dig and sow the soil of a Surrey hill to establish the first cell of the new Society, they were looked on without apprehension.[84]

These underground political and social influences will turn up often in our study of Bunyan's work. For the moment our object is to discover whether his conversion had a social significance, however vague and obscure. Did he—unconsciously—join the Dissenters so as to make cause with those who suffered like himself from their social status ? Did he unwittingly try to find in religion not only the path of spiritual salvation but also a kind of material satisfaction and social brotherhood ? Did he seek in the Baptist doctrine an expression of his grievances as a man of the people and a balm for his wounded

[79] C. H. Firth, *Cromwell's Army* (ed. *cit.*), p. 349.

[80] *Ibid.*, p. 357.

[81] Jack Lindsay, *John Bunyan, Maker of Myths* (London, 1937), p. 25. " In April of 1647 a spy had written that the army was one Lilburne throughout and more likely to give than to receive laws."

[82] W. T. Whitley, *A History of British Baptists* (2nd ed., 1932), p. 75. Having noticed the presence of many Baptists in the army, Whitley writes thus of the ' military Baptists '.

[83] C. H. Firth, *Oliver Cromwell and the Rule of the Puritans in England* (ed. *cit.*), p. 244.

G. P. Gooch, *English Democratic Ideas in the Seventeenth Century* (augmented ed. of H. J. Laski), chap. 5 : ' The Political Opinions of the Army '.

[84] G. P. Gooch, *op. cit.*, p. 181.

self-respect ?   Did he recognise from the start the social significance of the movement to which he rallied ?

As Bunyan has left us no detailed memories of his military life, we are not able to answer these questions with any certainty.   We have asked them merely so as to give some idea of the extent of the field of conjecture, and to show how many problems there are of the type psychologists would like to unravel.

In default of proof we can only offer a personal opinion.   We do not believe that political and social ideas had any influence over Bunyan's interior life at first, and we hope that our study of a soul's progress, even if it brings no decisive proofs, will at least uncover the sources of that soul's fervour so that others will share our conviction that his conversion was of quite another order.

Such was the awakening and formation of our author's personality. It owed nearly everything to life, to daily contact with people.   It was from them that he amassed the ideas and impressions that his genius afterwards made fruitful.   The struggle waged diffusedly throughout the nation was summed up in one individual soul and there acquired a vigour of expression which, one day, was to reveal itself to itself.   Both his *milieu* and his education favoured the first young flight of his innate sensibility and imagination; and the use he made of the riches he brought to the world was fixed by the circumstances of his life, within a given framework and at a given moment of history.

Bunyan was always nervous and highly-strung as a boy, and he became more nervous and highly-strung as he grew older.   The man inherited the child's tormented personality.   Some will say that the territory was indeed propitious for conversion,[85] and I fully agree; but that does not wholly explain the conversion.   If one reduces a man's psychology to the clinical study of his physiological disturbances one will inevitably misunderstand his spiritual life.

There is no need here to go into the arguments which divide those who favour experimental religious psychology from those who consider religious psychology to be irreducible to such researches.   A discussion of that kind does not enter into the scope of our work. On the other hand, we must take a position and state it, so as to show in what spirit we are pursuing our study of Bunyan's spiritual life.

[85] Cf. William James, *L'expérience religieuse* (Paris, 1906), p. 139.   H. Delacroix, *La religion et la foi* (Paris, 1922), p. 76.

We believe unreservedly in the interrelation of body and spirit, in the influence of the physical over the spiritual and *vice versa*. We know that conversion can follow or accompany certain bodily phenomena and certain physical or mental upheavals: but between the ascending curve of the spiritual life and the accidents of the body we do not see the relationship of cause and effect. Our opinion is that divine grace may perhaps work through a certain psycho-physiological determinism which, however, it infinitely surpasses.

We have already noted these physiological phenomena and the disturbances of the emotional life; and we shall do so again as research along these lines contributes to our knowledge of the personality we are studying. But we would not consider it permissible to draw from these observations an explanation valid for the total development of a conscience—a conscience which we feel to be directed and dominated by a teleology which goes far beyond particular phases.[86]

If the enthusiasm of some of Bunyan's readers has deprived them of their critical sense and blunted their psychological intuition, a purely scientific approach is still more risky, for it leads to a lack of understanding that is more radical because of its pretentiousness. The student of the life of a conscience should not approach it as if it were a matter of lines, planes and solids. He should bend over it seeking to be a lucid observer, mindful that it is a soul that is exposed before him, that great delicacy is required in drawing near to it, and that a little human warmth is essential if he is to understand it.

[86] Joseph Maréchal, *Etudes sur la psychologie des mystiques* (2 vols., Paris, 1937–1938), vol. I, p. 46.

3

The Valley of the Shadow of Death

Many have spoken of it, but none can tell what the valley of the shadow of death should mean until they come in it themselves. The heart knows its own bitterness.

BUNYAN

THE biographers date Bunyan's conversion from the year 1653.[1] But for us it starts almost with his birth. His whole life was a conversion—that is to say, a constant desire to pass from evil towards good, a thirst for perfection which moved side by side with a precocious sense of sin. He could have said with that nineteenth-century Puritan, Sir Edmund Gosse's mother, " If I must date my conversion from my first wish and trial to be holy I may go back to my infancy; if I am to postpone it after my last wilful sin, it is scarcely yet begun." [2]

The words " I have sinned " are the starting-point of many spiritual ascents; and Bunyan never ceased to repeat them from the moment he understood what they meant. Though, at least in his youth, he often gave them an exaggerated meaning. The God of his childhood and of his early manhood was a God who banished joy and condemned the most natural inclinations. Thus, like other fanatics of the period, Bunyan both exalted and falsified the Puritan conception of life. Later, when he was enriched by both personal and professional experience, he came to understand how immoderate his former exactions had been, and advocated an austerity which should discipline without mutilating nature. In this he conformed to the

[1] *Works* (ed. 1692), end of vol. : " And about 1652 (53) was by irresistible grace converted."

[2] Edmund Gosse, *Father and Son* (Heinemann's Windmill Library), p. 3.

49

ideals of such great Puritans as Milton, Marvell and Baxter. But in his youth, and before he had acquired this wisdom, he wanted to turn his back on all life's laughter, on games, dancing, profane reading and even the chime of bells. And we can see precisely in the detail of these renunciations his erroneous interpretation of the moral precepts of English Calvinism, which—whatever many writers may say[3]—never in fact demanded that a man should forswear all the healthy human impulses.

And here we have an opportunity of bringing fresh evidence to

[3] We have already mentioned Macaulay. See also the preface to Matthew Arnold's *Culture and Anarchy*; Sir Sydney Lee : " Puritanism was in fact a reactionary movement against the delight of the things of the senses." (*Great Englishmen of the Sixteenth Century*, quoted by Percy A. Scholes, *op. cit.*, p. 96); H. J. C. Grierson : " The more positive " notes " of Puritanism . . . the condemnation . . . of all popular amusements, of dancing, of music."

We could quote many other names, for the error is widespread. Literary critics especially, apparently oblivious of the works of historians, cling to what Joseph Crouch calls ' a popular fallacy '. *Puritanism and Art, an Inquiry into a Popular Fallacy*, London, 1910.

Those who want to prove the inhuman austerity of Puritanism quote W. Prynne : " Our Saviour whose doctrine no Christian dares control hath denounced woe to all those that laugh, that live in ease, jollity and carnall pleasures, etc." without taking into account Prynne's exceptional personality. For this eternally discontented man plunged straight in front of him, like a ' rhinoceros with blinkers ' (David Masson, *The Life of John Milton*, 6 vols., London, 1877, V, 449, footnote), and attacked Cromwell equally with Charles I; the Quakers, the Levellers, the Independents and the lay preachers equally with the Jesuits, the Episcopalians and Arminians ! (David Ogg, *Charles II*, 2 vols., Oxford, 1934, I, 25).

As for the Puritans' music, see Percy A. Scholes, *op. cit.*; Joseph Crouch, *op. cit.*; Ernest Walker, *History of Music in England* (1907), p. 122, and footnote p. 255. " In the ten years from 1650 to 1660 a great number of works issued from the press and, indeed, we may fitly date the never-ceasing stream of English music publications from the Commonwealth." In *Music in England* (Pelican Books) Eric Blom reluctantly recognises that the Puritans favoured the birth of English opera (p. 65), that Cromwell's Protectorate was a ' great period ' for English music, and that in 1650 John Playford was authorised to publish his first musical work, *The English Dancing-Master* (p. 69).

Cromwell liked music (C. H. Firth, *op. cit.*), and if it is objected that all this reveals the taste of ' gentlemen ' and not the Puritan ' vulgum pecus ', we must mention the humble tinker, John Bunyan, violinist and flautist. Cf. *infra*, p. 225.

bear on what we have already said regarding the first influence of the Puritan spirit on Bunyan.[4]

According to that eminent preacher, William Perkins, amusements and lawful games were refreshing both to mind and body and should be encouraged.[5]   And when in 1647 the Long Parliament suppressed the observance of Christmas, it granted the workers in return one day's holiday a month in which " to relax and amuse themselves ".[6]

It was only the violation of the *Sabbath* that the Puritans condemned, and this conformed to a twofold need of their character. First, by separating themselves from amusements for one whole day they practised the kind of renunciation their virile faith demanded; and secondly, it gave them an opportunity for observing the personal discipline that is especially dear to individualists.[7]   Games on the Sabbath were therefore forbidden, and the Sabbath thereby gained in dignity.   According to Cartwright and Baxter, these measures were necessary.   " If ", as Cartwright said before Parliament, " there be a bear or a bull to be baited in the afternoon, . . . the minister hurries the service over in a shameful manner in order to be present at the show." [8]   And Richard Baxter complained that the dancers showed no respect whatever for the churches, which they entered dressed in clownish clothes and with bells on their legs.[9] But, Sunday apart, the Puritans did not hesitate to amuse themselves when opportunity arose.   At the time of the marriage of his daughter Frances, Cromwell had his men and women guests dance until five o'clock in the morning to the strains of forty-eight violins.[10]   And

[4] Cf. *supra*, pp. 32 *et seq.*
[5] William Perkins, *Works* (3 vols., London, 1616–1618), I, 539, and II, 142, quoted by M. Knappen, *op. cit.*, p. 428.
[6] C. H. Firth, *Oliver Cromwell*, p. 353.
[7] S. R. Gardiner, *op. cit.*, III, 247.
[8] Quoted by P. A. Scholes, *op. cit.*, p. 305.
[9] This famous passage is given in Chamber's *Encyclopedia of English Literature*, vol. I, p. 412.
The Puritans fought against the licentiousness of which Philip Stubbs has noted an aspect in connection with the feasts of May : " I have heard it credibly reported (and that *viva voce*) by men of great gravity and reputation, that of forty, three score or a hundred maids going to woods over night, there have scarcely the third part of them returned home again undefiled." *Anatomie of Abuses* (1653), ed. F. J. Furnivall (New Shakespeare Society), pp. 148–149.
[10] C. H. Firth, *Oliver Cromwell* (ed. *cit.*), p. 462.

his son Richard, a devout rigorist, indulged in games, hunting and horse-racing.[11]   Colonel Hutchinson, a typical Puritan gentleman, was himself an expert musician and a friend of artists, and he had his children—both boys and girls—taught not only foreign languages and the sciences but also music and dancing.[12]

However this may be, Bunyan evidently believed that sin consisted not only in violating the Sabbath but in games themselves, in which he saw nothing but vanity and folly.   In his youth he strove to reach perfection through austerity, but this was all the more difficult for him as he was bound to the earth with all the ardour of a vigorous temperament.   Even when we have made allowance for the exaggerations of a penitent, we can still sense the attraction that the pleasures and fruits of the flesh—such as good food and women—had for him.[13]   The struggle that must have raged within him was terrible, but its very bitterness made its greatness.   If Bunyan moves us so vividly it is precisely because he had such difficulty in mastering himself.   The conversion of an angel (if the alliance of those two words were not absurd) would not touch us.   In Charles Péguy's words, we like sanctity to be wrenched, with all its roots, from the earth itself.[14]   The tragedy in Bunyan's case lies partly in the gulf that existed between his soaring ambition and the weight of his chains.

And we wonder how many readers of Grace Abounding have smiled, or at any rate faintly shrugged their shoulders with contemptuous pity, when confronted with an asceticism that to them seems simply morbid.   Morbid?   Undoubtedly, but it is something else and much more than a sickly flower.   It is expressive of the moral and intellectual severity that we find in all the great converts.   Indeed, it is the first phase of conversion.

11 Cf. *D. N. B.*, vol. XIII, pp. 186–192.

12 Mrs. Hutchinson, *op. cit.*, p. 348.

13 *G. A.*, pars. 21, 24, 45.   " . . . before I had well dined . . . and I made as much haste as I could to fill my belly with delicates . . . These [the Ranters] would also talk with me of their ways, and condemn me as legal and dark; pretending that they only had attained to perfection that could do what they would, and not sin!   Oh! these temptations were suitable to my flesh; I being but a young man, and my nature in its prime."

14 Charles Péguy, *Victor Marie, Comte Hugo* (N.R.F.), p. 90.

Evelyn Underhill,[15] after reminding us that E. D. Starbuck defined conversion as "a process of unselfing",[16] notes that all the adventurers in spiritual conquest have first to lay bare and then to tear out the interests which nourish and fatten 'the self'—however innocent these may seem in the eyes of the world. For them there is one rule only—the merciless rejection of everything that obstructs their path. Each is a judge for himself alone and knows for himself alone. Only the Curé d'Ars knew why he had to renounce the scent of roses. Only Bunyan knew why he had to stop dancing, playing bowls and ringing bells. But to anyone who knows anything about these souls, their petty renunciations, far from raising a smile, will seem like so many acts of heroism.

Among his sins Bunyan notes his habit of swearing, and Professor G. B. Harrison attributes the morbid tenacity of this weakness to a perverted form of the need for self-expression.[17] And when we come to know Bunyan well and have been struck a hundred times by the violence of his need for unburdening himself, we willingly accept this explanation. But perhaps, too, Bunyan swore by way of compensation and defiance. He swore because to him swearing was a kind of affirmation of virility.[18] He swore, too, to attract attention.[19] And, as St. Augustine put it, he took pleasure not only in the doing of the deed, " but in the praise ".[20]

And here we touch on the sin of which our author accused himself most often—pride. When a friend remarked one day on the excellence of the sermon he had just preached, Bunyan begged him not

---

[15] Evelyn Underhill, *Mysticism, a Study in the Nature and Development of Man's Spiritual Consciousness* (London, 12th ed., revised 1930), pp. 212–215.

[16] E. D. Starbuck, *The Psychology of Religion* (London, 1899), p. 127.

[17] G. B. Harrison, *John Bunyan, a Study in Personality* (London, 1928), p. 17. There was much swearing in the 17th century—that is well known. Arthur Dent who exercised such a lively influence over Bunyan notes it with distress : " For many there be, which cannot speake tenne words but one shall be an oath . . . Now adaies we cannot almost talke with a man but (in ordinary speech) he will belch out one oath or another." *Op. cit.*, p. 139.

[18] Cf. *Badman*. " He reckoned himself a man's fellow when he had learned to swear and curse boldly." II, 601.

[19] *G. A.*, par. 26 leaves this to be assumed.

[20] " *Et libebat facere non solum libidine facti, verum etiam laudis.*" *Confessions*, Book II, III, 7.

E

53

to say such a thing, for the devil had already whispered it to him before he left the pulpit.[21]   And once he asked whether anyone possessed even a thimbleful of the grace of humility.[22]

In *The Pilgrim's Progress* he gives us a transposition of his own life, and it is noteworthy that Christian had first to fight against the sins of the spirit.   He alone found the 'valley of humiliation' distressing, while Mercy, for example, found it sweet and peaceful.   And if Bunyan made Mr. Self-Satisfied the Devil's most redoubtable supporter in the epic of *The Holy War* it was because he himself had experienced the dangers not only of vanity but also of the nobler forms of pride—pride in work done in the service of God, pride in spiritual progress.   " I was proud of my Godliness, and indeed I did all I did either to be seen of, or to be well spoken of, by Man." [23]   Satan makes use even of the victories that the sinner gains over himself to distil his poisons, and his temptations are sometimes so subtle that man gives way to them without knowing that he is doing so.   And considering even the Poverello of Assisi wanted to be adored by the whole world,[24] how can we wonder that Bunyan sinned by pride even while in the act of humbling himself—as for example when he exaggerated the insignificance of his origins in order to exalt his destiny.[25]

Thus sensuality and pride—with the inbred intractability that the latter fault entails—constituted for Bunyan the fleshly man that he must, bit by bit, overthrow.

But his task was so burdensome that at first he despaired; and his ideal of the perfect life was so high that he was sure he could never attain to it.   And so he avenged himself on his over-exacting soul by revolting against God and wallowing in sin.   He made the most of his doom so as to accumulate the irreparable.   Since God cannot forgive a sinner such as I, he said to himself, I might as well be damned for a lot of sins as for a few.   And so, with death in his heart, he returned to his games: " I returned desperately to my game." [26]   Or perhaps he said to himself that if all other joy was to be denied him—if the joys of the Celestial City were beyond his reach—then all that was left him was to enjoy to satiety the pleasures of the

[21] George Offor, *Memoir of John Bunyan, Works*, I, p. lxx.
[22] *Christ a Complete Saviour*, I, p. 213.   [23] *G. A.*, par. 32.
[24] Paul Sabatier, *Vie de Saint Francois d'Assise* (2nd ed., 1894), p. 15.
[25] Cf. *supra*, p. I.   [26] *G. A.*, par 24.

stomach.[27] Thus the triumph of a sort of demoniacal perversity was narrowly linked to the defeat of his highest religious aspirations. He realised this thoroughly later when he said that atheists were perhaps those who had lost all hope.[28]

He sinned, therefore, to add flavour to a pleasure that nevertheless ceaselessly eluded him. In bleak little phrases, touchingly lacking in art, he admits the bitterness mixed with the taste of his laborious sins: " Now therefore I went on in Sin with great greediness of Mind, still grudging that I could not be so satisfied with it as I would." [29]

But if Bunyan sinned for sinning's sake, it may also have been because he was unknowingly following one of Luther's tactics— the desire to liberate oneself from an unspecified agony by giving it the shape of a known and catalogued serious sin, by throwing oneself against the concrete form so as not to feel the vague disquiet that gnaws secretly. There were times, Luther thought, when one should drink a drop too much, commit some sin in hatred and contempt of the devil so as not to give him the chance of turning trifles into a matter of conscience.[30] But whereas Luther thought himself cleverer than Satan, Bunyan was well aware that such subtle invitations to sin are the devil's supreme craft.[31]

We can see again the richness of Bunyan's precociously developed consciousness in the hatred he thought he entertained for religion. " In these days, the thoughts of Religion were very grievous to me. I could neither endure it myself, nor that any other should. . . . Then I said unto God," he continues, appropriating Job's words, " depart from me, for I desire not the knowledge of thy ways." [32]

There could be no better way of expressing man's dread of what attracts him most vitally. Obscurely Bunyan saw that if ever he set out on the path to God, he would want to go forward to the end.

[27] G. A., par. 24: " I found within me a great desire to take my fill of sin and I made as much haste as I could to fill my belly with delicates lest I should die before my desire."

[28] The Jerusalem Sinner Saved, I, p. 92.   [29] G. A., par. 26.

[30] Cf. Lucien Febvre, op. cit., pp. 269–270.

[31] Compare this idea of Père Lacombe : " Le plus grand sacrifice qu'on pouvait faire à Dieu était de commettre le péché qu'on avait le plus en horreur." Cf. E. Aegerter, Madame Guyon, une aventurière mystique (Paris, 1941), p. 104.   [32] G. A., par. 10.

He has excellently analysed in one of his books, though without a single direct allusion to his own life, this need to flee which is experienced by certain men at the moment when their conscience awakens. " An alehouse, a whorehouse, a playhouse, sports, pleasures, sleep, the world, and what not, so they may stave off the power of the word of God," [33] Bunyan wrote, analysing the basic reason for diversion. It is not from oneself that one turns away, but from God in the depths of oneself.

The hour had not yet come for Bunyan to change his way of life; and nevertheless this adolescent, who believed himself to be irreligious and claimed to sin with the greatest of pleasure, trembled with horror when he heard a supposedly devout man swear, or when he saw some wrong deed done.[34] This was because Bunyan knew with a vague certainty that he himself would be incapable of being a merely ordinary Christian. If he had the faith, then he would want his soul to be steeped in the divine message, " find his soul and Scripture together ",[35] and never rest until his life was in harmony with the Bible. " Thy life squared according to the Scriptures both in word and practice." [36]

But confronted by the vastness of the sacrifice required of him, he preferred not to accept the challenge. Not yet. And, since the two texts throw light on each other and open up vistas of thought, the tinker's groping progress gains by being offset by St. Augustine's more lucid advance. " But I wretched, most wretched, in the very commencement of my early youth, had begged chastity of Thee and said ' Give me chastity, and continency, only not yet.' For I feared lest Thou shouldest hear me soon." [37]

Not yet, " *Sed noli modo !* " " Then I said unto God : depart from me, for I desire not the knowledge of thy ways."

★

This respite was granted him. The army, though it strengthened in him the seeds that were later to grow, brought a diversion for a time. It was not until after his marriage that he was again torn by scruples. When we were examining the first influences undergone by Bunyan, we saw that his marriage represented a landmark in his life. And if we have put the study of those influences in a chapter apart, it is

[33] *Saved by Grace*, I, 350.   [34] *G. A.*, par. 11.
[35] *A Few Sighs from Hell*, III, 721.   [36] *Ibid.*, 720.
[37] *Confessions*, VIII, 7, 17.

precisely so that we need not be distracted here from the solitary struggle of a soul. Whatever share other people have in our interior lives, ultimately we have to carry our burdens, and the responsibility for our choice, alone. The voice of his wife need not have awakened an echo in Bunyan, nor need the love he received from her have touched his soul. And yet in fact Bunyan felt the wave of his first religious aspirations surge up within himself.

To begin with he attended Elstow church, where the Anglican rite was observed. The curate, Christopher Hall, though he baptised his son ' Oliver ' in honour of Cromwell and prohibited the profanation of Sunday by village games, remained faithful to the solemn rites of the Established Church, in spite of the recent inter-dictions.[38] And, by a delicious irony of fate, it was the beauty of the liturgy that carried away the future Baptist minister! The Puritan-to-be blossomed under the touch of profane ceremonial; and Rome's future enemy meekly trod Rome's path, which leads to the spiritual by means of sensuous beauty.[39] What a Catholic would this man have made, who trembled under the impact of majestic forms, rhythmic prose and the caress of song! In his bleak religion, Bunyan always felt an unconscious uneasiness.[40] Catholicism or High Anglicanism might perhaps have chased winter from his soul.

The return to church gave his spiritual life fresh impetus. His fear of being damned returned.[41] A sermon against Sunday games re-awoke his sense of guilt. He felt crushed under the weight of his sins: " greatly loaden therewith [42]. . . a great burden upon my spirit ".[43] Once more he was haunted by the vision of hell. And already the desire to be a saint was forming within him out of the fear of being an outcast; it seemed necessary to him to live better so as not to die. His longing to believe had something desperate about it. " Thou must believe," he wrote, " *because* thou canst not pray, *because* thou canst not do; thou must believe because there is nothing

---

[38] Cf. C. H. Firth, *Oliver Cromwell*, p. 361. The Anglican liturgy was forbidden in 1645, but the new discipline was never vigorously applied.

[39] *G. A.*, par. 16.

[40] See our chapter ' Why Bunyan Wrote '. Compare William James : " An imagination captured by splendour could not be satisfied with a purely personal religion. It needs majestic and complex institutions whose parts form a fine hierarchy." *L'Experience Religieuse* (Paris, 1906), p. 384.

[41] *G. A.*, pars. 18, 20.   [42] *G. A.*, pars. 18, 20.   [43] *G. A.*, pars. 18, 20.

in thee naturally that is good." [44]   By faith he would triumph over all the weakness and ailments of his soul.   After all, God was a doctor,[45] and "Christ's Church is an hospital of sick, wounded and afflicted people".[46]

It was at this time that he experienced a strange hallucination. In the full light of day he suddenly saw Jesus looking at him, and a voice that went through him like a dart said: "Wilt thou leave thy sins and go to Heaven, or have thy sins and go to hell?"[47]   Bunyan had just entered the realm of Law, and each day saw an increase in the number of his sins—as it is written: "God has given the Law that sins may abound."   He tells us that an 'outward reformation' started to work within him.[48]   We would call it an ethical reformation, and at first it brought him some happiness.   The more he set himself to study the divine requirements, the more he strove to satisfy them.   He stopped swearing, he stopped playing games, he stopped bell-ringing; but with each renunciation the Law seemed to demand yet more, and finally a panic, fed by all the superstitions of the day, took possession of him.[49]

For example, after he had given up the vain pleasures of a bell-ringer he still went to watch his comrades—until that, too, seemed to him to involve guilt.   He said to himself: "How if one of the bells should fall?" and forthwith found a safe place under a large beam, but was then seized with the fear that the fall of a bell might reach him even there.   So he retreated still farther and placed himself

[44] *The Doctrine of the Law and Grace*, I, 519.
[45] *The Jerusalem Sinner Saved*, I, 75.
[46] *No Way to Heaven but by Jesus Christ*, I, 327.
[47] *G. A.*, par. 22.
[48] *G. A.*, par. 30.
[49] Here is one that Bunyan knew well, as it is related in Clark's *Looking-Glass for Saints and Sinners* (1657), a book he liked and quoted from. "Not long since, in Bedfordshire, a match at football being appointed on the Sabbath, in the afternoon, whilst two were in the belfry, tolling of a bell to call the company together, there was suddenly heard a clap of thunder, and a flash of lightning was seen by some that sat in the church porch coming through a dark lane, and flashing in their faces, which much terrified them, and passing through the porch into the belfry, it tripped up his heels that was tolling the bell, and struck him stark dead; and the other that was with him was so sorely blasted therewith, that shortly after he died also." Quoted by George Offor in his "Memoir of John Bunyan", in *The Whole Works of John Bunyan* (London, 1862), vol. I, p. xiv.

at the door of the steeple, when suddenly a final fear took hold of him: " How if the steeple itself should fall ? " [50]

It was an absurd and groundless fear, without other cause than the disorder of a fevered spirit. But poor Bunyan often knew these nameless dreads, these terrors akin to madness.[51] Although he was married and on the point of becoming the father of a family—if he was not already one—he was still adolescent and passing through that period of " storm and stress " [52] which precisely characterises adolescence.

However, one day in a Bedford street he came across three or four poor women sitting in a doorway in the sun and conversing about God. He drew near and listened, and words that he did not understand reached his ears. " I heard but I understood not." [53] The conversation was about a new birth, about the work of God in their hearts, the corruption of human nature and the love of God which re-kindles souls: they also talked of the ' filth ' of mere effort, which was despicable in God's eyes. Assuredly Bunyan had already heard of justification by faith, but his inner territory had not been prepared to receive this doctrine. Now, after his exhausting efforts at moral reformation, it more than filled his need: the doctrine was able to penetrate within him and bear fruit. The more so as it touched him in a radiance of joy—these women seemed to be so happy. They knew the peace for which he longed.

This encounter with the women marked the beginning of a period of great intellectual ferment. All his thought became " fixed on eternity ".[54] He read the Bible furiously.[55] His longing for the divine became yet more ardent. He hungered for God.[56] Wherever he was—at home or out in the fields—he prayed.[57] His whole being

---

[50] G. A., par. 33.
[51] Cf. Mark Rutherford : " I was beside myself with a kind of terror which I cannot further explain. It is possible for another person to understand any emotion which has a distinct cause, but how shall he understand the worst of all calamities, the nameless dread, the efflux of all vitality, the ghastly haunting terror which is nearly akin to madness." *The Autobiography of Mark Rutherford* (13th ed. Fisher Unwin), p. 113.
[52] See E. Diller Starbuck, *op. cit.*, p. 213.
[53] G. A., par. 37.   [54] G. A., par. 42.
[55] G. A., par. 46. " I was then never out of the Bible."
[56] G. A., par. 56. " A vehement hunger."   [57] G. A., par. 56.

was lost in prayer. Spontaneous prayer which leapt hot from his heart " like the blood of a wound ",[58] or Biblical prayer, as when he lifted his heart and recited Psalm 51, which described so well his own spiritual climate: " Create in me a clean heart, O God! "

Hours of prayer and hours of joy. But aridity followed the refreshing shower. Anguish gripped him again with the two questions: " Have I the faith ? "   " Am I elected ? ",[59] and to these the human intelligence can bring no satisfying answer. They are questions which from time to time have driven people mad—people who lack the good fortune of benefiting from some inner enlightenment, whether real or imaginary. Calvin very properly said that the question of election should not be dwelt on, because " *le diable n'a nulle plus griefve tentation ne perilleuse pour esbranler les fidèles* ",[60] but how can one avoid thinking about it ? Bunyan believed that, if he had the faith and was numbered among the elect, he would be able to work miracles.[61] The temptation came to him on the road from Elstow to Bedford to make the puddles dry up and the dry part of the road become wet: " I must say to the puddles that were in the horse-pads, be dry. And to the dry places, be you puddles! " [62]

So we see that Bunyan's ignorance heightened the Puritan torment about election.[63] He did not know quite how to interpret the decree of predestination, and seemed almost to have an ingenuous picture of

[58] *I Will Pray with the Spirit*, I, 624.

[59] *G. A.*, pars. 47, 57.

[60] Calvin, *op.*, IV, 509, quoted by H. Bois, ' *La Prédestination d'après Calvin.*' *Revue de Métaphysique et de Morale*, special number, 1918.

[61] Edwards, *Gangraena* (error no. 145, part I), denounced the error of those who asserted that the gift of working miracles still existed.

A certain Matthew Coker claimed to have cured a leper, given the gift of walking to the halt, of sight to the blind. Cf. Robert Barclay, *op. cit.*, pp. 218–219. The ' ranter ' John Robins termed himself ' Almighty God ' and Lodowicke Muggleton 'the sole judge of men'. Cf. Whiting, *op. cit.*, pp. 243 and 252. When leaving prison the unfortunate James Naylor, too, believed himself to be God, ' Son of Justice and Prince of Peace ' and everyone knows about his entry into Bristol where his adorers threw clothes under his horse's feet. Cf. Robert Barclay, *op. cit.*, p. 425, and M. J. Milsand, ' Les Quakers ', in *Revue des Deux Mondes*, Apr., 1850.

[62] *G. A.*, par. 51.

[63] When Bunyan reviewed his past he admitted quite rightly that ignorance had added to his pain. " I was tossed betwixt the Devil and my own ignorance ", par. 52.

God as a sort of Lord Chief Justice who from time to time assembled his court and delivered his sentences. And he saw himself as thinking: " Aren't I too late ? Isn't the Day of Grace past and gone ? Won't God save only the good people of Bedford." [64] On almost every page we find expressions of his fear of solitude, as in the desperate cry: " I counted myself alone, and above the most of men unblessed." [65]

And here we must pause a little and try to trace some hidden orientation in the zigzag progress of this soul.

Bunyan had first been guided towards religion by outside influences: the personal influence of his wife and the institutional influence of the Anglican Church. By means of these the fresh and intimate sense of God was reborn within him. He subsequently set aside this visible world, which had led him to the invisible kingdom of the spirit, where sadnesses and joys followed in the wake of ' supernatural ' visitations, and every day buried himself more deeply within himself, until he was finally suffocated. [66]

Thus he next had to try to tear himself away from his interior universe, wherein, after flourishing, he now withered away. He had to return to the outside world, participate in the life of a group and form friendships. Bunyan needed human warmth and brotherhood. His unquiet soul needed the support of the approval of others. [67] And that was why the joy reflected in the eyes of the ' good people ' and ' poor women ' of Bedford stayed in his memory and awoke in his heart a longing for their brotherly sect. As he himself wrote, he felt a hunger and an urgent desire to have a place among ' the saints ' and to comfort himself "with the heat of their sun ". [68] Bunyan could never have gained peace had he not entered a Church capable of satisfying his need for human fellowship.

But the hour of peace had not yet sounded for a Puritan uncertain

---

[64] G. A., pars. 57, 66.
[65] G. A., par. 87.
[66] The knowledgeable reader will recognise our debt to Von Hügel here : *The Mystical Element of Religion as Studied in St. Catherine of Genoa and her Friends* (London, 2nd ed., 1909).
[67] G. A., par. 32. " Now, I was, as they said, become godly ; now, I was become a right honest man. But, oh ! when I understood that these were their words and opinions of me, it pleased me mighty well."
[68] G. A., pars. 53, 56.

as to his election. Phrases suddenly re-echoed in his mind coming from he knew not where. He no longer acted; he was acted upon. And he admirably translated these phenomena of sensory automatism into concrete terms: " I was almost *made* to see . . .," [69] " This scripture did also seem to me to *trample* upon all my desires . . .," [70] " That Sentence fell *with weight* upon my spirit," [71] " This Scripture . . . would sound so loud within me, yea, and as it were call so strongly after me, that once above all the rest, I turned my head over my shoulder, thinking verily that some Man had, behind me, called to me." [72]

His soul became a dwelling-ground where Biblical texts confronted each other. He felt as if he had a pair of scales inside his mind— now one end was uppermost, now the other, under the weight of scriptural texts.[73] He felt that life was slipping away from him [74] and that he was either going to faint with weakness [75] or become mad.[76]

But a beam of light occasionally penetrated this night of anguish. Words " broke " [77] upon his mind and brought him a little calm. " Go out into the highways and hedges, and compel them to come in, that my house may be filled." [78] Or perhaps a phrase "seized" his heart and " abode " there [79] so as to fill it with light: " Was ever any that trusted in the Lord, and was confounded ? " [80] And even in his worst moments a reflection of this light shone on him and gave him some warmth: " That word doth still, at times, shine before my face." [81]

So majestic were these threatening or consoling voices, so terrifying or intoxicating the emotion they excited, that Bunyan remembered

[69] *G. A.*, par. 71.   [70] *G. A.*, par. 58.   [71] *G. A.*, par. 62.
[72] *G. A.*, par. 93.   [73] *G. A.*, par. 205.   [74] *G. A.*, par. 58.
[75] *G. A.*, pars. 62, 116.
[76] *G. A.*, par. 61. That strict Calvinism involves for many people depression, melancholy and mental troubles is made plain enough by the documents of the time. See, *inter alia*, Richard Baxter, *Autobiography* (ed. *cit.*), " I was troubled this year with multitudes of melancholy persons." Very wisely he opposes those who put too many " fears, tears and scruples " into religion (p. 216). Cries and convulsions are not a sign of conversion, this moderate Puritan points out. Love is the sign : " Love is their best sign " (p. 217). And joy.
[77] *G. A.*, par. 68.   [78] Luke, xiv. 23.   [79] *G. A.*, par. 64.
[80] *G. A.*, par. 63.   [81] *G. A.*, par. 65.

the very place where he had heard them and even the position of his body at the time: it was in the middle of a game, just as he had struck the ' cat ' and was going to strike again; [82] or it was on the road from Elstow to Bedford; [83] or in a country lane. [84]   If the author of *Grace Abounding* seems sometimes unsure when outlining unexceptional memories, he is vigorous and lucid when following the curves of the heights and depths of his spiritual life.   The truth is that he never saw his ordeals as the pulsation of a private rhythm nor yet as the conflict of a divided soul; but as the war waged between God and the devil for the possession of a creature. [85]   It was the devil in person who tempted him. [86]   It was Jesus Himself who spoke to him.   Bunyan listened to Christ as if He were a contemporary: certain passages in the Bible were uttered for him, personally: " When the Lord Jesus did speak these words, he then did think of me." [87]   If Bunyan had been capable of thinking at that time that his sufferings and joys were caused merely by mental disorders he would really have gone mad.   The greatness of his faith saved him.   It is almost essential for a convinced Calvinist to believe in a personal call from Christ, and there are numbers among them who claim to have heard this call. We need only mention John Wesley, who tells us that at a quarter to nine on Wednesday, May 24, 1738, in the middle of a meeting in Aldergate Street, he received the assurance that Christ had " taken away my sins, even mine, and saved me from the law of sin and death ". [88]

So Bunyan's spiritual life moved forward, and the superficial reader who is surprised at the violent eddyings of this soul might think that Bunyan never made any headway; and Bunyan himself might well have thought so from time to time.   However, the wave that comes in is less strong than the one that goes out.   Though buffeted and sometimes submerged, our author did progress: " *Itus et reditus.*" Love for God, like love for a human being, requires this rhythm and

---

[82] G. A., par. 22.   [83] G. A., par. 51.   [84] G. A., par. 66.
[85] Compare Père Surin : " *Je sens que l'esprit de Dieu et l'esprit du Démon ont mon corps et mon âme comme champ de bataille et que chacun y fait ses impressions.*" *Triomphe de l'Amour* quoted by H. Brémond, *Histoire littéraire du sentiment religieux*, V, 253.
[86] G. A., par. 107, for example.
[87] G. A., par. 68.
[88] John Wesley, *The Journal* (ed. by Nehemiah Curnock, 8 vols.), I, 476.

alternation, these falterings and increasings.[89]   Pascal knew this when he said: " *L'attachement à une même pensée fatigue et ruine l'esprit de l'homme. . . . Il faut quelquefois ne pas savoir que l'on aime : et ce n'est pas commettre une infidélité car l'on n'en aime pas d'autres ; c'est reprendre des forces pour mieux aimer.*" [90]   If Bunyan retreated then, it was so that he could surpass himself.   From the depths of his despair he still cried to Christ to call him: " I cried to Christ to call me." [91]   And this high desire burnt in him like a flame.[92]

All this time he had never stopped seeing the ' poor women ' of Bedford and, through them, had made the acquaintance of their pastor, John Gifford, who exercised over Bunyan the strongest personal influence he underwent, if we except that of his first wife. Gifford was a convert from a life of profligacy, and therefore had the authority of personal experience when talking to Bunyan.   Other Baptists met at his house.   They talked about sin, and we know that as Bunyan became more and more enlightened about the fundamental corruption of human nature, he brought stricter and stricter judgments to bear upon himself.   His despair grew.   He deemed himself to be farther from God than ever, experienced the curious inhibitions we have described above [93] and started to envy the animals as unthreatened by divine wrath.   " Yea gladly ", he wrote, " would I have been in condition of Dog or Horse, for I knew they had no soul to perish

---

[89] Cf. St. Augustine : " *Quid est, quod haec rerum pars alternat defectu et profectu, offensionibus et conciliationibus ?   An is est modus earum ?* "   *Confessions*, VIII, 3, 8.

[90] *Discours sur les passions de l'amour*, complete works published in chronological order by Leon Brunschvig and Pierre Boutroux (Paris, 1908), vol. III, pp. 130–131.

[91] *G. A.*, par. 72.

[92] *G. A.*, par. 73.   " Thus I continued for a time, all on a flame to be converted to Jesus Christ."

[93] *G. A.*, par. 82.   " I durst not take a pin or a stick etc. . . . I could not now tell how to speak my words, for fear I should misplace them."   Cf. Baxter on the psychology of this family of souls to which Bunyan belonged for so long : " All their thoughts are contracted and turned inwards on themselves : self-troubling is the sum of their thoughts and lives. . . . He is endless in his scruples, afraid lest he sins in every word he speaketh and in every thought, and every look, and every meal he eateth," etc. *Christian Directory*, p. 313.

under the everlasting weights of Hell or Sin." [94] This is a strange admission, and yet Bunyan is not alone in making it.[95]

Meanwhile belief in justification by faith became every day more necessary and entered deep into his being—though farther into his heart than into his intellect. He felt he would never be able to satisfy the demands of the Law, that the shadow of a bad thought was enough to damn a man, and that Christ alone could save him, who alone was just in God's eyes. Yet, by a phenomenon of unconscious auto-suggestion, Bunyan always ended up by feeling what he passionately desired to feel. The current of his subterranean ideas invariably succeeded in rising to the level of his consciousness, and then in bursting forth into the daylight. We have the impression of feeling his secret life pulsate as if across a diaphragm; we hear the murmur of his buried thoughts and feelings and follow the process of their ripening until, when the ' vision' happens or the ' voice' breaks out, we almost exclaim to ourselves: "That is just what I expected!" Probably not the identical Bible text which recommended itself to Bunyan's soul, but a phrase with the same meaning and bearing the same message. This one, for instance, for which all his desires clamoured: "He hath made peace by the Blood of his Cross." [96] Or this: " Forasmuch, then, as the Children are partakers of flesh and blood, he also himself likewise took part of the same; that through death he might destroy him that had the power of death, that is, the Devil, and deliver them who, through fear of death, were all their lifetime subject to bondage." [97]

This phenomenon of unconscious auto-suggestion is particularly apparent in paragraphs 212 and 213 of *Grace Abounding*. Bunyan was at that time obsessed by a temptation that we shall examine further on—the temptation to "sell Christ" as Esau his birthright, and he tells us that his peace and joy depended entirely on whatever Biblical text he heard within himself. If it was a passage about Grace, he was in peace; if it was a passage about Esau, he was in agony.

[94] G. A., par. 104, and also par. 88 : " The beasts, birds, fishes, etc., I blessed their condition . . . they were not obnoxious to the wrath of God."

[95] See for example in William James, *op. cit.*, p. 133, a quotation from Henry Alline, evangelical of Nova Scotia : " Often I looked at animals with a feeling of envy. I ardently wished to be in their place, so as not to have a soul to lose."

[96] G. A., par. 115.   [97] G. A., par. 116.

"Lord, thought I, if both these Scriptures would meet in my heart at once, I wonder which of them would get the better of me." Immediately he was seized by an ardent desire that this experiment should happen. And two or three days later it did happen. The two 'scriptures' "bolted upon" him and struggled. At last the one about Esau waxed weak, withdrew and vanished, while the one about Grace prevailed in the radiance of joy.

On thinking it over, Bunyan was inclined to believe that that was a miracle. We, alas, are more sceptical! But what matters is not the ephemeral psychological phenomenon, but the upward progress, ever more steady, of a soul towards peace.

While praying that sacred texts might bring him light and comfort, Bunyan cultivated his unrest. If the sense of sin ever tended to weaken in his heart, he forced it back again.[98] The reason for this voluntary seeking-out of torture lies in Bunyan's growing familiarity with the fashionable theology of the day. He knew that sin was "the first step to salvation",[99] the gateway through which he could pass from the domain of Law to that of Grace. He knew that the "way to heaven lies by the gates of hell",[100] and that repentance must be desperate if Jesus is to hear it. He agreed with what Cromwell once put in lovely and virile words: "Our sorrow is the inverted image of our nobleness. The depth of our despair measures what capability and height of claim we have to hope."[101] This cult of the sense of sin is frequent with Protestants, and William James quotes Charles G. Finney, the American evangelical, who wrote in his memoirs: "I tried to revive my sense of my sin which, until then, had been weighing me down so heavily."[102]

However, Bunyan need not have feared that the sources of unrest would dry up. His sense of moral solitude[103] and his unsatisfied desire

[98] *G. A.*, par. 86. "And if it [my guilt] was going off . . . for the sense of sin would be sometimes as if it would die, and go quite away, then I would also strive to fetch it upon my heart again," etc.

[99] *The Saint's Knowledge of Christ's Love*, II, 28.

[100] *P. P.*, Part I, p. 59.

[101] Carlyle: *Oliver Cromwell's Letters and Speeches*, vol. I, p. 67 (London, 1846).

[102] William James, *op. cit.*, p. 183.

[103] *G. A.*, par. 87. "I counted myself alone and above the most of men unblessed."

to unburden himself in words kept them abundantly watered. To explain himself, to multiply his joy and diminish his pain by communicating both, was the craving of this self-educated man who was slowly shaping himself, who wanted to make his discoveries known and give voice to his wonderment. Above all, he wanted to spread around him the love that was growing in his heart so swiftly that he did not know how to contain it: " I could not tell how to contain it." [104] " I thought I could have spoken of his Love, and of his Mercy to me, even to the very Crows that sat upon the ploughed Lands before me." [105]

Though almost suffocated by the violence of his emotions, Bunyan was assailed by intellectual doubts. Were not the Scriptures, after all, " a fable and cunning story " ? [106] Did God really exist ? If God was love, how could He have left so many people in ignorance ? [107] And since the Jews, the Moors and the Pagans all thought their religion to be the true one, why should not ours, too, be " a think-so " ? [108] How could Jesus be man and God at one and the same time ? " Once I was much troubled to know whether the Lord Jesus was both man as well as God, and God as well as man." [109]

The devil, who, as Bunyan tells us, whispered these doubts to him, thereby proved once again that he lacks neither vigour nor subtlety ! Indeed, it is possible that he appeared as too good a dialectician for our tinker, and thus his shot misfired. He certainly failed to draw Bunyan into rational speculation. Remarkably gifted as Bunyan was, he never gave the intelligence an important rôle in religion.

He did not try to resolve these doubts by reasonings which a presentiment told him might turn back on him: " I quickly felt . . . such arguings as these would return again upon me." [110] One thing

[104] G. A., par. 92.   [105] G. A., par. 92.   [106] G. A., par. 96.

[107] G. A., par. 97. " And could I think, that so many ten thousands, in so many countries and kingdoms, should be without the knowledge of the right way to Heaven (if there were indeed a Heaven) and that we only, who live in a corner of the Earth, should alone be blessed therewith ? "

William Langland, of whom Bunyan often reminds us, could not believe that Aristotle was damned. Cf. J. J. Jusserand, L'épopée mystique de William Langland (Paris, 1893), p. 96.

[108] G. A., par. 97.   [109] G. A., par. 122.   [110] G. A., par. 98.

only he knew: that Christ was his unique consolation, and religion his whole life. Thus it was essential that Christ should be true. Life was not a work of the intelligence, but a construction of faith. By an irony of which he never became aware, Bunyan behaved like the Quakers whom he loathed. Like them, he ultimately followed interior inspiration; he listened solely to the reasons of the heart and made his feelings the criterion of truth. His final reason for a rejection or denial was if a suggestion were distasteful or unpalatable to his soul: " Only by the distaste that they gave unto my spirit, I felt that there was something in me that refused to embrace them." [111] The foundations of some people's religion reside solely inside themselves, and—what may seem the height of absurdity—so as the better to establish their convictions, they rely on the very legend whose authenticity they doubt. With them the imagination is so strong that it triumphs over reason itself. The complacent intellect then provides the firmness of line and the stability of a logical construction for the dreams that seduce it. " In the midst of the throne and the four beasts," he read in the Apocalypse, " and in the midst of the elders stood a Lamb." And it seemed to him luminous—" methought this did glister! " [112] It seemed to him that on the throne was His Godhead and in the midst of the elders His humanity. Thus Jesus was certainly man and God at the same time.

Bunyan's exegesis is simply one particular form of the eternal *credo quia absurdum* which, strictly speaking, means—as Miguel de Unamuno has pointed out—*credo quia consolans*.[113] From Tertullian [114] down to Bunyan we have the same triumphant affirmation of irrationality, of faith and of life. For them there are even not enough mysteries in religion in which they can lose themselves and from which they can draw strength.[115]

In spite of all this, Bunyan did not always succeed in his battles,

[111] *G. A.*, par. 100.   [112] *G. A.*, par. 122.
[113] Miguel de Unamuno, *The Tragic Sense of Life*. N.R.F. (Paris), p. 63.
[114] One finds in Tertullian phrases like these : *"Credibile quia ineptum est."* (*De Carne Christi.*)
[115] Cf. Sir Thomas Browne : " Methinks there be not impossibilities enough in Religion for an active faith. . . . I love to lose myself in a mystery. I can answer all the objections of Satan and my rebellious reason with that odd resolution I learned of Tertullian, *Certum est, quia impossible est.*" *Religio Medici*, 1st part (Everyman ed.), pp. 10, 11.

especially when his tempter laid sentimental rather than intellectual snares. It was along these lines that Satan tried to persuade him to "sell Christ", to "exchange him for the things of this life".[116] "The temptation lay upon me for the space of a year," he tells us, " and I was not rid of it one day in a Month." He was assailed for hours on end.[117] " Sell him, sell him, sell him ! " These words swept over his mind like a whirlwind, so that he was reduced to a state of stupor and lassitude in which he no longer knew whether he had accepted their suggestion or not. Convulsions shook him.[118] " In labouring to gainsay and resist this wickedness, my very body also would be put into action or motion by way of pushing or thrusting with my hands or elbows, still answering—as fast as the destroyer said, *Sell him*—I will not, I will not, I will not." [119] Until finally one morning in bed, Bunyan, like all obsessed people, set himself free by giving way to the obsession.[120]

What was the meaning of this strange outburst? It is by no means impossible that at a certain point of his life Bunyan felt a desire for social promotion and a thoroughgoing enjoyment of the world's riches. It is not impossible that the obsession which seems absurd and gratuitous on the surface was the manifestation of obscure and repressed desires. The radical distrust Bunyan sometimes showed for society's favours suggests that he perhaps exaggerated his rigorism the better to triumph over temptations that attracted him. When Bunyan's first biographer and friend offered an apprenticeship to his son so as to assure him a better future, Bunyan replied that God had not sent him into the world to assure the preferment of his family, but to preach the Gospel.[121]

---

[116] *G. A.*, par. 133. [117] *G. A.*, par. 136.

[118] Bunyan had already experienced such. " And in so strong a measure was this temptation upon me, that often I have been ready to clap my hand under my Chin, to hold my Mouth from opening; and to that end also I have had thoughts at other times, to leap with my head downward, into some Muck-hill hole or other, to keep my Mouth from speaking." *G. A.*, par. 103.

[119] *G. A.*, par. 137.

[120] *G. A.*, par. 139. Cf. Richard Baxter : " The very pain of their fears draws their thoughts to what they fear. . . . And oft-times they feel a vehement urgency, as if something within them urged them to speak such or such a blasphemous or foolish word; and they can have no rest unless they yield." *Christian Directory*, p. 314.

[121] *A New and Authentic Account of the Life and Death of Mr. John Bunyan,*

The critic, limited to conjecture, can but pose questions and offer tentative answers, in the hope of throwing some light on the mystery of the moral crises that Bunyan sometimes referred to as " storms ".[122]

After this ordeal Bunyan collapsed. " For the space of two hours, I was like a man bereft of life." [123]   He did not know that he had just touched the bottom of the abyss and that his fall was to be followed by an ascent.   But before ridding himself of his straitness and self-concentration, so that Grace could act upon him, Bunyan still had some time to pass in the valley of darkness.   According to him, he lived for another two and a half years in a night-time of anguish; [124] but sorrowful hours appear long.   Perhaps Bunyan unconsciously elongated this period of terror, even while living it, measuring time by this slowest rhythm of his life.   And from a distance, in his retrospective exploration, it must have seemed still more drawn out.   A long past, as St. Augustine said, is perhaps nothing but " a long memory of the past ".[125]

Throughout twenty paragraphs Bunyan repeats himself untiringly, as in the past the sad days repeated themselves.   " And now was I both a burthen and a terror to myself [126]. . . . Oh! none knows the terrors of those days but myself." [127]   His pain was deepened by his reading the life of Francis Spira, an Italian who said he had ' denied Christ ',[128] lost all faith,[129] had been possessed by ' legions of demons '.[130]

Moral anguish is accompanied by physical anguish.   He experienced such a sensation of burning that he sometimes felt as if his chest were being torn in two.[131]   These were nervous phenomena,

late Minister of the Gospel at Bedford, written by a friend to the cause of true Religion—an entire new edition to which are now added notes by W. Mason (London, printed for Alex. Hogg, at the King's Arms (No. 16) Paternoster Row), p. 31.

[122] Cf. G. A., par. 96: ". . . a very great storm came down upon me."
[123] G. A., par. 140.   [124] G. A., par. 142.
[125] Confessions: XI, 28, 37, " sed longum praeteritum longa memoria praeteriti est."   [126] G. A., par. 149.   [127] G. A., par. 153.
[128] A Relation of the Fearful Estate of Francis Spira in the Year 1548 compiled by Nath. Bacon Esq. (London, 1653), p. 28. The reading of Spira was almost a tradition in certain Puritan circles. Cf. R. Baxter: " The reading of Spira's case causeth or increaseth melancholy for many." Christian Directory, p. 312.
[129] Ibid., p. 29.   [130] Ibid., p. 33.   [131] G. A., par. 164.

70

no doubt, bearing a resemblance to the heartaches of St. Theresa of Avila, the inner fire from which she suffered, and the tearing of her being by " sharp teeth ".[132]

But in spite of these hours of motionless torture which give the impression that Bunyan was making no progress at all, we cannot help our conviction that the moment when he gave way to temptation and ' sold Christ ' marked a turning-point in his life.

To begin with, the direct encounter with Luther in the *Commentary on the Epistle to the Galatians* must have helped him a lot even if he did not realise it.   He must have learnt, or more correctly re-dis-covered,[133] not to be surprised at finding the residue of the old corrup-tion still within him.[134]   A Christian, according to Luther, " is not he who hath no sin, but he to whom God imputeth not his sin through faith in Christ ".[135]   The warmth and good cheer in the dialogue in Luther's divided soul must have been sweet to Bunyan: " Martin, thou art not without sin, for thou hast flesh." [136]   And sweeter still the assurance that the hour of Grace is eternal,[137] and that " God is the God of the humble, the afflicted, the oppressed . . . and His nature is to exalt the humble, to feed the hungry, to give sight to the blind, to comfort the broken-hearted, to justify sinners, to quicken the dead." [138]

But, with or without Luther, the temptation and the defeat in themselves offered the possibilities of an ultimate victory.   " When all refuge fails," Bunyan once said, " and a man is made to see that there is nothing left him but sin, death and damnation unless he flies to Christ for life; then he flies, and not till then." [139]   Everything was lacking to Bunyan, and the hour of flight was at hand.   Dead—" bereft of life "—he was going to be able to revive.   By the laby-rinth of its paths the Valley of the Shadow of Death leads to the heights where there is irradiating light.

---

[132] Cf. James H. Leuba, *Psychologie du mysticisme religieux*, translated by Lucien Herr (Paris, 1925), p. 219; a book to study with prudence.

[133] For he had heard it said, and Arthur Dent, to whom he owed so much, had shown him that the second birth does not bring perfection.   Cf. Arthur Dent, *op. cit.*, p. 14.

[134] Luther : *A Commentary on St. Paul's Epistle to the Galatians* (London, ed. 1940), p. 102.

[135] *Ibid.*, p. 72.　　　　　　　　　　[136] Luther, *op. cit.*, p. 336.

[137] *Ibid.*, p. 214.　　　　　　　　　　[138] *Ibid.*, p. 194.

[139] *Come and Welcome to Jesus Christ*, I, 248.

4

The School of the Cross

The school of the cross is the school of light.

JOHN BUNYAN

RETURN UNTO ME![1] This was the resounding call that soon fell on Bunyan's ears, and so urgent was it that he stopped and looked back over his shoulder to see if the God of Grace was following him, a pardon in his hand.[2]

His night was no longer at its darkest when this call rent him. His ascent towards the light, though still painful, was nevertheless an ascent, and the slopes were fanned by breezes from the summit.

If remorse for his 'big' sin took hold of him, a voice would sweep by on the wind asking: " Didst ever refuse to be justified by the Blood of Christ?"[3] and the ever more firmly established answer " No " brought the silence of peace to his heart.

Though he did not admit it, he was beginning to realise in the depths of his heart that the man who experienced such visions could not be an outcast. More than ten years later he was still dazzled by their memory, and his body still glowed. Even then he dared not investigate the mystery of such grace, but his innermost feelings remained unchanged: the sudden breeze was like the coming of an angel.[4]

Of course he still went through hours of torment. The fear of hell had weighed too heavily on him to leave him unscathed. But joy beat within the sadness, and the union of these two gave his soul its characteristic note. Anguish was there, but within a plenitude of love. The day was coming when, wanting to comfort others and with an eye on his own past, he would say: " Thy fears are born of an

[1] *G. A.*, par. 173.　　　　　　　[2] *G. A.*, par. 173.
[3] *G. A.*, par. 174.　　　　　　　[4] *G. A.*, par. 174.

excess of love." "Thou art sick of love." [5] That was everything for him. Anxiety was still there to trouble belief, but then belief, according to Luther's experience, is ' fighting' certainty.[6] Indeed, in reading Bunyan we might well think that God bestows faith only where there is fight—at least in the case of those of His children whom He has created for combat. Luther said that God was a mighty stronghold. Bunyan wanted to hurl himself into a sort of hand-to-hand battle for heaven—" to wrestle for heaven ".[7] Even the most timid of his heroines, Mercy, knocked at the gate of the Kingdom as if she wanted to take it by storm. [8]

It would seem that God sets little store by our moments of fervour, our fleeting triumphs when we stand erect and push upwards. He demands an ever-indecisive struggle on which man must bend himself with relentless perseverance. For it is in perseverance that man's supernatural life is made manifest. This was one of the lessons that Bunyan learnt from reading St. Paul,[9] as well as from his own self-searchings and his experience of human beings. " O it is hard continuing believing, continuing loving, continuing resisting all that opposeth; we are subject to be weary of well-doing," he wrote in his manual *Christian Behaviour*.[10] " There is not so much of a Christian's cross in the beginning of a work as there is in a continual, hearty, conscientious practice thereof," and in loyalty to the chosen Master.[11]

This was why Bunyan continued to be " tossed like a broken Vessel." [12] But the rhythm of his interior life, having slowed down during the hopeless days that followed his renunciation of Christ, now became more rapid. There was never a week without its consolation; twenty times in one hour he felt that God was upholding him when he was in danger of giving way to despair.[13]

His visions continued to enlighten him. One day when he was sitting on a bench in a town not far from Elstow, lost in one of those reveries so precious to his life and genius, he felt that the sun " did grudge to give light ",[14] and that the stones in the streets and the tiles

---

[5] *Come and Welcome*, I, 282.
[6] Cf. Jean Wahl, *Etudes Kierkegaardiennes* (Paris, 1938), p. 299.
[7] *The Strait Gate*, I, 369.   [8] *P. P.*, Part 2, p. 177.
[9] St. Paul, *Gal.*, vi, 9.   [10] *Christian Behaviour*, II, 570.
[11] *Ibid.*   [12] *G. A.*, par. 186.
[13] *G. A.*, pars. 191, 205.   [14] *G. A.*, pars. 187, 188.

on the houses menaced him. He asked in a loud voice " how God could comfort such a wretch as I ", and heard an answer like an echo saying: " This sin is not unto death." Joy swept over him and gave him strength.

One day the voice murmured the following consoling words: " I loved thee whilst thou wast committing this sin ";[15] on another occasion Jesus seemed to pierce the roof of his dwelling to look on him,[16] and yet another time he saw with his soul's eyes Christ on the right hand of the Father, and a voice cried: " Thy righteousness is in Heaven." This was the supreme deliverance. The chains and shackles fell from him just as the burden fell from the shoulders of his pilgrim.[17]

These visions remained in Bunyan's memory, and with the passing of time seemed to gain in size and take greater possession of his soul. An echo of past joys, exquisitely sweet and tender, can often be heard in his latter works. He asked one day of a listener whether Jesus Christ had ever appeared to him even for a minute: " Hast thou not sometimes as it were the very warmth of his wings overshadowing the face of thy soul ? "[18]

Thus if a psychologist studies only *Grace Abounding*, and so comes to the conclusion that Bunyan's religion was that of a diseased soul, he receives and propagates an impression that is altogether false. *Grace Abounding* reflects only one phase of the tinker's spiritual and religious life. After the tempest, calm returned. Indeed, this is foreshadowed in the autobiography. The attentive reader will notice that even during the period that Bunyan could have called his ' dark night ' there is that swift alternating from joy to grief, from despair to hope, which constitutes the rhythm of our author's life and perhaps, in varying intensity, of every human life. If Bunyan exaggerated the horrors of his darkness it was perhaps because he demanded the impossible in desiring always the supreme tension of his being; " There is love, that should be in us as hot as fire. . . . But who finds this heat in love so much as for one poor quarter of an hour together ? "[19]

He emerged so exhausted from his struggle with himself that

[15] *G. A.*, par. 191.   [16] *G. A.*, par. 207.   [17] *G. A.*, par. 229.
[18] *Come and Welcome*, II, 229.
[19] *Christ a Complete Saviour*, I, 213.

there were grounds to fear that he had consumption,[20] very common in England at that time, according to Richard Baxter.[21] Sometimes he was so weak that he thought he could not live.

Satan profited from his illness to make one last assault,[22] but it did not have a deep or lasting effect. Hope refused to be extinguished, and health returned. Joy took possession of him and brought untold energy and vitality in its wake. " I could scarse lie in my Bed for Joy, and Peace, and Triumph, through Christ." [23]

From then onwards Bunyan was ready to bear witness to his Saviour. In offering himself for persecution he advanced towards a fresh deepening of his spiritual life; the boundaries of his soul's understanding fell back, and he achieved his possession of God in the ultimate possession of himself.

★

When Bunyan was arrested on November 12, 1660, he could have fled.[24] When brought before the Judge he could have obtained his liberty.[25] He could have left prison if he had wanted to.[26] He did not want to. And Froude lets it be understood that Bunyan showed such obstinacy that the Government could hardly be blamed for leaving him for twelve years in Bedford gaol.[27]

Was Bunyan obstinate? Yes, but what high motives inspired his obstinacy! To begin with, he believed in the value of example. He knew that by one's own life one could bear witness to Christ. How could his faith be a living reality for his children, his friends, the people of the parish, if he did not show them that it was first and foremost a living reality for himself? This is what he described so admirably in the *Relation* of his imprisonment. " For what will my weak and newly converted brethren think of (my flight) but that I was not so strong in deed as I was in word? " [28] And again: "Seeing

[20] G. A., par. 255.
[21] Richard Baxter, *Autobiography* (ed. *cit.*), p. 11.
[22] G. A., pars. 257, 260.   [23] G. A., par. 263.
[24] *A Relation of the Imprisonment of Mr. John Bunyan*, p. 402. " But had I been minded to have played the coward I could have escaped. . . ."
[25] *Ibid.*, p. 405. " If I could come to him [the justice] and say certain words to him I should be released."
[26] *Ibid.*, pp. 416 *et seq.*
[27] J. A. Froude, *op. cit.*, chap. 5, pp. 64 *et seq.*
[28] *A Relation of the Imprisonment of Mr. John Bunyan*, p. 402.

that God of his mercy should chose me to go upon the forlorn hope in this country, that is to be the first that should be opposed for the Gospel, if I should fly it might be a discouragement to the whole body that might follow after." [29] Bunyan found it natural to endure persecution with inflexible firmness because he believed that to fear man was to forget God.[30] " Ay, say some, that is because he is headstrong, obstinate and one that will hear no reason. No, say I, but it is because his spirit is in the hand, under the conduct and preservation of a Creator." [31] A Creator who upholds him so that he might remain bound to Him.

Bunyan's faith did not derive from simple cerebral knowledge, but —as Faithful, one of the heroes of *The Pilgrim's Progress*, explains to the false pilgrim Talkative—from the knowledge of the heart.[32] " Not a notional and historical assent in the head." [33] Not an intellectual notion [34] but " a principle of life, a principle of strength ".[35] The Bible was his light and his laughter,[36] and it was through the heart that he understood it. Moreover, his convictions had an indescribable power and brightness. He was " more than sure ".[37] He found stronger evidence for the truths of the Gospel than for everyday reality. " I saw ", he said, " it was the blood shed on Mount Calvary that did save and redeem sinners, as clearly and as really with the eyes of my soul as ever, methought, I had seen a penny loaf bought with a penny." [38]

Bunyan's fervour was heightened by his belief in the approaching return of Christ and in the establishment of God's Kingdom on

---

[29] *A Relation of the Imprisonment of Mr. John Bunyan*, p. 402.

[30] *The Saints' Knowledge of Christ's Love*, II, 13.

[31] *Seasonable Counsel*, II, 728.

[32] *P. P.*, Part I, p. 77. " There is therefore knowledge and knowledge. Knowledge that resteth in the bare speculation of things, and knowledge that is accompanied with the grace of faith and love."

[33] *A Few Sighs from Hell*, III, 718.

[34] *The Doctrine of the Law and Grace*, I, 493. " And so study them until thou . . . do not only get the notion of the one and of the other in the head. . . ."

[35] *Christian Behaviour*, II, 551.

[36] See *G. A.*, almost on every page : " This did glisten," par. 122 ; " I had a sweet glance from that in the 5th of 2nd Cor.," par. 113.

[37] *G. A.*, par. 282.

[38] *The Doctrine of the Law and Grace*, I, 549.

earth. The apocalyptic enthusiasm of many of his contemporaries recalls that of the fourteenth and sixteenth centuries in Germany, and Bunyan shared their faith for at least a part of his life.[39] In his *Celestial City*, written in prison, he asks himself whether he will live long enough to see the New Jerusalem, and he ends his *A Few Sighs from Hell* with an act of faith that resounds like a clarion call: " God's hand is up. . . . The judgment-day is at hand." [40]

Such a living faith tends to be deepened by action. To study Christ [41] meant for Bunyan to steep himself in the lesson of His life and to achieve, by the ardour of his soul and the power of his imagination, that ' contemporaneousness' with Jesus, both in fortitude and grief, that Kierkegaard judged necessary for the true Christian. One might almost say that Bunyan did not read the Gospel but heard it fall from the lips of the Master. And while awaiting his Master's return he brushed away the centuries, lived at His side, and placed himself among His disciples. " Methought I was as if I had seen him born, as if I had seen him grow up, as if I had seen him walk through this world, from the cradle to his cross." [42] Moreover, the presence of Christ shines from his work as it shone from his life. Not a glorious Christ so much as a Christ " weeping and mourning under the lashes of justice ",[43] a Christ " betrayed, apprehended, condemned, spat on, scourged, buffeted, mocked, crowned with thorns, crucified, pierced with nails and a spear ".[44]

St. Paul had taught him that we must live in Jesus if we want to possess Him. " So long as sinners can make a life out of anything below Christ, so long they will not close with Christ." [45] From St. Paul, too, he learned that the Son of God completes His Passion in His saints, each one being for Him, in the magnificent words of

---

[39] Robert Barclay points out that all those who believed in the advent of a ' Fifth Monarchy ' (and they were very numerous because belief in the millennium was widespread) must not be confused with the few enthusiasts who in history are called ' Fifth Monarchy men'. *Op. cit.*, p. 182, footnote.

[40] *A Few Sighs from Hell*, III, 722.

[41] *Prison Meditations :* I, 64. " My mind is free to study Christ."

[42] *G. A.*, par. 120.

[43] *The Greatness of the Soul*, I, 131, and compare *G. A.*, par. 128.

[44] *Ibid.*

[45] *The Doctrine of the Law and Grace*, I, 543.

Elisabeth of the Trinity, an additional humanity where He can again suffer for His Father's glory.[46]

Moreover, from the day that he felt that God loved him, he was ready for any sacrifice. "Had I a thousand gallons of blood within my veins, I could freely then have spilt it all at the command of my Lord and Saviour." [47] And when he preached to men deaf to the word of God he thought how sweet it would be to die if his death might be the instrument of their conversion.[48] Thus for years Bunyan built up his courage so as to be worthy of his mission. We could say of him what he said of St. Paul—that he was ready to die before his enemies were ready to kill him.[49]

However, the sacrifice was not unaccompanied by anguish. His unconquerable soul was rich in human love. He wrote that in spite of all the help that he had had from heaven " I found myself a man, and compassed with Infirmities. The parting with my Wife and poor Children hath often been to me in this place as the pulling of the Flesh from my Bones; and that not only because I am somewhat too fond of these great Mercies, but also because I should have often brought to my mind the many hardships, miseries and wants that my poor Family was like to meet with, should I be taken from them, especially my poor blind Child, who lay nearer to my heart than all I had besides. O the thoughts of the hardship I thought my Blind-one might go under would break my heart to pieces ".[50]

So in this creature, always engaged in dialogue with himself, there began a new and tragic debate, and in his soul, always engaged in warfare, a yet more terrible conflict. " Poor Child, thought I, what sorrow art thou like to have for thy portion in this world! Thou must be beaten, must beg, suffer hunger, cold, nakedness, and a thousand calamities, though I cannot now endure the Wind should blow upon thee. But yet recalling myself, thought I, I must venture you all with God, though it goeth to the quick to leave you. O, I saw in this condition I was a man who was pulling down his House upon the Head of his Wife and Children; yet, thought I, I must do it, I must do it." [51]

[46] Cf. Pierre Messiaen, art. *cit.*   [47] *G. A.*, par. 192.
[48] *G. A.*, par. 281.   [49] *Seasonable Counsel*, II, 702.
[50] *G. A.*, par. 327.   [51] *G. A.*, par. 328.

Must, because Christ had ordained it, because his own salvation was at this price, and all human afflictions were as nothing compared with the holy anguish of the soul.[52] So Bunyan reasoned, torn between his religious longings and his paternal love, between the demands of God and those of human morality; and finally he accepted the call of faith. There was no life for him outside Christ. " Give me Christ on any terms." [53] " Father, mother, husband, wife, lands, livings, nay, life and all, shall go rather than the soul will miss of Christ." [54]

Those who talk of Bunyan's obstinacy could—with the same superficial plausibility and the same fundamental incomprehension—likewise talk of his selfishness [55] and describe with precisely that epithet his infinite concern for his own soul. Bunyan never could express all his respect and wonder for the soul—" God's breath, God's desire, God's image ",[56] the only living reality, with the faith that fills it and God who created it.

Concern for himself, yes, but a concern which, as we have seen, found its perfect expression in a total forgetfulness of self. A selfishness that gave birth to every kind of charity—for it is from his esteem

[52] G. A., pars. 85, 325.
[53] The Doctrine of Law and Grace, I, 544.
[54] Ibid., I, 544 and G. A., par. 325. " I was made to see, that if ever I would suffer rightly, I must first pass a sentence of death upon everything that can properly be called a thing of this life, even to reckon myself, my wife, my children, my enjoyments, and all, as dead to me, and myself as dead to them. He that loveth father or mother, son or daughter, more than me, is not worthy of me."
Bunyan had not the modern sentimentality with regard to Christ and did not emasculate His message.
[55] Bunyan's present-day enemies do not fail to make this accusation. We need quote only Alfred Noyes who, in a sketchy and superficial article pretentiously entitled " Revaluation ", calls the author of Pilgrim's Progress ' Caliban ' and portrays him thus : " He stares at us with those pitiful insane eyes burning with little hatreds, and as we look at them, under that stunted and narrow brow, the water may well stand in our own eyes." The Bookman, Oct., 1928.
This furious attack caused a sensation. The article was widely quoted in the English and American press. The Bookman devoted most of its Nov. issue to answers from Bunyan's admirers and a further statement from Alfred Noyes. For our part we do not mind these poor articles from a co-religionist, for they prove our author's vitality. One does not attack furiously (nor defend vigorously) those who are not alive.
[56] The Greatness of the Soul, I, 114–115.

for himself that a man draws the respect and love he owes to others. The selfishness that is a task confided by God to man—" to find what we are ",[57] and when we have found it, to accept it and will it. That was the whole of Bunyan's spiritual life.

But before we take a general view, let us examine Bunyan's state of soul at the moment when he was risking his life. A final doubt—his old, old doubt—assailed him: that of his election. Would death bring him eternal consolation or eternal torment? This was the most tragic moment in a life where tragedy had certainly not been lacking. Agonising dilemma. His whole life was suspended. Then the act of faith, " the stroke of Will in the night ".[58] He would venture his eternal state with Christ, whether he had comfort here or not. " If God doth not come in, thought I, I will leap off the Ladder even blindfold into Eternity, sink or swim, come Heaven, come Hell. Lord Jesus, if thou wilt catch me, do; if no, I will venture for thy Name." [59] Bunyan had need of this risk which raised him to the heights of tragedy. It was by this act of supreme heroism that the genesis of a new life was made possible.

After this sacrifice, this upbounding of a prayer which was an absolute submission to God, Bunyan, like St. Peter, knew an indescribable peace and joy, " joy unspeakable and full of glory ".[60] " Now was my Heart full of comfort . . . and I hope I shall bless God for ever for the teaching I have had by this trial." [61] We are reminded of Jacob Boehme, that other remarkable and inspired artisan, who said: " Leaning on my own nothingness I give glory to the eternal being. . . . The treasure of treasures for the soul is to pass from the Something into this Nothingness from which anything can be born." [62] The whole of mystical literature [63] says the same thing in varying forms, that from nothing everything is born. One must die to be reborn. *Periissem nisi periissem.*

[57] *Seasonable Counsel*, II, 694.
[58] Arriaga, *Viva*, quoted by Henri Delacroix, *op. cit.*, p. 121.
[59] *G. A.*, par. 337.
[60] *A Few Sighs from Hell*, III, 692, and I Peter, i, 8.
[61] *G. A.*, par. 339.
[62] Quoted by William James, *op. cit.*, p. 351.
[63] On the question of Bunyan's mysticism (or absence of mysticism) see *infra*, Conclusion.

At first Bedford gaol seemed more beautiful than a palace and Bunyan felt able to sing:

> For though men keep my outward man
> Within their locks and bars,
> Yet by the faith of Christ I can
> Mount higher than the stars.[64]

He saw the Scriptures with a new eye.[65]   Certain verses, the meaning of which had been obscure, became clear.   The invisible world, in which St. Paul had ordered him to believe,[66] became more and more real to his soul's eye.   Just as the three children of Babylon [67] beheld God's Son walking by them in the fire, and Daniel saw angels placing their hands in the lion's jaw, so Bunyan saw and " felt " Jesus; [68] he saw the Celestial City in jasper and gold; he heard the music of the angels and, " the mist of our carnality " having dispersed,[69] he already dwelt in a climate radiant with reflections of eternity.

"We let go shadows, and take hold of immortality." [70]

Such were the ecstatic moments punctuating with fiery points the path of his never-completed conversion.   As we have already said, Bunyan's life was like a series of successive conversions, conversions within conversions, a slow march towards the possession of himself and God.   He always sought to pick out the essential element of his being from among his potentialities, to capture the basic note in the tumult of his soul, and to distinguish the principle of order in chaos.   The process of conversion, then, consists surely in an act of self-choice, in willing oneself in one's necessity, in staking one's life on the true ' me ', whatever the consequences, " come heaven, come hell ".

And this act of supreme will is the supreme revelation of oneself to oneself.   Indeed, Bunyan had not existed in his fullness until then.   Keats said that the earth should not be called " a vale of tears " but " the vale of soul-making ".[71]   Bunyan understood that, for by each renunciation he made, by his tears and voluntary suffering, he was

[64] *Prison Meditations*, I, 64.
[65] *G. A.*, par. 321.
[66] *G. A.*, par. 326.
[67] *Seasonable Counsel*, II, 701.
[68] *G. A.*, par. 321.
[69] *Holy City*, III, 418.
[70] *Prison Meditations*, I, 65.
[71] J. Keats, to George and Georginia Keats, 14th Feb. 1819, letter 114, ed. Maurice Buxton Forman (2 vols., Oxford, 1931), II, 114.

ceaselessly individualising himself, giving himself a soul, creating himself. By his final surrender he achieved the perfection of the human task—the genesis of self through self. And meanwhile new interior illumination was granted him. For if one must go to God so as to know oneself (" They come to Him for a more clear discovery of themselves to themselves "),[72] then it follows that one must lose oneself in Him to reach a complete revelation of self. And it was at that point that Bunyan seems to have felt that in the depths of his being there was not only himself; in the depths of his soul, where he touched his very essence, he touched God, too. God revealed by the love burning in His creature [73] and by the joy throbbing within him and literally drowning him: " I am drowned." [74] For joy is the essence of the divine nature, and joy in us is the gift of God.[75]

Not all converts have tasted the peace that Bunyan knew in prison, for not all have so triumphantly succeeded in stripping themselves of their secondary ' me '; not all have moved so far towards achieving that harmony of being which, according to Bunyan, can be realised only in Heaven. " In this world there cannot be that harmony and oneness of body and soul as there will be in Heaven." [76] But all converts follow the same path and move in the same direction; they make their way towards all that is truest in themselves. We have only to read certain passages of St. Augustine to feel that the law of conversion may well lie in a man's progress in the search for his own essence. " But thou, O Lord, while he was speaking, didst turn me round towards myself, taking me from behind my back, where I had placed me unwilling to observe myself." [77] And again: " Myself verily either way; yet more myself, in that which I approved in myself, than in that which in myself I disapproved. For in this last, it was now for the more part not myself, because in much I rather endured against my will, than acted willingly." [78]

---

[72] *Christ a Complete Saviour*, I, 225.
[73] *Ibid.*, I, 222. " God is love; and he that dwelleth in love, dwelleth in God and God in him." [74] *Ibid.*, I, 218.
[75] *Ibid.*, I, 218. " He is in himself most happy . . . and all true happiness is only to be found in God, as that which is essential to his nature; nor is there any good or any happiness in or with any creature or thing but what is communicated to it by God."
[76] *Saved by Grace*, I, 342.
[77] St. Augustine, *Confessions*, VIII, 7, 16.　　[78] *Ibid.*, 5, 11.

With Bunyan, as with many other converts, the human side of conversion lay in the working of the will. " Inflame your will," he said, [79] " the will is all." [80] And although sometimes he seemed to be a kind of automaton, giving way to every whim of his imagination, and the slave of a sick sensibility, in fact his will never disappeared for long. And actually it was the will that prepared its own eclipses by encouraging the very unrest [81] and anguish that caused the disorder favourable to automatism, to visions, and even perhaps to the mysterious action of Grace. But, even while wilfully submitting to this fever, Bunyan was able to take solitary, lucid and decisive actions: his return to the Church, the moral reformation of his life, his friendship with the ' poor women' and with John Gifford, and finally his resistance to civil power and the affirmation of the rights of the spirit by which conversion is achieved. Then his spiritual life blossomed in peace and joy, and the whole man seemed to grow.

James Bissett Pratt, the psychologist, holds that Bunyan's conversion was purely emotional [82] and contrasts it with so-called " conversions of the will ". It is obvious that he has not studied Bunyan's complete works, and has given *Grace Abounding* a much too cursory reading.

Grace Abounding provides another lesson about Bunyan's spiritual life. His conversion was a return to his earliest and most vivid longings, to the perfumed paradise of his childhood. His precocious feeling for religion,[83] his taste for moral uprightness [84] and his respect for holiness were sentiments that were originally fashioned by his education and social *milieu*. Roughly between his fifteenth and twentieth year these were stifled; but little by little they broke upon his life again and deepened his conversion.

Everyone who has studied these psychological problems has made similar observations and reached the same conclusion, namely, that man changes only in his continuity. " *Dieu n'écrit pas en nous comme sur une page blanche*." [85] Obviously the page bears the imprints of our childhood. Once again the convert hears the gushing of the springs of his youthful years. He knows that he has found again the

---

[79] *The Heavenly Footman*, III, 286. [80] *Ibid.*, 283.
[81] Cf. *supra*, p. 66. [82] J. B. Pratt, *op. cit.*, p. 151.
[83] Cf. *supra*, Part I, chap. 3, p. 55. [84] Cf. *supra*, p. 52.
[85] H. Brémond, *John Henry Newman* (1932 ed.), p. 193.

being that he is. And much of the peace that dwells within him comes from this knowledge.

Let us sum up and draw our various threads together. Bunyan's conversion was a triple victory. In again finding himself, the convert found himself and found God.

It was a classical Puritan conversion, in which Bunyan himself saw three stages.[86] First " the conviction of sin ", black shame and anguish. Next, the evangelical revelation, the " hungerings and thirstings " after Christ. Finally, the personal call of Jesus, " a special call ", answering to the sinner's expectation. And the conversion was influenced by the spiritual climate of a given society and a whole religious tradition.

But this graph, this vague curve, marks only three moments of a long process with any precision. It represents, not only Bunyan's conversion, but that of a thousand unknown Puritans. It is not paradoxical to say that it is true for each and true for none. This frozen impersonal line does not convey the whole life of a consciousness, its subtle interplay of colour, the modulations of its voice.

Thus it is true and untrue to say that Bunyan's conversion resembled many others. To insist on the resemblances so as to prove that the tinker was unoriginal would be to betray a lack of understanding of the soul and an incapacity to discern the quality which makes each one irreplaceable.

[86] *P. P.*, Part I, p. 77.

PART II

THE WRITER AND MAN OF ACTION

*Be ready always to give an answer to every man
that asketh you a reason of the hope that is in you.*
ST. PETER

*Audiendo ergo praecepta Dei illuminati non sunt
faciendo illuminati sunt.* ST. GREGORY THE GREAT

WHY BUNYAN WROTE

BEFORE embarking on a study of Bunyan's work, we should try to discover the law by which that work came into being and grew in the depths of his heart. We should try to find out what force pushed the uninstructed tinker to write.

But was Bunyan uninstructed? Even before reading his major works and recognising the vital juices by which they were fed, we know that our passionate reader of the Scriptures was not without culture. The Bible had already provided a metaphysic, an ethic and a psychology for his meditation, and it had already moved his spirit with the strong gust of its poetry.[1]

In his *History of my Time* Gilbert Burnet says that the people of Scotland had such vast learning that the peasants could pray *ex tempore*.[2] Puritanism has always brought this vast learning to intelligences capable of understanding it. Bunyan was rich in popular culture. Our study of his work will make this plain; but our study of the man and his *milieu* has already shown that he breathed in a dust of knowledge merely by breathing the air of the period. The thoughts, dreams and feelings of a people entered into Bunyan and worked out their synthesis within him, his experience of life wiping away any discrepancies, and his soul beating its own inimitable mark on all the rudiments collected there.

A thinking and striving nation showered its intellectual and sentimental nourishment on Bunyan, and it was above all in solitude that he transformed these into another flesh and blood. Thus all Bunyan's solitudes—his interior solitude (" I counted myself alone ")[3] and his

---

[1] S. T. Coleridge has so justly written : " The fears, the hopes, the remembrances, the anticipations, the inward and outward experience, the belief and the faith of a Christian, form of themselves a philosophy and a sum of knowledge, which a life spent in the grove of Academus, or the Painted Porch, could not have attained or collected." *Aids to Reflection* (ed. by H. Nelson Coleridge, London, 1848), pp. 146–147.

[2] Quoted by Daniel Neal, *op. cit.*, vol. III, p. 101.

[3] *G. A.*, par. 85.

material solitude in gaol—were creative, for they helped the man to know himself and the writer to put the stamp of his individuality on everything he ' borrowed '.

In this way was Bunyan formed and, in a broad sense, cultured. Inevitably culture had to become a weapon for a man of such fight and fervour. If every neophyte burns to convert the world, the Puritans above all seem to have been on fire with this duty. Their will, proceeding from grace [4] and renewed by God, had to spend itself in the service of God. Moreover, they believed that God worked through their will. " God is the author " of our works, wrote Calvin.[5] He puts in us the desire to do the good and the strength to accomplish our desire. " *Il s'ensuit donc que si l'homme attribue aucune chose, ou en la volonté ou en l'éxécution, qu'il desrobe autant à Dieu.*" In all humility Bunyan could proclaim himself " God's instrument ".[6] He preached and wrote so as to spread the word of his Master.

But perhaps another more personal reason impelled him to talk and write. Ever since his childhood he had been tormented by the need to confide. His sins, as we have seen, were often nothing but a sort of perversion of his need for expression. He wanted to free himself by opening his heart; to cure himself of his painful adolescence by projecting outside himself the spectres that had assailed him. But their shadows still lingered in the dark recesses of his soul, so he had perpetually to shed more light on that deep dwelling-place; he perpetually had to unburden himself and repeat himself. Repeat his reasons for believing; reassure himself that faith alone justified and that Christ's blood really had been shed on purpose to wash away the sins of His miserable creature, John Bunyan; repeat the comforting texts that Jesus whispered to him; pick up the Bible yet again because its sacred words offered inexhaustible enlightenment. Even when he was addressing others he was really talking to himself, and throughout the whole length of his work there runs this hidden moving personal dialogue.

For no one convinces himself so well as when he is trying to convince others. " Preach the faith until you have it," [7] said Boehler to Wesley. Bunyan was well aware of this and knew Paul's words to

[4] J. Calvin, *Institution de la religion chrétienne* (original text of 1541 reprinted under the direction of Abel Lefranc, 2 vols. Bibliothèque des Hautes Etudes, Paris, 1918), vol. I, p. 76.

[5] J. Calvin, *ibid.*, I, 76.   [6] *G. A.*, par. 273.

[7] John Wesley, *The Journal* (ed. *cit.*), vol. I, p. 442.

Timothy, " that if he put the brethren in mind of the truths of the gospel, he himself should not only be a good minister of Christ, but should be nourished up in the words of faith and of good doctrine ".[8] Finally, it was in order to convince himself that Bunyan welcomed controversy. Like Luther,[9] he enjoyed the heresies that gave him an opportunity to fight. He probably felt that opposition showed him where he stood and that he was most certain of his own truth when revolting against a lie perceived outside himself. A thought which only yesterday might have been germinating in the depths of his soul, would suddenly grow and formulate itself under the shock of an encounter or a clash of personalities. Action reveals; to fight, to preach, to write was to secure his own development.

And finally Bunyan could not take cognisance of the richness of his spiritual drama all at one go. Though life is lived forwards, as Kierkegaard noted, it is only understood backwards. Bunyan never ceased to recreate his life and to marvel at his destiny. There was a treasure hidden in every nook, and each had to be explored. His memory was an enchanted palace to him, for he could have said with St. Augustine: " There also meet I with myself " (" *ibi mihi et ipse occurro* ").[10] It was a precious palace, and more precious still the memories it contained. The human adventure engraved on its walls has become immortal through him. Curiously enough, Bunyan never imagined heaven or hell without reference to the earth. The joys of paradise and the torments of hell were perhaps nothing but the heightened memory of our joys and torments on earth. In hell one word would re-echo ceaselessly, lugubrious and importunate like the toll of a death-knell: " Remember ". It was the terrifying word that Bunyan had meditated on at such length, the word said by Abraham to the bad rich man: " Father Abraham, have mercy on me . . . for I am tormented in this flame. But Abraham said: Son, remember that thou in thy life-time receivedst thy good things and likewise Lazarus evil things." [11]

[8] *Christian Behaviour*, vol. II, p. 570.
[9] Cf. Lucien Febvre, *op. cit.*, p. 124. Bunyan: " It is very expedient that there should be heresies among us that thereby those which are indeed of the truth might be made manifest." *A Vindication of Some Gospel Truths*, p. 181.   [10] *Confessions*, X, viii, 14.
[11] Luke, xvi, 24–25. The whole of *A Few Sighs from Hell* is a meditation on this text. See especially pp. 685–691.

In heaven, wrote Bunyan, " our memory will be so enlarged to retain all things that happened to us in this world, so that with unspeakable aptness we shall call to mind all God's providences, all Satan's malice, all our own weaknesses, all the rage of men, and how God made all work together for his glory and our good ".[12]   Thus if our supra-terrestrial destiny is nothing but the reflection of our carnal life—but magnified and written in eternity—by tirelessly re-living that life down here we are already participating in eternity.   Bunyan wrote so as to experience this exaltation and felicity.   Memory is the soul of his work as it is the soul of his thought; but so is meditation, or rather the dream of the future, the vast perspectives of which are illumined by the light of the past.

The universe of memory was more real and richer in significance; the universe of the imagination more real and more beautiful.   So Bunyan wrote in order to recapture the threads of his dead life and weave them together again so as to understand better the texture and pattern of his past, so as to achieve a keener perception of himself, and so as to possess himself more fully through the works that revealed himself to himself; but he also wrote in order to forget the miseries of a drab and corrupt world.   For Bunyan, as for all artists, literature was a compensation for life.   He wrote so as to console himself, to possess in dream what he lacked in life.

The persecuted tinker no longer noticed his gaol, for he was lost in the vision of the Holy City where God would come to deliver the elect and punish the cruel.[13]   The Baptist Church was grey indeed to an imagination gripped by splendour, but the magic of the dream coloured it in the jasper and gold reflected from the Celestial City.[14]   The Baptist Church was dumb indeed to a musical sensibility, but he made it sing and hum with the melodies of heaven.[15]   Bunyan refused to ring the bells of Bedford and of Elstow, but his work re-echoes with the joyful peal of chimes.[16]   He refused to dance, and yet the

[12] *Saved by Grace*, vol. I, p. 342.

[13] *Holy City*, vol. III, p. 406, and *A Few Sighs*, pp. 685, 687.

[14] *Holy City*, pp. 404, 405, 407, for example.

[15] Cf. *infra*, pp. 156 and 191.

[16] " Here also they had the city itself in view, and they thought they heard all the bells therein to ring to welcome them there to." *P. P.*, I, p. 147.   Mr. G. B. Harrison says of the bells in *The Holy War* : " There are some interesting details in the first triumphant entry of Prince Emmanuel

page he was writing often leapt with farandoles and roundelays.[17] He scorned earthly pomp, yet he was carried away by the thought of heavenly magnificence.[18]

Thus Bunyan achieved a task which, according to Edward Dowden,[19] is always difficult for Puritans. He gave to ideas and feelings the body and plastic form which alone can interpret them artistically to the outside world. We know the penetrating analysis in which the author of *Puritan and Anglican* contrasts the Puritan dualism of visible *versus* invisible, the sensory sphere *versus* the spiritual sphere, with the Catholic conception which unites them in a universal sympathy and understanding. For us in France to-day Claudel's work enlarges on the English critic's thesis. Claudel's metaphysics and mystical realism magnify that synthesis of elements always drawn together or united by the alchemy of poetic catholicism. Claudel says that there is no radical separation between this world and the next;[20] things are a partial, intelligible and delectable image of God;[21] so we can discern the mark of the spirit in the sensory world, and through the senses convey spiritual messages. And surely Claudel's thought lies, more or less darkly, more or less openly, at the heart of all Catholic mystical poetry.

Salut donc, ô monde nouveau à mes yeux, ô monde maintenant total !
O credo entier des choses visibles et invisibles, je vous accepte avec un coeur
    catholique.
Où que je tourne la tête
J'envisage l'immense octave de la création.[22]

We have only to read these lines to see the gulf which separates the

---

which suggest that Bunyan's sense of humour, though acute in small details, was not widely developed. The young men are ordered to ring the bells for joy, etc. . . . " We are surprised to find these lines written by such an intelligent critic as Mr. G. B. Harrison; the matter, as we have seen, depended on something quite other than a more or less lively sense of humour.

[17] Cf. *infra*, pp. 192–193.
[18] " King Emmanuel was clad in his golden armour, he rode in his royal chariot, the trumpets sounded about him, the colours were displayed." *Holy War* (ed. Mabel Peacock, Clarendon Press), p. 113.
[19] *Puritan and Anglican* (London, 1900), pp. 5, 6 et seq.
[20] *Positions et Propositions* (N.R.F., 2 vols., 1928 and 1934), I, 174.
[21] *Ibid.*, p. 88.
[22] *Cinq grandes Odes, L'esprit et l'eau.*

Puritan, absorbed in the anguished contemplation of his sin and invisible reality, from the Catholic who embraces the whole world " as everlasting nourishment and as a fruit that we grip with our teeth ".[23] We can recognise at once the advantage the Catholic has over the Puritan when both are in search of an image to give form and feature to the abstract.

But if by some miracle the Puritan does succeed in re-creating his fervour and vision in a concrete form, then he, too, will be an artist; and, by virtue of his temperament and conception of the world, a great artist.

Like every Christian, a Puritan such as Bunyan lived in his daily life the conflict that Christianity engenders in all men—but with him it was perhaps more urgent and intense. And the two dramatic advantages that Claudel has discovered in the Christian religion obtain equally in its Puritan manifestation. The first is born of the turning-in of the Christian on himself, the examination of conscience which scrapes away his filth and humiliates him in God's eyes, thus creating deep currents of thought and feeling; the second derives from the opposite movement which forces man away from introspection and offers for his contemplation the end he should attain.[24] " We know that we are not interesting in ourselves; what is interesting is the end which we have been shaped to attain." [25]

The pathos linked with these two movements of the interior life, and which is essential to the richness of Christian literature, was never absent from Bunyan. And he already had at his disposal a whole world of concrete forms necessary, as we have seen, for his artistic expression. There were the spectres that haunted his spirit, the demons that tried to drag him to hell, the angels who wrapped him round with light and warmth. There was nothing abstract in the personal drama of this man. The phantasms of his imagination found a body and a voice. His thoughts took to themselves limbs and muscles and raiment. A study of his sermons and stories will show us how he transposed his inner conflict, projected these demons and angels outside himself. He enlarged his soul to the dimensions of the universe, so much so that his universe seems to be born by satanic

---

[23] Claudel, *Théâtre* (Mercure de France), vol. I, p. 278.
[24] *Positions et Propositions*, vol. I, p. 142.
[25] *Ibid.*

and divine giants, and his own lyricism seems amplified into a sort of cosmic lyricism.

Hence everything predestined Bunyan to write: his apostolic ardour, his restlessness that had to be appeased, his sensibility reaching out for human contact, his imagination bent on realising its dreams, and his soul avid for self-contemplation.   And always there was his fervour, compelling him to proclaim his faith, his love, his faults, all his victories, and to seek in prayer the directing inspiration of his life.   For Bunyan went down on his knees before writing.   " I with a few groans did carry my meditations to the Lord Jesus for a blessing which he did forthwith grant." [26]

[26] *Holy City*, III, 397.

1

Bunyan, Controversialist and Preacher

I. THE CONTROVERSIALIST

WHEN Bunyan's Bedford 'brethren' gave him permission to bear witness to Christ, first at their private meetings and then in public, he almost immediately came up against the Quakers, who were fairly numerous in the district. The first encounter took place at Bedford on May 23, 1656. Other skirmishes followed, and so Bunyan decided to put his arguments and convictions on paper in the form of a tract. *Some Gospel Truths* was the first statement of the 'confession of faith' which henceforth guided his life, and, as controversy, it revealed to the world and himself his gifts as a writer. And this fact is significant in a man who had always battled his way forward. In our view, his polemical works are of interest only in so far as they throw light on his intellectual development and illustrate a new phase in what we have called 'the genesis of self through self'.

Bunyan was a great dreamer with a mystical temperament, but we shall now see him striving to escape from his inward quest. He is searching for God not in his own depths but in militant action.

Some Gospel Truths and the tract which he wrote the following year [1] in reply to Edward Burrough—the Quaker who had made himself the spokesman of his sect—may help us to discover the value of oratorical warfare on Bunyan's development.

In both the pamphlets we come up against a passionate temperament. Bunyan was a new convert, and as yet uncertain as to whether his faith was properly 'racinate'. Twenty years later, fortified by

[1] *A Vindication of Gospel Truths*, II, 178 *et seq.*

94

experience, he was able to defend it with a calmer authority, since he had learnt to estimate the strength or weakness of his adversary's position; and, above all, because he was certain of his own. But in 1656 and 1657 the slightest assault from anyone seemed to him to threaten the whole Kingdom of God : whence the bitterness and false-sweetness of his pamphlets. There was no room in that passionate century for shades of charity ! As he himself was treated roughly,[2] he answered or attacked unsparingly.

" Friend," he said to Edward Burrough, " what harm is it to join a dog and a wolf together ? A fawning dog and a wolf in sheep's clothing; they differ a little in outward appearance, but they can both agree to worry Christ's lambs." [3] Though we do not know whether the dog or the wolf represents the Quaker, we can appreciate the amiableness of the words! Bunyan never put himself out to be courteous. " Would a parishioner learn to be proud ? " he said, directing his shafts this time against the ministers of the Established Church, " he or she need look no farther than to the priest, his wife and family. Would the people learn to be wanton, they may also see a pattern among their teachers. Would they learn to be drunkards, they may also have that from some of their ministers." [4]

Incidentally we notice that in the heat of argument his wit sharpened, his language became more vivid and spicy, and the instrument that later served for *The Pilgrim's Progress* and *The Life and Death of Mr. Badman* was forged and polished. " Other lame arguments thou tumblest over," he said, " like a blind man in a thicket of bushes "; [5] or again, " like a man in the dark, in seeking to keep thyself out of one ditch, thou art fallen into another ".[6]

[2] Even in the title of the pamphlet Edw. Burrough called Bunyan a soldier of the army of Gog !

[3] *A Vindication of Gospel Truths*, II, 182. Edw. Burrough had protested against Bunyan's equation : Quakers = Ranters. " Between Quakers and Ranters there is no more union than betwixt light and darkness, good and evil." *Truth (the strongest of all) Witnessed forth in the Spirit of Truth, against all Deceit* (London, 1657), p. 8. George Fox makes his hostility to the Ranters quite plain in his journal. As far back as 1649 he had been shocked to hear them call themselves God. " They said they were God; but we could not bear such things." *Journal* (Leeds, 1836, 2 vols.), I, 122.

[4] *Some Gospel Truths*, 178.

[5] *Ibid.*, 193.

[6] *Ibid.*, 201.

But these felicitous expressions are rare. Bunyan had not yet found his style. He charged into the fray like a medieval knight— the first onslaught was swift, but his armour, shield and lance were so heavy that they enforced a slower rhythm. We need not go into this here because later his sermons will give us the opportunity for a more detailed study of his oratorical technique as a preacher.

But what was the central argument of this lively dispute? Bunyan would say that the whole of God's Kingdom had been threatened as well as the edifice of his own personal faith. He had found peace in belief in Christ's sacrifice, and here were the Quakers throwing doubt on Christ's very existence.[7] As against the Carpenter, Mary's Son, crucified and risen from the dead, they upheld a " Christ within " who, crucified within each man, dies within him, rises within him, and makes His ascension within him. Jesus's sacrifice, they said, was not a historical event, valid for everyone and efficacious in itself; it had to be renewed in each creature. The spirit of Christ penetrates man, saves him, and up to a point deifies him. " Some of them call themselves Christ." [8]

Such was the doctrine that caused Bunyan's whole being to revolt, and it made his own conception of the truth clear to him. He had such great need of historical certainties, and he saw them suddenly undermined; the authority of the Holy Books on which he had been bred fell to the ground.[9] He had weighed up his own unworthiness and nothingness, and now they wanted him to believe that man could find redemptive force within his own self. Against the pretensions of this Quaker doctrine he had the irrefutable evidence of his own experience, his own interior certainty. He did not, of course, deny the existence of interior illumination, but this was not Christ's spirit; it was merely the moral conscience. And surely implicit in the con-

[7] *Some Gospel Truths*, II, 134, 135.

[8] *Ibid.*, 163.

[9] Although Burrough declares : ". . . For we own Him [Jesus Christ] as He is ascended far above all heavens who fill all things, yea and without us too," (*op. cit.*, p. 8), yet I think we must agree with J. Milsand (art. *cit.*) that Quakerism was only really christianised with Robert Barclay. The 'Christ within' of Fox could well have been the natural morality of the deists, or the divine emanation of the neo-Platonists. For Robert Barclay 'the inward Christ' was nothing other than the grace deriving from Christ's merits.

ception of a " Christ within " was the spirit which engenders the belief in a " Christ without ".[10]

" Christ without ", " God-man ", " the Man-Christ "—Bunyan multiplied the terms expressive of his faith in a historical Christ. The " heresy " of the Quakers gave him the opportunity of re-telling himself the whole story of the Bible. His sense of wonder at those mysteries seems to have been always fresh and young. He retraced Christ's life; he placed Him, concrete and strong, in front of him. It was in Him that he found peace, not in the mirages of personal deification. Of all the Quaker blasphemies, this one struck him as the worst, perhaps because, as a dreamer and a visionary, he felt its attraction more deeply. He tore himself away from that delectation by binding himself to the Scriptures. He wanted to use his fervour not in the ecstasy of being lost in God, but in a person-to-person dialogue with the Father or the Son. Meanwhile he awaited the Son's return. " I will show you ", he wrote in *Some Gospel Truths*, " that his coming will be very shortly." [11] To deny, like the Quakers, a second Incarnation was to rob Bunyan of one of his most consoling dreams.

Finally our author sensed a moral danger in George Fox's doctrine.[12] Quaker mysticism seemed to him very near to that of the Ranters, and he knew by experience that the doctrines and sentiments of those enlightened people could justify an unleashing of the worst instincts.[13] Whoever thought himself equal to God, or believed himself to be God, saw no sin in the satisfaction of his appetites.[14] " Hypocrisy ! " Bunyan cried. It was the lie of the wolf

[10] *Some Gospel Truths*, II, 173.

[11] *Ibid.*, 162.

[12] And a danger of leakage among the Baptists who might be seduced by George Fox's ideas. In fact this man made many converts among Bunyan's co-religionists in different parts of the country. Cf. W. T. Whitley, *op. cit.*, " Whole baptists churches changed their views," p. 84. Certainly Bunyan felt, like Richard Baxter, that his controversies helped his brothers to remain united. Cf. F. J. Powicke, *A Life of Richard Baxter* (London, 1924), p. 107.

[13] *G. A.*, par. 43.

[14] W. Preger quotes this text : " *Quod homo unitus Deo peccare non possit . . . quod nihil sit peccatum nisi quod reputatur peccatum . . . Oscula virorum et mulierum solutorum non esse peccatum . . . Animam esse de substantia Dei.*" *Geschichte der Deutschen Mystik* (1874), p. 463. Here is another text quoted by M. Delacroix : " *Qui cognoscit Deum in se*

who makes himself a sheep the better to devour the flock! Bunyan was mistaken, but we can hardly blame him. It was impossible for him to perceive either the sincerity of these people or their conception of divine love—which, incidentally, the historians of mysticism allow us to appreciate to-day.

> La liberté en Dieu peut être conçue aussi bien comme l'affranchissement de tout désir que comme le droit de laisser en le coeur affluer tout le désir. Les hommes qui de leur identité avec Dieu ont conclu la necéssité du renoncement et ceux qui ont conclu l'obligation d'agir selon l'instinct et la passion ont ceci de commun, qu'ils ont aspiré les uns et les autres à vivre de la vie divine; seulement ils se sont figuré Dieu de differentes manières: les uns l'ont cherché dans son expansion, les autres dans son abstraction.[15]

Bunyan saw a difference between the ' Ranters ' and the Quakers, but it seemed to him a superficial and hypocritical one:[16] whereas the former, pushing their faith to its logical conclusions, lived according to their pleasure, the latter practised an asceticism the rigours of which were odious to the tinker.

It is even open to question which of the two irritated him more acutely. The anarchy of the first exasperated his respect for order,[17] and the asceticism of the second offended the healthy sensuality which he wanted to allow to flower after the excessive severity of his years of " storm and stress ". He distrusted the Quakers, who were content with bread and water, who tore the ribbons from their hats, and—a

---

omnia operari, etiam si fornicationem faceret, non peccaret. Non enim sibi attribuere debet, sed totum Deo quod facit." Essai sur le mysticisme spéculatif en Allemagne au XIVe siècle (thesis, Paris, 1899), p. 50. George Fox himself described himself as freed from all sin, cf. Milsand, art. cit.

[15] Henri Delacroix, op. cit., p. 94.

[16] " . . . The very opinions that are held at this day by the Quakers, are the same that long ago were held by the Ranters. Only the Ranters had made them threadbare at an alehouse, and the Quakers have set a new gloss upon them again, by an outward legal holiness, or righteousness." A Vindication of Gospel Truths, II, 183.

Richard Baxter thinks no differently from Bunyan : " The Quakers, who were but Ranters, turned from horrid profaneness and blasphemy to a life of extreme austerity on the other side." Autobiography (ed. cit.), p. 73.

[17] Cf. infra. The political and social thought of Bunyan.

still more serious sin in the eyes of this good father of a family—
refused to marry.[18]   To abstain from the lawful pleasures of the flesh
was to mutilate man and offend against God's goodness.[19]   Bunyan
agreed with Milton:

> Our Maker bids increase ; who bids abstain
> But our destroyer, foe to God and Man ? [20]

Bunyan's opposition to the Quakers, then, was born of intellectual
antagonism and a clash of temperaments.   This controversy pushed
him in the direction of his desires—towards the realisation in himself
of the type of man and saint he admired.

★

From time to time Bunyan let fly more arrows at the Quakers,
for example in his treatise on the *Resurrection of the Dead* in 1665,[21]
and in a polemical work that we shall now study: *A Defence of the
Doctrine of Justification by Faith in Jesus Christ*, written in 1672.

In that year Bunyan had got hold of a work which was much
discussed in his neighbourhood: *The Design of Christianity*.[22]   Its
author, Edward Fowler,[23] was an M.A. and a Doctor of Theology
and had been the Presbyterian chaplain to Annabella the Dowager
Duchess of Kent.   In 1656 he obtained the parish of Norhill in
Bedfordshire.

---

[18] *Some Gospel Truths*, II, 153.
[19] *Ibid.*, II, 153, where Bunyan gives his opinion with regard to marriage :
" which God hath created to be received with thanksgiving."
[20] Milton, *Paradise Lost*, IV, 748–749.
[21] George Offor, a conscientious but colourless admirer of Bunyan, makes
a surprising mistake with regard to this work : Bunyan, he writes in his
introduction to *Some Gospel Truths*, does not renew his attacks against the
Quakers in his " admirable treatise on the Resurrection of the Dead ", which
belongs to the " latter part of his life " (cf. II, 130).   But Bunyan does come
to grips with the Quakers in this tract.   And can we say that our author was
entering the latter part of his life in 1665 ?   He had another 23 years to live.
The hostility between Baptists and Quakers ceased only with the Hanoverian
dynasty.   Cf. W. T. Whitley, *op. cit.*, p. 24.
[22] *The Design of Christianity*, by Edward Fowler (4th ed., London, 1760).
The first ed. was in 1671.
[23] Cf. article in the *D. N. B.*, vol. XX, p. 84.   Consult, too, John Tulloch,
*Rational Theology and Christian Philosophy in England in the Seventeenth
Century* (2nd ed., London, 1874, 2 vols.), II, pp. 35 *et seq.*, and II, pp. 437
et seq.

When the Act of Uniformity came into force in 1662, this ex-Presbyterian turned Anglican seems to have been undecided at first as to what to do. His father and brother, who had been driven from presbytery and Cambridge college respectively, had given him an example of resistance. But Edward Fowler was less rigid: he contented himself with leaving his town for two years, and then he submitted and returned to his flock.

He was a great admirer of the Cambridge theologians, of Whichcote, Smith and Cudworth, and in 1670 published *A Free Discussion between two Intimate Friends*, in which he laid down, without much clarity or depth, " the principles and practices of certain ministers of the English Church injuriously called Latitudinarians ".[24] Then in 1671 he wrote the treatise which aroused Bunyan's indignation.

" I know you not by face," wrote the tinker, " much less your personal practice." [25] He was not, however, wholly ignorant of Fowler's career, since he accused him of having a " weathercock spirit ",[26] and, suddenly caustic, slipped some personal allusions into his doctrinal criticism: " Here you may hop from Presbyterianism, to a prelatical mode; and if time and chance should serve you, backwards, and forwards again. . . . Behold you have then, good reader, a glorious Latitudinarian, that can, as to religion, turn and twist like an eel on the angle; or rather like the weathercock that stands on the steeple." [27]

The present-day critic who looks back on this quarrel of three centuries ago finds no difficulty in being impartial. Bunyan did not really understand Fowler; [28] not that he read him carelessly, for the quotations he makes are numerous and accurate, but what he knew of the author added to his already hostile attitude towards a theology so foreign to his spirit. Moreover, Bunyan needed a new quarrel. And fantastic and alarming rumours were circulating everywhere

[24] Edward Fowler, *The Design of Christianity* (ed. *cit.*), preface, xxxi.
[25] *A Defense of the Doctrine of Justification*, II, 313.
[26] *Ibid.*, 314.
[27] *Ibid.*, II, 322.
[28] Other Puritans were more just towards Fowler. Baxter wrote a few pages to explain to his readers the real meaning of his doctrines. In his autobiography he speaks of Fowler as a moderate and conforming Anglican, " a very ingenious sober conformist " (ed. *cit.*, p. 216). Calamy said of Fowler : " He is a man very worthy of esteem." See *D. N. B.*, vol. XX, p. 84.

THE VALLEY OF
THE SHADOW OF
DEATH

Engraving from the 1830
edition, after a painting
by John Martin

FRONTISPIECE
By J. M. W. Turner to the edition of 1838

about the Latitudinarians; in the taverns, in the streets, in the churches, they were being accused of every kind of sin.[29]

So Bunyan again felt that the Kingdom of God was threatened. He must again engage in battle. Fowler and his book appeared at just the right moment; and, if they had not appeared, it is probable that the tinker would have found another target. In his militant ardour he was quite capable of " setting up men of straw and then fighting with them ", as Fowler himself put it.[30]

Bunyan saw the *Design of Christianity* across the mist of prejudices and false interpretations which were weighing down the Cambridge school. He even went so far as to compare the vicar of Norhill's insipid treatise with the *Leviathan*. It is doubtful whether Bunyan had ever read Thomas Hobbes, but this allusion to him helps us to guess at the views held about Latitudinarianism in Dissenting circles, and the degree to which it was thought to be dangerous.

Fowler was all the more indignant as he had taken a stand against the materialism of Hobbes,[31] but since we are interested in Bunyan's intellectual development, even this bad quarrel is precious. How far this village artisan had travelled! What knowledge he had acquired! In spite of the fact that his arguments were often biased and confused, they give us a singular respect for his intelligence. Having arrived at religion through the heart and the will, Bunyan stabilised his faith forever in these discussions—discussions in which the still all-powerful sentiment seeks the support of reason to express itself more forcefully.

---

[29] Cf. Tulloch, *op. cit.*, II, 36. " The name of Latitude-men is daily exagitated amongst us, both in taverns and pulpits, and very tragical representations made of them. A Latitude-man, therefore (according to the best definition I can collect), is an image of clouts, that men set up to encounter with for want of real enemy ; it is a convenient name to reproach a man that you owe a spite to."

This passage was borrowed by Tulloch from a pamphlet by Samuel Parker (future Bishop of Oxford) published in 1665. Fowler himself, in his *Free Discussion*, had foreseen Bunyan's attacks : " I have heard them represented as a generation of people that have revived the abominable principle of the old gnosticks ; as a company of men that are prepared for the embracing of any religion, and to renounce or subscribe to any doctrine, etc." Cf. Tulloch, II, 37.

[30] See *Dirt Wip't Off, or a Manifest Discovery of the Gross Ignorance, Erroneousness and most Unchristian and Wicked Spirit of One John Bunyan Lay-Preacher in Bedford* (London, 1672), p. 27.

[31] Tulloch, *op. cit.*, II, 38.

Fowler believed in the purity of human nature which Christ " originally seated in the soul ".[32] It was so as to restore this pristine holiness to man that Christ had come and died. He was incarnate in order to offer us a model of life, and the whole Gospel aims solely at telling us of the straight and clear paths we should follow. " Holiness is the only design of the precepts of the Gospel." [33] He held that there could be no more fallacious doctrine than justification by faith! Belief in Christ's merits was not enough. There was no forgiveness for the unrepentant sinner.

We can imagine what was at stake in the battle Bunyan waged. He had found peace both in the recognition of his personal unworthiness and powerlessness, and in the merits of his saving faith before Christ the Redeemer.

This controversy had such reverberations in Bunyan's spirit that we can hear its echoes even in *The Pilgrim's Progress*. Bunyan had risked and lost all his worldly happiness—his wife and children— for his faith, and he saw before him a man apparently prepared for every compromise. For the Bedford preacher, attentive only to the demands of his religion, the world did not count. But the vicar of Norhill, when confronted with the world's demands, seemed to forget the imperatives of his faith.[34]

[32] Fowler, *op. cit.*, sect. I, chap. 1, p. 4.
[33] *Ibid.*, sect. I, chap. 3, p. 16.
[34] This explains why Bunyan thought he saw Hobbes' influence in certain passages of Fowler : " Far from committing sin when we submit ourselves to obviously innocent usages and to the inoffensive customs of our compatriots and neighbours, or to the will of our governors when they demand this submission, to refuse to obey would be sin," *Design of Christianity* (ed. 1760), p. 204. But the curate had plainly indicated that he was referring only to usages that did not deprave man and about which the Gospel says nothing. And he added (p. 206) : the whole difference between the Mosaic law and the law of the Gospels rests precisely in this, that the first imposed or prohibited a mass of indifferent things, whereas the second imposes that which is necessary. Passionate and blinded, Bunyan retorted : Thus man can do all that seems to him good, even if he lives in the most corrupt country (p. 322). And again : " How then, if God should cast you into Turkey, where Mahomet reigns as Lord . . ." (p. 322).
The distance which separates Fowler from Thomas Hobbes is so great that there is no need to insist on this point. Let us only recall this passage from the *Leviathan* : " But what (may some object) if a King, or a senate, or other soveraign person forbid us to beleeve in Christ ? . . . Profession with the

They exchanged sharp blows. Bunyan called Fowler "a brutish, beastly man", "this thief", "a bat", "an angel of darkness", and all the epithets which two hundred years later astounded his worthy editor, George Offor.[35] The vicar called Bunyan "pestilent Schismatick", and "black-mouthed calumniator".[36] A creature like you, he said to the tinker, is as powerless to discredit my works as dogs are incapable of causing an eclipse of the moon by barking at it, or of sullying palaces by putting their paws against the walls.[37] And finally he was surprised at the Government's toleration of such a "firebrand" and so subversive a criminal.[38]

★

Bunyan made no answer. Already he was occupied with another controversy—not of his own seeking this time—with his London co-religionists. We need not go into this in detail because in our opinion this new passage of arms had no formative influence on Bunyan. The works which it led him to write are interesting from another point of view, and it is as religious messages that we shall study them later on. At this point it is enough to recall the occasion which caused them.

In 1672 Bunyan had published a sort of "credo", ample and clear, called *A Confession of my Faith and a Reason of my Practice*. At the end of this tract he said that he did not think it proper to make the baptism of an adult by water the condition *sine qua non* of his admission into the sect. Baptism was only a symbol for the baptised person, an aid given to him.[39] It should be judged that such-and-such a person was worthy to enter into communion by the faith he professed and the

---

tongue is but an externall thing, and no more then any other gesture whereby we signifie our obedience; and wherein a Christian, holding firmly in his heart the faith of Christ, hath the same liberty which the Prophet Elisha allowed to Naaman the Syrian . . . This we may say, that whatsoever a subject as Naaman was, is compelled to in obedience to his soveraign, and doth it not in order to his own mind, but in order to the laws of his country, that action is not his, but his soveraigns." *Leviathan*, chap. 42, 'Of power ecclesiasticall' (p. 270, Everyman ed.).

[35] *Works*, II, 279.
[36] *Dirt Wip't Off*, p. 2.
[37] *Ibid.*, The Preface to the Reader.
[38] *Ibid.*, p. 70.
[39] *Confession of Faith*, II, 610.

works he accomplished.[40] And here Bunyan quotes St. Paul: "For he is not a Jew, which is one outwardly; neither is that circumcision, which is outward in the flesh. But he is a Jew, which is one inwardly; and circumcision is that of the heart, in the spirit, and not in the letter ".[41] Similarly, there was baptism and baptism. " He that believeth in Jesus Christ . . . and is dead to sin . . . hath the Heart, Power and Doctrine of baptism; all then that he wanteth, is but the sign, the shadow, or the outward circumstance thereof." [42]

Although he had not yet expressed these ideas in his work, Bunyan had doubtless always believed them. Indeed, his master, John Gifford, discouraged any discussion of this question, which seemed to him secondary.[43] Faith in Christ and holiness of life—those were the essentials. The first members of the little Baptist sect of Bedford, who had come from the Established Church and been baptised as babies, had no desire, either, that baptism should be a cause of interior quarrels. Finally, the Bedford group came under the influence of the curate of the neighbouring parish of Yelden, William Dell, sometime chaplain to Fairfax's army. William Dell [44] maintained that it was important to distinguish between John's baptism, which was the baptism of the body, and Christ's baptism, which was the baptism of souls. John's water-baptism was to last only until Christ's fire-baptism. Neither Christ nor Paul had baptised. This rite should not become a condition of the union of Christians.

Bunyan's position was the same as Dell's. For years the 'strict-communion Baptists' of London had reproached him with this,[45]

[40] *Confession of Faith*, II, 607.
[41] Rom. ii, 28–29.
[42] *Works*, II, 609.
[43] See *The Church-Book of Bunyan Meeting* (fac-simile ed. 1928) : " Faith in Christ and holiness of life, without respect to this or that circumstance, or opinion in outward and circumstantiall things. By which meanes grace and faith was incouraged, love and amity maintained ; disputings and occasion to janglings and unprofitable questions avoyded and many that were weake in the faith confirmed in the blessing of eternall life." And also his beautiful letter (ff. 2–4) : " In your assemblies avoide all disputes which gender to strifes ; as questions about externalls, and all doubtful disputations." f. 3.
[44] John Brown, *op. cit.*, p. 236.
[45] " Assault, I say, upon this congregation, by times, for no less than 16 or 18 years, Yea, myself they have sent for, and endeavoured to persuade to break communion with my brethren." *Works*, II, 618. The " strict and

and William Kiffin, Thomas Paul and Henry Danvers had, naturally enough, profited by the publication of Bunyan's *Confession of Faith* to attack him publicly through his books.

In two works—*Differences in Judgment about Water Baptism No Bar to Communion* in 1673, and *Peaceable Principles and True* in 1674—Bunyan answered his critics and restated his beliefs. " I will not let water-baptism be the rule, the door, the bolt, the bar, the wall of division between the righteous and the righteous.[46] . . . Baptism was certainly a right of God but God never ordered that it should be made a partition to separate the saints from the saints.[47] . . . I tell you I would be, and hope I am, a Christian. . . . And as for these factious titles of Anabaptists, Independents, Presbyterians or the like, I conclude that they came neither from Jerusalem, nor Antioch, but rather from hell and Babylon." [48]

Twelve years of prison had enabled Bunyan to weigh the principles for which he had suffered: " To weigh and pause, and pause again, the grounds and foundation of those principles for which I thus have suffered." [49] He was detached from everything which seemed to him secondary, and he had bound himself only to fundamental principles. And if it is true, as we have said, that Bunyan liked to tilt with words and polemic, it is equally true, as he himself said, that he despised doing so.[50] He was always ready for the fray so as to lay heresy low, but he was equally ready for conciliation so as to unite all those who recognised the authority of the Bible to the exclusion of all human additions in one and the same love, one and the same mission.

---

particular baptists " were Calvinists and refused to communicate with anyone whatsoever outside the members of their Churches. The " open and particular baptists ", like Bunyan, were Calvinists but denied, as we have seen, the absolute necessity of baptism and showed themselves to be much more liberal in their communion with others of the faithful. There were still two other groups, the " seventh-day and particular baptists ", Calvinists too but who did not recognise Sunday as the Sabbath, and the " general baptists " who were not Calvinists.

Towards 1660 there were about 115 assemblies of general baptists, and 131 of particular baptists. The general Baptists were the first to appear in England. The particular ones broke away in 1633. See C. E. Whiting (*op. cit.*, pp. 83 *et seq.*), who outlines the matter clearly and concisely; and also W. T. Whitley, *A History of British Baptists* (2nd ed., London, 1932).

[46] *Works*, II, 629.   [47] *Ibid.*, II, 648.   [48] *Ibid.*, II, 649.
[49] *Ibid.*, II, 593.   [50] *G. A.*, par. 284.

II. THE PREACHER

Many who came as mere spectators, for novelty's sake,
rather than to be edified and improved, went away well
satisfied with what they heard, and wondered, as the
Jews did at the apostles, viz. whence this man should
have these things.

A CONTINUATION OF MR. BUNYAN'S LIFE

A fiery tear he put in every tone.
'Tis my belief God spoke ; no tinker has such powers.

ROBERT BROWNING

THOUGH Bunyan carried the good news unhesitatingly to his
enemies, he was only really happy when addressing his brethren.
He found contact with the Puritan masses sweet and profitable above
all else.   In talking to them he broke his isolation, if not his solitude,
for that was interior and inseparable from the human condition.

When his Bedford friends first implored him to preach, Bunyan
was immured, and silent.   But the walls immediately crumbled, and
joy flooded in through the cracks.   He was happy only when fulfilling his task or, as he put it, exercising "his gift": "I could
not be content unless I was found in the exercise of my gift." [51]
The faith he awakened in others rebounded on himself and brought
him comfort: "The tears of those whom God did awaken by my
preaching would be both solace and encouragement to me." [52]   His
confidence in himself grew when he found himself surrounded by
affection and respect.[53]   Success did not go to his head,[54] but it
brought him the stimulus essential to a man of action and an artist.
There is probably no exaggeration in saying that if he had not joined
the Church and felt the warmth, fellowship and admiration of others [55]

[51] *G. A.*, par. 269.   [52] *G. A.*, par. 275.
[53] *G. A.*, par. 273.   [54] *G. A.*, pars. 269, 300.
[55] In 17th-century England all believers, whether Arminians or Calvinists,
gave to the sermon a place of honour in religious life.   The preacher's influence
over the masses was thus considerable.   Cf. David Ogg, *op. cit.*, I, 100,
"Throughout the reign of Charles II, and especially during the popish plot,

he would never have found peace.   In converting others he deepened his own conversion.   His personal experience dictated his sermons, but once his words were spoken and no longer a part of himself, they flocked back to him charged with the emotions they had aroused in his listeners.   And so his work, while born of his life, had a constructive influence over his life.   This is what a study of his sermons will help us to understand.

1   *His Oratorical Method*

We do not possess the exact text of his sermons.[56]   It is probable that they were improvised, that Bunyan allowed himself to be led by the inspiration of the moment and the needs of his public, and that he wrote them down from memory afterwards.[57]   His small publications

---

the sermon was one of the most potent influences on the masses." What it meant to the Puritans in particular is plainly shown in a little work of the period, *The Character of an Old English Puritane or Non-conformist*, by John Geree, M.A., and Late Preacher of the Word at Saint Faiths (London, 1646). " He accounted preaching as necessary now as in the primitive church . . . He was a man of good spiritual appetite, and could not be contented with one meal a day.   An afternoon sermon did relish as well to him as one in the morning."   P. 2.

[56] Except the last, preached two days before his death : *Works*, II, 155 *et seq*.   Briefly, this sermon, by a Bunyan already ravaged with fever, is of little interest.   Probably it was taken down during the service by an admirer. On this question of the stenography of sermons see W. Fraser Mitchell, *English Pulpit Oratory from Andrewes to Tillotson* (London, 1932), pp. 31 *et seq*. This well-documented work has a comprehensive and clear bibliography, is easy to read and full of interest.   It is particularly helpful in the study of the relationship between the sermon and the ' treatise '.   W. Fraser Mitchell quotes on p. 27 a passage from Playfere in which the latter explains that he delivered a sermon in the temple " as filled up the ordinary time of an houre ; but that was scarce halfe the Sermon.   I uttered no more, to avoid the offense of the hearer ; I wrote no lesse, to procure the profit of the reader . . . I thought good in publishing this sermon rather to inlarge it to the comprehension I have conceived and meditated in my minde, then to scant it according to that strict compasse of time which I was tied to in the pulpit." Epistle dedicatory of *The Sick-Manscouch* in *The Whole Sermons*, 1623.

[57] If we are to believe his friends Chandler and Wilson : " It being customary with him to commit his sermons to writing after he had preached them."   Preface, *Works*, 1682.   This statement of Chandler and Wilson throws light on this passage from the *Relation* of the imprisonment : " I would willingly take the pains to give any one the notes of my sermons."   P. 421. That Bunyan often improvised his homilies there is no doubt : Cf. " The

are merely developments of the original sermon in the form of tracts or little treatises. However, here we have the substance of his oral discourses in book form, and also their structure and rhythm.

Bunyan gives us to understand in *Grace Abounding* that a certain change took place in his style some two years after he started preaching.[58] At first the sermons of the new and still frightened convert drew their sustenance from his agitation: the groans of his soul passed into his words. Then later, becalmed, he probably strove to recreate the face of Christ the Redeemer for his audience, and bring confidence to sinners.

And in fact we find reflections of Bunyan's spiritual life in his work which enable us to divine his progress towards greater peace, if not absolute serenity; but our findings do not enable us to indicate the precise moment at which his style as a preacher changed. The fact is that the change did not take place in a continuous line, and Bunyan never really modified his view of life nor altered the essential features of his oratorical method.[59] Since his newly-acquired tranquillity was always quivering and anxious, the themes, thoughts and sentiments of his work remained like to themselves. His climate

---

Epistle to Four Sorts of Readers," *The Holy City*, III, 397. " But at that time I felt myself, it being my turn to speak, so empty, spiritless and barren, that I thought I should not have been able to speak among them so much as five words of truth with life and evidence." Then inspiration came and he spoke. See too *G. A.*, pars. 277, 292, 293.

However, it is not impossible that he sometimes prepared notes before preaching. Here there is a whole question of technique which was of great importance in the 17th century. Cf. W. Fraser Mitchell, *op. cit.*, pp. 19–26. As an interesting document of the period consult : *The Works of that Famous and Worthie Minister of Christ in the Universitie of Cambridge*, Th. William Perkins (Cambridge, 1609), vol. II. *The Arte of Prophecying*, pp. 731 *et seq.*, and in particular chap. 9 : " of memorie of preaching ", pp. 758 *et seq.*

[58] " I preached what I felt, what I smartingly did feel, even that under which my poor soul did groan and tremble to astonishment." Par. 276.

[59] It is nevertheless customary for critics to maintain, without providing any proof, however, that there was an ' amazing ' change. See for example a fairly recent study by Austen Kennedy de Blois, *John Bunyan the Man* (Philadelphia, 1928) : " The change that immediately came in his method of preaching was amazing," p. 155.

We have purposely taken most of our ' terrifying ' examples from Bunyan's posthumous works, probably the last he wrote.

did not alter, but the seasons advanced and winter gave way to spring: but a spring with some cold and squally days, in whose air hung the memory of past storms.

In practically all Bunyan's sermons two stages are distinguishable. In the first he condemned the flesh and extolled the threat of the Law—he "preached terror",[60] as he himself said; and afterwards he soothed and comforted the soul sickened with fear. First he showed it Christ's omnipotence, and then the infinitude of His love. The method was not original; indeed, it seems to have been the common property of a large number of Protestant preachers.[61] It reproduced the two great phases of conversion as it proceeded, and showed the preacher attempting to lead his listeners along the path that he himself had trodden.

Thus Bunyan's sermons, like his spiritual life, present us with two poles. Fear is crystallised round the one, while the other is radiant with confident clarity. There is a continual oscillation from one to the other, a constant interplay of light and shade.

But first he always had "to preach terror", make his audience listen to the "burning words"—"brennyng wordys", as they said in the Middle Ages.[62]

One first phase had for its theme the unworthiness of humanity, with Bunyan's personal experience and the Holy Scriptures for orchestration. For he found in the Scriptures the poetic expression of everything he had experienced or observed. He let the prophets speak for him: "Acknowledge thine iniquities, that thou hast transgressed against the Lord thy God, and hast scattered thy ways to the strangers under every green tree." [63]

When his eyes looked upon human corruption, they penetrated deep into the heart and uncovered its rottenness and hypocrisy with the sadness of Pascal. He noted that even in prayer "the heart and the tongue do not go along jointly".[64] The words we utter condemn

[60] *Doctrine of Law*, I, 495.

[61] H. Delacroix, *La religion et la foi*, p. 75.

[62] John Myrc : "The Apostolys, and all othyr prechours aftyr hom schold speke brennyng wordys." *Festiall*, quoted by G. R. Owst, *Preaching in Medieval England* (Cambridge, 1926), p. 334.

[63] *No Way to Heaven*, I, 327. This treatise was published after his death, in 1688.

[64] *I will Pray with the Spirit*, I, 628 ; publication of this "discourse", 1662.

the very faults of which we are most fond.[65]   And which of us wants
to do God's will if it brings about our temporal downfall?[66]   A lie
may issue from a man's mouth at the very moment when he is feigning
the greatest sanctity.[67]   The creature's love for God should burn
like an unquenchable fire; yet it is like a " little flash ".[68]   As for
humility, who possesses a thimble-full of it?[69]

And again, with still more desolating lucidity: the sincerity of the
best of us is " mixed with dirt ".[70]

Bunyan sometimes wished that remorse would gnaw at us ruth-
lessly: he wanted our prayers to be one prolonged groan.[71]   His
sermons, as well as *Grace Abounding*, give him a place in penitential
literature, and his fervour recalls that of the psalmist whose violence
he admired: " Every syllable carrieth a mighty vehemence in it."[72]

More or less united to this theme of human unworthiness was the
one which introduced " the flaming sword " of the Law[73]—the Law
which condemns irrevocably because it demands of the creature a
total and constant respect for the ten commandments; in other words,
it demands the impossible.[74]   In the eyes of the Law there is no
" little sin ".[75]   One fault only in the whole of a human life brings
with it the certainty of death,[76] and, worse still, the shadow of an evil
thought damns a man for ever.[77]

And what a damnation!   A third theme describes its nature and
gives us an insight into hell.   Later on we shall study the value of
these descriptions which could be inscribed with Dante's words:

> Fearful indeed art thou, vengeance of God!
> He that now reads what mine own eyes with awe
> Plainly beheld, well may he dread thy rod![78]

Man is therefore incapable of saving himself by his own strength
alone.   Only Christ can assure him salvation because only Christ

---

[65] *I will Pray with the Spirit*, I, 630.   [66] *Ibid.*   [67] *Ibid.*
[68] *Christ a Complete Saviour*, I, 213, published posthumously, 1692.
[69] *Ibid.*
[70] *Ibid.*, I, 213: " Simplicity and godly sincerity also, with how much
dirt it is mixed in the best."
[71] *I will Pray with the Spirit.* See vol. I, pp. 631, 635, 636.
[72] *Ibid.*, I, 624.   [73] *The Strait Gate*, I, 368, published in 1676.
[74] *The Doctrine of Law and Grace*, I, 500 *et seq.*
[75] *Ibid.*, I, 542.   [76] *Ibid.*, I, 501.   [77] *Ibid.*
[78] *The Inferno*, Canto 14, line 16 *et seq.* (Sayers' translation).

can satisfy the justice of God. This was the second phase of Bunyan's sermons and treatises, " solempne and mervaylous swete ", in the great tradition of the Christian homily.[79]

Bunyan aroused terror in his listeners only so that they could better savour the peace of love; for man must not have only an intellectual knowledge, but an intimate experience, of the Scriptures; he must know them with his heart.[80] Finally, all our preacher really wanted to do was to bring consolation, to fight the despair which does the creature so much harm. He never tired of quoting and commenting on certain words that always held new depths of meaning for him. " Come unto me, all ye that labour, and I will give you rest. . . . I have come to call not the just but sinners to repentance. . . . God is love, and he who dwells in love dwells in God and God in him."

2 *The Structure of the Sermon*

Fear, then love. Bunyan constructed his sermons around these two emotions and the thoughts they evoke. It was a massive structure, with all its framework open to view.

There was generally a prelude in which he placed the Biblical quotation that was to be expounded in its context. Thus in *Come and Welcome to Jesus Christ*, which has these words of John as their text: " All that the Father giveth me shall come to me; and him that cometh to me I will in no wise cast out," Bunyan starts by recalling that the disciples had gone in a ship towards Capernaum; but the wind was contrary, and in the fourth watch of the night Jesus came to them walking upon the sea, and they were afraid.[81]

There followed some preliminary remarks which outlined the development strictly speaking. For example, in *Come and Welcome*: " The text, in the general, standeth of Two Parts, and hath special respect to the Father and the Son; as also to their joint management of the salvation of the people. . . . The first part of the text, as is evident, respecteth the Father and his gift; the other part the Son and his reception of that gift. . . . These things might be spoken to at

---

[79] Whitford of Syon : " A solempne and mervaylous swete sermon, makyng speciall mencion of love, unitie, peace and concorde." *A Werke for House-holders* quoted by G. R. Owst, *Preaching in Medieval England*, p. 345.
[80] *The Doctrine of Law and Grace*, I, 493.
[81] *Come and Welcome*, I, 240.

large . . . but I shall choose to speak to the words, FIRST by way of Explication, SECOND by way of Observation." [82]

In this way the listener could see at a glance the ground that was to be covered. The scheme was clearly mapped out by a man accustomed to speaking. He knew that his listeners liked to be led with a strong hand, that they needed landmarks on the road, and preferred counsel and instruction to be summed up in advance, then delivered, and afterwards repeated. So Bunyan kept watch over his chain of ideas and reinforced the links. Examples offer themselves on every page: " The description of the coming to Christ divideth itself into two heads. First, etc. Second, etc. To speak to the first. . . ." [83] And in another treatise, taken at random, we find: " I now come to the second doctrine that I gathered from the words . . . There are 4 things in the words that do prove this doctrine . . ." [84] And so the sermon made its way, marked at every joint by the same formulas. Nobody could fail to feel the weight of such a rhythmic advance.

And here, too, side by side with his own born-orator's instinct, Bunyan was following in the tradition of all sacred oratory, whether popular or learned, whether addressed to simple people or to the lettered. [85] In his excellent study, G. R. Owst tells us that if there is one point on which all the medieval preachers agreed it was on the importance of dividing up a sermon, the " processus thematis ". [86]

[82] *Come and Welcome*, I, 241.   [83] *Ibid.*, I, 241.
[84] *Some Gospel Truths*, I, 136, then 143, 144 and 146.
[85]   " *A la simple gent*
                Ai fait simplement
                Un simple sermon
                Ne l' fiz as letrez
                Car il mit assez
                Escriz et raisum."

Quoted by Lecoy de la Marche, *La Chaire française au moyen age*, p. 283.

[86] G. R. Owst, *Preaching in Medieval England*, p. 321. See too W. Fraser Mitchell, *op. cit.*, p. 112 : " . . . the extraordinary attention paid to ' method' by preachers, particularly puritan preachers, in the first half of the 17th century. A man's methods was a recognised property which was commented upon, by his hearers . . ."
The author quotes a passage where the celebrated Puritan, John Dod, expounds his personal method. The established divisions and sub-divisions are so numerous that they obscure what they want to throw light on—and Bunyan seems a timid ' logician ' compared with Dod !

After reading Bunyan and other Puritans of his period we can appreciate the truth of the eminent medievalist's observation: " Sometimes the subsequent careful notes and scoring, the rare erasures, the names entered by later hands in these very sermons and handbooks, seem to give almost tangible evidence of the continuity of use. Their influence stalks on silent but wonderfully real and alive from generation to generation, troubling little about the noisy clash of theologians and parties without. For round the family board and in the hearts of the peasantry, the Reformation meant no such break with the past as many would have us believe." [87]

The monotony of Bunyan's sermons and treatises was increased by the countless repetitions.[88] Some of these were intentional. Bunyan was addressing humble people, and knew the pedagogic value of repetition: " I insist," he said, " for the better understanding of those that are weak of apprehension." [89] Like all the " mechanick "

---

[87] G. R. Owst, *Preaching in Medieval England*, p. 280. On the same page we read : " This after all is where our stubborn puritan temper comes from —not from protestant Geneva or Wittenberg, but medieval York-Shire. It is the vigorous unsacerdotalism of Rolle, coupled with the strict religious discipline of the household which he handed on from St. Edmund Rich and others, that re-emerges, by means of this homely literature, in the sturdy sixteenth and seventeenth century yeomen of England. His mystical fire may burn low for a while ; but it will leap again in Bunyan and in Penn."

On the Puritan sermon see Bunyan's biographer, John Brown, *Puritan Preaching in England* (London, 1900), a rather rapid and sometimes disappointing book, particularly the article on Bunyan ; see too W. Fraser Mitchell, *op. cit.*, pp. 255 *et seq.* " The Non-Anglicans to 1660." In both these books there is mention of Thomas Adams, whom Southey called the prose Shakespeare of Puritan theologians. Adams was minister at Willington, four miles from Bedford. About the sermon (on the banquet to which Satan summons his friends) which John Brown analyses (pp. 92 *et seq.*), G. R. Owst says that it betrays a fundamentally medieval spirit. Cf. *Literature and Pulpit in Medieval England* (Cambridge, 1933), p. 101.

[88] The Dominican Thomas Walleys gave this advice : " *Et in magis ponderandis magis immoretur, ut, si necesse videatur, ea bis vel ter replicet.*" Quoted by G. R. Owst, *Preaching in Medieval England*, p. 353. Compare Richard Baxter : " Nay, I find, if we not purposely dress out the matter into such a length of words and use some repetition of it,—that they may hear it inculcated on them again—we do but overrun their understanding and they presently lose us." (" They " represents " the ignorant sort of people ".) See Powicke, *A Life of the Reverend Richard Baxter* (London, 1924), p. 285.

[89] *Doctrine of Law and Grace*, I, 511.

preachers, the tinker's concern was for the ignorant, the "lewede men" towards whom that other great dreamer, William Langland, leant with such solicitude. And the rural and working population, which formed the bulk of Bunyan's audience, needed time to accept an idea. They needed to walk round an idea, take it up in their hands, like the faithful tools they were handling every day. And it was these people that Bunyan wished to serve. Each of his books was an act into which the desire to make a work of art simply did not enter. He spoke and wrote for "those who have but shallow purses, short memories and but little time to spare".[90]

Other repetitions derived from his respect for the Bible, which was for him the authentic record of the word of God. As he considered everything in it to be of equal weight, he did not have to select. He multiplied the quotations which he thought proved his point, and marked time instead of advancing.[91]

And yet his repetitions had still another and deeper cause. He re-iterated Biblical texts because for so long they had been circling round in his own sick head. And if debating-points were always arising in his work, it was because at the dawn of each day they arose in his mind. Bunyan's sermons were the mirror of his life. His apologetics, as we shall see in the course of our study, followed the pattern of his life.

A patient reading of his sermons reveals numerous digressions, though 'digression' is hardly the right word for these meanderings. They are not discussions of points foreign to the spirit of the subject under treatment, but they are secondary branches, whole growths of saplings. We feel that the thought proceeds under a forceful organic logic, not at all the prescribed logic of a work of art. In spite of the divisions in his sermons which we have outlined, their joints and numberings constitute a natural growth, as in so many Anglo-Saxon works. And their interior unity is only strengthened by the continual resounding of the basic theme—for example, Christ's redemptive Grace in *Come and Welcome*.

[90] *The Perpetuity of the Seventh Day Sabbath*, II, 361.
[91] And we could say too what Mark Rutherford said of Luther: "The iterations we find are not those of mumbling torpor but of a prophet too much in earnest to be diversified." *Op. cit.*, p. 107.

3 *His Imagery*

The weighty structure of the sermons is fortunately adorned by numerous images taken from the Bible and daily life.

If consolation were needed, then Bunyan drew on the joyful harmonies of the *Song of Songs*; indeed, if we did not know that he was equally familiar with the whole Bible we would conclude that he knew this beautiful and poetical book the best. He hardly transposed or adapted his quotations, but usually let their melody of divine love speak for itself. " He inviteth thee to a banquet of wine, yea, to come into his wine-cellar, and his banner over thee shall be love." [92] And the New Testament offered him images of an infinite sweetness, enriched by his whole life of memories and meditation.

The imprecations and threats were often taken from the Psalms or the Apocalypse: but all the Bible was food for his ' terrifying ' sermons.

In *Come and Welcome* Bunyan asks us what Christ's refusal to welcome the sinner implies ? To be abhorred and despised like the " filthy rags " and mud of the street; to be shut out from God's presence and damned to eternal shame like the " fallen angels "; to be cast into the press of divine anger, into the " lake of fire ", the " bottomless pit ", the " outer darkness ", the " fiery furnace ". [93]

Bunyan liked these strings of quotations, each casting its light or shade over the next, and all mounting in a terrifying crescendo. [94]

In *The Strait Gate* he pointed out that only eight people were saved at the time of Noah or, more exactly, seven, since Ham was damned after escaping from the flood. And from the land of the Chaldeans only Abraham was called. From Sodom and Gomorrah, from Admah and Zeboiim, yes, from the four cities, only Lot was saved. And were not the elect compared to a handful of corn, to a lily among thorns, to gleaning after the vintage ? Moreover, only a fool could

[92] *Come and Welcome*, I, 281. Cf. *Ca.* ii. 4.

[93] *Ibid.*, 271.

[94] The Puritan preacher always quoted his scriptural texts with rigorous precision : " If we are prophets we are God's messengers and must preach God's word as God's word and deliver it as we received it. For as many men mar a good tale in the telling, so we must see to it lest we take away the power and majesty of God's word in the manner of delivering it." William Perkins, quoted by J. Brown, *Puritan Preaching in England*, p. 78.

forget how ephemeral life is, and worry about the things of this world, when this very night he may die.[95]

Here Bunyan certainly followed a very old tradition of religious oratory, but his fervour, in his best moments, made it seem new. He depicted frightful scenes in his sermons, but this was not because people had always done so but because he himself had lived through the terror he described. Thoughts about the grave and about hell ran through his preaching because they were always present in his mind. And because his own desperate desire to live had grown out of his fear of perishing, he made the immense shadow of Death pass over his audience.

In *A Few Sighs from Hell* he tells us that a sinner's torments begin even before he has drawn his last breath.[96] Then come the demons that look like lions. But sometimes these appear to him as he is dying, so that while still undergoing temporal suffering the eternity of his agony is revealed to him.

He tells the sinner that he should live with this moment always before his eyes. He should carry the picture of his deathbed within him, when he would have " the sight of an ill-spent life " spread out before him—" thy sins flying in thy face, thy conscience uttering itself with thunder-claps against thee, the thoughts of God terrifying of thee, death with his merciless paw seizing upon thee, the devils ready to scramble for thy soul, and hell enlarging herself and ready to swallow thee up." [97]

No short phrases here, but flowing periods. Instead of the homely images of a rustic muse, we have the fresco of a visionary painter. A diligent anthologist would probably have no difficulty in proving that Bunyan borrowed everything—even that final touch about Satan's kingdom seeming to become larger. But who else has portrayed this scene with such bold beauty, hoisting it, or rather wafting it to the top of his picture on the rhythmic flow of his prose ?

The scene becomes vaster and vaster as page follows page, as if a cluster of lights were casting their beams farther and farther, lighting up successive planes of horror.

Indescribable torments of " a never-dying worm ", of the " fiery

[95] *The Strait Gate*, I, 379.   [96] *Works*, III, 680.
[97] *Ibid.*, III, 682.

VANITY FAIR
By George Cruikshank
from the edition of
1838

CHRISTIAN AND
HOPEFUL ESCAPE
FROM DOUBTING
CASTLE

An engraving by H. Melville from the edition of
1838

furnace ", the " bottomless pit ", the " unquenchable fire ", and the lake of flames.[98]

The tortures of memory, which enable the damned to see all the past and suffer remorse " as if thy belly were full of pitch and set on a light fire ".[99]

The agony of solitude when he is removed from all familiar things and surrounded by snarling demons who roar at him and madden him with fear.[100]

But the fresco does not take on its full proportions unless placed in its true perspective—eternity.   Bunyan tried to make us feel this infinitude by accumulating images of spatial immensity, like that mentor of his adolescence, Arthur Dent.   " When thou hast been in hell so many thousand years as there are stars in the firmament, or drops in the sea, or sands on the sea-shore, yet thou hast to lie there for ever.   O, this one word EVER, how it will torment thy soul! " [101]

And in an effort to describe the indescribable (" O I am set, I am set, and am not able to utter what my mind conceals of the torments of hell "),[102] the gentle Bunyan, the indulgent father,[103] the loyal husband, sought out words of appalling cruelty to describe the damned, scorned and abandoned by friend and neighbour who turn their backs.[104]

It is this sort of passage that is pinned on to prove Bunyan's in-humanity—Caliban escaped from the legendary island to enter the reality of history.[105]   But surely we know that this harshness—theoretical rather than practical—was common to nearly everybody at that time and not only to certain groups.   And Puritans who imagined they would enjoy vengeances to come merely followed in a tradition. G. C. Coulton reminds us that Dante did not dare to snatch unbaptised

[98] *Works*, III, 683.   [99] *Ibid.*   [100] *Ibid.*, 684.
[101] *Ibid.*   Compare Arthur Dent : " When as many hundred thousand yeares are expired as there be stones by the seaside yet still there be so many more to come."   *Op. cit.*, p. 364.   " Yet shall a man sooner empty the sea by taking out a spoonfull once in a hundred thousand yeares, than the damned soule shall have any ease."   P. 365.
[102] *A Few Sighs*, III, 684.
[103] " For he was both a loving and tender husband and an indulgent father, perhaps somewhat to a fault."   *A New and Authentic Account of the Life and Death of Mr. John Bunyan.   Written by a Friend to the Cause of Religion*, p. 28.
[104] *A Few Sighs*, III, 705.
[105] See Alfred Noyes, art. *cit.*, cf. *supra*, p. 79.

children from hell; while St. Gregory, St. Bonaventure and St. Thomas Aquinas believed, like our tinker, that the spectacle of the wicked in the flames would be one of the joys of the blessed.[106]

But whether cruel or tender, suffused with light or plunged in darkness, Bunyan's pictures have the strength and grandeur of the invisible which they reveal. Over his descriptions of the fight between God and Satan, between the devils and the angels, there blows the breath of what we have called his cosmic lyricism. The human drama seems like a particular aspect of a universal conflict, the only side we see of the war between the Eternal One and the Prince of Evil.

Thus when one of the elect dies, devils foregather to devour his soul, but angels descend from heaven and carry it up to the bosom of Abraham.[107] Thus, too, conversion is a planetary drama. On one side there are God and His creatures, on the other all the strength of the devils, all the power of Satan, who " is called a god, a prince, a lion, a roaring lion ".[108] All the temptations of the earth and all the corruptions of the flesh rise up against the elect. But, though feebler than a moth, this creature of God stands erect, defends himself and triumphs, wondering at himself and causing the world to wonder.[109]

' Wonder.' It is this emotion that makes Bunyan, in his best moments, a poet. With religious respect he takes the word ' Creator ' in his hands. He weighs it—as he often weighs words—and finds it so fraught with meaning, so radiant with power that, in a kind of ecstasy, he contemplates through it the unspeakable reality that it signifies.[110]

' Creator.' That is to say, He on whom the whole universe reposes. ' Creator '—the source of all life. Who would have thought that three children could live in a burning furnace, that Daniel could be safe among lions, that Jonah would return from the whale's belly, and that Christ could rise from the dead ? [111]

In marvelling at these things, Bunyan was not merely recounting remembered happenings in a book, he was assisting at the Genesis. We might say of him what Charles Péguy said of Victor Hugo:

[106] G. G. Coulton, *op. cit.*, p. 61. See too Perry Miller and Thomas H. Johnson, *op. cit.*, p. 7.
[107] *A Few Sighs*, III, 680.
[108] *Saved by Grace*, I, 340.
[109] *Ibid.*
[110] *Seasonable Counsel*, II, 727.
[111] *Ibid.*

" *Il avait ce don unique, entre tous les hommes, il avait reçu ce don, plus jeune que les anciens avant les anciens, il avait reçu ce don de voir la création comme si elle sortait ce matin des mains du Créateur* ".[112]

And even when the wings of his dream did not transport him to the first dawn and the first awakening of things, there was always a part of Bunyan present in the far reaches of history. If doubts or worries assailed him, then immediately there rose up before him comforters from the historical, poetical and prophetical books, not like great shadows, but like beings throbbing with life. And they arranged themselves in pictures, the majesty of his memories holding dispute with their homeliness. The scene that appeared to Bunyan's mind's eye was always steeped in religion and yet glinting with England's tepid sun or swept by her storms, according to the subject. These pictures, at once very near and very remote, have the charm of a view that is new to us.

But much of the power of his concrete eloquence came from purely realistic imagery. Sketches of rustic and family life were more frequent than large frescoes. Bunyan was a visionary only at times. But he was practically always a keen observer of daily life and often amused by it.

He was always ready to portray intimate scenes of home life, to pause a minute to watch insects at play in the air,[113] or the galloping of a race-horse, or the slow pace of a pony ambling along.[114] He depicted the lively scene of a " court of judicature " where the accused answers to the call of his name: " Here, Sir," then, elbowing his way through the crowd, " Please give way; I am called to the Court." [115] He noticed the smiling flowers in a spring garden, and listened to the song of birds.[116] He painted the village forge with " the smith's dog at the foot of the anvil, though the fire sparks fly in his face ". Two lines only, and the scene rises before our eyes, warming the heart of any village- or peasant-loving person.

We could multiply these examples, which occur over and over again in his sermons. The tact and lightness of touch are always there, indispensable in the blending of day-to-day things with eternal things, in interweaving earth's coarse brown linen with the gold and

[112] Charles Péguy, *Victor Marie, comte Hugo* (N.R.F.), p. 121.
[113] *Come and Welcome*, I, 252.   [114] *Ibid.*, 252.
[115] *The Jerusalem Sinner*, I, 89.   [116] *Holy City*, III, 409.

silk of heaven.   Bunyan was aware of the essential solemnity of our actions in the sight of God, and he also knew by intuition that every kind of love is essentially the same, that the inconceivable and terrifying God is also the Father to whom we can turn " with frank and filial trust ".   And thus he managed to blend the visible and the invisible in one stroke.

4   Other Elements in his Style

The variety of his images and tones necessitated variety in the construction of his sentences and in the general tempo of his prose.

There are pages uniformly grey where hard argument follows hard argument, often with a purely verbal logic.   In our examination of the structure of a typical sermon we have already seen those chains of proofs dragged along as it were at ground level,[117] with every link numbered: " First objection . . . answer . . . second objection . . . answer."

On certain points of doctrine he wrangled with the tenacity of a cunning rather than a subtle lawyer.   For example, in *Come and Welcome* he twisted John's text in the effort to prove, like Calvin and various others,[118] that ' all ' does not mean the totality but the part, and that when Christ said: " All that the Father giveth me shall come to me," He meant only the elect.[119]   We cannot help recalling Samuel Butler's malicious satire:

> He was in *Logick* a great Critick
> Profoundly skill'd in Analytick.
> He could distinguish and divide
> A Hair 'twixt South and South-West side.[120]

In the worst examples of this kind of thing the phrase stands still, and even in the rest of the sermon proceeds at a slow pace.   This tempo is inevitably bound up with Bunyan's temperament, his personal needs and the didactic necessity of repeating himself.   The style of the sermons and the treatises is an explanatory style, for his

---

[117] Cf. *supra*, p. 112 ; and again : " I shall now lay down a few arguments and afterwards answer two or three objections . . ." *Doctrine of Law*, I, 539.

[118] Calvin : " *L'apostre parle de tous etats, et non pas d'une chacune personne*," quoted by H. Bois, art. *cit.*

[119] *Come and Welcome*, I, 242.

[120] *Hudibras*, Part I, canto I, 65 *et seq.*

own sake as much as for other people's. The rhythm is that of a man who is listening to himself speaking (not necessarily with complacency). We feel that we can justly apply to the language of these works G. D. Bone's remark on the English of William Tindale and other writers of his period: " Each sentence looks backward as it were—adds something fitting to what has gone before. In our new prose each sentence leans forward; seems to be getting more and more deep into the argument, to be leading to something really interesting. . . . The old prose sentences settle comfortably into their positions . . . you read the new prose pressing on to the end of the sentence. . . . In the old prose you took each part, section or sentence, piece after piece, fully understanding and consuming one part before moving on to consider the next." [121]

We would not go so far as to agree with Mr. Bone that this kind of prose is more " savourous ". For pleasure depends on content as much as on rhythm, and we—assiduous readers of Bunyan—are well acquainted with the heaviness of his treatises.

But Bunyan belonged also to the future, as a study of the style and thought of his major works will show. We will find that he too made phrases " that lean forward ", indeed in the best moments of his sermons and treatises his phrase goes at quite a sharp pace, and, as he grew older, these good moments became more frequent. The fact is that style changes with the man whom it reveals. And although his convictions about the small number of the elect and the damnation of the outcast multitudes remained theoretically the same, in practice he worried less and less about the clash between his intellectual conviction and his unavowed feeling (which he did in fact half-avow) that all would be saved who wanted to be. The comprehensive suppleness and diversity of life had blunted a little the contradictions it had not been able to resolve. The heart often spoke louder and more urgently than the reason.

So there were brisk phrases, phrases spontaneously furnished with the simplest of words. Bunyan addressed himself to humble people " in words easy to be understood." " Do not affect high expressions," he said, " they will drown your children." [122] Speak " as God spoke

[121] G. D. Bone, 'Tindale and the English Language', *The Works of William Tindale*, by S. L. Greenslade (London and Glasgow, 1938), p. 63.
[122] *Christian Behaviour*, II 558.

to His children ".[123]   There should be no borrowings from the
Fathers of the Church, nor from Aristotle or Plato.[124]   Bunyan made
his intentions plain, as did the friend who wrote the preface of *A Few
Sighs from Hell*: " If there be that which some may call tautology, be
not displeased by it . . . for that word that may not fasten upon thy
heart in one page, may in another." [125]

Bunyan knew so well the shock words can have on a soul.   He
had experienced this himself before trying it out on others, and his
findings as an orator only reinforced his personal experience: " I
have observed ", he wrote, " that a Word cast in by the by hath done
more execution in a Sermon than all that was spoken besides; sometimes also when I have thought I did not good, then I did the most of
all; and at other times when I thought I should catch them, I have
fished for nothing." [126]

We could find very many examples [127] to show that Bunyan, like
a hundred other popular preachers, desired to be simple and personal.

Personal?   " I have never endeavoured to, nor durst make use of,
other men's lines." [128]

We can concede to Bunyan that he re-thought other people's
ideas.   His own experience was so vivid that it enabled him, as we
have shown in this chapter, to infuse freshness into old themes, and
this may well have enabled him to conceal even from himself his
debt to his forerunners and his contemporaries.   The ideas that we
encounter in our youth and which, as it were, grow up with us, easily
seem to be our own personal property, inseparable from our inmost
being.   And perhaps we are not altogether wrong, if it is true that
nature is only an initial habit.

We must grant Bunyan all this, and yet, without wanting to be

[123] *Christian Behaviour*, II 558.

[124] *The Doctrine of Law and Grace*, I, 495.

[125] *A Few Sighs from Hell*, III, 672.

[126] *G. A.*, par. 287.

[127] " Sir, I suppose, in your reading of this discourse, you will be apt to
blame me for two things : first, because I have not so beautified my matter
with acuteness of language as you could wish or desire.   Secondly because
also I have not given you, either in the line or in the margent, a cloud of
sentences from the learned fathers . . .

" . . . Words easy to be understood do often hit the mark when high and
learned ones do only pierce the air."   *Holy City*, III, 398.

[128] *G. A.*, par. 285.

disrespectful, we cannot forget that solemn denials of borrowing formed a part of the recipe of the trade.[129]   Each " prophet " affirmed his own " immaculate conception ", as Mr. York Tindall would say. And by dint of affirming it he probably ended up by believing it, if he did not believe it at first.   Has anyone ever been able to trace in a man the dividing line between sincerity and lies ?

However this may be, the " mechanick preachers " glorified their ignorance so as to exalt their divine mission.[130]   In 1644 the Baptist, Samuel Howe, said that human knowledge could never make a man a minister of the Gospel, neither could it enable him to understand the spirit of God in His Word.[131]   And George Fox [132] proclaimed that the Lord had revealed to him that study at Oxford and Cambridge was not enough to make a good minister of God.

It was this holy ignorance that Edwards denounced as the 127th and 128th heresies,[133] while Samuel Butler smilingly remarked that the " fanatic " owed all his gifts to his ignorance, just as beggars owe their alms to their poverty.[134]

---

[129] Read the advice of William Perkins (*op. cit.*) : if one quotes a profane author, he says, one must not mention his name (p. 751) because " humane wisdome must be concealed . . . because the preaching of the Word is the testimonie of God ", p. 758.

[130] See the conclusion of par. 285 of *G. A.* which we were quoting just now : " For I verily thought and found by experience that what was taught me by the word and spirit of Christ, could be spoken, maintained and stood to by the soundest and best established conscience."

The title of Evans' biography is significant : *An Eccho to the Voice from Heaven, or a Narrative of the Life and Manner of the Special Calling and Visions of Arise Evans.   By him published in discharge of his duty to God, and the satisfaction of those who doubt* (Long Alley, Blackfriars, 1652).

And when the preacher does not sufficiently emphasise his exceptional destiny, his friends do it for him.   Cf. ' Mr. Burton's epistle to the reader ', *Some Gospel Truths Opened* : " This man is not chosen out of an earthly, but out of the heavenly university, the church of Christ, etc. . . .", p. 140. William Perkins says that one must preach in such a way that " all, even ignorant persons and unbeleevers, may judge that it is not so much he that speaketh, as the spirit of God in him and by him." *Op. cit.*, p. 759.

[131] Samuel Howe, *Sufficiency of the Spirit's Teaching Without Human Learning* (1644), p. 2.

[132] George Fox, *The Journal* (ed. *cit.*), I, 88.

[133] Ths. Edwards, *Gangraena*, errors 127 and 128.

[134] Samuel Butler, *Characters and Passages from Notebooks*, ed. by A. R. Waller (Cambridge, 1908), p. 85.

The lay-preacher, as well as wanting to be ignorant, wanted to be simple. He cultivated simplicity. The desire for personal success demanded it and—we can hardly insist too much on this point—popular tradition required it. Wycliffe urged his disciples to scorn pompous words [135] and make use of a unified language, " *plana elocutio* ".

We can measure the success of Bunyan, Benjamin Keach,[136] Vavasor Powell and other " mechanick preachers " by the proposals that Roger L'Estrange drew up in 1663 with a view to " regulating " the Press. We must destroy, he said, these great masters of popular style who play so exactly on the capacity and humour of the masses.[137]

To-day Bunyan occupies a unique place among these " great masters ", for he is the only one who still finds readers outside the professionally erudite. In his time his reputation was not exceptional, though it was very high. His friend, Charles Doe, went as far as to call him a " new Paul ".[138] He saw thousands of Christians converted by the tinker showing their joy by tears.[139]

Certainly the power of irradiating faith was very strong with Bunyan, but it would have been less so without his oratorical art, and especially without his skill in using what we may call the tricks of the trade. The sad or funny anecdote, dialogue, proverbs—the whole traditional procedure was known to him; but in the rapid analysis we are going to make we shall not draw attention at every moment to similarities between our author and his forerunners or

---

[135] " *Grandia verba . . . color rhetoricus.*" See Victor Vattier, *John Wyclyff, sa vie, ses oeuvres, sa doctrine* (Paris, 1886), p. 239. Consult too Dyson Hague, *The Life and Work of John Wyclyff* (revised ed., London, 1935), p. 69; and the monumental study by Herbert B. Workman, *John Wyclif, a Study of the English Medieval Church* (2 vols., Oxford, 1926), p. 212, for example.

[136] This Buckinghamshire tailor who was first a ' general baptist ' then a ' particular baptist ' was so well known that the historian of the sect, W. T. Whitley, has written : " When Bunyan died in 1688, except that Keach had no version of his books into Dutch and Welsh, it might well be doubted which was the more popular author." *Op. cit.*, p. 140.

[137] Roger L'Estrange, *Considerations and Proposals in Order to the Regulation of the Press* (London, 1663), p. 10. York Tindall, too, quotes this passage, *op. cit.*, p. 167.

[138] Ch. Doe, *The Struggler*, ed. Offor, III, 766.

[139] *Ibid.*

contemporaries. After all, what does borrowing matter? Don't we all know, at least since Pascal, that the ball is not so important as the way of throwing it? Bunyan's friends recognised this, and noticed in him " a peculiar phrase to himself ".[140] His vivid personality knew how to impress its individual stamp on everything he consciously or unconsciously borrowed.

Humour came naturally to this man of the people who liked the taste of words that smack of the soil and homely turns of phrase. " The formalist ", he wrote, " has lost all of religion but the shell." [141] As for the conviction of the Latitudinarians, they are merely a reflection of the time; their religion " is always like the times turning this way and that way, like the cock on the steeple ".[142]

But Bunyan's wit was never livelier nor more robust than when hitting out at hypocrites, with their ready-made faith, their false show of love, the assumed gravity of their faces, and their beautiful words just for Sunday. " Their feigned faith, pretended love, glorious carriages, will stand them in little stead. I call them holiday ones, for I perceive that some professors do with religion just as people do with their best apparel—hang it against the wall all the week and put it on on Sundays. For as some scarce ever put on a suit but when they go to a fair or a market, so little house religion will do with some; they save religion till they go to a meeting, or till they meet with a godly chapman." [143]

So we see that his desire to make himself understood by the roughest countryman, with no artistic preoccupation, nevertheless gave birth to art, to a clear style and expressive metaphors. His use of simile was determined by the need to convince. " Similitudes, if fitly spoke and applied, do much set off and out any point." [144] He also made use of the terse comparison reduced to its most suggestive elements, as our recent examples show. Sometimes, however, he developed them, as in *The Heavenly Footman*, where the whole work is built round the analogies between a footman and the Christian who goes

[140] See the ed. of works (1692) by Ebenezer Chandler and John Wilson : " The author indeed had a peculiar phrase to himself in expressing the conceptions of his mind; his words were his own . . ." *To the serious, judicious and impartial reader*, folio A.

[141] *The Strait Gate*, I, 388. [142] *Ibid.*, I, 389.

[143] *Ibid.*, I, 377. [144] *The Holy City*, III, 409.

to heaven. Such an extension of the comparison seems forced and clumsy to the cultivated reader, but it spoke very plainly to slow minds attached to concrete things. " If thou wouldst so run as to obtain the Kingdom of Heaven then be sure that thou get into the way that leadeth thither . . . Set the case that there should be a man in London that was to run to York for a wager; now though he run never so swiftly, yet if he run full south he might run himself quickly out of breath, and be never the nearer the prize! " [145] And again: " It is but a vain thing to talk of going to heaven if thou let thy heart be encumbered with those things that would hinder. Would you not say that such a man would be in danger of losing, though he run, if he fill his pockets with stones, having heavy garments on his shoulders, and great lumpish shoes on his feet ? So it is here; thou talkest of going to heaven, and yet fillest thy pocket with stones, i.e. fillest thy heart with this world, lettest that hang on thy shoulders, with its profits and pleasures." [146]

To make his meaning still clearer, Bunyan favoured the anecdote which would insinuate what he had to teach into the dullest mind and, as a first step, arouse attention: " I heard once a story from a soldier who, with his company, had laid seige against a fort, that so long as the besieged were persuaded their foes would show them no favour, they fought like madmen," [147] and the anecdote runs on to the inevitable moral application.

And finally this " fisher of souls " made use of all the formulas which help the memory: proverbs, antitheses, repetition of the same words. In speaking of the man who always agrees with those around him, he said: " He can be anything for any company, he can throw stones with both hands, he is a frog of Egypt and can live in the water and out of the water; he will hold with the hare and run with the hounds; he carries fire in the one hand, water in the other." [148]

Proverbs are homely. For solemn effects Bunyan chose the more noble antithesis: " Dost thou understand me, sinful soul? He wrestled with justice, that thou mightest have rest; he wept and mourned, that thou mightest laugh and rejoice; he was betrayed, that thou mightest go free; was apprehended, that thou mightest

[145] *The Heavenly Footman*, III, 383.　　　[146] *Ibid.*, III, 384.
[147] *The Jerusalem Sinner*, I, 78.　　　[148] *The Strait Gate*, I, 389.

escape; he was condemned, that thou mightest be justified; and was killed that thou mightest live." [149]

One feels here, despite the obvious sincerity, the conscious eloquence of a preacher who is master of himself. But it sometimes happened that Bunyan was carried away on a wave of oratory that he had not planned. At such times there was no studied crescendo, but rather a flat, single-stringed litany:

But I am a great sinner, sayest thou.
" I will in no wise cast out," says Christ.
But I am an old sinner, sayest thou.
" I will in no wise cast out," says Christ.
But I am a hard-hearted sinner, sayest thou.
" I will in no wise etc. . . ." [150]

We seem to hear Bunyan reciting that as if in a trance, re-living the hours when Bible contexts were re-echoing twenty times a day in his sick head. In common with all primitive people, Bunyan liked hammering away at the same words, and their magic incantation.[151] At those times he was speaking more to himself than to others, or rather he let words that were hardly his pour forth both for his own and their benefit. He had a feeling that an angel was upholding him.[152] He lay himself open to the prophetic inspiration that descended on him.

We must, however, be on our guard against insisting on this aspect of Bunyan's genius, or we might falsify his moral and literary physiognomy. Moments of trance were rare with him. For the most part he was keen and wary, as we have seen, knowing whither he was going and calculating his effects.

★

In these quotations we can hear the lyrical note that we noticed in our study of the seer, painter of heaven and hell. Bunyan always strove to capture his inmost self, and this passionate quest is the very essence of lyricism. Personal experience underlies and gives body to Bunyan's style in his best passages, as well as giving it a soul.

[149] *The Greatness of the Soul*, I, 131.
[150] *Come and Welcome*, I, 280.
[151] See the constant repetition of the word ' run ' in *The Heavenly Footman*.
[152] *G. A.*, par. 282; see too par. 287.

And hence his dialogue has a spontaneity which makes a search after forerunners and models superfluous. Style is not only a matter of recipes, a fact critics who are always tracing sources seem to forget; it is a matter of sensibility and vision. The dialogue-form with questions and answers is a repetition of the inner monologue which is often nothing more than an implicit dialogue. Bunyan certainly realised how much the authors he had read and the preachers of all time benefited from this form. His instinct as an educator enabled him to see that at once; and to follow this method he had only to abandon himself to the movement of his thought and reproduce the debates between heart and reason, *animus* and *anima*, that were always coming to fresh life within him. "I would say to my soul, 'O my soul! this is not the place of despair: this is not the time to despair in'." [153] No matter what sermon we glance at, we shall be sure to find this self-with-self dialogue—even when the preacher is at pains to efface himself. For Bunyan, knowing that every man has in his heart the key which opens the hearts of others, and that if the individual is not the universal he is at least a means to it, endeavoured to change over from the 'I' to the 'one'. It was not only *his* story that mattered, but the story of the human soul. "Poor coming soul, thou art like a man that would ride full gallop, whose horse will hardly trot! Now the desire of his mind is not to be judged by the slow pace of the dull jade he rides, but by the hitching and kicking and spurring as he sits on his back . . . Thy flesh is like this dull jade; it will not gallop after Christ." [154]

The soul . . . the flesh. . . . These were the general terms in the preacher's abstract discussion, just as they are the eternal enemies in the concrete struggle of all mankind.

But Bunyan was not altogether successful in concealing his own vibrating self behind other entities, however vast and majestic. The very nature of his mission, like that of his faith, was not such as to permit of a complete forgetfulness of self: Calvinism was too concerned with the original character of each person, the Puritan crowds too urgently desirous to touch on a unique experience. In that trembling colloquy on which he embarked with his listeners, even the most modest preacher sometimes had to lay bare his soul. Whence in sermons those relapses from 'one' to 'I', as moving as the contrary

[153] *The Jerusalem Sinner*, I, 92.　　[154] *Come and Welcome*, I, 252.

effort to rise from the personal to the indefinite: " I speak by experience, I was one of these lousy ones; one of these great sin-breeders." [155] Sometimes one little phrase, testifying to the personal method, creeps into a lengthy impersonal unfolding, and snaps it. And this unrestrainable upsurge reveals the strength of the underlying current that gives to Bunyan's best passages their vibrating quality. Here is the conclusion of *Come and Welcome* :

> Coming sinner . . . God hath prepared a mercy-seat . . . a golden altar for thee to offer thy prayers and tears upon. He hath strewed all the way from the gate of hell, where thou wast, to the gate of heaven, whither thou art going, with flowers out of his own garden . . .
>
> Now thou hast at this time a sweet and stiff gale of the spirit of God, filling thy sails, drawing thee beyond thyself and also above all thy fear and temptations . . .
>
> Hast thou not now and then a kiss of the sweet lips of Jesus Christ ? I mean some blessed word which drops like a honeycomb upon thy soul ? Does not Jesus Christ sometimes give thee a glimpse of himself ? . . . And hast thou not sometimes as it were the very warmth of his wings overshadowing the face of thy soul ?
>
> All these things are the good hand of thy God upon thee . . . that thou mightest in the end be saved." [156]

Not once does Bunyan mention his own experience here, but everyone who has read *Grace Abounding* knows the secret source from which the emotion and poetry have been drawn.

When Bunyan consoled the poor believer and threatened the rich powerful unbeliever he was first and foremost bringing the hope of peace and justice to himself. Word and pen, sermon and book were his revenge and his consolation. Only a patient reading can really bring out his egocentricity, can really enable us to judge the inadequacies of the preacher's art and the fragmentary character of his genius. The critical analysis which is at pains to point out the beauties of his work runs the risk of overlooking its faults.

To read from one end of Bunyan's tracts and treatises to the other

[155] *The Jerusalem Sinner*, I, 79.   [156] *Come and Welcome*, I, 299.

is an exacting task, in spite of the strong appeal which at long intervals alleviates the wearisome unfolding, and in spite of the lyrical
inspiration and visionary fervour: islands of beauty in a monotonous
ocean, gusts of poetry in the still air of a logician's theology. Painter
and poet when moved, Bunyan was but a rhetorician of the third
order when he let the voice of methodical rationality cover up the
song of his emotions.

2

Poetry and Truth in *Grace Abounding*

Ce qu'on dit de soi est toujours poésie.

ERNEST RENAN

EVEN the reader who is out to discover the psychological revelations of *Grace Abounding* cannot be altogether blind to its formal beauty. No book which uncovers a human experience with such firmness and delicacy, which captures and prolongs the tremulous quality of a soul, perceiving both its harmonies and discords, can fail to acquire the secret movement and tension which make for great works. In this chapter we shall study the autobiography from a literary point of view, having first indicated the circumstances of its genesis and publication.

Bunyan had been in prison for ten years before he wrote it, and its purpose was to edify and help the 'brethren' from whom he had for so long been separated.[1] Here again, people say, he was following in a tradition: new converts had a habit of relating the history of their conversion to their co-religionists. The existence of this custom is confirmed by the archives of the Baptist community of Bedford. In order to gain admittance the neophyte had to give the faithful an account of the work of grace on his heart; and then in the course of a subsequent meeting he was received into the Church.[2]

---

[1] *G. A.*, preface. "Children, grace be with you, amen. I being taken from you in presence, and so tied up that I cannot perform that duty that from God doth lie upon me to you-ward, for your further edifying and building up in faith and holiness."

[2] The exceptions are rare: Alice Clark, however, " was propounded and received into our fellowship both at the same meeting not as a precedent for others but because she feared she might be hindered her duty if her husband heard it." *The Church-Book*, f. 85.

That Bunyan thought this practice excellent is made plain in *The Pilgrim's Progress*. One of the heroes, Faithful, says that a confession of one's own experience is necessary to convince others of the faith.[3] But this custom usually involved a simple verbal confession only; and although some Baptists wrote accounts of their lives,[4] the autobiographical tradition was less living among them than among the Quakers.[5] So, if Bunyan had not been Bunyan, the need to write which took hold of him some thirteen years after his entry into the communion would not have presented itself as a duty. In fact he was not bowing to custom so much as using custom in the interest of his inmost needs. And as psychology and art are very closely interlinked on this point, we must lay special emphasis on this need.

It was the outcome first and foremost of the very nature of the Protestant faith,[6] as Newman once described it in a passage we shall quote without comment: " . . . I do not mean to say that Christ is not mentioned as the Author of all good, but that stress is laid rather on the believing than on the Object of belief, on the comfort and persuasiveness of the doctrine rather than on the doctrine itself. And in this way religion is made to consist in contemplating ourselves, instead of Christ; not simply in looking to Christ, but in *seeing* that we look to Christ." [7] Obviously Bunyan's religion was quite different from that, but it was that too.

And further examination shows us a second kind of inner need. Bunyan was haunted by the desire to survey his whole life in one glance, to hold his soul in his hands, the better to possess himself. He never named this need; he neither perceived it nor singled it out in his moral life, but he nevertheless succumbed to it. He did not, like a psychologist, probe into the craving lodged within him; he simply threw himself into a passionate quest. He thought he was being prompted by motives of religious propaganda and the sweetness of unburdening himself; he never analysed the true nature of his delight. But we can see farther than he, thanks to his sincerity and his art: we know him better than he knew himself. If we sharpen our perceptions and read *Grace Abounding* rapidly from beginning to

---

[3] *P. P.*, I, p. 78.   [4] Cf. *supra*, Part I, chap. 1.
[5] York Tindall, *op. cit.*, p. 29.   [6] Only in one of its aspects, naturally.
[7] Newman: *Lectures on Justification*, quoted by H. Brémond, *op. cit.*, p. 138.

end, receptive to the rhythm of this confession and ready to be carried away by it, then we can probe its author's deepest needs, feel them and understand them.   Bunyan strove to recapture all the threads of his past at one go, and knot them to a present that was always slipping through his fingers; he wanted to press his past to him, wrap it around him, to ensure that it really was his.

It has been perhaps exaggeratedly maintained that Bunyan's sincerity entitles him to a place among the first of the moderns.[8] But his modernity lies rather in his trembling, obscure desire to assure himself of his own identity; yet whereas we see more or less plainly the motives which compel us to plunge into our past, Bunyan mis-construed his motives or else did not guess at them at all.   But his writing seems to know his motives for him, and it conveys them to us. Sometimes it runs, loses its breath, makes a fresh start, lingers a little at some turning-point, rebounds again, always jerky, always leaning towards a miraculous prize, towards events which are for their author (the prose shows it) familiar and yet mysterious at the same time.[9]

Familiar, yes, for he had re-lived them ten or twenty times already. He had made confessions in works written before 1666. Though these were fragmentary, or else simple proofs of the theological argument under discussion, they had nevertheless provided Bunyan with a source of deep personal happiness—quite apart from their apologetic value.   And gradually there had grown in him the need to tap that source again, and when, in the solitude of prison, it became irresistible, the new work burst spontaneously forth.   If we agree with Charles du Bos that works of art are divided into two distinct groups, those that have been ' contrived ' and those that have been ' given ',[10] then certainly *Grace Abounding* belonged to the second category, where *The Pilgrim's Progress* was soon to join it.

Familiar yet mysterious, events, we were saying.   For surely there are always new aspects to be uncovered in a " wondrous " past ? Even when his autobiography appeared to be completed, Bunyan re-opened it to append some further details the pathos or providential

---

[8] M. P. Willcocks, *op. cit.*, p. 125.

[9] *G. A.*, par. 174. " But as to my determining about this strange dispensa-tion, what it was I knew not : or from whence it came I know not.   I have not yet, in twenty years' time, been able to make a judgment of it."

[10] Ch. du Bos, *Approximations*, 4th series (Paris, 1930), p. 50.

significance of which he had not previously appreciated. And he did not merely take his past up again, but enlarged on it in his effort to describe it truthfully. While meaning only to re-live it, he partially created it; [11] not only did he discover more of himself in himself, but he even perfected his development while writing. And as for the past which he did not alter in recapturing it, it remains nevertheless an enchanted past. Truth is poetry reborn to existence in a memory that is warmer, intenser and vaster than the reality. The march forward down the course of the years offers fewer surprises than the voyage backwards into the soul where lie the voyager's first horizons. So art flourishes in the story when it grows out of the natural, and everyday life despoils itself so as to rise to the eternal.[12] It did not matter that Bunyan had no literary ambition: in spite of himself he achieved the work of a great writer.

In the first place, he tells the story of his life without ever raising his voice. He felt instinctively that eloquence would be a lapse of taste as well as a kind of profanation. " I could ", he wrote, " also have stepped into a Style much higher than this in which I have here Discoursed, and could have adorned all things more than here I have seemed to do; but I dare not." [13] The style of *Grace Abounding* is thus very different from the style of his sermons: there are no phrases encumbered with dry logic and no emotional crescendo, no mocking smile and no invective. The homely image is not sought out and as it were cultivated, but now and then it springs naturally from the pen of this man of the people: " My heart would not be moved to mind that that was good . . . it would now continually hang back in every duty: and was as a Clog on the Leg of a Bird to hinder her from flying." [14]

[11] On all this question see Part I, chap. I, in which we studied the biographical value of the alterations added to *Grace Abounding*. We are interested here only in the relation between psychology and art.

[12] The excellent critic, John Livingston Lowes, denies this, however. He writes of *Grace Abounding* : " It is molten stuff which is not yet moulded —a profoundly significant human document, but not a work of art. It is intensely personal, but it is not universal." ' *The Pilgrim's Progress*, a study in immortality ', *Of Reading Books* (London, 1930). There are works of art and works of art—but we hope to prove that *Grace Abounding* contains great artistic qualities.

[13] G. A., Preface, p. 295.   [14] Par. 77.

The sentences, grasping his thought and pliant to the lilt of his emotion, acquire a singular strength. The vocabulary is especially expressive because of its rustic flavour, its frankness, and, as it were, its concrete solidity: " Their talk and discourse went with me; also my heart would tarry with them . . .[15] This, for that instant, did benumb the sinews of my best delights . . .[16] The sentence stood like a mill post at my back . . .[17] I have found my unbelief to set, as it were, the shoulder to the door to keep him out. . . ."[18]

Bunyan's words are successful in conveying the phenomena of automatism and hallucination which he experienced: " That sentence fell with weight upon my spirit [19] . . . bolted upon me." [20]   The Bible shone and sparkled for him: " That word doth still at times shine before my face . . .[21] Scriptures were in those days made to spangle in mine eyes . . ." [22]

Vocabulary and syntax weld their effects together to express our author's amazements. The style attains an almost miraculously expressive power at those moments, and Bunyan—a psychologist without knowing it—makes us feel the existence of a sort of pure ' ego ',[23] with man's personality and all his intimate warmth and life as something external. In the soul where it takes refuge this pure ego is watching. It is like a gaze untroubled by any emotion. It is apparent in many places in the book, lucid in the midst of tumult. The passage which we quote below has already been used for another purpose, and we repeat it deliberately:

" By these words I was sustained, yet not without exceeding conflicts, for the space of seven or eight weeks; for my peace would be in and out, sometimes twenty times a day; Comfort now, and Trouble presently; Peace now, and before I could go a furlong as full of Fear and Guilt as ever heart could hold; and this was not only now and then, but my whole seven weeks' experience; for this about *the sufficiency of Grace*, and that of *Esau's* parting with his Birthright,

---

[15] *G. A.*, par. 40.   [16] Par. 21.   [17] Par. 189.
[18] Par. 81.   [19] Par. 62.   [20] Pars. 22, 213.
[21] Par. 65.   [22] Par. 235.
[23] In the sense understood by Paul Valéry in his *Introduction à la Methode de Léonard de Vincy* (*Variété*, I), Paris, 1924.   When we read *Grace Abounding* for the first time, the analysis of the author of *Cimetière Marin* came to mind in spite of ourselves.   And we were gradually forced to see that Bunyan's text could often provide valid examples for Valéry's thesis.

would be like a pair of Scales within my mind, sometimes one end
would be uppermost, and sometimes again the other; according to
which would be my peace or trouble " (§ 205).

" And I remember one day, as I was in diverse frames of spirit, and
considering that these frames were still according to the nature of the
several Scriptures that came in upon my mind; if this of Grace, then
was I quiet; but if that of *Esau*, then tormented; *Lord*, thought I,
*if both these Scriptures would meet in my heart at once, I wonder which
of them would get the better of me.* So methought I had a longing mind
that they might come together both upon me; yea, I desired of God
they might " (§ 212).

" Well, about two or three days after, so they did indeed; they
bolted both upon me at a time, and did work and struggle strangely
in me for a while; at last, that about *Esau's* birthright began to wax
weak, and withdraw, and vanish; and this about the sufficiency of
Grace prevailed with peace and joy. And as I was in a muse about
this thing, that Scripture came home upon me, *Mercy rejoiceth against
judgment* " (§ 213).

Bunyan's language, mainly composed of monosyllabic Anglo-Saxon
words, is a little hard: " Peace now, and before I could go a furlong
as full of Fear and Guilt as ever heart could hold; and this was not only
now and then, but my whole seven weeks' experience." Judged
according to the rules of scholastic rhetoric, his language could be said
to be clumsy; but schoolroom standards are here derisory. With
Bunyan it is the very clumsiness that is beautiful. It is the absence
of polish, the jerky rhythm, the lowliness of the words and the
roughness of their contours which achieve this impression of absolute
sincerity and perfect union between thought and expression. Stark
and nervous, the style clothes the man and vibrates with him. In
his conflicts: " If ever Satan and I did strive for any Word of God in
all my life, it was for this good word of Christ; he at one end and I at
the other. Oh, what work did we make! It was for this in John,
I say, that we did so tug and strive; he pulled and I pulled; but, God
be praised, I got the better of him, I got some sweetness from it." [24]
In his ecstasies: " And being now ready to sink with fear, suddenly
there was, as if there had rushed in at the Window the Noise of wind
upon me, but very pleasant, and as if I heard a voice speaking, *Didst*

[24] G. A., par. 215.

136

thou ever refuse to be purified by the Blood of Christ? " [25]   And this sentence suggests a sort of nostalgia for the invisible kingdom that Bunyan has seen: "O, the mount Sion, the heavenly Jerusalem, the innumerable company of the Angels, and God the Judge of all, and the Spirits of Just men made perfect, and Jesus, have been sweet unto me in this place.   I have seen that there, that I am persuaded I shall never, while in this world, be able to express." [26]   In these lines the 'last vision' of the *Pilgrim* is foreshadowed, and the dream-filled concluding phrase with its sustained melancholy: "And after that, they shut up the Gates; which when I had seen, I wished myself among them." [27]   For Bunyan, as for Augustine, this country was not an object of contemplation but a fatherland. [28]

The emotion is finally crystallised in certain terms which are always recurring and seem to foreshadow some of the *Pilgrim's* imagery: "And so went home with a great burden upon my Spirit [29] . . . I was a burden to myself [30] . . . the burden that was upon me . . . ! " [31] We can hardly be surprised that Bunyan later conceived the idea of a Pilgrim with "a great burden upon his back".   And the representation of despair in the guise of an allegorical slough must have suggested itself quite naturally to the man who had already said: "I found myself as on a miry bog that shook if I did but stir," [32] and again: "I knew not what ground was sure enough to bear me." [33]   The constant recurrence of certain images cannot fail to strike the attentive reader.

As usual with Bunyan, the Biblical reminiscences mingling with personal memories introduce a graver note into the style and bring a quality of solemnity to the confession: "I can remember my Fears, and Doubts, and sad Months with Comfort; they are as the head of Goliath in my Hand.   There was nothing to David like Goliath's Sword, even that Sword that should have been sheathed in his Bowels; for the very sight and remembrance of that did preach forth God's Deliverance to him." [34]

Sometimes the Bible merely suggests an idea that his imagination seizes on and transforms.   When he wrote in paragraph 42: "My

[25] G. A., par. 174.   [26] Par. 322.   [27] P. P., p. 148.
[28] Confessions, VII, 20.   [29] G. A., par. 20.   [30] Par. 149.
[31] Par. 165.   [32] Par. 82.
[33] Par. 220.   [34] Preface, p. 295.

Mind was now so turned that it lay like a horse-leech at the Vein, still crying out, *Give, Give*," he was thinking for a moment of a text in the Book of Proverbs: "The horse-leech hath two daughters crying, Give, give." But the symbolism of the image is totally different in the two contexts. Bunyan makes use only of the concrete and expressive quality of the text, adds the realistic touch "at the vein", and then gives it an entirely new figurative meaning. In the Bible the horse-leech stands for concupiscence. Bunyan was describing his thirst for meditation and his hunger for divine things.

The next example is even more characteristic. Bunyan wrote: "Thus by the strange and unusual assaults of the Tempter, was my soul like a broken vessel," [35] which reminds us all of the Psalm: "I am forgotten as a dead man out of mind, I am like a broken vessel." [36] Now, Biblical contexts were always hovering in Bunyan's memory, and he was probably set going by the rhythm and roll of the text. But he did not have in mind the psalmist's sense of the word 'vessel'. The psalmist was thinking of a broken vase, whereas Bunyan let his sensibility play round the vision of a disabled ship, which he could do easily enough, like every Englishman who knows the sea. [37] "My Soul was like a broken Vessel driven as with the Winds. . . . I was but as those that jostle against the Rocks."

Thus in his borrowing from Biblical imagery, Bunyan sometimes reinforced a line, sometimes omitted one, sometimes touched up a colour and sometimes expunged it. *The Pilgrim's Progress* will provide us with further examples to make our point clearer; for the autobiography, while making way for a better understanding of the *Pilgrim's* spiritual significance, also prepares the ground for its literary form. The dream-form of *The Pilgrim's Progress* might seem to the uninitiated reader an old if not worn-out trick even in Bunyan's time; but to the reader of *Grace Abounding* it will seem quite natural, for this confession makes it clear (even when it does not say so) that dreams are the writer's daily bread and the invisible world the only one that counts.

Men like George Fox and Wesley commented on things and people in their private diaries. But Bunyan was turned in on himself, trying to cup his past in his hands and embrace with a conscious effort the

[35] *G. A.*, par. 186.   [36] Psalm XXXI, 13.
[37] *G. A.*, par. 12. "For once I fell into a creek of the sea. . . ."

unconscious rhythm of his being, and he neglected these material contingencies so as to bind himself to what was imperishable. In his book he does not, like Dante, " wear the body that I've always worn " (" *E con col corpo ch'i ho sempre avuto* "),[38] but he wears the soul that he will always wear.

Bunyan lived enclosed within his vision of the world above, and if dreams were the poetry of his work, it was because they were first the poetry of his life. He had always woven golden threads over the drabness of the things of this world. His autobiography often says as much: " So one day I walked to a neighbouring Town and sat down upon a Settle in the Street . . . and, after long musing, I lifted my head, but methought I saw as if the Sun that shineth in the Heavens did grudge to give light, and as if the very stones in the Street, and the Tiles upon the Houses, did bend themselves against me . . . [39] Then . . . in the bitterness of my soul I said to myself, with a grievous sigh *how can God comfort such a wretch as I*. I had no sooner said it but this returned upon me as an echo doth answer a voice, *this sin is not unto death*." [40]

But there are passages in *Grace Abounding* which enable us to see the spontaneous genius with which Bunyan dramatised his experiences. " But upon a day the good providence of God did cast me to Bedford, to work on my Calling; and in one of the Streets of that Town, I came where there were three or four Women sitting at a door in the Sun, and talking about the things of God " (§ 37). " And methought they spake as if Joy did make them speak; they spake with such pleasantness of Scripture Language, and with such appearance of grace in all they said, that they were to me, as if they had found a new World " (§ 38).

Some pages farther on Bunyan takes up the same theme: " About this time, the state and happiness of these poor people at Bedford was thus, in a Dream or Vision, presented to me. I saw, as if they were set on the Sunny side of some high Mountain, there refreshing themselves with the pleasant beams of the Sun, while I was shivering and shrinking in the Cold, afflicted with Frost, Snow, and dark clouds. Methought, also, betwixt me and them, I saw a wall that did compass about this mountain; now, through this wall my soul did greatly desire to pass; concluding, that if I could, I would go even

---

[38] *Inferno*, XXIII, 96.   [39] *G. A.*, par. 187.   [40] Par. 188.

into the very midst of them, and there also comfort myself with the heat of their Sun " (§ 53).

"About this wall I thought myself to go again and again, still prying as I went, to see if I could find some way or passage, by which I might enter therein; but none could I find for some time. At the last, I saw, as it were, a narrow gap, like a little doorway in the Wall, through which I attempted to pass. Now the passage being very strait and narrow, I made many efforts to get in, but all in Vain, even until I was well nigh quite beat out, by striking to get in. At last, with great striving, methought I at first did get in my head, and after that, by a sidling striving, my Shoulders and my whole Body. Then was I exceeding glad, and went and sat down in the midst of them, and so was comforted with the light and heat of their Sun " (§ 54).

Paragraphs 37 and 38 tell of a tinker busy about his trade in a little town of Puritan England. It is a fine day. Some housewives are talking on their doorsteps, their grave, pure conversation dictated by a radiant Calvinist faith and reflecting the thoughts and feelings of the period.

In paragraphs 53 and 54 the Bedford street has disappeared. The scene takes place on some height which might be anywhere or nowhere. The spring sun has changed into a symbolical sun, resplendent like the countenance of God. The little group of women united in a common belief has become a whole people whose evangelical faith puts them apart and separates them from a corrupt and damned world.

Thus a particular experience becomes a generalisation. Bunyan's method is still personal, but we feel that he is on the way to transposing, effacing the ' me '. We mean that we have here, as it were in the raw, the natural process by which the history of one man, a certain John Bunyan, becomes transformed into the journey of a Christian pilgrim; an autobiography into an allegorical work of fiction. The images, dreams and signs of the Bible become joined to those of life. One Puritan conversion is about to be transformed into a drama of universal import.

3

The Pilgrim's Progress

I. THE PLOT AND THE SYMBOLISM: A Critical
Summary of the Text and an attempt to interpret
the Allegorical Meaning.

> *Take heed, also, that thou be not extream*
> *In playing with the outside of my dream.*
>
> BUNYAN

> *It is in my conviction incomparably the best ' Summa*
> *theologiae evangelicae' ever produced by a writer not*
> *miraculously inspired.* S. T. COLERIDGE

THE opening scene of *The Pilgrim's Progress* is painted with firm
strokes of the brush. The author is lying asleep in a den. In a
dream he sees a man clothed in rags; his face is turned away from his
home, he has a book in his hand and a heavy burden on his back, and
is crying out: "What shall I do?" He has just read in his book
that the "City of Destruction" will be burnt by fire from heaven.
Despair takes hold of him, and at first he wants to keep quiet about
what he knows, but after a while his grief breaks out and he throws
everyone—his relations, friends and neighbours—into a state of con-
sternation. His fervent awakening to the religious life seems to them
madness. We can imagine the malicious gleam in Bunyan's eye when
retailing the opinion of unbelievers tainted with science: "a frenzy
distemper in his head ",[1] "craz'd-headed coxcomb ",[2] "a brain sick
fellow ".[3]

They shower advice on the sick man so that he can only stop up
his ears and flee. "Fly . . . Go to yonder Light shining over that

[1] *P. P.*, p. 12. [2] *P. P.*, p. 14. [3] *P. P.*, p. 14.

Wicket-gate," [4] a certain Evangelist had said to him one day when he was wandering in the fields.

The ragged man therefore leaves the city. Pliable, a decent fellow without much initiative, goes with him, and talking together they make their way towards the Gate. But before reaching it they fall into a miry bog called the Slough of Despond. The advance now becomes extremely difficult. Pliable turns back. The desire for a better life had slipped up to the surface of his soul, but his will had not really been engaged. In this way he serves as a foil to his companion, who wallows in the mire but nevertheless goes forward.

By this time we have discovered the identity of our brave pilgrim. He is no longer "a man" or "he", but Christian; [5] no longer an indefinite quantity lacking dimension or colour, but a man with a name.

So, by means of struggle and sorrow, this man has wrenched himself away from anonymity. Who was he in the doomed city? What did he do? The author does not say. For him the city is already dead; and as it exists only as it were on reprieve, the crowd which struts and frets there is not really alive. In the City of Destruction individual behaviour does not count. It is a cemetery of the dying where each acts like everyone else and loses himself in the mass. One must leave it if one is to become dimensional. One must fight to be worthy of a name.

Hence Bunyan gave us an example of 'muscular Christianity' long before Kingsley. Before Kierkegaard he demonstrated that the man who is really alive is the man who is moving forward; he may stumble, but he gets up again; he is fervent and full of will; he is very much here and yet at the same time he is elsewhere, because his gaze is fixed on a horizon that is always receding.

The truth is that there are no new conceptions of life. It is only our vocabulary that alters. We look for the spiritual food in contemporary writers that we could easily find in Bunyan, for example—if only we cast off our prejudices with regard to him and had the wisdom not to be taken in by the new flamboyant terminology of the fashionable writers.

[4] Summary of the words on p. 13 : " Do you see yonder wicket-gate ? . . . Do you see yonder shining light ? . . ."

[5] *P. P.*, p. 14.

Christian is wallowing, then, but presently there comes towards him a man called Help. He offers him his hand, puts him on the road and is surprised that the traveller has lost his way. For indeed there are good and substantial landmarks placed in accordance with Jesus's promises.[6] That is how Bunyan expressed the conviction of his maturity—the conviction that the Christian who follows the Gospel should not find despair on his path. If we have to pass by despair in order to leave the doomed city, it should be met with no more on the path of true pilgrims.

Abandoned by Pliable, Christian is soon joined by Mr. Worldly-Wiseman, a notable of the town of Carnal-Policy. This city-dweller is surprised to see a poor ragged man laden with so heavy a burden. Why does he clutter himself up for his journey? Why doesn't he dress properly and have his shoulders free? Mr. Worldly-Wiseman obviously has a more cushy idea of the journey and, in a delicious satire which is another *Pilgrim's Progress*, Nathaniel Hawthorne has depicted the grandson of this man-of-the-world and given him a still more refined love of comfort.[7] He makes him travel by train. His burden goes in the luggage-van, and he chats cosily with his fellow-pilgrims, like a respectable citizen; and, as they are all well brought-up, they never dream of mentioning religion, although that is—naturally—what they are all thinking about.

The Worldly-Wiseman advises Christian to go and live in a village called Morality: the rents are not high, the market is well stocked, and the neighbours are agreeable. The village is at the foot of a near-by mountain. The road there is good. Christian allows himself to be tempted. But as he approaches, the mountain looms larger, until it perilously overhangs the road and a storm breaks out on its slopes. It is Sinai, the Kingdom of Law. Christian trembles. Sweat beads his brow.

Then Evangelist appears again and speaks to him. The just live by faith, he says; all will be pardoned to the brave man who gains the Strait Gate. The negative honesty of the village of Morality

---

[6] *P. P.*, p. 17.
[7] Nathaniel Hawthorne, *The Celestial Railroad, Works* (6 vols., Edinburgh, 1883), vol. II; this story has often been published in anthologies of short stories.

cannot assure anyone's salvation. What is needed is heroic renunciation.[8]

Then Evangelist makes flames spurt from the side of the mountain in confirmation of his words. And at this point we sense the conviction with which Bunyan is writing his story. Indeed, he ends up by believing in the physical reality of his symbols as much as in the doctrine which they express. And it is this childlike faith, coupled with his rich human experience, that makes him a great poet.

Christian is afraid, but peace returns to him when he sees Evangelist, who gives him one smile.[9] The virile sweetness of this smile is one of the happiest inspirations of the book.

So the pilgrim goes on his way, comforted. He reaches the Gate. He knocks and knocks until it is opened by Good Will. There is genius here too—in this strong name with moral overtones. Whoever seeks and knocks will find, as Arthur Porter points out in an excellent meditation on this passage.[10] Good Will always responds to man's good will in the end. And the same critic justifies the symbolism of the Gate in these words: "The Christian life is an expression of dynamic will. One cannot drift into it. The spiritual man is not a mere outgrowth of the natural man." [11] We might say that the Gate marks an end and a beginning. It is the dividing-line between two conceptions of life and almost two universes. A supreme tension of the being is necessary to pass from one to the other. There must be the desire to cross the threshold and the desire to knock loudly.

Perhaps Bunyan did not perceive all this as clearly as his commentators, but he felt it, and expressed his feeling in his allegory. As happens with all men of genius, his art knew more than he knew himself. That is why the cultivated reader of the *Pilgrim* savours a more lively pleasure of the intellect than, for instance, a Scottish peasant.[12]

[8] This long interview between Evangelist and Christian occupies pp. 22–25.

[9] *P. P.*, p. 25.

[10] Arthur Porter, *The Inside of Bunyan's Dream, the Pilgrim's Progress for the Man of To-day* (London, 1927), p. 61.

[11] Arthur Porter, *op. cit.*, p. 62.

[12] Mark Rutherford advises us to forget all other books before opening *The Pilgrim's Progress*. And yet he dreams of Virgil on Christian's road

So the pilgrim, having passed through the Gate, pushes on, and arrives at a dwelling named the House of the Interpreter, and here he has to knock again. The whole of the *Pilgrim* re-echoes with the blows that Christian makes on door after door, because he is always advancing in a new light.[13]

Who is this Interpreter? Perhaps he is the Holy Spirit? Like Good Will, he is erect, large, and silhouetted against a sort of halo. As a commentator has observed,[14] the spiritual impression is preserved precisely because of this reticence as to his identity.

Christian is well received, and led into a room decorated with symbolical pictures which, by the problems they pose, stimulate his intellect and bring him an " illumination ".[15]

The pilgrim leaves this house reluctantly and continues on his way, following a highway " somewhat ascending "; but, strengthened by the Interpreter, he goes boldly forward and runs to the top, where stands a Cross. There, miraculously, the burden falls from his shoulders. Three shining angels ("the Shining Ones") appear to him; the first tells him that his sins are forgiven, the second gives him new garments, and the third a Roll with a seal upon it—a safe-conduct for the Celestial City.

Thus the Cross is a prize as well as a trial of strength, and rises up at a late stage of the journey. Bunyan's thought is clear: the

---

and quotes Goethe : " [*Wir*] *haben schrecklich viel gelesen*." H. White, *John Bunyan by the Author of Mark Rutherford* (1st. ed., 1905, o.p. London, 1923), pp. 25 and 130. Certainly we have read a great deal and we could not wipe this culture away even if we wanted to. However, Mark Rutherford's error is that of love and of the intelligence. The simplicity of the story seems to him so richly expressive that he dreads to see it tarnished by too many erudite commentaries. On the other hand some sin against Bunyan by their idiocy—they see depth only in dissertations stiff with technical terms, and the story of Christian seems to them " la gravure d'Epinal du symbolisme ". And Augustin Filon, the author of this remark, continues : " In time gone by this book was the property of peasants and children. Ought we not to give it back to them? " (Quoted by Jules Pacheu, *De Dante à Verlaine* (Paris, 1897), p. 255.) In times gone by? Perhaps Filon did not know that Swift, Cowper, Samuel Johnson, to mention a few, had read ' this book ' with love and admiration?

[13] Arthur Porter, *op. cit.*, p. 71.
[14] John Kelman, *The Road, a Study of John Bunyan's Pilgrim's Progress* (2 vols., London, 1917), I, 52.
[15] *P. P.*, p. 29.

Gospel must be understood and Grace received before we deserve to reach this gallows of glory and sorrow.

Beyond the Cross the road winds towards a valley where three men, their feet in chains, are sleeping—Simple, Sloth and Presumption. Christian goes towards them to help them, but they refuse his aid. " I see no danger," says Simple; " Yet a little more sleep," says Sloth; and Presumption: " Every fatt must stand upon his own bottom." [16]

Puzzled and hurt, Christian leaves them to their fate. Soon he meets Formalist and Hypocrisy, and accompanies them as far as Hill Difficulty, where there are three paths. One, rugged and with no turnings, climbs towards the summit of the hill. The two others go to the right and left at the bottom of the hill. Christian chooses the narrow path upwards; his companions separate, tempted by the charms of the roads of the plain.

We can interpret this symbolism in several ways, as everything else in the book. This rich vagueness is surely the peculiar property of symbolism. Herbert Eveleth Greene says that in the arbitrary allegory the sense is exact, and one guesses it once and for all, whereas in symbolism the meaning is never really exhausted.[17] And, using the *Pilgrim* as a sort of model of a symbolic journey, Albert Thibaudet gives this definition of symbolism: " It is not merely the reverse side of a drawing, but a poetical reality which lives freely and spontaneously in its own right." [18]

But perhaps this passage has never been read with more sensitive intelligence than by Kelman. Formalist and Hypocrisy, he contends, have to go round the hill, that is to say, they have to prolong their journey—just as in life the distance of many journeys is increased because the traveller wants to spare himself the trouble of scaling even a modest hillock. Notice, too, he says, that the two friends bid each other good-bye—the hill separates them. " Difficulty is the common lot, and it unites those who face it bravely; while each man seeking to avoid it has to find out his own solitary, sinuous path." [19]

---

[16] *P. P.*, p. 38.
[17] H. E. Greene, *The Allegory as Employed by Spenser, Bunyan and Swift*, P.M.L.A. (1889), p. 157.
[18] A. Thibaudet, *Le liseur de romans* (Paris, 1925), p. 98.
[19] John Kelman, *op. cit.*, I, 84. Nathaniel Hawthorne's pilgrims got a tunnel built under Hill Difficulty, having thrown a bridge across the Slough !

After studying the symbolism and literary technique of this passage, Kelman turns his attention to the manner of Christian's ascent; for, having started at a run so as to climb the hill, he soon slows down into a walk, and finally is forced to proceed on his hands and knees.[20] This apparent retrogression, Kelman says, brilliantly suggests the ever-rougher ascent. "The apparent anti-climax really gives a brilliant suggestion of climax in the increased steepness of the way." [21]

While Christian is climbing, his two companions lose themselves, one in a forest and the other in a vast field full of sombre mountains,[22] which Coleridge rightly thought ridiculous.[23] Living in a plain and having seen nothing higher than the modest range of the Chilterns, some miles from Elstow, Bunyan is never at his best when painting a mountain landscape.

On reaching the top of the hill, the pilgrim encounters Mistrust and Timorous, who, tired and frightened, are retracing their steps. Christian too has to turn back, but for quite a different reason: he has left his Roll in an arbour where he paused for a little while and fell asleep. He retraces with bitterness the path which should have been joyful—and all because he rested too soon. Athlete and soldier, the Christian has not the right to cease his effort before reaching the end of the struggle.

However, after this incident the pilgrim presses on, and suddenly sees the outline of a palace called Beautiful. He goes towards it, but in proportion as he approaches it the road becomes narrower, and he sees that two lions are guarding the entrance to the Palace. He pauses, but then, encouraged by the porter, Watchful, he continues on his way. The lions roar, but do him no harm, for they are chained.

This incident, so serious in its moral import, shows that Bunyan's spirit, in spite of its maturity, was young and charmingly naïve. If we really wish to appreciate the *Pilgrim* we must put on a new soul—as we do when looking at primitive pictures or medieval illuminations. Bunyan, we might say, has the same childlike vision as those bygone

[20] *P. P.*, p. 41.
[21] John Kelman, *op. cit.*, I, 85.
[22] *P.P.*, p. 41.
[23] S. T. Coleridge, *Notes on English Divines* (ed. by Derwent Coleridge, 2 vols., London, 1853), vol. I, p. 343.

painters who dressed the workmen of the Tower of Babel in fifteenth-century Italian costume.[24]

Always attentive to the symbolism, Kelman dwells on this passage only so as to stress its moral significance: that when one is going towards God it is never impossible to find a way through.[25] Our author certainly intended this, but the adventure was for him so full of transposed memories, sheer delight and spiritual significance, that we shall have to come back to this later on.[26]

Watchful welcomes Christian, questions him, and introduces him to a " grave and beautiful damsel " named Discretion, who does not ask him his name, but whence he has come, whither he is going and why he ever started: for the pilgrim's behaviour is now much more important than the identity it has conferred on him.[27] Moved by his answers, the wise damsel smiles and " the water stood in her eyes ".[28] She calls her sisters, Prudence, Piety and Charity, who invite the pilgrim to cross the threshold.

He enters and describes his adventures in detail exactly as the Elstow tinker had described them to the " poor women " and other faithful of the Baptist community of Bedford. The *Pilgrim* is always in the image of Bunyan's lived experience, but, from a literary point of view, these excursions back into his own life are valueless because they teach us nothing new. We must admit that it was almost an effort to read Bunyan with simplicity at this point, almost an effort not to demand of him more than he could give, and to put aside—in the interest of a true historical perspective—the memory of modern techniques in which these flashbacks to the subject at the heart of the development are so rewarding. But, after all, if the *Pilgrim* invites the critic to make comparisons in spite of himself, and of which he is immediately ashamed because he knows them to be unfair, it is because Bunyan carried the art of story-telling so far that one has to pull oneself in so as not to demand yet more.

Having finished his confession, Christian sups with his hostesses,[29]

---

[24] Arthur Ransome, *A History of Story-telling* (London, 1909), quoted by Frank Mott Harrison, *Some Illustrators of the Pilgrim's Progress, part one* (reprinted by the O.U.P. from *The Library*, 1936).
[25] John Kelman, *op. cit.*, I, 89.
[26] Cf. *infra*, " The Origins of the *Pilgrim* ".
[27] Cf. *supra*, p. 142.   [28] *P. P.*, p. 45.
[29] About this supper see *infra*, " Realism in the *Pilgrim* ".

and then goes to rest in a large room on the first floor open to the rising sun. The next day they show him the " rareties " of the Palace: records and other historical testimonies to the Lord of the Kingdom. They show him the rod of Moses, the hammer and nail with which Jael slew Sisera, the ox's goad with which Shamgar slew six hundred men, the jawbone of Samson's ass, and David's sling. . . . A curious passage, which illustrates Bunyan's fervent Biblical literalism and at the same time his pleasure in amassing threats.

Finally, the next day they take him to the top of the Palace. It is a clear day, and he sees the Delectable Mountains in the distance. So great is the magic of this name that we hardly notice certain unlikely details: those woods and vineyards, flowers and fruits, springs and fountains which Christian can see at such a distance! The radiance of the spiritual content of this passage obliterates these improbable minutiae.

The Palace Beautiful is the Church as Bunyan conceives it: a sort of *home* where one draws refreshment in communion with God and brotherly fellowship. His Church is social, if one can accept this use of the word. It is also militant: Christian will be armed when he leaves it. He entered a civilian, and will depart a soldier.

Finally, the Church is, for Bunyan, a spiritual summit, one of the landmarks on the pilgrim's road. It has often been noticed that Christian proceeds from height to height, physically as well as morally. Since leaving the city, he has made his way towards ever-wider horizons. His taste for physical effort and his love of the earth are thus brought together at the call of interior illumination. *The Pilgrim's Progress* is redolent of the country: but the rustic odours are never more fragrant than in the moments of religious revelation.

As *The Pilgrim's Progress* reproduces in its topography, though with the stylisation of art, the pattern of spiritual progress, it is natural that valleys and hills alternate. On coming out of the Palace Beautiful, Christian descends into the Valley of Humiliation. There he encounters the monster Apollyon, to whom he gives battle; but it would be premature to study at this point a fight the moral significance and literary value of which will be clearer to us in our examination of the origins of the story.

One plain succeeds another, and their names change with the landscape. After Humiliation, there is the Valley of the Shadow of

Death—solitude, wilderness, treacherous sands—where the Christian passes alone and no man has his abode. It is the symbol of the dark night of the soul in which God seems so distant and hell so near! At the same time it is a symbol of hope and courage: " I will walk in the strength of the Lord God," [30] cries Christian, and the demons who were preparing to attack him fall back.

Then light returns and the valley comes to an end in a vision of horror: the ground is strewn with mutilated corpses and skeletons. The fact is that near by there are the caves of two giants, Pagan and Pope. The first has been dead for some time, the second is so decrepit that he remains at the cave's mouth " biting his nails ".[31]

By now the road is winding up, and Christian sees Faithful, a traveller whose name has a double sense: faithful—that is to say, rich in faith, and also loyal. Christian joins him. His solitary adventures are now at an end.

Is this second genuine pilgrim necessary to liven up the narrative ? Perhaps, but his arrival seems to us to be due to psychological rather than literary causes. *The Pilgrim's Progress* could well have continued, grim and gay by turn, but always alive, centred round one hero at grips with natural dangers, enemies and false brethren. But Bunyan felt that one person could hardly give a complete picture of the really virile man—his gravity, his courage, and also (for our author does not make utopian portraits) the diversity of his weaknesses.[32]

We consider that Bunyan, a story-teller through and through, was obeying the need to personify " the infinite directions of his possible life " [33] in several men. Faithful, too, is the tinker, just as Hopeful will be later on in the narrative.

United in friendship, the two pilgrims make their way towards the same goal but not the same destiny. Together they meet the Puritan, Talkative, whose hypocrisy Bunyan denounces as energetically as would Samuel Butler or any Cavalier writer. Together they make their way into Vanity Fair, a large city and a flourishing com-

---

[30] *P. P.*, p. 60.   [31] P. 62.

[32] We are enlarging here on one of John Kelman's ideas : " The author feels the insufficiency of any one human life as an all-round portraiture of manhood. To crowd into one personality all the virtues were to create a figure at once unnatural and unhelpful." *Op. cit.*, I, p. 161.

[33] Cf. Albert Thibaudet, *op. cit.*, p. 6.

mercial centre, the description of which is a masterpiece of satirical humour and realism which we shall study later on.

Christian and Faithful are indifferent to the seductions of wealth and do not stop, but their purity is an object of scandal to the traffickers of Vanity Fair, and also a secret reproach. So the two travellers are arrested, chained, imprisoned, submitted to a parody of a trial and condemned to death; but whereas Faithful is tortured straight away, Christian is taken back to gaol. Is this a whim on the part of the tormentors? Are they weary of cruelty? The material reason is not important to Bunyan, since he knew that the powerful of this world are merely instruments of the Lord. In his dream he sees Faithful snatched from his scene of torment and carried by angels towards the Celestial City. He understands that God has other designs for Christian when he sees him escaping from prison and departing with a new companion, Hopeful, a citizen of Vanity Fair converted by the self-sacrifice of the martyred Faithful.

Each reader can interpret this new episode as he likes. Our favourite commentator, John Kelman, thinks that at this point the allegory illustrates St. Paul's words about hope being born of experience.[34]

Our two companions now meet the shifty By-ends, a canny man whose aims are dubious, and whose shrewdness and resourcefulness arouse the admiration of hypocrites (and lovers of good literature) and the suspicion of honest folk. This character has grown little by little in Bunyan's hands. It was not until the second edition of *The Pilgrim's Progress* that he acquired his juicy genealogy,[35] and the third edition that he was reflected in the minds of his friends as in a hall of mirrors. In twice touching-up this portrait Bunyan was probably indulging the pure and simple joy of polishing up his satire on a detested creature and not, as Sir Charles Firth suggests, stressing his distrust of the false brethren.[36] Talkative was a false brother, whereas By-ends was a " man of latitude " as our author conceived such a one to be. But we are anticipating.

[34] " Knowing that tribulation worketh patience; and patience, experience; and experience, hope," Rom., v, 3-4 (Authorised Version).
[35] Concerning the first version of the *Pilgrim*, see Appendix C.
[36] Charles H. Firth, essay quoted. The English Association, leaflet No. 19, Oct., 1911.

Having shaken him off, our two travellers cross " the delicate plain called Ease ",[37] and arrive at a silver mine that Hopeful very much wants to visit. R. L. Stevenson [38] comments on this point that envy and avarice are temptations of the ageing, and that our pilgrims have indeed gradually aged. However, Christian, who is as indifferent to the goods of this world as Bunyan himself, holds his companion in check, and it is then that they see before them a pillar of salt bearing the inscription " Remember Lot's wife ",[39] and both of them marvel. Belief in the conservation of this monument was very widespread in the Middle Ages, and was one of the many things that formed Bunyan's medieval heritage.[40]

The pilgrims refresh themselves at the river of God, rest on its banks, and then find themselves on a rough road. Weary, they leave it, climb over a stile and walk on to grass, a " by-path meadow ", where they lose themselves.

This error on the part of the tried wayfarers, this softness from our hardened pilgrims, surprises the attentive reader; for, after all, this rough road [41] was nothing compared with Hill Difficulty. Granted, answers Arthur Porter,[42] but this rough road comes after the delicate plain called Ease, whereas Hill Difficulty came after the Cross. At that time effort had strengthened their energy for new exertions, whereas now the pilgrims have been softened by a period of ease. For our part, we would like to add that the road is to a great extent what pilgrims make of it. Its ascents and descents, its dangers and its charms vary according to their faith and their courage. The world is the screen on to which we project our interior landscape.

Lost in the meadow, Hopeful and Christian are overcome with remorse. Too late! Giant Despair arrests them and throws them into a dungeon of his Doubting Castle. Then, urged by his wife Mrs. Diffidence, he batters them with redoubled blows and gives them a piece of advice—suicide. Christian might have followed this advice, but is deterred by Hopeful.

[37] *P. P.*, p. 98.
[38] R. L. Stevenson, *Bagster's Pilgrim's Progress, Works* (Swanston ed., vol. XXII).   [39] P. 100.
[40] Sir John Mandeville, *Travels*, chap. 9. "At the right side of the Dead Sea the wife of Lot still stands in likeness of a salt stone, because she looked behind her when the cities sunk into hell."
[41] P. 103.   [42] Arthur Porter, *op. cit.*, p. 232.

Then one day Christian regains his resilience of spirit and remembers that he has in his possession a sort of master key called Promise, and he decides to try it. No sooner said than done. The lock of the dungeon yields; that of the iron gate is " damnable hard ",[43] but finally gives way. The pilgrims are free.

This incident almost at the end of the *Pilgrim* recalls the initial adventure of the Slough of Despond. Despair spreads its slime or erects its prison as soon as the Christian forgets the promises of the Gospel and permits the spirit of the Law—an ethic without light—to rear up within him. Everyone can see that this Giant and his wife dwell in the very heart of man.

And when they come out of this hell, how much more beautiful seem the Delectable Mountains, and the lands and gardens, orchards and vineyards, slopes running with living water! The lambs of the Lord are grazing there, and Bunyan sees in his dream with the intensity of a visionary the two pilgrims, leaning on their staffs, chatting with the shepherds at the side of the road.

The symbolism of these Delectable Mountains is perhaps the richest of the story, not only because it contains a deep spiritual meaning, but also because it implies a conception of psychological life, the subtlety of which seems not to have been perceived.

In fact, these mountains, though having such a gentle name, are singularly terrifying. One of them, even in this paradise, bears the skeletons of heretical Christians who deny the resurrection of the body (i.e. the Quakers: Bunyan never forgot old quarrels). A second is a graveyard where blind and hopeless people wander about among the tombs, and from the very side of the hill is the descent into Hell. Only the third is a sort of new Eden.

This trinity at the centre of delectability is the symbol of our most exquisite delights which are always mixed with bitterness. The waves of joy that sometimes submerge us are always tinged with misgiving. Only in very exceptional circumstances is the soul at one with itself. It is a whole world of feelings the fringes of which unite or detach themselves according to secret affinities or repulsions. All is innuendo and reflection, an unending game of light and shade, in the very wake of great currents known and recog-

[43] " Damnable hard ", p. 109. This ' damnable ' from the pen of a Puritan who held swearing in horror is really delicious !

nised by everyone. For us these are oft-repeated truths, but it is remarkable that Bunyan should have grasped the complexity of psychological life. *Grace Abounding* is a proof of this, and justifies our interpretation of the symbolism.

★

Let us pause a while on the hill called Clear. It is there that the pilgrims take their Glass so as to be able to see the Celestial City. However, their hands shake; and we would have preferred Bunyan to attribute this display of emotion less to the memory of recent horrors than to the awe, in which fear and exultation are blended, of the man to whom the divine is about to be revealed.

John Kelman, for his part, sees in the mountains a symbol of the Church, no longer in its character of social institution and temple of the cult (Palace Beautiful), but as the summit of spirituality.[44] The critic points out that, as in Browning's *Paracelsus*, the pilgrim's path is constantly being shortened by the vision of future truths. From the Palace Beautiful one sees the Delectable Mountains, and from the pinnacle of these mountains one glimpses Heaven.

The end is near, and the companions must set forth again. They meet, coming from the country of Conceit, a very vital young man called Ignorance, whom we confess to finding sympathetic—in spite of Bunyan. To pass the time Christian recounts the story of Little-Faith, the only badly-named character of *The Pilgrim's Progress*. He is a timid, restless man in whom faith never expands, although it has deep roots. The poor fellow has been plundered on the road by three robbers, Faint-Heart, Mistrust and Guilt. Once again Bunyan is giving concrete shape to his own intimate feelings, for where do these brigands seek refuge if not in the too frail soul of Little-Faith? Yet hardly have we written the word ' frail ' than we regret it, for a certain complexity of character is always conveyed by Bunyan, however rapid his sketch may be. Little-Faith prefers to beg rather than sell the jewel that the robbers have overlooked, for they are jewels of heavenly promise. So he is possessed of constancy, which is surely a great strength.[45]

Christian finishes his account of Little-Faith on arriving at a fork

[44] John Kelman, *op. cit.*, II, 66.

[45] On the way in which this second narrative is inserted into Christian's story see *infra*, " The *Pilgrim* as a work of art ".

in the road. Not knowing which fork to take, he asks "a man black of flesh" [46] called Flatterer; it is doubtful why, since he abstains from all flattery! Perhaps this apparent lack of significance is in itself revealing: this Flatterer does not exist outside Christian himself; he is the presumption that still lingers in his heart. But this is a psychological explanation, not a justification from the literary point of view: it does not obscure the fact that Bunyan has failed to give form to this character and has contented himself with pinning a label on to a dummy.

In all this part of the story the invention and what R. L. Stevenson calls the " energy of vision " [47] slacken. Whereas up to this point " the piety [of the author] was baffled by his genius, and Bunyan of Parnassus had the better of Bunyan of the conventicle ",[48] now the theologian and the controversialist triumph over and stifle the story-teller. Reason holds forth precisely where the imagination should give birth to people and create symbols.

After being led astray by Flatterer, the pilgrims are put on the right road again by an angel who scolds them and whips them. They meet with Atheist, another fleshless person, and arrive at the " enchanted ground ", a country the air of which makes people drowsy. In order to resist this languor, Christian questions Hopeful about the origins of his conversion, and the confession that follows reads like a summary of *Grace Abounding*. But we have already made the point that all the heroes of *The Pilgrim's Progress* represent Bunyan in varying degrees.

This enchanted ground is a vast country, and our heroes have to go on talking so as to fight sleep. Which is why they wait for Ignorance to catch them up, for they have talked with him already, and can go on with their theological discussion. Once again they quarrel and separate. Then Christian comments at length on the behaviour of another acquaintance of his.

These successive discourses are drawn out over many pages. The

---

[46] *P. P.*, p. 122.

[47] R. L. Stevenson, *Bagster's Pilgrim's Progress* (ed. and vol. quoted), p. 189.

[48] We are quoting here a fragment of a phrase of S. T. Coleridge in his article on the Allegory in *Miscellaneous Criticism*, ed. Ths. Middleton Raysor (London, 1936), p. 31. Coleridge is considering the whole of the *Pilgrim* in this passage and not the particular episode we are studying.

allegory is forgotten. We are no longer reading a story, but a tract.[49]

At long last the theologian withdraws into the background. Imagination again takes flight: we have Beulah and the Land of the Bride and Bridegroom, where the song of birds goes on forever and the flowers bloom afresh every morning; the sun shines " night and day ",[50] and " as the Bridegroom rejoyceth over the Bride, so did their God rejoyce over them ".[51]

They are not yet in the Celestial City, though they are bathed in its splendour. While still in time, they find themselves absorbed into eternity. Personal memories blend with memories of the Bible, and thence emerges the description of the ecstasies that Bunyan has known.

The Pilgrim's Progress is reaching its conclusion. Only the river has now to be crossed—that is to say, Death. Hopeful goes fearlessly forward. Christian remembers his sins and, under the weight of his fears, all but sinks to the bottom. But his comrade holds him up and enables him to cross the deep waters.

Does Christian really nearly sink? No, but his " burden " is on him again, much heavier now than at first. The sense of his own unworthiness never bowed him down so much as in the moment when he is at last going to see God face to face.

In this Bunyan's intuition was the same as Dante's. It is not at the foot of the hill of Purgatory, as Mary W. Smyth points out,[52] that the Italian poet experiences the most vivid sense of sin, nor later when he strikes his breast three times, but at the top, in the veiled presence of Beatrice.

Shining angels are waiting to receive Christian and Hopeful on the other side of the river, and then come the King's musicians, clothed in white raiment. The very heavens echo with the blast of

[49] For the really pious readers of the period, the Pilgrim was a tract. In the sequel that Thomas Shermann (T. S.) wrote to Bunyan's allegory, he describes the work as " that necessary and useful tract " (the author's apology for his book); see infra, " How the Pilgrim was written; the Problem of sources ".

[50] P. P., p. 141.

[51] P. 141, and Isaiah lxii, 5, which Bunyan quotes.

[52] 'Puritan Bunyan and Catholic Dante', in The Nineteenth Century, Aug., 1928, vol. 104.

the trumpets, " as if Heaven itself was come down to meet " the pilgrims.[53] When at the gate of the City, the travellers are transfigured and arrayed in clothes that shine like gold. A crown is placed on their heads, and the music of harps sounds in their honour. All the bells in the City ring for joy, and Bunyan hears them (" I heard ") [54] in his ecstasy. The City shines like the sun, the roads are paved with gold, the angels sing without intermission " Holy, Holy, Holy is the Lord." " And after that," the author adds, " they shut up the Gates: which when I had seen, I wished myself among them." [55]

This phrase, so brief, so bare, coming at the end of a long description, betrays resignation and nostalgia, melancholy and hope. There is more dream in these few commonplace words arranged in such a familiar order than in all the rest of the book. The effect derives from the position of the phrase in the context, from its humbleness and colourlessness after so much light and gold, and perhaps too from its slightly halting, faintly abrupt rhythm: " And after that, they shut up the Gates: which when I had seen, I wished myself among them."

The Pilgrim's Progress should stop there so that the sustained tremor of this phrase might go on vibrating within us. But, though Bunyan was a writer and far from ignorant of the rules of his trade, he was never an artist first and foremost. He evidently did not feel the beauty of this conclusion. One lesson still remained to be put across—so this had to be done, whatever the literary shortcomings involved, whatever the collapse or weakening of the dramatic effect.

So in his dream the author sees his enemy Ignorance approaching the river, reaching its yonder bank, coming right up to the Gates of the City. Angels finally put an end to this scandal, seize the wretched man and lead him to hell which is connected to the Hill as it was to the City of Destruction: " Then I saw that there was a way to hell, even from the gates of heaven, as well as from the City of Destruction," [56] writes Bunyan in a phrase that has become almost a proverb, like many others in The Pilgrim's Progress, owing to its zestful vigour.

The dreamer may then wake up, and the story comes to an end.

[53] P. P., p. 146.   [54] P. 147.
[55] P. 148.   [56] P. 148.

Bunyan of the conventicle has won a final victory over Bunyan of Parnassus.

The Second Part of The Pilgrim's Progress

We can make a much briefer analysis of the second part of the *Pilgrim*. The road is the same, and stopping-places are unchanged; just certain characters and various incidents are new. And yet this sequel is not a repetition, but a conclusion.[57] Both in its differences from, and its resemblances to the first part, it reveals Bunyan's advancement in the knowledge of the soul.

The dreamer who the first time was sleeping in a den now sleeps in a wood. In this way we are immediately led to expect a less sombre atmosphere, a lightness that will touch the slumbering author and intertwine itself with his dream. Bunyan sees an old man, Sagacity. He dreams that he gets up, walks beside him and questions him about Christian's family. Thus the story is given us at second hand; but Bunyan is not a subtle enough craftsman to take advantage of the indirect vision and put a certain mystery between himself and the narrator. He simply wants to make a variation, but it is so insignificant that the reader hardly notices it and the author himself soon tires of it. " And now," he writes, " Mr. Sagacity left me to dream out my dream by myself." [58] So with this charming ingenuousness he gets rid of the old man who is embarrassing him.

Christiana is converted at her fireside, if one can so put it, simply by the memory of her husband. Evangelist does not appear to her. His message has become a living reality in the person of Christian, whose adventures remain in the memory of those who have known him.

Christiana recalls the sorrows of her husband, his renunciations, his perseverence, and she understands the lesson of his life, although she did not previously understand the meaning of his words.

She dreams, too, for Bunyan always set great store by *signs*, and would gladly have appropriated Sir Thomas Browne's belief that we

[57] This is what many readers (starting with James Anthony Froude, *op. cit.*, p. 171) do not feel. Whence those useless discussions about whether the first part of the *Pilgrim* is better or worse than the second. The two books are different and can be appreciated for totally different reasons. Cf. *infra*, " The *Pilgrim* as a Work of Art ".

[58] *P. P.*, p. 174.

are a little greater than ourselves when asleep, the languor of our bodies merely awakening our souls.[59]   Thus Christiana sees heaven and hell in a dream, as in a dyptich.   The next day an angel visits her while she is praying and invites her to follow the same path as Christian.   She gathers her children around her, prepares them for the pilgrimage, and leaves her home before the neighbours have time to hold her back.   A very young woman, Mercy, decides to go some of the way with the traveller so as to take the edge off the parting: " I think to walk this sun-shine morning a little way with her to help her on the way." [60]

" This sun-shine morning " somehow presages an easier pilgrimage. Perhaps Bunyan had noticed, like certain modern psychologists, that the conversion of women is usually less violent.[61]   In the exercise of his function as a minister and in his dealings with people, he had acquired a very delicate understanding of souls.   He knew that a conversion could be calm and yet genuine, and also, as that other admirable Puritan Richard Baxter said, that tears and lamentations are not the signs of a regenerated soul so much as love and joy.[62]

The Slough of Despond presents scarcely any dangers for women and children aware of Christ's promises, and the travellers arrive at the wicket Gate.   In spite of the furious growlings of Satan's dog, Christiana knocks hard.   She and her son are admitted first, and while she is interceding for Mercy, Mercy herself, though weakening, knocks with redoubled blows.   Good Will cannot do other than smile with tenderness in admitting the young woman.[63]

A shady path now stretches before the pilgrims, running alongside a big wall.   On the other side of the wall is the devil's garden the trees of which stretch their fruit-laden branches over the wall so that the ripe fruits fall on to the path, and the children pick them up and eat them.   Two rogues accost the women and try to violate them, but they push them away, shout, and their cries reach the porter's lodge, who sends relief.   Their Reliever asks them why they

[59] *Religio Medici*, Part II (p. 120 in Blackie's little ed. of the classics).
[60] *P. P.*, p. 172.
[61] Cf. E. D. Starbuck, *op. cit.*, p. 95.   " Conversion for males is a more violent incident than for females."
[62] *The Autobiography* (ed. Lloyd Thomas, Everyman classics, p. 217).
[63] " When he heard your lumbring noise, he gave a wonderful innocent smile," p. 177.

have no guide, saying that they are too weak to face the dangers of the road and that he will implore his Master to grant them a conductor.

After saying this he withdraws and the pilgrims proceed towards the house of the Interpreter, who is delighted to see them. This house is still happy and full of wonders—symbolical pictures of which we shall speak later. A friendly welcome, supper, and—a new detail—a bath. If Bunyan did not consider baptism by water a necessary sacrament, he nevertheless looked on it as a beneficial ceremony which he gladly introduced into this new story.

When the travellers depart from here they are accompanied by Great-heart. Some people think that Great-heart's presence deprives the story of its dramatic tension. For whereas in the first part we were uncertain as to whether Christian was going to win, we are sure that Christiana will henceforth run no great risk. This obvious remark, however, does not amount to much, for if the suspense does not lie exactly where it did, it nevertheless exists. We cannot, for example, guess how Great-heart's final triumph will be achieved; and throughout the furious battle the spectator, trembling with the combatants, is hardly aware of the foregone conclusion—indeed he completely forgets it.

In its literal acceptance the allegory thus retains its attraction, and a new symbolic value gives the impression of conclusion that we were talking about just now.

In the first part of the *Pilgrim*, Christian was almost alone, and in all the decisive moments he fought without assistance. He was alone on Hill Difficulty, alone in the Valley of the Shadow. Faithful's martyrdom was capable of stirring a soul still ignorant of its vocation, and Hopeful was snatched out of Vanity Fair; but Faithful could not heighten the courage of Christian, who was prepared to face the same sacrifice himself. As for Hopeful, though he did console Christian in the Giant's dungeon, he did not give him any essential help. Indeed, it seems that Christian received essential help only twice: when he was given a hand out of the Slough, and when Hopeful saved him from drowning in the River of Death.

The lesson we learn from the first part of the *Pilgrim* is hence similar to that of *Grace Abounding*: that conversion is a solitary pilgrimage. Writing in the thick shadow of personal memories,

Bunyan agreed with Kierkegaard that " one absolutely cannot be accompanied when going into these regions ".[64] But his experience as a minister had gradually enlarged his human horizon and modified his early certainties.   He had learnt that there are weak people whose sincerity and will should be guided and upheld by a spiritual director—for instance, his treatment of the Fearful family is sympathetic.[65] For the development of one man, then, he substitutes that of a group. If the first part of the work taught men how to die, the second teaches them how to live.   After the great solitary battles come the warmth of fighting shoulder to shoulder and the sweetness of wider fellowship.

While going on their way, Great-heart teaches his flock, and catechism takes the place of allegory.   However, allegory soon reappears, and the destiny of some of the characters in the first part is revealed to us.   Thus the travellers pass near the gallows where Simple, Sloth and Presumption are hanging.

Hill Difficulty, Palace Beautiful—all these names turn up again, and the old memories become associated with new episodes.   A giant now guards the road with the lions, and Great-heart engages him in combat.   At the Palace the pilgrims rest for a long time in the absence of their guide, who has been recalled by his Master. Mercy looks after the religious instruction of the children, or else pays amused attention to her sweetheart, Mr. Brisk.   The whole passage scintillates with humour.

There follows the famous incident of Matthew's illness.   The child is seized with violent internal pain.   The doctor asks if he has taken any unwholesome food.   Yes, everyone remembers that he ate the fruit of Satan's garden.   Only one remedy will be efficacious: pills composed " *ex carne et sanguine Christi* ".[66]

It is unfair to isolate this passage, as Alfred Noyes does,[67] and see in it a characteristic example of Bunyan's bad taste.   Undoubtedly the symbolism is poor.   Those intestinal pains, vomiting, purges and pills are too crudely physical to express the suffering of the soul and the virtue of the Eucharist.   The episode has some redeeming

[64] Sören Kierkegaard, *Crainte et tremblement* (Aubier, 1935), p. 113.

[65] " Little-Faith " (first part), " Ready-to-halt ", " Feeble-mind ", " Mr. Despondency " and " Much-afraid " (second part).

[66] *P. P.*, p. 213, Bunyan adds : " The Latin I borrow."

[67] Alfred Noyes, ' Bunyan, a Revaluation ', *Bookman*, Oct., 1928.

features, however. If we forget that we are reading an allegory (which is not difficult—we forget it over and over again in reading the *Pilgrim*), we find ourselves present at a realistic scene sparkling with good-fellowship and humour. It is a charming *genre* picture.[68]

But the story as an account of the pilgrim's journey has a serious fault at this point. Matthew's illness is almost unexplainable. Days and days have passed since the child ate the poisonous fruit. The road from the wicket Gate to the Palace Beautiful is long, and they have already been in the Palace over a month before the child falls ill.[69] The belated consequences of the fruit-eating seem improbable. But the improbability in itself is not so very serious—there are many improbabilities in the *Pilgrim*, and we forget them, even supposing we notice them. No, the fault is significant because it shows up Bunyan's incapacity to reproduce duration of time in his narrative. To realise that the road is long and that days have passed we have to calculate mathematically: the sensation that time has elapsed is lacking. Christian's children have no spiritual life, and we hardly believe in their physical existence. Mercy remains the same from beginning to end, a pure and courageous woman; and Christiana does not develop at all in the course of the pilgrimage. Her spiritual growth has taken place—the manner in which this is suggested, by the way, is great art—during the six years' silence which divides the two parts of *The Pilgrim's Progress*.

Bunyan was successful in bringing home to us the fact of Christian's ageing, or rather his growth towards the fulness of maturity. He was unable to create another character endowed with such a deep capacity for living.

But let us get back to the Palace Beautiful before the pilgrims leave it. There we shall hear birds singing for Christiana—birds that her husband missed. Similarly, the Valley of Humiliation will be a " fat ground " for these new pilgrims,[70] and they will be greeted by shepherds where Christian saw nothing but desolation and was attacked by Apollyon.

By these means Bunyan has delicately expressed his feeling that in the soul's progress through this world " it is not the places that

[68] Cf. *infra*, " The Principal Characters ".
[69] *P. P.*, p. 207.
[70] P. 220 : " It is fat ground."

change but the traveller ",[71] and the deeper the spiritual life grows, the more beautiful the world appears. The Delectable Mountains and the country of Beulah are at the end of the road.

The Valley of Humiliation, though it smiles on the women and children, retains traces of Christian's fight. For once, the evocation of the past is not mere repetition; it makes the exploits that we witnessed seem even more admirable. " See," says the guide, " how they did beat the ground with their feet . . . how with their by-blows, they did split the very stones in pieces." [72]

At the end of the second Valley—Death—where Christian had seen the two giants Pagan and Pope, Christiana and her party see only one giant, Maul, whose task it is " to spoil young pilgrims with sophistry ".[73] What is the significance of this change ? There are bigoted Protestants only too ready to think that Bunyan, the second time, represented Paganism and Catholicism as one and the same error. From many points of view, Kerr Bain, for example, says, the religion of Rome is the Paganism of Christianity; its tactics, its arrogance, its insolence, its lack of charity, its barbarous pomp . . . etc. [74] We must cut the passage short, or its violence might make us doubt the intelligence of a critic who has some good qualities.

But we could propound a contrary interpretation. We have been led to notice that Catholicism plays a very small part in our author's work, and this perhaps inclines us to agree with Sir Charles Firth " that Bunyan had perceived by some kind of intuition that the noisy struggle between Protestantism and Catholicism was but a sham fight after all, and that the question whether England was to be Protestant or Catholic had been already decided. The real conflict, he seems to suggest, is between Protestantism and Rationalism." [75] So perhaps Giant Maul represents the Rationalism that was threatening; and in assuming this we do not necessarily endow Bunyan with prophetic intuitions!

[71] Jean Wahl, *Etudes kierkegaardiennes* (Paris, 1938), p. 283.
[72] *P. P.*, p. 223: Bunyan, always exact, uses the word " by-blows "—blows which miss their aim.
[73] P. 226.
[74] J. A. Kerr Bain, *The People of the Pilgrimage*, 2nd series (Edinburgh and London, 1888), p. 465.
[75] C. H. Firth, ' Bunyan's Holy War ', *The Journal of English Studies*, Jan., 1913, p. 146.

After the prolonged delay in Palace Beautiful the story regains its naïve liveliness in the fight between Great-heart and Maul. Bunyan's face always lights up at the prospect of a struggle between a man and a giant. Then the excitement calms down again in the meditation which follows Great-heart's victory, to be again revivified by the arrival of Father Honest, who is certainly the most vivid of the episodic characters. For ourselves, we cannot think of this good-natured fellow without being reminded of Thomas Hardy's peasants—the strength, good sense and humour are almost the same. This entire passage does not read like an allegory, nor like an old-time story in which the portraits, cracked with age, represent bloodless figures with stiff gestures, but like a romantic story very near to our own time. No other moment of *The Pilgrim's Progress* confirms us more strongly in our conviction that, before Defoe, Bunyan was the father of the modern English novel.[76]

The pilgrims then proceed to an inn, one of those inns where the food is excellent and the sheets are scented with lavender, as Izaak Walton describes them, Bunyan's charming contemporary, who, like him, loved the country and let gusts of fresh air blow through his pages.[77]

The pilgrims stay with Gaius, the innkeeper, for over a month.[78] So the second part is drawn out by these lingering halts. These new pilgrims know nothing of Christian's passionate urgency. But if the book was written for the author's pleasure, perhaps no section delighted Bunyan more keenly than that in which Father Honest is introduced.

The author seems to be enjoying himself more openly than elsewhere. The allegorical purpose, if not forgotten, seems not to be dominant. With a wholly unconscious lack of respect, the author competes with God the Father and abandons himself to the joy of creating human beings. Now we have the Bunyan described by

[76] Concerning Bunyan and Defoe see Paul Dottin, *Daniel De Foe et ses romans* (Paris, 1924), pp. 325–326.

[77] It is even possible that Gaius' inn had its walls papered with ballads like the one where " the compleat angler " slept, but Bunyan refrains from mentioning it, through that " charming hypocrisy " that Harold Golder denounces. (See H. Golder, ' John Bunyan's Hypocrisy ', *North American Review*, 1926, vol. 223.)

[78] *P. P.*, p. 245.

Robert White [79]—a man who smiles on life and allows himself a little harmless malice. To the swift and tense spiritual drama of the first part, there has succeeded a bourgeois novel.

They chat around a table laden with rustic fare. Matthew and Mercy marry (which is really rather surprising, since it was only the other day that the young woman was teaching her husband the catechism and thinking of all sorts of ruses to make him take a pill). Then James marries Gaius' daughter, and the two attractive cronies, Feeble-mind and Ready-to-halt, dance merrily in spite of the latter's crutches.

So in a completely new spirit of serenity a wider conception of life comes into being, a friendship with the good things of the earth, a pity and love for human beings—and this has a moral and religious lesson for us. As Bunyan more or less says himself, the harmonies of the treble have taken the place of the graver notes of the bass; and he points out that we must always tend in that direction, towards the clear harmonies of the trumpet and the harp. [80]

We will not follow the pilgrims any farther. Suffice it to say that they all reach the river, though the young ones remain on the bank. " Shall it be my Lot to go that way again I may give those that desire it an Account of what I here am silent about; meantime I bid my Reader Adieu." [81]

So we see that Bunyan played with the idea of writing a third part, but had the wisdom not to do so. [82] What could he have written about a second generation which was always foreign and a little

---

[79] See Appendix D.

[80] " The first string that the musician usually touches is the bass, when he intends to put all in tune. God also plays upon this string first, when he sets the soul in tune for himself. Only here was the imperfection of Mr. Fearing, he could play no other musick . . ." P. 235.

[81] *P. P.*, p. 290.

[82] An apocryphal " third part " was published in 1693 : " *The Pilgrim's Progress From This World to That which is to Come—The Third Part—Delivered Under the Similitude of a Dream—to which is added the life and second part, this compleating the whole progress*—London—printed by E. Millet for J. Deacon at the Angel in Giltspur-street without Newgate, J. Back at the Black-boy on London Bridge and J. Blare at the Looking-glass on London Bridge, 1693."
Nathaniel Ponder protested against this fraud. Cf. Frank Mott Harrison, art. *cit.* Nathaniel Ponder.

unreal to him ? He would certainly have been bored in following the sons of his hero—in other words, he would have committed a sin unpardonable in an artist.

II. How *The Pilgrim's Progress* was Written and Published : The Problem of Sources.

> *Give me a ballad, a news book, George on horseback, or Bevis of Southampton ; give me some book that teaches curious arts, that tells of old fables.*
>
> BUNYAN

> *It is not fantastic to assert that it was the Puritan culture as much as Bunyan that produced The Pilgrim's Progress.* Q. D. LEAVIS

DELIVERED at the Stationers' Hall on December 22, 1677, and authorised to appear by the censorship on February 18, 1678, *The Pilgrim's Progress* was published in London in the spring of that same year by Nathaniel Ponder at the Sign of the Peacock in the Poultry.[83] But when was it written ? As we are reduced to conjecture on this point, we will restrict ourselves here to outlining the most solidly established of these conjectures,[84] and will examine the other hypotheses elsewhere.[85]

In the " Apology " in verse which serves as a preface to his work, Bunyan tells us that the idea of the *Pilgrim* came to him suddenly while he was engaged on another book about " the War and Race of Saints ".[86] The very subject of this book, the idea of a road and runners, gave birth to the allegory of the pilgrimage. Captivated, the author immediately started making notes of the ideas that poured into his mind, but they came so thick and fast that they destroyed the

[83] Cf. Frank Mott Harrison, *Nathaniel Ponder, the Publisher of The Pilgrim's Progress* (reprinted by the O.U.P. from the transactions of the Bibliog. Society, *The Library*, 1936).

[84] We owe this hypothesis to John Brown, *op cit.*, pp. 261–262.

[85] Cf. Appendix A.

[86] " The author's Apology for his book," lines 7–8.

unity and balance of the work in hand. So he had to put them aside by themselves, these ideas that flew "like sparks from the coals ".[87] And so *The Pilgrim's Progress* was written in the joy of a sort of illumination. "Thus I set Pen to Paper with delight." [88]

But which of his books is that one about the Way and Race of Saints ? The work which by and large shows the closest resemblance to the *Pilgrim*, and seems to contain the allegory in potentiality, is *The Heavenly Footman*.[89] But as this was probably written [90] between 1666 and 1671, it could not be the work out of which the *Pilgrim* so forcibly sprang into being.[91]

We are therefore led to consider *The Strait Gate* (1676), the last theological treatise published by Bunyan before the story of Christian's mystical pilgrimage.

Although there is insufficient family likeness or true community of feature in these two works to prove beyond doubt that they saw the light simultaneously, they nevertheless have certain related ideas. It is tenable that the meditation on the gate and the narrow way foreshadows the wicket Gate or, better still, prefigures the rough path followed by Christian. The sharpness of the doctrinal work [92] is in tune with the severity of the first part of the *Pilgrim*. It might be said that Bunyan seems a dry and bigoted logician in the former whereas in the latter he seems a kindly theologian : but the transition from one literary medium to another so different from it is enough to explain this change in the author. And finally *The Strait Gate* contains the seed of some of the *Pilgrim's* characters: Mr. Legality,[93] the Formalist,[94] and above all Talkative,[95] Worldly-Wiseman,[96] Ignor-

---

[87] "The author's Apology for his book," line 14 : "Like sparks that from the coals of fire do fly." [88] *Ibid.*, line 29.

[89] For a comparison of *The Heavenly Footman* and *The Pilgrim's Progress*, cf. *infra*, p. 178. [90] Cf. Appendix B.

[91] Unless we admit that *The Pilgrim's Progress* was started much earlier than is generally supposed. Cf. Appendix B.

[92] Bunyan does not fail to emphasise in the preface : " The text calls for sharpness, so do the times." I, 363.

[93] The legalist comes next, I, 388 ; and Mr. Legality (*P. P.*, p. 20).

[94] Neither is the formalist exempted, I, 388 ; Formalist (*P. P.*, p. 38).

[95] " A prating-tongue will not unlock the gates of heaven," I, 388 ; compare Talkative " the son of one Saywell, he dwelt in Prating-row ", *P. P.*, p. 72.

[96] " Poor covetous worldly man," I, 386, and Worldly-Wiseman (*P. P.* p. 18).

ance,[97] and By-ends.[98] From some points of view, then, the allegory seems like the poetic development of several abstract themes in the treatise. We might have expected to find more numerous and obvious similarities between the two books, but will anyone ever understand the mystery of inspiration? *The Strait Gate* is near enough to the *Pilgrim* for us reasonably to assume that it was its immediate pretext; that it produced in the author's mind the necessary shock for the birth of the allegorical story.

In his preface-apology Bunyan tells us that when the *Pilgrim* was finished he hastened to show it to his friends. Some of them were shocked by so light a treatment of divine things: the reader might see in the allegory no more than what Montaigne called " a simple and pleasing story ". He might be perfectly satisfied with " the outside of the dream ", to use Bunyan's own words.[99]

> Some said, John print it; others said, Not so!
> Some said it might do good; others said, No ![100]

Bunyan let himself be led by his own instinct and experience. He was convinced that the message of his pilgrim would stick in people's memories like burs on clothes;[101] so he listened to the arguments of others, but heard only his own.

> Since you are thus divided
> I print it will; and so the case decided.[102]

His vivacity, his very impatience, incline us to think that he would

---

[97] " There is also the wilfully ignorant professor . . . He is one of the many that will seek to enter in, and shall not be able," I, 389. The lad Ignorance sought to enter too. He crossed the river but did not manage to escape Hell. Cf. *P. P.*, p. 148.

[98] Cf. *infra*, " The Characters ".
We could find other points of contact between the two books. The following passage could describe the porter at Palace Beautiful or Good Will at the wicket Gate : " There were placed at these gates porters, whose office was to look that none but those that had right to enter might go in thither," I, 367. And this immediately reminds us of the torments inflicted by the inhabitants of Vanity Fair on the two pilgrims : " The world will seek to keep thee out of heaven with mocks, flouts, taunts, threatenings, jails, gibbets, halters, burnings and a thousand deaths." I, 370.

[99] Cf. " The Conclusion ", p. 149, line 8.

[100] " The Author's Apology," p. 4, lines 39–40.

[101] *Ibid.*, p. 9, line 217 : " They will stick like burs."

[102] *Ibid.*, p. 4, lines 43–44.

not have delayed in sending his manuscript to the publisher. If we want to make a good guess as to how events fell out we can do no better than read the *Pilgrim* with John Brown's attentive mind.[103]

For, after having described the scene where Christian and Hopeful leave the shepherds of the Delectable Mountains, Bunyan writes: " So I awoke from my Dream." [104]   Then in the following paragraph he rather clumsily repairs the broken thread: " And I slept and dreamed again, and saw the same two Pilgrims going down the Mountains along the High-way towards the City."

Now, this curious rupture in the narrative is the only one in the book, and is totally unjustified: both the art and the story suffer. Hence John Brown is probably quite correct in seeing in it the simple statement of a fact: the narrative was interrupted because at that point the author came out from the 'den' of dreams.[105]   On this basis two-thirds of the book would have been written in prison and the last third in the course of the year 1677.

The Pilgrim's Progress had an immediate popular success.   Two editions were sold out in the first year.   In 1679 a third appeared which contained notable additions and seems to have been an almost complete version of the allegory such as we know it to-day.[106]

Bunyan hoped to write a counterpart to the portrait of Christian and give a portrait of a man condemned.   After the pilgrimage to the Celestial City, the journey towards Hell.   Thus in 1680 there appeared *The Life and Death of Mr. Badman*; but the public wanted a sequel to the *Pilgrim* and did not see this at all in the new book.

A certain ' T.S.' published a second part to the *Pilgrim* in 1683. This was by no means an ordinary forger, but a holy man more serious than Bunyan himself.   Far from wanting to be thought to be the tinker, he strove to correct his mistakes.   He especially wanted to suppress the laugh that the story sometimes gave rise to.[107]

---

[103] John Brown, *op. cit.*, p. 262.

[104] *P. P.*, p. 113.

[105] It is in the 3rd ed. (1679) that Bunyan makes it plain in a marginal note that we must read ' prison ' where the story says ' the den '.

[106] The Worldly-Wiseman was introduced in the 2nd ed. of 1678.   The psychology of By-ends is considerably enriched in the 3rd ed. (1679) by the conversation he has with his friends.   Concerning the original version of the *Pilgrim*, cf. Appendix C.

[107] " To deliver the whole in such serious and spiritual phrases that may

Enlightened now as to what his public wanted, Bunyan continued with his dream, and in the beginning of 1685 [108] published the authentic sequel to the *Pilgrim*.

★

As soon as the allegory was published, the author was accused of plagiarism. Bunyan himself tells us:

Some say the Pilgrim's Progress is not mine.[109]

And ever since that time sources from which the work could have been taken have been discovered. Always conscientious, George Offor took note of all these imputations and made a study of more than fifty texts.[110] Other learned men interested themselves in the matter, and at least three of them deserve to be known: James Blanton Wharey, Sir Charles Firth and Harold Golder.[111] We will note down those points in their work which may be useful for a better appreciation of the allegory.

J. B. Wharey's attention was particularly drawn to *Le Pèlerinage de l'Homme*, by Guillaume Deguileville, and *The Isle of Man*, by Richard Bernard.

The latter work, which has too many resemblances to *The Holy War* for Bunyan not to have read it, exercised no appreciable influence

---

prevent that lightness and laughter which the reading some passages therein occasions in some vain and frothy minds." The Author's Apology for his Book, *The Second Part of The Pilgrim's Progress from this Present World of Wickedness and Misery to an Eternity of Holiness and Felicity*, The Second edition with additions, London, printed by G. Larkin for Tho. Malthus, at the Sun, in the Poultry, 1684.

[108] 1684, old style.

[109] "An advertisement to the reader," *Holy War*, p. 252.

[110] Cf. his ed. in 3 vols. of the complete works of Bunyan, III, pp. 29–62.

[111] James Blanton Wharey, *A Study of Bunyan's Allegories, with Special Reference to Deguileville's Pilgrimage of Man* (Baltimore, 1904). C. H. Firth, *John Bunyan* (The Eng. Assoc. leaflet No. 19, Oct., 1911), published again in *Essays Historical and Literary* (Clarendon Press, Oxford, 1938). Harold Golder:

(a) 'John Bunyan's Hypocrisy' (*North American Review*, 1926).
(b) 'Bunyan's Valley of the Shadow' (*Modern Philosophy*, Aug., 1929).
(c) 'Bunyan and Spenser' (*Public Modern Lang. Assoc. of America*), vol. 45, 1930.
(d) 'Bunyan's Giant Despair' (*Journal of Eng. and Germ. Philol.*, Oct., 1931).

on the *Pilgrim*.[112]   As for the allegory written by the French monk Deguileville in 1330–1331, it probably never passed through our author's hands.   Translated by John Lydgate in 1426, and then 'modernised' in the seventeenth century, it was circulating at this time in manuscript form.   It is this last version that Bunyan is supposed to have read, according to William Aldis Wright.[113]   But since it is unlikely that a manuscript would be confided to a tinker, and since the parallelism between *Le Pèlerinage de l'Homme* and *The Pilgrim's Progress* is very slight, we may perhaps safely conclude that Bunyan had not read his forerunner.   On the other hand, it is very possible that he was familiar with other allegorical stories inspired by the works of Guillaume Deguileville.[114]

Of the long line of authors [115] who depicted man's spiritual life as a journey towards Jerusalem, Bunyan was among the last.   Towards the middle of the seventeenth century, the idea of a pilgrimage had become common property and its treatment conventionalised.   Bunyan could not have failed to be in touch with this popular religious literature, whether through personal reading or talk with friends.   He borrowed a framework from his forerunners.[116]   For detail he was above all indebted to the Bible and to the wonderful adventure stories that charmed his youth.   It was an immense debt, on which

[112] J. B. Wharey, *op. cit.*, pp. 78–90.

[113] W. Aldis Wright, *The Pilgrimage of the Lyf of the Manhode from the French of Guillaume de Deguileville*, printed for the Roxburghe Club, London, 1869, preface, x.
On this question consult : *The Ancient Poem of G. de Deguileville, Entitled Le Pèlerinage de l'homme, compared with the Pilgrim's Progress of John Bunyan*, edited from notes collected by N. Hill, with illustrations, London, 1858. Hill's thesis is examined by Katharine B. Locock in her intro. to John Lydgate's text of F. J. Furnivall's ed., Roxburghe Club, London, 1905.   See the intro. : " Lydgate and Bunyan," pp. liii *et seq.*

[114] J. Blanton Wharey, *op. cit.*, pp. 64–66.   Concerning Deguileville see too C. S. Lewis, *The Allegory of Love*, pp. 264 *et seq.*

[115] See Gerald T. Owst, *Literature and Pulpit in Medieval England*, pp. 104–105, the comparison between *The Pilgrim's Progress* and *The Weye to Paradys*, written at the end of the 14th or beginning of the 15th century. The manuscript is illustrated and we can see a man who has a heavy load on his right shoulder crossing a plank thrown over an abyss.   It is the pilgrim who is going towards the City.   In this old text there is also something about a " slough of hell ".

[116] J. Blanton Wharey, *op. cit.*, p. 136.

Sir Charles Firth and the American professor, Harold Golder, in a series of detailed works,[117] lay special stress.

The discovery of all these borrowings would have no interest for us were it not that they help our understanding of the texts. Long before we knew about all Bunyan's literary reminiscences, we suspected that the *Pilgrim* was not unique either as to form or purpose. Only, as John Livingston Lowes has pointed out,[118] the stories by which our author was inspired lie buried beneath the dust of the British Museum, whereas the adventures of Christian are read by millions of people. An examination of the sources is fruitful only in that it throws light on the genesis of the work.

III. THE MAKING OF *THE PILGRIM'S PROGRESS*: The Marvellous: Profane and Biblical. The Characters of the Creative Imagination

> *For lewed people loven tales olde*
> *Swich thinges can they wel reporte and holde.*
> CHAUCER
>
> *I seek to please.*
> BUNYAN

MR. HAROLD GOLDER'S studies [119] are indispensable for the specialist, and after them any further detailed study of the parallels between the *Pilgrim* and the romances of chivalry seems superfluous. One or two comparisons will be enough to show Bunyan's debt to popular literature and the way in which he made use of his borrowings; the characteristics of his creative imagination will thus be apparent and the 'marvellous' elements explained.

In the stories a stronghold often stands at the top of some height.[120]

[117] See the bibliography.
[118] J. L. Lowes: 'Essay on The Pilgrim's Progress,' *Of Reading Books* (London, 1930), p. 10.
[119] See the bibliography.
[120] Cf. for example: *The Seven Champions of Christendom*, by Richard Johnson. We have sometimes used the 1755 ed. (2 vols., London), and

The brave Montelion, for example, climbs "a rocky hill of great largeness", [121] from which there rises an extremely imposing palace; but two lions are guarding the passage, and roar savagely. You must have this knight's courage if you want to go on. At his approach, however, the lions suddenly lie down at his feet as if to venerate him.

Episodes of this kind are so frequent in the romances of chivalry, Harold Golder says, that we would need a catalogue to list them all.[122] And there can be no doubt that memories of them lay somewhere in Bunyan's mind, but these memories mingled and harmonised with Biblical ones. For example, Bunyan's lion—in *The Strait Gate* and other works—is also the image of the Law.[123] He had met with lions in the *Song of Songs* ; [124] and in his period of hallucinations, when he endured such personal dread, Satan must have roared within him like a wild beast. Certainly wild beasts made part of his life at that time. So the impulse to describe his imprisonment as the adventure of a man caught between lions' jaws came spontaneously to him: "I thank God upon every remembrance of you; and rejoice, even while I stick between the teeth of the lions in the wilderness." [125]

He always makes his borrowings vivid and his own. There is no

---

sometimes, for some references, the J. J. Harvey Darton ed. (London, 1913). This last has the disadvantage of being very free but on the other hand combines Richard Johnson's text with that of the Chap-books.

[121] Cf. Harold Golder, 'John Bunyan's Hypocrisy', *North American Review*, vol. 223, p. 327.

[122] Cf. Harold Golder, *Bunyan and Spenser*, P.M.L.A. (1930), vol. 45, pp. 226–227.

One could mention many other similarities. The four lovely and virtuous sisters of Palace Beautiful recall the four sisters of our "sawles warde" (G. R. Owst, *op. cit.*, p. 107). Christian does not leave this hospitable dwelling before being taken into the armoury and given the wherewithal of a true knight. In the same way the enchantress Kalyb armed St. George (cf. Johnson's *Seven Champions*, ed. Harvey Darton, p. 36). It is a classical precaution : "As we that ben everyday walkyng a iorney, towarde the londe of lyghte amonge all oure enmyes . . . Therefore . . . cloth we us in armure, oure enmyes to mete, that we may wythstonde the dynt of the devele." MS. Roy 18 B XXIII, f. 153 b, quoted by G. R. Owst, *op. cit.*, p. 107. It is unnecessary to recall the Palace of Truth and the Palace of Falsehood in *Piers Plowman*.

[123] *The Strait Gate*, I, 368.

[124] *G. A.*, preface ; and *Song of Songs*, IV, 8.

[125] *G. A.*, p. 293.

image, however well-worn it may be, that does not take on some new spiritual significance in the warm familiar atmosphere that he provides. Symbolical transpositions make themselves. How could he have failed to believe in his moral allegory with the " energy of faith " that Stevenson so admired ? [126]

Another interesting example of the fusion of profane and Biblical images, brought together in the crucible of a religious life, is apparent in the valleys of the *Pilgrim*. In the tales of chivalry there are often two valleys following after each other. Arthur of Little Brittany [127] arrives in a large, deep and sombre valley. Some woodcutters immediately come running up to him to warn the gentle knight for the love of God to go back, for if he goes on he will die. The valiant knight naturally pushes on all the same and gives battle to giants, lions and griffins. Afterwards he penetrates into the darkness of a second valley, and passes near " a greate pitte " and " a greate hideous fyre ". [128]

To all Bunyan's readers the parallelism between the *Pilgrim's* episodes and those of the tales of chivalry must be obvious. In the Valley of Humiliation Christian has to fight the fiend Apollyon; and then, at the entry of the Valley of the Shadow of Death, two men accost him and implore him to turn back.[129] Darkness, satyrs, dragons, the pit, flames, hideous noises, all the terrifying apparatus of the popular stories is given us. When the sun rises Christian can see that the ground is stained with blood and strewn with bones, ashes and mutilated bodies—just as St. George, after delivering the princess, came to a ravine where the bones of dead knights glimmered white and terrible.[130]

But here again the popular imagery is tinged with the Bible. Job felt the shadow of death weighing upon him,[131] and the psalmist

---

[126] R. L. Stevenson, *Lay Morals and Other Papers* (London, Chatto & Windus, 1911), p. 185.

[127] Harold Golder, ' John Bunyan's Hypocrisy ', art. *cit.*, p. 329.

[128] *Ibid.*   [129] *P. P.*, p. 58.

[130] *The Seven Champions* (ed. *cit.* Harvey Darton), p. 56. Note that Spenser borrows the background elements for his *Faerie Queene* from the same stories as Bunyan, which explains the similarities in their works. Cf. Harold Golder, *Bunyan and Spenser* (1930), vol. 45, pp. 216 *et seq.*

See too C. S. Lewis, *op. cit.*, p. 311.

[131] *P. P.*, p. 59 and Job, III, 5.

wandered in a dark valley: [132] David trembled before the " quag ",[133] and Jeremiah knew that " wilderness, a land of pits . . . a land of drought and of the shadow of death ".[134]

Christian is not waylaid by simple woodcutters, as in *Arthur of Little Brittany*, but by the sons of those explorers who were sent by Moses into the land of Canaan and returned with false reports.[135]

Thus with Bunyan the Bible invades popular legend and transforms it. The valleys of the *Pilgrim* are no longer merely the setting for fabulous exploits, but the mystical path that its author has trodden. " I have been in my spirit so filled with darkness." [136]

As Harold Golder points out, the Bible and the tales condemned by the Puritans make strange bed-fellows.[137] But then for Bunyan the Bible was an adventure story, a kind of tale of chivalry, as Harold Golder again has shown with much subtlety.[138]

The author of *The Pilgrim's Progress* would probably turn in his grave to hear our opinions—unless in the next world we learn to see ourselves with absolute clarity. For, if Bunyan's intelligence saw the Bible as the only authentic record of God's word, his imagination, unknown to him, most certainly fed on more human adventures— human even in their marvellous heroism.[139] And then where do the frontiers between the marvellous and the real, between history and legend, lie ? [140] In the Middle Ages and much later, and particularly for our Bunyan, these realms which are distinct to-day formed one and the same territory open to action and to dreams.

After his conversion Bunyan strove to deny himself the blending of fiction with Scripture, since his faith condemned it: he tried to tear himself away from profane reading as from all other pleasures. Then later these repressed instincts suddenly broke out and the spirit of childhood burst forth and blossomed in the mature man. We select these explosive verbs on purpose: the *Pilgrim* was born in a

---

[132] *P. P.*, p. 59 and Ps. XXIII, 4.   [133] P. 59 and Ps. LXIX, 16.
[134] P. 58 and Ps. II, 6.   [135] P. 58 and Numbers, XIII, 32.
[136] *G. A.*, Conclusion, p. 397.
[137] Harold Golder, 'Bunyan's Valley of the Shadow', *Modern Philology* (1929), vol. XXVII, p. 66.
[138] *Ibid.*, p. 68.
[139] Cf. *supra*, p. 149, the enumeration of the heroic figures of the Bible in the *Pilgrim*.
[140] Cf. *supra*, p. 152.

sort of dazzled violence, ideas flew like " sparks ", and multiplied so rapidly (" did breed so fast ") that they threatened to devour the religious work in progress—" eat out the book ".[141]

To this eruption of childhood and liberation of repressed artistic ideas are due the equilibrium and serenity which become more marked as the *Pilgrim* advances, particularly in the second part. A psychologist would say this work of art worked a ' catharsis ' in Bunyan.

So by uniting the profane ' marvellous ' with the sacred ' marvellous ' and making a moral or religious symbol of adventure, he could abandon himself to his delight with no scruples, and experience the new Spring or second adolescence [142] which, according to Goethe, are the artist's privilege.

And anyone who can read the book without experiencing some of the delight that the author felt in its creation must indeed have a grey soul and a joyless heart; so must the reader who fails to grant " a willing suspension of disbelief " to the artist who believed with such energy in his own allegory. So, finally, must the man who fails to feel the charm of a work in which morality, metaphysics and theology borrow, by a sort of miracle perhaps unique in literature, the laughs, games and fears of childhood.

All the same, it must be admitted that however much the Frenchman who reads the book for the first time in his twenties strives towards an intelligent familiarity with the text, he will never enjoy it so much as the English and Americans, who find it on their nursery shelves. Samuel Johnson [143] wished that it was longer, and Macaulay [144] knew all its climbs and descents, all its refuges and perils, and always retained the terrifying vision of the Valley of the Shadow.

Now let us consider the fiend Apollyon, who provides such a curious example of artistic creation. The name is to be found both in a favourite story of Bunyan's—*Bevis of Southampton* [145]—

---

[141] " The Author's Apology," lines 17, 18.

[142] Charles du Bos, *Approximations*, 6th series, p. 119.

[143] Boswell, *Life of Johnson* (edited by G. B. Hill, revised by L. F. Powell, 6 vols., Oxford, 1934), II, 239, footnote.

[144] T. B. Macaulay, *Essays and Lays of Ancient Rome* (London, ed. of 1889), p. 198.

[145] " Then said the Saracen—this is the day of Crist his mass, first day of yule—(and he laughed). But what is that to us who only serve Mahomed and great Apollyon ? " p. 10 in *The Romance of Sir Beves of Hamtoun, newly*

and in the *Revelation* of St. John the Divine.[146] Winged, covered with scales and breathing fire, he recalls all the dragons of popular imagination, for example the one in Richard Johnson's story about St. George.   When he fights, he fights like a giant.[147]   And if the monster speaks we seem to be hearing the voice of Satan, such as the tragic dialogues of *Grace Abounding* have taught us to recognise it.[148] Certainly Apollyon was only too real to Bunyan, and certainly it was in this form that devils had always appeared to him.   A thousand disparate elements go to make the child's imagination of Satan, and James Bisset Pratt puts on record that two American boys were known to take their ideas of the devil " from the pictures on devilled ham! " [149]

> It [the *Pilgrim*] came from mine own heart, so to my head,
> And thence into my fingers trickled;
> Then to my pen, from whence immediately
> On paper did I dribble it daintily.
> Manner and matter too was all mine own.[150]

Bunyan was not lying.   He did not plunge into books before writing, but drew from his own life.[151]   We can hardly blame him

---

done into English prose from the metrical version (by Eustace Hinton Jones), Southampton (undated).

[146] Apoc., IX, 2.
In the 17th century Apollyon frequently stood for the devil or sin.   See for example Jeremy Taylor : " Sin is the Apollyon, the destroyer," *Holy Dying*, Bohn's Libraries, p. 315.

[147] *The Seven Champions* (ed. 1755), vol. I, pp. 80–82.
The giant Blanderon has nothing less than an oak-tree for a weapon " an oaktree upon his neck " (p. 80).   Note how the fight starts and continues : " what fury hath incensed thy overboldned mind, thus to adventure thy feeble force against the violence of my strong arms ?   Therefore betake thee to thy weapon, which I compare to a bulrush, for on this ground will I measure out thy grave . . ." (p. 81).   " For every stroke the giant gave, the root of his oak entered at the least two or three inches into the ground " (p. 82). Compare Bunyan: *P. P.*, II, pp. 226–228, the fight between Great-heart and the Giant Maul, and p. 223 where Great-heart speaks of Christian's fight with Apollyon : " . . . with their by-blows they did split the very stones in pieces."

[148] For example *P. P.*, p. 55.

[149] James Bisset Pratt, *The Religious Consciousness*, p. 96, footnote.   And also : " One boy says he got his ideas of the devil from a Punch and Judy show."

[150] " An advertisement to the reader " in *The Holy War*, p. 253.

[151] We have shown (cf. *supra*, p. 137) that with Bunyan emotion crystallised itself spontaneously in specific images, such as the image of the

if he failed to notice the constructive influence that a whole literature exercised over him. He had carried " the manner and the matter " within him for so long that he saw them as his own personal property.

Ever since *The Heavenly Footman*, which, as we have said, is the most obvious precursor of *The Pilgrim's Progress*, Bunyan had made up his mind to describe the path that the Christian has to tread and the landmarks by which he has to pass.[152] " The way is long," he wrote, " and there is many a dirty step, many a high hill, much work to do, a wicked heart, world and devil to overcome. Thou must run a long and tedious journey, through the vast howling wilderness, before thou come to the land of promise." [153] Christian's whole itinerary is outlined here. And in an imaginary dialogue between his reader and himself Bunyan again disclosed the various aspects of the spiritual battle that the Pilgrim would one day have to wage:

Reader: . . . But if I should set in, and run as you would have me, then I must run from all my friends; for none of them are running that way . . . But if I run this way, then I must run from all my sins.

Author: That is true indeed; yet if thou dost not, thou wilt run into hell-fire.

Reader: But if I run this way, then I shall be hated, and shall lose the love of my friends and relations, and of those that I expect benefit from . . . and I shall be mocked of all my neighbours.[154]

So the groundwork of the book had been decided on and the ideas conceived: he only had to give them a concrete form. Throughout the following ten years a whole crystallisation of memories formed

---

" slough "; these unsafe boggy lands he had found in his life. The famous episode of the *Pilgrim* is prefigured in the biography, and let us remember that the " romances " contained similar incidents : " St. Andrew left the path in order to take a shorter way across a bend in the track. The moment he was off the path he sank in the ground almost up to his waist . . . the whole green meadow was a treacherous quaking bog, with only this one way through it," *The Seven Champions* (ed. Harvey Darton, pp. 155 and 156).

[152] It is the very name of the work.
[153] *Heavenly Footman*, p. 270.
[154] *Ibid.*, p. 260.

around the ideas. Life was to give them body and feature; the dialogue between one man's heart and his reason was to develop into a drama for many characters.

Ten years. Let us look back at this period of gestation from our vantage point and pick out some of the landmarks. 1675: "I am persuaded," wrote Bunyan in *Saved by Grace*, "that God hath visited some of you often with his Word . . . and you have thrown water as fast as he hath by the Word cast fire upon your conscience." [155] 1676: now we have *The Strait Gate*, where we read, "Such poor sinners are much like to the wanton boy that stands at the maid's elbow, to blow out her candle as fast as she lights it at the fire. Convinced sinner, God lighteth thy candle and thou puttest it out." [156]

The brief metaphor made in the first theological treatise has become a vivid and homely picture in the next, but this one illustrates the idea rather than suggesting it. We pass from the concrete to the abstract by the ordinary steps of rhetoric.

1678: "The Interpreter took Christian by the hand, and led him to a place where was a Fire burning against a Wall, and one standing by it always, casting much Water upon it to quench it; yet did the Fire burn higher and hotter." [157]

Here we have the foreground of a scene that stretches backwards. If we go behind the wall we find a man who in the privacy of his retreat is constantly pouring oil on the fire. This fire is the work of Grace in the heart, the person who throws the water is Satan, and the Man standing behind the wall and spreading the oil of His Grace is Christ.

Three attempts—and what was a mere figure of style illustrating a point of argument has been transformed into a scene detached from all discursive development. It is a riddle presented to our intuitive curiosity, and also a little picture that has its own life; we can look on it as a sort of model allegory.

Bunyan borrowed this literary form from a practice very much in vogue in his time: the emblem.[158] The Frenchman Menestrier

---

[155] *Saved by Grace*, I, 351.   [156] *Strait Gate*, I, 387.   [157] *P. P.*, p. 32.
[158] Since the publication of my book in 1948, Miss Rosemary Freeman has produced an excellent work, *English Emblem Books*, in which there is an important study of Bunyan. I should like also to mention a very interesting article by Mr. Roger Sharrock 'Bunyan and the English Emblem Writers' (*R.E.S.*, vol. XXI, No. 82, Apr., 1945).

defined the emblem as " a sort of teaching by pictures ",[159] and the Englishman Francis Quarles as " a silent parable ".[160] The emblem joined drawing and poetry together in the service of morality or religion. A few lines of poetry pointed out the lesson of an engraving and made a concrete scene appear as the emblem of a way of life or a virtue. Peacham, George Wither, Geffrey Whitney and above all Francis Quarles, acquired a lively popular fame by their emblems. Milton's nephew, Edward Philips, said of Quarles that he was " the darling of our plebeian judgments ".[161] As a true plebeian, Bunyan liked emblems, too, and composed some himself.[162]

But now we come across other landmarks in the making of the book. In *The Holy City* (1665) and *The Heavenly Footman* [163] there are already the forked roads and the pleasant but twisting paths that chequer the territory of the *Pilgrim*.

The episode of Christian falling asleep in an arbour midway up the hill [164] can be found in potentiality some ten years earlier in this question: " What will become of them that are grown weary before they are got half way thither . . . Friend, it is a sad thing to sit down before we are in heaven, and to grow weary before we come to the place of rest." [165]

The creation of the Palace Beautiful seems—from this distance— almost inevitable to anyone who has read *The Heavenly Footman* with its: " Thou shalt have a good and easy lodging, good and wholesome diet, the bosom of Christ to lie in, the joys of heaven to feed on." [166]

---

[159] Menestrier, *L'art des emblèmes* (Paris, 1584) quoted by Elbert N. S. Thompson, *Literary Bypaths of the Renaissance* (Yale Univ. Press, 1923), p. 33.

[160] Francis Quarles, Epistle to the reader, *Emblemes* (1635).

[161] Text quoted in *The Chambers's Encyclopaedia of English Literature*, vol. III, p. 232.

[162] Cf. his collection: *A book for Boys and Girls or Country Rhymes for Children* (1686)—in 1701 the book was published again by a Puritan who took the liberty of leaving out 25 poems and correcting others (see the copy in the Bodleian Library). In the following editions the title of the work was changed: *Divine Emblems*.

[163] " It is Antichrist that hath brought in all those crossings, bye-lanes and odd nooks, etc." *The Holy City*, III, 437. " Though the way to heaven be but one, yet there are many crooked lanes and by-paths, shoot down upon it, as I may say," *The Heavenly Footman*, p. 276.

[164] Cf. *supra*, p. 147, and *P. P.*, pp. 41–42.

[165] *Heavenly Footman*, p. 293.

[166] *Ibid.*, pp. 290–291.

Our author did not know at that time that he would one day write the *Pilgrim*, but if one can so put it, the allegory wanted to be born and Bunyan was moving darkly towards it. Unawares, he was already groping after this lapidary formula, that clear-cut outline. How, for instance, could he portray hypocrisy in the most arresting way? In 1672 we saw the Latitudinarian twisting and turning like the eel at the end of a line, or rather like a cock on the top of a steeple.[167] Four years later he turns up again. The same comparison is used, but features are added that will soon be integrated into the character of By-ends.[168] Finally, with the *Pilgrim* this celebrated personality comes to life, but by this time his author has realised that the captive fish and vacillating weathercock call to mind the mischief-making fool rather than the more considered activities of a hypocrite. Hence he selects a more accurate image from the vast storehouse of popular rhetorical imagery. By-ends ingenuously admits that he has made his fortune in emulating his grandfather, the waterman, " who looked one way and rowed the other ".[169] This is a proverbial joke,[170] but so cleverly grafted on to the narrative that it gains all the vigorous irony necessary to sum up the character.

In 1658 Bunyan made mention of the procession of angels who escort the elect to the Celestial City: " The angels of the Lord come from heaven to watch over and conduct the soul . . . into Abraham's bosom." [171] In its bare outline we have here the theme of consolation that Bunyan's life of meditation is going to enrich to provide the sumptuous orchestration of Christian's last moments.

Thus the *Pilgrim* grew little by little within Bunyan, probably with-

---

[167] *Defence of the Doctrine of Justification*, II, 322.

[168] *Strait Gate*, I, 389. " He can be anything for anybody . . . he is a frog of Egypt and can live in the water and out of the water . . . he will hold with the hare and run with the hound, he carries fire in the one hand and water in the other."

[169] *P. P.*, p. 92.

[170] Cf. Samuel Butler :

> " Or rowing scull, he's fain to love
> Look one way, and another move."
>
> *Hudibras*, I, canto 3.

And Sir Thomas Overbury : A water-man : " For like a fellow that rides to the pillory, he goes not that way he looks." *Works* (edited by Edw. F. Rimbault, London, 1856), p. 136.

[171] *A Few Sighs*, III, 680.

out his even suspecting it. Yet it was this secret unfolding that explains the sudden and imperious manner in which the work imposed itself on its author when the time came. He could let his pen run on; there were no halts nor hesitations nor omissions. He was gathering a ripe fruit.

★

A study of the genesis of a book usually involves some revelation as to the nature of its author's creative imagination; and Bunyan's sometimes seems to us to be endowed with vigour of precision rather than richness and variety of invention.

An artist's imagination never composes the pictures it offers us *ex nihilo* ; no, but the imagination of the greatest writers pushes the dissociation of borrowed elements farther and reassembles them with a freer fantasy. Their imagination is the free and lightsome flight of a bird whose wings have been bred on a thousand thoroughly assimilated substances. Whereas with Bunyan we often have the lumbering flight of a bird whose booty is still in its claws.

Thus in his *Celestial City* we can discern the raw materials borrowed from St. John's *Apocalypse*: the mountain (XXI, 10), the tree of life (II, 7), the throne of judgment (XX, 11), the white garments of the elect (III, 4), the absence of death, sorrow and pain in the new heaven (XXI, 1–4). To the First Epistle to the Thessalonians [172] he owes the coming of the Lord in the clouds with the sound of trumpets. Then, having joined all these details together with yet more culled from the Bible, Bunyan enlivens his fresco with the song of bells, joyful music and all the fervour of his faith; but he is not original. As M. Emile Legouis has remarked, a Giles Fletcher or a Shelley painted the joys of paradise with greater freedom and ravishment.[173]

However, if we should not exaggerate our author's inventive gifts, we certainly should not commit the graver error of belittling them. Far from labouring his effects, Bunyan thought in images. He never really grasped his idea until he saw it personified; and so Biblical metaphors came to populate—literally—the universe he created. The " filthy rags of righteousness " [174] became Christian's

---

[172] Bunyan gives all his references himself.

[173] E. Legouis and L. Cazamian, *Histoire de la littérature anglaise* (Hachette), p. 326.

[174] " And all our righteousnesses are as filthy rags," Is., lxiv, 6. Authorised Version.

clothing, and the " burden of sin " really bowed down his shoulders.[175]
Religious literature commonly speaks of " the water of life ", [176]
" the bread of salvation ",[177] and " the light of the Gospel ",[178]
and—literally—the pilgrims when prisoners at Doubting Castle
lacked water, bread and light. It is said, too, that despair " comes
and goes in fits " [179] and Giant Despair suffered from fits of epilepsy.
We speak of " the keys of the Kingdom of Heaven ",[180] and Christian
carried on him the keys which set him free from the dungeon.

The simple words of the Scriptures, then, were enriched by concrete notation, and sometimes one little phrase suggests a whole
episode. " Two women shall be grinding at the mill; the one shall
be taken, and the other left," writes St. Matthew.[181] The ring of
these words was so vivid to Bunyan that he forthwith described the
arrival of Christiana and Mercy at the wicket Gate, the furious barking
of the watchdog, Christiana's knocking which leads to her admittance,
while her companion is left on the threshold; the intercession of
friendship, Mercy's fears and subsequent banging as if she wants to
take the kingdom by storm, and finally her fainting while the keeper's
face lights up with a smile of wonderful innocence.[182]

All these examples abundantly prove that Bunyan's imagination,
while lyrical in his sermons, was here essentially dramatic. Our
author was creating a drama. He saw every detail of it with a pro-
digious intensity, and this gives his work its vital and dimensional
quality.

From his prison he endowed the ideal world of the Bible with the
clear forms of the terrestrial universe, and recreated the concrete world,

[175] " For mine iniquities are gone over mine head : as an heavy burden
they are too heavy for me." Ps. XXXVIII, 4.
[176] " I will give unto him that is athirst of the fountain of the water of life
freely." Apoc., XXI, 6.
[177] Or the bread of life : " I am the bread of life," John, vi, 35. Or the
bread of God, see John, vi, 33.
[178] " The light of the glorious Gospel," II, Corinth., iv, 4.
[179] Concerning despair W. Perkins says : " It hath its fittes after the manner
of an ague." *A Declaration of Spirituall Desertions*, Works, 1612, I, 418.
See too H. Golder's article on Giant Despair, *Journal of Eng. and Germ.
Philol.*, Oct., 1931, p. 367.
[180] Matt., xvi, 19.
[181] Matt., xxiv, 41. Bunyan suggests all his thought, *P. P.*, p. 177.
[182] *P. P.*, 174 *et seq.*

from which he was excluded, with a precision of line if possible greater than there was in fact. He took the real in his vigorous grasp and brought it into his dreams; and this energy of gesture and vision is the better part of his genius.

IV. REALISM IN *THE PILGRIM'S PROGRESS*

As ideal as Spenser, as real as Defoe.

GEORGE SAINTSBURY

I. THE BACKGROUND

OUR study of the sources and genesis of *The Pilgrim's Progress* brought into relief the important part played in the allegory by the 'marvellous'; but the *Pilgrim* is also realist. Before Swift and Defoe, Bunyan had integrated the imaginary with the real. We would not go so far as to say that he discovered for himself the laws governing a literary *genre*, nor that a sure instinct made him see that fiction must be blended with history and dream with life so as to give authority to both. No, he simply had to give way before the twin forces of his double love—love for the realities of dream, and love for the realities of the concrete universe.

Hence the pilgrims' way is not only a mystical path but a good Roman road mounting straight up Hill Difficulty,[183] or cutting across " the delicate plain called Ease ".[184] Coming as we do after other critics, and particularly Sir Charles Firth,[185] we shall content ourselves with briefly noting various aspects of this road, already familiar to whomsoever is well versed in the seventeenth century.

At one point a high wall runs alongside it, over which hang branches laden with fruit.[186] Watchdogs bark when travellers approach,[187] and God knows how many do pass along, chatting together as on Chaucer's road. Elsewhere a meadow lies beside the road and there is a stile by which to cross over the fence.[188] A " fine pleasant green

---

[183] *P. P.*, p. 40.
[185] Art. *cit.* (The Eng. Assoc.), Oct., 1911.
[187] P. 174.

[184] P. 98.
[186] P. 179.
[188] P. 103.

lane " [189] sometimes runs into it, along which it is sweet to wander when the "rattling of Coaches and the rumbling of Wheels " [190] become unbearable, as they do to Mercy.   At the foot of a hillock is a spring muddied by careless walkers.   Those who want to drink must draw the water in an earthen pot and let it stand.[191]   There the valley is filled with the song of a young shepherd.[192]   Love of nature —of the peaceful nature that a Bedfordshire man would know—is expressed with a fervour foreshadowing the outpourings of the Romantic period.   " Here," wrote Bunyan about Mr. Fearing, " he would lie down, embrace the Ground, and kiss the very Flowers that grew in this Valley.   He would be up every Morning by break of Day, tracing, and walking to and fro in that Valley." [193]

In another work our author, whose imagination was always enriched by the things of the earth, endowed this smiling and flowery nature with eternity, for the " Holy City " of his dreams was to be a sort of celestial Bedfordshire: " Now also will all the pretty robins and little birds in the Lord's field most sweetly send forth their pleasant notes, and all the flowers and herbs of his garden spring." [194]

However, in the seventeenth century the roads were by no means consistently agreeable.   In some villages two " honest parishioners " were detailed to police the highway, elected for one year on the Tuesday and Wednesday of Easter Week.[195]   It fell to them to

---

[189] *P. P.*, p. 114.   [190] P. 222.   [191] P. 199.   [192] P. 220.

[193] P. 234.   Cf. Izaak Walton: "As I thus sate, these and other sights had so fully possest my soul, that I thought as the poet has happily exprest it :

'I was for that time lifted above earth
And possest joyes not promis'd in my birth.'"

The Compleat Angler as it was Originally Published (Elliot Stock, London), p. 63.

Let us remember that the first Quaker, George Fox, goes much further than Bunyan and attains to veritable ecstasy that recalls Blake.   " Now was I come up in spirit through the flaming sword into the paradise of God.   All things were new; and all the creation gave another smell unto me than before, beyond what words can utter . . . the creation was opened to me." *Journal* (2 vols., Leeds, 1836), I, 105.   For Bunyan the doors of perception never opened in this way.

[194] *Works*, III, 409.

[195] Eleanor Trotter, *Seventeenth Century Life in the Country Parish* (Cambridge Univ. Press, 1919), pp. 120–121.

compel the rural proprietors to come and mend the roads with waggon, spade and pick,[196] and these thought it quite sufficient—and with a bad grace at that—to throw stones into the holes without breaking them up or levelling them down.[197] The ruts were four feet deep in some places, if we are to believe Arthur Young.[198] A contemporary of Bunyan's declared the roads to be " very dangerous to the lives and limbs both of men and horses ".[199] Celia Fiennes found that the miles seemed longer in Bedfordshire than anywhere else ! [200] And our author's admirer, Agnes Beaumont, noted that she hesitated to mount her horse with a neighbour " the wayes being soe dirty and deepe ".[201] When it rained the road was often flooded, and it is on record that the only way of getting along at such times was to swim ! [202]

Such slow methods of travel were favourable to robbers, some of whom went on foot (footpads) and others on horseback (highwaymen). Cambridge students making their way to London trembled on the edge of Epping Forest, and those of Oxford on the outskirts of ' Maidenhead Thicket '.[203]

So Christian's road was a truly English road, and more especially a truly Bedfordshire road, with its swamps, narrow causeways and deep ditches. If we wanted to push our point farther we could prove that the famous " slough " lay near to Dunstable,[204] and that Hill Difficulty rose up six miles from the village of Elstow, and so on—but we would be taking the innocent pastime of local archaeologists too seriously.

We find more realism on the *Pilgrim's* marvellous and mystical

[196] Eleanor Trotter, *Seventeenth Century Life in the Country Parish* (Cambridge Univ. Press, 1919), pp. 120–121.

[197] E. Lipson, *The Economic History of England* (London, 3 vols., 5th ed., 1929), II, 442.

[198] Quoted by Lipson, *ibid.* Young's evidence (18th century) shows that no progress whatsoever had been made.

[199] *Ibid.*

[200] Celia Fiennes, *Through England on a Side Saddle in the Time of William and Mary* (ed. used, London, 1888), p. 290.

[201] *The Narrative of the Persecution of Agnes Beaumont in 1674* (ed. by G. B. Harrison, London, 1929), p. 19.

[202] E. Lipson, *op. cit.*, II, 443.

[203] Macaulay, *The History of England* (Everyman), I, 294.

[204] Charles G. Harper, *The Bunyan Country—Landmarks of the Pilgrim's Progress* (London, 1928), p. 72.

road when robbers attack Valiant-for-Truth [205] and plunder Little-faith. Three " sturdy rogues " on horseback come galloping up to this sleeping pilgrim. " With threatening language they bid him stand. At this, Little-faith looked as white as a Clout, and had neither power to fight nor fly. Then said Faint-heart, Deliver thy Purse; but he making no haste to do it (for he was loth to lose his Money) Mistrust ran up to him, and, thrusting his hand into his Pocket, pull'd out thence a bag of Silver. Then he cried out, Thieves, Thieves. With that Guilt, with a great Club that was in his hand, strook Little-faith on the head, and with that blow fell'd him flat to the ground, where he lay bleeding as one that would bleed to death." [206] Here Realism becomes Romanticism—the Romanticism of daily life in the century when women fell in love with bandits and begged them for mercy! [207]

It is again from the life of the period that Bunyan borrowed the scene of his Vanity Fair, in which the precision of his observation is topped off with a streak of satire.

It goes without saying that Bunyan was well acquainted with the fair of Elstow village; and it seems almost certain that he had also visited that of Stourbridge, near Cambridge. It is possible, too, that he knew St. Bartholomew's Fair, to which Ben Jonson has given literary fame.

At any rate, like all the fairs of the period, Vanity Fair is divided up by streets or rows along which stalls are ranged.[208] It has its " lord ", and its lawcourts are based on the ' Piepowder Court ' of Stourbridge and elsewhere.

In this microcosm everything is for sale, and Bunyan's list is of a bitter diversity: " Houses, Lands, Trades, Places, Honours, Preferments, Titles, Countries, Kingdoms, Lusts, Pleasures and Delights of all sorts, as Whores, Bawds, Wives, Husbands, Children, Masters, Servants, Lives, Blood, Bodies, Souls, Silver, Gold, Pearls, Precious Stones, and what not." [209]

As in all fairs—and in the world—the following things can also be obtained: " Jugglings, Cheats, Games, Plays, Fools, Apes, Knaves, and Rogues, and that of every kind. Here are to be

[205] *P. P.*, pp. 269 *et seq.*   [206] P. 116.
[207] Macaulay, *op. cit.* (Everyman), I, 296.
[208] Cf. E. Lipson, *op. cit.*, I, 229.   [209] P. 82.

seen, too, and that for nothing, Thefts, Murders, Adulteries, False-swearers, and that of a blood-red colour." [210]

Confronted with man's greed and dishonest commerce, Bunyan's gorge heaved, and a fair seemed to him a miniature of the world he loathed. He could hardly have chosen better, for these large annual fairs apparently provided a spectacle of vice triumphant, in spite of the injunctions delivered in the opening speech that all sellers of wine, pale or brown ale, must use legal measures such as the gallon, the half-gallon, the quart and the pint; that no eating-house keeper, baker or hawker, whoever he may be, may sell or put up for sale victuals which are not good and healthy for the human body. [211]

Bunyan's protest, as will be apparent in our study of his social thought, was a traditional one. It was the one Ben Jonson had heard in the mouth of Zeal of the Land Busy: " Look not toward them, hearken not! . . . The wares are the wares of the devil, and the whole fair is the shop of Satan." [212]

Surely we hear an echo of these words in this passage from the *Pilgrim*: " But that which did not a little amuse the Merchandizers, was, that these Pilgrims set very light by all their Wares, they cared not so much as to look upon them: and if they called upon them to buy, they would put their fingers in their ears, and cry, Turn away mine eyes from beholding vanity; and look upwards, signifying that their Trade and Traffic was in Heaven." [213]

The description of the pilgrims' trial is no less realist. Bunyan may have had in mind a method of popular literature, [214] but it is more likely that he was recalling his own experience and that of his co-religionists. His judge, Hate-good, behaves like the Earl of Dorset at the trial of William Prynne, [215] or like Lord Jefferies later at that of

---

[210] *P. P.*, p. 83.

[211] Lipson, *op. cit.*, I, 215.

[212] *Bartholomew Fair*, act. III, sc. 1.   [213] *P. P., p.* 84.

[214] Cf. C. H. Firth, art. *cit.*, p. 21 on the various anti-Catholic pamphlets where the trial form is used by the author on account of its dramatic value.

[215] " I will not set him at liberty no more than a plagued man or a mad dog; who though he can't bite will foam; he is so far from being a social soul, that he is not a rational soul. He is fit to live in dens with such beasts of prey as wolves and tigers like himself; therefore I condemn him to perpetual imprisonment; and for corporeal punishment I would have him branded in the forehead, slit in the nose and have his ear chopped off." (Cf. D. Neal, *op. cit.*, I, 570.)

Richard Baxter.[216]   A delicious irony underlies all the parts of this parody of justice in which the witnesses, without realising it, praise the accused: "My Lord, This man, notwithstanding his plausible name, is one of the vilest men in our Country; he neither regardeth Prince nor People, Law nor Custom: but doth all that he can to possess all men with certain of his disloyal notions, which he in the general calls Principles of Faith and Holiness.   And in particular, I heard him once myself affirm, *That Christianity and the Customs of our Town of Vanity, were Diametrically opposite, and could not be reconciled.*" [217]

Anyone who has read Bunyan's controversy with Edward Fowler can hear an echo of it here.   But the furious diatribe of 1672 has now been succeeded by the calm in which the artist calculates his effect; and if this trial of the theories of Fowler and Hobbes mixed up together [218] lacks depth, it certainly has a fine comic vigour.

So we see that some of the events of the period are woven like a watermark into the narrative.   We could almost read in it the evolution of the religious situation in England.

At the time of Bunyan's conversion about 1655—we mean when Christian reaches the Palace Beautiful—the lions, symbol of the danger threatening Dissenters, are chained.[219]   We are at the height of the Commonwealth.   But when Great-heart and his charge arrive at the same place, the wild beasts, now backed by Giant Grim, who personifies civil power, are so terrible that the path has become quite unused and is all grown over with grass.[220]   This was because in 1684, the year of the publication of the second part of *The Pilgrim's Progress*, the persecution had redoubled its force.

---

[216] See Richard Baxter, *Autobiography*, ed. by Lloyd Thomas (Everyman), Appendix I.   And particularly p. 261 : "Come you, what do you say for yourself, you old knave ! come, speak up: what doth he say ? " Cf. *P. P.*, p. 88 : "Sirrah, Sirrah, thou deservest to live no longer, but to be slain immediately upon the place ; yet that all men may see our gentleness towards thee, let us see what thou hast to say."

[217] *P. P.*, p. 87.

[218] Cf. *supra*, " The Controversialist ".

[219] Lions have another meaning besides (cf. *supra*, p. 173).   It is precisely the property of symbolism, as we have said (cf. *supra*, p. 146) to have this richness.

[220] *P. P.*, p. 203.

We cannot help noticing that the spring at the foot of Hill Difficulty is clear when Christian passes and muddy when his wife wants to drink there. From this we can infer that doctrine was pure when the Dissenting Church, at Bedford as elsewhere, had only a small number of faithful, and corrupt when black sheep had slipped in among the many converts.[221]

If we want to find evidence concerning the futility of royal tyrannies, we shall find it in the conversion of Hopeful, who is awakened to the religious life by the martyrdom of Faithful. We shall have even better proof when the new pilgrims come to Vanity Fair, for even there the Church has built itself " a very fair Dining Room " [222] and has prospered.[223]

Examples could be multiplied, but these are quite sufficient to show the allusions that contemporaries could find in *The Pilgrim's Progress*. But we believe that the majority of readers, especially outside Nonconformist circles, would hardly have noticed them. Even if the people who read it had a sharpened political sensibility, they would have had sufficient freshness of spirit to abandon themselves to the charm of a fine story without bothering to trace the arabesques of subtle allusions in its texture. And if our study has made it plain that *The Pilgrim's Progress* was rich enough in new harmonies to stimulate the attention and charm the heart, while conforming sufficiently to literary tradition not to upset the humble who prefer the forms they are used to, we shall see that the success of the book for a profoundly religious people lay precisely in the supremely felicitous alliance of new finds and old reminiscences.[224]

Mr. York Tindall is quite right [225] when he hears the echoes of

---

[221] The Dissenting Church at Bedford had 12 members at first, 26 when Bunyan joined in 1655 (*Church-Book*, f. 5) and 120 in 1676 (cf. Brown, *op. cit.*, p. 303). The archives show some black sheep and false brethren : in 1673 John Rush, who became drunk as an animal, was excluded, f. 53 ; in 1677 communion had to be refused to Edward Dent who contracted debts he could not pay (f. 54) ; and in 1680 John Wildman calumniated all the faithful including the pastor (f. 68).

[222] *P. P.*, p. 254.

[223] " For it was not now as in former times wherefore the Pilgrims grew acquainted with many of the good people of the town . . ." p. 258.

[224] Cf. *infra*, p. 310, and Elie Halévy, ' La Naissance du methodisme en Angleterre ', *Revue de Paris* (1906).

[225] York Tindall, *op. cit.*, pp. 43, 51, 58, 62, 67.

Bunyan's controversies in *The Pilgrim's Progress*, but we can hardly believe that the majority of his contemporary readers were aware of the book's polemical aspect. The success of the work was too big for that; it swept beyond the Puritan body.

We wonder whether the ordinary reader, apart from those in Dissenting circles, ever, for instance, interpreted the songs of the *Pilgrim* as hidden propaganda for the singing of psalms—which the Bedford church refused to tolerate.[226] More especially as Bunyan makes his own feelings abundantly clear by causing vocal and instrumental music to be heard at the supper given by the Interpreter.[227]

We can thus see many aspects of Puritan life reflected in the mirror of the allegory. There is nothing more touching and instructive than those pictures of family life in which Bunyan foreshadowed the work of Wordsworth and George Eliot. For we must see the Puritan in his home if we really want to understand him: only then a whole legend collapses! If we expect to find the monastic gloom in which we have believed so long on the strength of a few historians,[228] we shall be disappointed.

We are not allowed to see the father actually in the midst of his children, since Christian has left them so as to obey the call of the Lord: but the image is given us by reflection, for Great-heart is identified finally with Bunyan. He is the medieval knight, fearless and blameless and rather stiff in his armour, but he is also the loving father. His heart expands in the atmosphere of the home.

He takes the children by the hand and knows how to use the coaxing tone that encourages them: " Come, my pretty boys, how do you do ? "[229] If he teases them, it is with kindliness, and the mockery of his words is lost in the smile of his eyes: " How now, my Boys, do you love to go before when no danger doth approach, and love to come behind so soon as the Lions appear ? "[230]

And he is not so austere that he does not know the price of dainties for the children. After an absence he celebrates his return by giving

---

[226] John Brown, *op. cit.* (ed. Frank Mott Harrison, 1928), p. 232 (marginal note).

Frank Mott Harrison, *John Bunyan, a Record of Recent Research* (MS. Bedford Library), p. 27.

[227] *P. P.*, p. 189.　　　　[228] Cf. *supra*, p. 38.

[229] *P. P.*, p. 200.　　　　[230] P. 202.

them figs and raisins.[231] There is no scorn in this humble family for the good things of the world. Without being greedy, they can take delight in a good meal. After "a dish of milk well crumbed " [232] they do justice to " a dish of Butter and Honey ".

The fact is that Bunyan loved good food. Christian made an excellent meal at Palace Beautiful; and if the dishes served him remind the reader that they are spiritual food, their adjectives— " fat things ", [233] " well-refined wines "—contrive to give a sensual appeal to the symbol.

We suspect the tinker of having had all Cromwell's contempt for " French quelquechoses "! [234] This man of the roads needed substantial fare—" solid substantiall food " [235] such as Thomas Fuller had praised before Defoe. Christian and Great-heart owe their physical strength to beef and beer, too. And perhaps Great-heart owes his gaiety to them.

For although Great-heart sometimes preaches, as the father of a family should, he is a very jovial man. And it is with an approving eye that he watches young and old dancing—for Ready-to-halt, though old, cannot resist the appeal of music. " True he could not dance without one Crutch in his Hand, but I promise you, he footed it well." [236]

Bunyan's work vibrates with music, and we are never allowed to forget how much he loved it—he who had made a metal violin for himself and fashioned a flute from one of the legs of his prison chair.[237]

In *The Pilgrim's Progress* all the women are musicians. Prudence has " a pair of excellent virginals ", on which she accompanies herself when she sings.[238] Christiana plays the viol and Mercy the lute.[239] So women bring the inspiring grace of art to the home. " Wonder-

---

[231] *P. P.*, p. 217. [232] P. 243. [233] P. 50.

[234] C. H. Firth, *Oliver Cromwell and the Rule of the Puritans in England* (1st ed. 1909, ed. used 1933), p. 458.

[235] Thomas Fuller, *Selections* (Oxford, Clarendon Press, 1928), see the portrait of the " good yeoman ". [236] *P. P.*, p. 263.

[237] P. 78. " There is no reason for disbelieving the tradition that it was Bunyan's, although there is no evidence yet available definitely to establish its connection with him." This is the opinion of Mr. J. Whiting, curator of the Bunyan Museum, about the flute, and of Mr. Frank Mott Harrison; cf. Percy A. Scholes, *op. cit.*, p. 385.

[238] P. 217. [239] P. 263.

ful! Musick in the house, musick in the heart and musick also in Heaven." [240]

Christian and Great-heart fight; Christiana and Mercy irradiate beauty and tenderness. Where woman is, there is the home and the sanctuary of peace, as Ruskin said.[241] Bunyan's realist descriptions convey all that so well that in reading him we can see the justice of the opinion of J. R. Green, the historian, when he points out that the home such as we conceive it now was a creation of the Puritans. With them life gained in moral grandeur, in a feeling for the dignity of man, in order and in equity. The wider sociability of the previous century was replaced by an intense love in the narrower circle of the home.[242]

These Puritans of good stamp, however, also had a sense of hospitality and mutual help. Persecution had folded them in on themselves; but within the limits of their little groups they showed ardent friendship towards each other. The days spent in Palace Beautiful are devoted to prayer, serious conversation, or else music and games of riddles. They give a picture of how beautiful the world can be in the warmth of fellowship. This meant so much to Bunyan that in his view one of the greatest joys of Heaven would be the loyalty of man to man, the union of heart and soul.[243]

We have only to open the archives of the Bedford church to see where Bunyan first conceived the vague and imperfect outline of his dream:

" 1658, 28th of the 6th moneth. It is agreed that a speedy course be taken either by publick petition or some private way to gather a sume of money for the release of our Sister Deane. It is agreed also that next fourth day of the weeke come fortnight be set apart to seeke God by prayer.

" 1st day of the 8th moneth. It was agreed that two brethren should be made choyce of every monethly meeting to go abroad to visit our brethren and sisters; and to certify us how they doe body

[240] *P. P.*, p. 206.

[241] Ruskin : " This is the true nature of home : it is the place of peace. . . . And wherever a true wife comes, this home is always round her . . . and for a noble woman it stretches far round her." *Sesame and Lilies*, 2nd lecture : ' Of queens' gardens.'

[242] Cf. John Stephen Flynn, *op. cit.*, p. 75.

[243] See *Holy City*, III, 409.

and soule; and to stirre them up to come (especially at our monethly meetings) to us to Bedford; and to let them know if they come not, the Church will expect an account of the reason of their absence . . .

" The latter part of the 9th moneth. . . . In respecte of the present distresse of many of our friends, upon whom God's hand of visitation lyes, it is thought fit and agreed that our brethren doe according to their severall abilityes deposite something in the hands of our bro: Spencely: who is desired to spend the same to and for our severall distressed friends use.

" 25th of the 10th moneth: . . . Information was also given to the Church of the miscarriage of bro: Oliver Dicks of Milton which was very great: for he (as he saide) having lost a sheep and a sheep being staide in another field, he was sent to owne it if it were his: and he came and owned it; and tho' by the way (as he himself expressed) he judged in his Conscience that it was not his; yet did not carry it back againe, but tooke it away and kept it, and sold the fleece and would have sold the sheep, there being not above 4d. or 8d. difference in bargaining: But the sheep being owned he was brought before a Justice where he restored the sheep and 20d. for the fleece to the party whose owne it was. And all this to the great dishonour of God, the wounding of his owne soule and great scandall to the Church of Christ, of which he is a member. Upon consideration thereof, being sent for by the Congregation; after a full debate and things aforesaide prooved to him, besides some confession of his owne; his evill also being opened and charged home upon him, he was by generall consent withdrawne from for the present." [244]

These Bedford church archives, drawn up in artless prose, throw light on the life of a Puritan community in the seventeenth century and indirectly on one aspect of *The Pilgrim's Progress* background.

II. THE PRINCIPAL CHARACTERS

THE principal character is, of course, Christian. He dominates all the others by his moral stature, and the book is ordered around him. Our summary of *The Pilgrim's Progress* consisted in following Chris-

---

[244] This long passage from the archives is quoted by John Brown *op. cit.*, pp. 104, 106. We will of course find these extracts, at the dates indicated, in the fac-simile ed. that we owe to G. B. Harrison, *The Church book of Bunyan Meeting* (London, 1928).

tian on his way, watching him live, and understanding him. All we need do now is remind ourselves of what we noticed. At first Christian is a troubled man; but his disquiet recalls less the morbid worries described by Bunyan in his autobiography than the nobility of an over-exacting soul. His burden is perhaps less a load of remorse hinged on to the past than anguish concerning the future. The sin on his back weighs less in act than in potentiality. This feeling is not only inseparable from life; it constitutes its beauty.

It is because of his restlessness that Christian undertakes and pursues his pilgrimage. It is only dross that falls and rolls on the ground in front of the Cross—the fear which is mere fear, the terror of punishment. The awe which necessarily accompanies respect and love when these judge themselves to be imperfect persists right up to the end.

Christian's disquiet thus draws part of its strength from the imagination. Though still on earth, he is already living in the invisible: and having formed his own picture of the City from the first moment he set out,[245] he goes towards it with energy and conviction.

In this passionate energy the stubbornness and pride of not giving in play their part. The greater his solitude, the harder the road, the more exalted his effort. In the Slough,[246] and when faced with the lions, giants and monsters, his will and his courage wax stronger. He wavers only when his intelligence is taken unawares, and thus it is that Worldly-Wiseman's arguments tempt him to stray from the path.[247]

He is a man whom struggle intoxicates. In fact he finds peace of soul only in the tumult of battle, forgetting danger in the moment of facing it. It is painful and inauspicious for him to cease to be doing. Perhaps others may lawfully rest in an arbour half-way up a hill, but if he does so it is at his peril.[248] And despair threatens to defeat him only once—when he is cast into the dungeon.[249]

He has the impatience of nervous people or of those whose lively intelligence makes them irritated by the slowness of less gifted minds. He snubs his friend Hopeful roundly and treats him as a nit-wit;[250]

---

[245] *P. P.*, p. 15.
[246] " Wherefore Christian was left to tumble in the Slough of Despond alone but still he endeavoured to struggle . . ." P. 17.
[247] P. 19 *et seq.*   [248] P. 41.   [249] P. 106.   [250] P. 117.

but on the other hand he can recognise his own mistakes and apologise with simplicity of heart.[251]

Though he is harsh towards himself and often harsh towards others, being blinded by certain prejudices (for example he unjustly snubs "the brisk lad" Ignorance), he does not lack sensitivity. To argue from his abandonment of his family that he has no heart seems to us unfair. We should not judge his heroic renunciations by the standards of middle-class morality. There are probably two reasons for his reserve concerning his abandoned family. First, that to revel in his grief would have softened his courage and drawn attention to his sacrifice. And second, that by keeping silent he resisted the twofold temptation of despair and pride, to both of which he would have found it very sweet to give way. Christian was one of those proud and imaginative creatures who know how to extract bitter enjoyment from suffering, a self-satisfaction that Bunyan would have considered satanic; and Christian had enough insight into his own character for us to presume that he understood or guessed at himself as much as a man ever does.

Good insight, yes, for he was able to size up Talkative immediately and uncover the secrets of his heart: "Know him! Yes, better than he knows himself." [252] And his sympathy for Little-faith testifies to his penetration into souls as much as to his charity.[253]

And Christian is learned, as Hopeful respectfully points out; [254] he speaks his language with precision and knows how to make a discursive statement—both signs of intellectual clarity and vigour.[255] His prejudices to which we referred just now come not from a limited intelligence but from a mind blinded by fervour; they are the inevitable outcome of passion.

And his apparent selfishness is also linked to his passionate zeal. When confronted with the choice between heaven and the world, he does not hesitate; yet his love of God by no means kills his love of people: it imposes a direction on it, and boundaries. Christian never refuses proffered friendship. It is he who first goes towards

---

[251] *P. P.*, p. 104.
[252] P. 72, and also "Take my advice do as I bid you, and you shall find that he will soon be sick of your company . . ." p. 75.
[253] P. 115.　　　　　　　　　　　　　　　[254] P. 100.
[255] Cf. pp. 39 and 97, for example.

Faithful and speaks to him with words in which affection is tempered with respect (" Honoured and well Beloved brother, etc.").[256]   Christian never shows anyone a warm and over-indulgent affection, but he always has a friendly and reverent curiosity about others.   He knows how to question and how to listen, as his conversations with his two brother pilgrims show.

Here, then, we have Christian—all fervour, will and courage with plenty of intelligence; but proud, hard, irascible and sometimes unjust.

We must not, however, pretend that we know Christian as we know some of the characters in modern novels.   When we shut the book he does not continue to walk by our side.   But Bunyan was able to endow him with that interior truth and coherence which gives life to the creatures of fiction.

Christian owes much to his author.   In fact he is his author, his author detached from himself and looking back on himself over the passage of years.   So that whereas Bunyan the tinker was at the mercy of life's torrential course, Bunyan the artist could control and direct it.   He can see lucidly into his past.   He no longer confuses Satan's voice with his own nor frets about the blasphemies which he now knows he never uttered.[257]   And since he divines by instinct that the truth of art is not the truth of everyday existence, he is far from making Christian's pilgrimage a carbon-copy of life.   For example, he allows the wounds inflicted by Apollyon on the pilgrim to heal immediately,[258] whereas there is no miracle of this kind in the autobiography.

Hence it is in the person of Christian that we can best measure the relationship between *Grace Abounding* and *The Pilgrim's Progress*. *Grace Abounding* is life lived again in an effort at faithful remembering: *The Pilgrim's Progress* is life retraced and dominated in the joy of an original creation.   *Grace Abounding* is the resurrection of a man who comes towards us and introduces himself: *The Pilgrim's Progress* is the work of an artist who effaces himself behind the creatures whom he has brought to life.

And side by side with Christian, Faithful and Hopeful make their way.

[256] *P. P.*, p. 63.
[257] P. 60: " Christian made believe that he spake blasphemies, when twas Satan suggested them into his mind."   [258] P. 57.

JOHN BUNYAN

Faithful has will and courage. His steadfast spirit during his martyrdom causes many of the inhabitants of Vanity Fair to awaken to the religious life,[259] but he does not possess either the intelligence, imagination or sensibility of Christian. No burden rests on his shoulders, he does not have to cross the Slough,[260] and for him the lions do not even deign to roar.[261] After a sudden and definitive conversion he goes tirelessly forward with an energy and determination that enable him to catch up and outstrip his companion. But if Christian's straying is foreign to him, he knows nothing of the joy of the second birth: the Interpreter does not show him into his room of rarities.

This robust pilgrim has to fight against the temptations of the flesh only. Satan does not appear before him in the guise of Apollyon, but as Madam Wanton.[262] And yet his pride is stronger than his sensuality—his human pride which, as Bunyan knew, is salutary as well as dangerous. Faithful resists Wanton by means of pride: in one fleeting vision he glimpses at the future and sees himself married to her and the slave of her desires. That is enough, and he shakes off the Old Man.[263]

Faithful's conduct shows a virility that we would admire unreservedly if we did not suspect that he himself was so satisfied with it. Faithful is rather like a continental European's impression of those Englishmen who, not content with being ' manly ', want above all things to appear so. He is one of those in whom self-respect often degenerates into respectability and priggishness. So it is not Apollyon—loathsome, but not without a certain greatness—that he encounters in the Valley of Humiliation, but dwarf-like creatures called Discontent [264] and Shame.

Whereas Apollyon makes his attack with his claws, Discontent and Shame proceed by insidious suggestions: Is it not disloyal to leave honest friends and give up an advantageous social position so as to follow worthless, enthusiastic and ignorant men?[265] (Here we recognise the habitual reproach levelled by the prosperous Anglican against the impecunious Dissenter.) Is it not *shameful* to groan over one's sins? (Groaning, indeed, for a ' manly ' Englishman!);[266]

[259] *P. P.*, p. 91.　　　[260] P. 64.　　　[261] P. 66.
[262] P. 65.　　[263] P. 66.　　[264] Pp. 67–68.　　[265] P. 68.
[266] " He said that a tender conscience was an unmanly thing." P. 68.

and contempt for the rich and powerful is a *shame* just as much as are the religious brotherhoods of the poor.[267]

We expected a verdict other than 'shame'. We expected the Conservative to reproach the Puritan with being a cause of social unrest; but Shame's reasoning turns short, and the conclusion is not what the premises prepared us for. Does he fight shy of certain words? Or does he want to give his discourse the appearance of those moralising speeches which never fail to stir the Anglo-Saxon mind?

Bunyan inserts impossible confessions into Shame's prosaically exact facts and statements.[268] This character reveals his inmost thoughts with a candour and frankness so foreign to his nature that the effect is irresistibly comic in a discreet way, for example, when he admits that it is shameful " to ask my neighbour forgiveness for petty faults, or to make restitution where I had taken from any ".[269]

But when this shrewd twister becomes so virtuously indignant at virtue and bases his most reprehensible actions on moral principles, the satire surely goes farther than even Bunyan thought. Without knowing it, our author is making fun not only of Shame but of a whole aspect of a national character.

Is it necessary to point out that Faithful, Discontent and Shame all dwell in the same man? They are three aspects of his being, presented in dramatic form; they bring before us the private debate which they are always holding in the soul of their birth. Here Bunyan profits with great virtuosity from the possibilities of allegory: it really seems quite natural for him to be breaking up a personality and restoring life to the fragments in amusing incarnations. He achieves the desired scenic effect without altering the probability or destroying the unity of the character: for every attentive reader is a creator the other way round, and the three phantoms join up again in him, the three phantoms which make up the said Faithful—proud and limited, yet solid, pure and zealous.

This rapid portrait is one of the most vivid in the book; but the reader would push his collaboration with the author too far if he attributed a greater process of 'becoming' to Faithful than he has got.

[267] *P. P.*, p. 68.
[268] Concerning the attitude of the dissenting Puritans and the Anglicans respectively. [269] P. 68.

To hold—as John Kelman does—that Christian's and Faithful's friendship changes them mutually, that Christian acquires more vigour and Faithful a wider human sympathy, is to see more in the characters than is really there.[270]

Hopeful is insubstantial and colourless beside the two other pilgrims. He is a composite character, some of whose characteristics probably come from a Bedford brother, and others from the author himself. An original and lively personality could have been born of this fusion, but Bunyan has not succeeded in creating it. His failure is not surprising. For Hopeful was introduced into the allegory only so as to enliven the dialogue and personify a Christian virtue. He had been inside the author for a short while only, and his birth does not seem to have been preceded by a period of gestation.

Indeed, Hopeful is so little real to Bunyan that in telling his story he contradicts himself. After having explained that the pilgrim's conversion was sudden and that its apparent human cause was Faithful's and Christian's steadfastness of soul,[271] Bunyan later describes him as having gone through a long evolution [272] similar to his own; and just as the tinker had opened his heart to John Gifford, Hopeful informs us that he had sought advice from Faithful, whom he knew well.[273] There is great improbability here. Faithful was a stranger to Vanity Fair, and was arrested almost

[270] Cf. John Kelman, *op. cit.*, I, 162. Most of Bunyan's critics crush the *Pilgrim's* charming sketches under the weight of forced commentaries. The most guilty is Alexander Whyte (*Bunyan Characters*, London, 1893, 3 vols.), but even the more delicate and vigorous minds of John Kelman and Arthur Porter, for instance, dangerously inflate the more firmly drawn characters. John Kelman bases his opinion about Faithful which we mention in the text on the fact that Faithful ends by calling Christian ' good Brother ' (p. 66), whereas at first he had said ' dear Friend ' (p. 63). This gives to a fortuitous change of address a value that it has not in fact got. For we might just as well point out that Christian passes from ' My honoured and well beloved Brother ' (p. 63) to ' Neighbor Faithful ' (p. 64) without in the least ceasing to be fraternal.

[271] " Now I saw in my dream, that Christian went not forth alone, for there was one whose name was Hopeful (being made so by the beholding of Christian and Faithful in their words and behaviour, in their sufferings at the Fair) who joyned himself unto him." *P. P.*, p. 91.

[272] Pp. 126–127.

[273] " I could not tell what to do, till I brake my mind to Faithful; for he and I were well acquainted." P. 128.

on arrival and very soon condemned. No one could have known him intimately.

A moment ago we were talking about a fusion of diverse elements in the portrait of Hopeful; but, as our analysis proceeds, the word seems inapt. If the moral characteristics attributed to the pilgrim had really been blended, a genuine soul would have emerged. But Hopeful is made up of bits and pieces ill joined together. Instead of drawing selectively on his own conversion to develop a psychology suitable to his creature, Bunyan systematically reproduces the whole of his own religious evolution. Indeed, he sometimes takes whole phrases from *Grace Abounding* almost without changing a word. " Yea, I thought, that had I now a thousand gallons of blood in my body, I could spill it all for the sake of the Lord Jesus," [274] cries Hopeful, echoing much too nearly his author's voice: " Then I thought had I had a thousand gallons of blood within my veins, I could freely then have spilt it all at the command and feet of this my Lord and Saviour." [275]

Hopeful is a ghost among richly vital characters.

Christiana is a very sensitive woman. She did not set out at the same time as her husband, no, but this cannot be interpreted as a failure of love. Christian, less than anyone, would commit the error of such an interpretation—he knows that conversion does not come to order. One has to set out in one's own good time when the call of God resounds in the depths of one's being. Christiana suffered from being obliged to wait, and the memory of her absent husband often made her cry.[276] But it was not until this memory really took possession of her and she had meditated on Christian's words, conduct and person that she was led to follow in his footsteps.[277] Her conversion was a movement of human love [278] and of the intelligence upheld by divine grace.[279]

[274] *P. P.*, p. 131.   [275] *G. A.*, par. 192.
[276] P. 164.   [277] P. 164.
[278] Arthur Bryant writes of the 17th-century English woman : " The thoughts always hovered round its kindly mysteries [of religion]; its pieties were her pieties, the sermons of its divines . . . her everyday reading. ' I pray to God,' writes a little bride of the year 1629 on her wedding day, ' I have got an onast religas man.' It was the motif of the whole age." *The National Character* (London, 1934).
[279] Cf. *supra*, the critical summary of the *Pilgrim*.

For Christiana has a lively and intuitive intelligence—" a woman of quick apprehension ".[280]   She grasps in a moment the meaning of the Interpreter's pictures, and for her explanation often seems superfluous.   And her need for light only testifies to an integrity and a wideness of spirit superior to the intelligence.[281]   In talking to Great-heart at the beginning she says, " Pray make that appear," [282] and she remains faithful to that attitude.

This good wife is also an excellent mother.   Her love spreads over her children.   The obedience she gets from them is the fruit of persuasion and love.   Bunyan forgets both himself and his allegory a little when he describes Christiana at the bedside of her ill son. His feeling for the dignity of life is so vital that poetry seems to spring from the most commonplace scenes; while his smiling malice tempers compassion with humour; but here is an example:

" When this potion was prepared, and brought to the Boy, he was loth to take it, tho' torn with the Gripes, as if he should be pulled in pieces.   Come, come, said the Physician, you must take it.   It goes against my Stomach, said the Boy.   I must have you take it, said his Mother.   I shall vomit it up again, said the Boy.   Pray Sir, said Christiana to Mr. Skill, how does it taste ?   It has no ill taste, said the Doctor, and with that she touched one of the pills with the tip of her Tongue.   Oh, Matthew, said she, this potion is sweeter than Hony.   If thou lovest thy Mother, if thou lovest thy Brothers, if thou lovest Mercy, if thou lovest thy Life, take it." [283]

Much tact and freshness were needed to sketch this scene and no thought of a possible smile from the sophisticated.   If the symbolism is inadequate to the spiritual requirements,[284] it is a charming picture, and Christiana appears as simple and affectionate.

The picture we get of her is of a loving and worthy woman with a suggestion of vivacity in her disposition and a great deal of courage. When circumstances demand it she can defend herself and strike at the adversary.[285]   Was Christiana suggested to Bunyan by his second wife, Elisabeth ?   It is very possible.

[280] *P. P.*, p., 185.
[281] Ker Bain understood that too; cf. *op. cit.* (1st series), p. 252.
[282] P. 194.   [283] P. 213.
[284] Cf. *supra*, the critical summary of the *Pilgrim*.
[285] " Christiana waxing very wroth, spurned at them with her feet." P. 180.

Mercy seems more fragile than Christiana, more charming, too, with her youth and her pretty face—often blushing with humility.[286] It seems that, in order to paint her, Bunyan temporarily forgot his doctrinal convictions concerning the fundamental corruption of human nature. Mercy has no dreams nor visions nor sense of crushing guilt;[287] her conversion is a movement of the whole soul: like water from a spring tranquilly following its slope. She is worried for others rather than for herself. Her fear of not being received by the Lord makes her faint at one moment, but her fervour enables her to recover and knock so hard at the door that the Lord has " a wonderful innocent smile ".[288]

She is charitable and hard-working and always occupied in making some garment for others;[289] yet she is not without a touch of mischief; for instance, when she teases her sweetheart, Mr. Brisk.[290]

Bunyan has put much tenderness into his portrait of Mercy, and nostalgia for his own youth. She is born of the union of reality and dream, of literary reminiscence and life. She is the ideal virgin of popular stories made flesh in a Puritan girl. She makes us think of Bunyan's first wife as we imagine her to have been across the reticences of *Grace Abounding*; or yet again of Margaret Charlton at the time when Baxter first met her.[291]

III. THE SECONDARY CHARACTERS

THE secondary characters testify to the same qualities of observation, and particularly moral observation. Though Bunyan was perfectly capable of seeing the concrete, he could easily overlook it when dealing with men, through his predilection for making straight for the soul. He treats the appearance of his characters in a very general way.

Great-heart and his friends recognise that Honest is a pilgrim by his " Clothes and his Staff and his Girdle ".[292] These are tradi-

---

[286] *P. P.*, pp. 171, 210, 190. [287] P. 198.
[288] P. 177.   [289] P. 210.   [290] Pp. 210–211.
[291] Cf. Richard Baxter, *Breviate of the Life of Mrs. Margaret Baxter* (1681); and J. M. Lloyd Thomas, *The Autobiography of Richard Baxter* (Everyman), appendix II; *Richard Baxter's Love-Story and Marriage*, pp. 267–277.
[292] P. 229.

tional hall-marks. Bunyan knew that rather than saw it. Ready-to-halt has two crutches.[293] Ignorance is " brisk ".[294] All that is vague enough. Unlike the naturalist novelists, Bunyan does not bother about physical details, but when he does select one it is usually characteristic and captures the imagination. But for the most part his characters benefit by the reader's additions.

Just once there is a portrait with a precise descriptive note. It is of Madam Bubble,[295] who wears " a great Purse by her Side ", into which she often puts her hand, " fingering her Money ".[296] This habit says a great deal about this woman's soul. Just one physical characteristic, and her heart is almost laid bare.

Other revealing touches give life to the portrait. Madam Bubble is no longer young, but " a tall comely Dame, something of a swarthy complexion ".[297]

When she speaks to the rich she punctuates each sentence with a smile,[298] but she laughs the poor to scorn.[299]

In spite of her important air and beautiful clothes, it is easy to guess what she is: she is a whore who offers to everybody who comes " her Body, her Purse, and her Bed ".[300] " Commune as the cart-wey ",[301] as Langland said of Bubble's forebear, Lady Meed.

But Bunyan usually concentrates on words rather than externals, and he paints his characters by what they say.

Pliable, as John Kelman [302] has so rightly said, gives a succinct summary of himself when he cries out: " I begin to come to a point." [303] What a delicious and incongruous alliance those two verbs make! Action may be preceded by long, critical examination in a thoughtful and resolute man, but the decision itself when it comes is swift. With Pliable, however, the very decision is drawn out, in fact it drags on and is never concluded. He acts when he is pushed into it, but without engaging his will.

[293] *P. P.*, p. 252.   [294] P. 113.
[295] The name is pretty, but it was common to associate the ' vanity ' of the world with the fragility of an air or soap bubble; cf. Francis Quarles, *Emblemes* (London, 1639).
[296] P. 281.   [297] P. 280.   [298] P. 281.
[299] P. 281.   [300] P. 280.
[301] Langland, *Piers the Plowman*, C passus IV, line 168, and B passus LII, line 131.
[302] John Kelman, *op. cit.*, I, 6.   [303] P. 14.

One word is enough to reveal such a spineless character, but we must be ready to catch it. Bunyan was endowed with delicate hearing and swift sight, and he further possessed the art of condensing his observations into the one stroke of irony or humour which brings them into relief. In making us accomplices in his fun, the writer almost succeeds in convincing us that we are as good psychologists as he is. We can feel intuitively at every moment how much Bunyan's writing does service to his observation. Not only has he got an exact vocabulary but he knows just how a rhythm, a mood or tense of a verb, can translate a thought or a state of mind.

Each sentence uttered by Obstinate starts with an exclamation. "What! . . . leave our friends," [304] "Tush! . . . away with your book!" [305] "What, more fools still!" [306] There are people whom one can never advise because they have invariably made up their minds in advance; and there are those who know about everything beforehand. Even if they listen to what is said to them they do not really hear. Their monotonous initial interjections show that from the first minute they have erected an impenetrable partition between themselves and the reasoning of others.

Mr. Worldly-Wiseman, similarly, paints himself by his conversation and slowly builds himself up before our eyes. This process of progressive synthesis once again makes Bunyan the precursor of the modern novelists.

We have only to hear this substantial citizen greeting Christian condescendingly in the second person singular: "How now, good fellow, whither away after this burdened manner?" [307] Then eulogising a tranquil life in a village where rent and food are not dear, where the neighbours respect the conventions, laws and morality of the moment, and carry on their affairs far from the Strait Gate.

But he says everything in such a circumspect way: "I would advise thee then," [308] "I could direct thee to the obtaining of," [309] "There I say thou mayest . . ." [310] Worldly-Wiseman always uses the conditional, for, despite his kindly words, he is profoundly indifferent to the fate of others. He expounds his own methods without really caring whether they are adopted by anyone else or not.

[304] *P. P.*, p. 14.   [305] P. 14.   [306] P. 14.
[307] P. 19.   [308] P. 19.   [309] P. 20.   [310] P. 20.

Talkative is a Puritan, at least in words. This inhabitant of Prating-Row can expatiate on the new birth, on the insufficiency of works and the need of Christ's righteousness. And what eloquence in his oratorical flow! I will talk, he says, of " what you will: I will talk of things Heavenly, or things Earthly; things Moral, or things Evangelical; things Sacred, or things Profane; things past, or things to come; things foreign, or things at home; things more Essential, or things Circumstantial." [311] He can string texts together by the hundred if necessary to establish a single point of doctrine. [312]

" For to talk of such things," he said, " is most profitable, [313] for by so doing a Man will get Knowledge of many things . . . besides, by this a man may learn by talk, what it is to repent, to believe, to pray, to suffer, or the like." [314]

But Christian does not allow himself to be taken in by these speeches. Probably he knows Talkative of old. [315] He knows that this saint-abroad is a devil-at-home; that he is harsh, dishonest and teaches deception to his children; and that his eloquence varies according to the amount of beer he has in his " crown ". [316]

However, even if he had never met him before, he would see through him at first glance. For Christian, truth is something you are, not something you know. One does not imagine religion, one lives it. So he is never the dupe of empty words. Strict in language as in actions, he soon notices the speciousness of Talkative's discourse. And even Faithful is aware of the frothiness of his opinions.

Talkative: Where the grace of God is in the heart, it causeth there a great outcry against sin.

Faithful: I think you should rather say, it shows itself by inclining the soul to abhor sin.

Talkative: Why, what difference is there between crying out against, and abhorring of sin ? [317]

[311] *P. P.*, p. 72. Compare Bunyan's vivid and active portrait with the sketch his master, A. Dent, makes of chatterers : " They are all in words, nothing in deeds. They promise mountains, and performe molehills. They will speak well of religion, and practise nothing. They will give faire words to their friends and doe just nothing for them." *Op. cit.*, p. 154.

[312] P. 72. [313] P. 71. [314] P. 71.
[315] P. 72. [316] P. 73. [317] P. 76.

But Christian and Faithful know the gulf that separates the thought from the deed, a living religion from a dead religion; and for Bunyan Talkative's hypocrisy is more odious than Worldly-Wiseman's conformity; so his satire is less merry than that of Samuel Butler; [318] the latter is making fun of an adversary, the former is lashing a false brother.

But the comic note is struck again when By-ends appears on the scene. Bunyan does not give us, as he did with Pliable and Obstinate, a mere sketch in which the line, though suggestive, remains inconclusive, but a thorough-going picture in which the colour completes and heightens the design.

By-ends is a bourgeois of short standing. His grandfather was a simple water-man and made his fortune in the individual way that we have mentioned. [319] Like a true upstart, By-ends has married into the nobility and without knowing it he gives everyone he meets the amusing impression that he is naïvely and continually astonished by his recent social promotion. Familiarly we might say that he hasn't yet recovered from it. Listen to him detailing the merits of his wife whose good breeding is so exquisite that she is equally at ease with prince or peasant, [320] and notice with what complacency he gives his family connections: My Lord Turn-about, my Lord Time-server, my Lord Fair-speech, not to mention the parson, Mr. Two-tongues and the other rich citizens. [321]

Like Dickens Bunyan excels in the choice of names, and the humour underlying these bursts forth merrily when their owners begin to speak.

By-ends' hypocrisy is so ingrained that he is unaware of it and admits with a sort of candour: " 'Tis true, we somewhat differ in religion from those of the stricter sort, yet but in two small points. First we never strive against Wind and Tide. Secondly we are always most zealous when Religion goes in his Silver Slippers; we love much to walk with him in the Street, if the Sun shines and the people applaud it." [322]

[318] Whatever was the nature of Samuel Butler's profound sadness (Dowden spoke of the gulf of gloom that opened beneath his soul) he was singularly gay on the surface. Cf. Edw. Dowden, *op. cit.*, " His jests were flashes of merriment which played over a gulf of gloom." *P. P.*, p. 279.

[319] Cf. *supra*, the critical summary of the *Pilgrim*.

[320] P. 92.   [321] P. 92.   [322] P. 92.

This is satire, yes, but it is also excellent psychology. When Bunyan puts such ingenuous words into the fellow's mouth he is amusing himself and, as happens with humorists, he is making us accomplices in his fun. But the comic element derives its piquancy from keen observation. The most cautious man sometimes lets such avowals escape him, so why not By-ends, who plays Tartuffe with almost the heaviness that Monsieur Jourdain would bring to the part?

But Bunyan goes further still in revealing the man by what he says. By-ends says that he met " a couple of far country-men ".[323] Here we have an authentic term that Bunyan has noticed, not one he has invented. By-ends tosses off this remark in a colourless voice and in so doing sums up his whole relationship with the true pilgrims. He feels that fervent Christians always dwell in another world even when they are beside him; and as John Kelman says, every Christian can make his own " the beautiful words with which Bacon closes his *New Atlantis* . . . 'for we are here in God's bosom, a land unknown' ".[324]

For By-ends, again according to John Kelman, the Church is a society with limited responsibilities; and the reference naturally is to the national Church which bestows privileges and advantages. By-ends is a Latitudinarian of the Fowler school, and probably we have in him the portrait of a type with characteristics observed in others superimposed. It is an unjust portrait. Christian, climbing his steep path, was incapable of understanding those Anglican pilgrims of the *via media*, or of appreciating their sincerity. Though he thought he was painting a Latitudinarian, in reality Bunyan was simply painting a hypocrite. What does it matter? The portrait is excellent.

This character belongs to that wealthy class that Bunyan hated in his youth and still mistrusted in his maturity. The ignominious titles that he gives the noble relatives are a further sign of his feelings. It is *lords* who deserve the titles Time-server and Turn-about. We are not dealing with vulgar jealousy here, not with ordinary prejudice, but with the astonished indignation of a man who by vocation chose the poverty that his birth had previously imposed on him. Like the Interpreter in *The Pilgrim's Progress* Bunyan cried out all his life: " Give me not riches." [325]

The satire continues in the portrait of By-ends' childhood friend

[323] *P. P.*, p. 94.   [324] John Kelman, *op. cit.*, II, 16.   [325] P. 185.

Hold-the-world who was, like him, a pupil in the school of Mr. Gripe-man who taught them the art of go-getting either by violence, flattery, lying or hypocrisy. He strings quotations, proverbs and other observations of popular wisdom together like the butler of a comedy. " I can count him but a fool, that having the liberty to keep what he has, shall be so unwise as to lose it. Let us be wise as serpents: 'tis best to make hay when the Sun shines; you see how the Bee lieth still all winter and bestirs her then only when she can profit with pleasure. God sends sometimes Rain, and sometimes Sunshine; if they be such fools to go through the first, yet let us be content to take fair weather along with us." [326] None of these remarks proves anything and yet they are put forth as highly rational. That is the dart that Bunyan lets fly—for did not the Latitudinarians always confront the blind faith of the Puritans with their rational beliefs ?

Money-love's remarks are shrewder. He is a hypocrite of another stamp—he is not his own dupe. Which is all the more reason to dupe others. The intelligent knave always has a surfeit of arguments. The casuist is never short of proofs. Money-love demonstrates that it is good for an ecclesiastic to aim at fat livings just as he proves that tradesmen are right to feign piety. After all has not Providence set benefices before the minister ? Will not his desire for a benefice increase his zeal, make him a better man and hence serve God ? So a minister " that changes a small for a great, should not, for so doing, be judged as covetous, but rather . . . as one that pursues his call, and the opportunity put into his hand to do good ". And if the tradesman becomes religious he acquires a virtue that is good whatever the motives.[327]

Our gallery of false pilgrims would not be complete without Ignorance.

It is not that this portrait is a masterpiece of humour in Bunyan's best manner, but it is curious and wrapped in an element of mystery that makes us wonder why the author was pleased to paint it.[328]

The fact is that the Puritan, proudly convinced that he possessed

---

[326] *P. P.*, p. 95.   [327] P. 96.

[328] Since this book was written, Mr. Maurice Hussey has published an important essay, ' Bunyan's Mr. Ignorance ' (*Modern Language Review*, vol. xliv, No. 4, Oct., 1949). Mr. Hussey has abundantly shown how hateful ignorance was to Puritans. He is right and we have been aware of

the truth, looked on ignorance as " a most dangerous thing " as Arthur Dent taught Bunyan.[329] The *summa theologiae evangelicae*, which the *Pilgrim* is, thus necessarily had to include one article—we mean one character—representing this major sin of the damned.

But as this task was accomplished rather as a pastoral duty, it did not inflame Bunyan's inspiration as felicitously as usual. Christian does not conceal the fact that his conversation with Ignorance is merely to pass the time: " Let us talk away the time in this solitary place." [330] This character's entry on to the scene is very lively, however. " They met a very brisk lad " [331] says the narrator and we expect to see an alert and witty fellow who will liven everything up by his presence. " A brisk lad." We had hoped for further strong characteristics after this sharp personal observation of Bunyan's: but it is likely that the phrase was a sort of commonplace, for the notion of ' ignorance ' has often been associated with that of quickness in pace and lack of maturity in mind. When Samuel Butler made the portrait of Pert—who was also very ignorant—he too described him as ' brisk ' [332] and he wrote in a notebook: " Ignorant and Sottish people are never to be prevayld upon, by those who have the greatest abilities of Reason, but by such as are nearest to their own Latitude, and have but ever so little more Sense and Capacity, as Duckes are never to be Drawn into a Decoy but by other Duckes of their own kinde." [333]

---

this for some time, but this knowledge of a historical fact does not in any way prevent us from considering the character " Ignorance " an artistic failure. We must avoid confusing different points of view.

Among other papers of Mr. Hussey I should like to mention : ' Arthur Dent's Plaine Mans Path-way to Heaven ' (*M.L.R.*, vol. xliv., No. 1, Jan., 1949). ' John Bunyan and the Books of God's Judgements ' (*English*, vol. vii, No. 40, Spring 1949).

[329] Arthur Dent. *op. cit.*, pp. 323–324. In his book, *The Progress of Sin*, in which memories of Bunyan's allegory are many, Benjamin Keach, the Baptist tailor, pastor and rival writer of our author, makes Madam Ignorance a cousin of Apollyon, thus bringing out the tinker's thought. Cf. Benjamin Keach, *The Progress of Sin or the Travels of Ungodliness* (4th ed., London, 1707), p. 61. This book was published in 1684.

[330] *P. P.*, p. 132. [331] P. 113.

[332] Samuel Butler, *Characters and Passages from Note-Books* (Cambridge Univ. Press, 1908), p. 201. " A Brisk man—Pert—Knows nothing of himself . . . he has nothing in him that is properly his own but confidence . . ."

[333] *Ibid.*, p. 455.

"A brisk lad," "a youngster." [334] Bunyan writes these words without seeing his man so he does not succeed in evoking one of those characters whose presence we sometimes seem to feel; however he gives a very precise idea of his opinions.

At first Ignorance seems like an honest citizen who respects the laws and customs. "I pay every man his own; I pray, fast, pay Tithes, and give Alms." [335]

Calm, reserved, very English, he is astonished to see Christian and Faithful accost him in such an untimely way and try to make him share their beliefs which revolt him. The Lutheran doctrine of the *sola fides* seems to him capable of leading to moral anarchy,[336] and mysticism worries him no less. Ecstasies? Visions?—mere symptoms of madness! [337]

His own faith is more reasonable. "I believe that Christ died for sinners, and that I shall be justified before God from the curse, through his gracious acceptance of my obedience to his Law." [338] In this way he associates his own works with the merits of Jesus who would have died in vain unless we led worthy lives. By His sacrifice Christ has given back a meaning to His creatures' efforts towards sanctity. He permits them to work in all confidence for their salvation.

Thus no burden weighs down Ignorance's shoulders and his path is "a fine pleasant green Lane ".[339] One could not put him off his stride by telling him that man is corrupt to the heart; has he not secret and unanswerable evidence of his fundamental goodness ? [340]

He lives in hope, a hope that is happier and sunnier than Hopeful, who nevertheless incarnates the second theological virtue. The rational character of his faith satisfies him and the intuition of his heart enlightens him yet more. "My heart tells me so." [341]

When we meditate a little on him (for Ignorance is not boldly enough drawn to impose immediate judgments on us) we see that he achieved within himself the realisation of the harmony between

---

[334] *P. P.*, pp. 113, 131.   [335] P. 114.

[336] "This conceit would loosen the reins of our lust." P. 135.

[337] "What ! You are a man for revelations ! I believe that what both you and all the rest of you say about that matter, is but the fruit of distracted brains." P. 135.

[338] P. 134.   [339] P. 114.

[340] "Mine [my heart] is a good one." P. 132.   [341] P. 132.

sensibility and intelligence. He is as remote from aridity as from unbalanced effusion and he offers the spectacle of admirable poise because he is a really manly man. And it is this unpedantic sage, this aristocratic spirit who seeks only the company of his equals,[342] this likeable and tolerant personality that Bunyan wants us to detest!

What does Ignorance represent? Who is he? According to John W. Draper he is a disciple of natural religion which took the form of Deism at that time.[343] He personifies the bourgeois sentimentality which was to lead to Shaftesbury.

Optimism, belief in natural goodness, belief in the intuitions of the heart—these are characteristics common to Bunyan's false pilgrim and the author of the *Essay on Man*. But need we mention Shaftesbury? Ignorance recalls rather Fowler and through him the Cambridge masters. In painting the " brisk lad " Bunyan really has succeeded in giving us a portrait of a Latitudinarian, whereas in sketching the portrait of By-ends he gave us nothing but a hypocrite. In his horror of ' enthusiasm ', his insistence on Christian morality and his tolerance, Ignorance makes us think of Henry More, John Smith and particularly of Robert South, whose " ways of Pleasantness " [344] and wisdom evoke the " fine pleasant green Lane " along which Bunyan's " youngster " makes his way.

And soon there appears Father Honest who is not bewildering in any way and who is very much alive.

He is an old man who shows himself from the beginning as being both grave and prudent.[345] He does not see the point of uselessly seeking out an enemy but is ready to fight till he drops when necessity arises.[346] As Great-heart nicely puts it (let us note in passing that his vocabulary has the flavour of that of the damned) [347] he is " a cock of the right kind ".[348]

---

[342] " I do take my pleasure in walking alone, even more a great deal than in company, unless I like it the better." *P. P.*, p. 132.

[343] John W. Draper, ' Bunyan's Mr. Ignorance ', in *Modern Language Review* (1927), vol. xxii, p. 18.

[344] Robert South, *The Ways of Wisdom are Ways of Pleasantness, a sermon preached at court*, vol. I of the ed. of sermons of 1737 in 6 vols. The date of this sermon is not given.

[345] *P. P.*, p. 229.　　　　　　　　　　　　[346] P. 229.

[347] He evokes the cock-fights condemned by the Puritans.

[348] P. 229.

PART OF THE FOLDING PLATE

From *The Works of John Bunyan*, Vol. 3, edited by Geo. Offor, published by Blackie & Son, 1855

Then said Evangelist, If this be thy condition, why standest thou still? He answered, Because I know not whither to go. Then he gave him a parchment-roll, and there was written within, "Fly from the wrath to come!"

The man therefore read it, and looking upon Evangelist very carefully, said, Whither must I fly? Then said Evangelist (pointing with

Then said Evangelist, pointing with his finger over a very wide field, "Do you see yonder wicket-gate?"

his finger over a very wide field), Do you see yonder Wicket-Gate? The man said, No. Then said the other, Do you see yonder shining light? He said, I think I do. Then said Evangelist, Keep that light in your eye, and go up directly thereto, so shalt thou see the Gate; at which, when thou knockest, it shall be told thee what thou shalt do.

So I saw in my dream, that the man began to run: now he had not run

far from his own door, when his wife

Evangelist. "Keep that light in your eye, and go up directly thereto." So I saw in my dream that the man began to run.

and children, perceiving it, began to cry after him to return; but the man put his fingers in his ears, and ran on, crying, Life, life, eternal life! So

He had not run far from his own door when his wife and children began to cry after him to return; but the man ran on, crying, "Life, life, eternal life!"

he looked not behind him, but fled towards the middle of the plain.

The neighbours also came out to see him run, and as he ran, some mocked, others threatened, and some cried after him to return; and, among those that did so, there were two that were resolved to fetch him

There were two neighbours determined to bring him back by force.

A page from the edition published by Samuel Bagster in 1845, illustrated by Eunice Bagster

Hence Honest is robust but his strength is undoubtedly that of an old man. Bunyan knows how to communicate a sense of the great age of this man; and to anyone who knows the difficulties of creating living people in fiction this success will seem so great that it is superfluous to underline it.

Everything conspires together to give this feeling of age. First of all—an easy method but one which the writer was right not to reject—the cumulative effect of the repetition of the words: " Old Honest," " Father Honest," " Old Father Honest." Next, the swift but sure description of a posture: in the course of a long vigil Honest begins " to nod " and become " drowsy ".[349] And above all the indefinable tone of his remarks which reveal both experience and wisdom [350] and a freedom of behaviour sanctioned by old age: he alone [351] permits himself to give a fraternal kiss to everyone outside the church.[352]

Having seen much, remembered much [353] and encountered like everyone else the kindly whore named Bubble,[354] Honest preserves enough freshness and ardour of soul to blush.[355] The touch is so light that the painter might have put it there in play; until one suddenly realises that this bright stroke was all that was needed to bring life to the canvas, light to a countenance, and a sense of nearness and friendliness to someone hitherto a stranger.

In the course of his life Honest has learnt to see people. He is the only one of all the pilgrims who is interested in physical detail and knows how much of the soul a face can reveal. It is to him that we owe the vivid description of Madam Bubble and it is he who guesses the relationship between Mr. Fearing and Feeble-mind. Have they not both got the same " whitely look ", the same cast in the eye and the same " speech " ? [356]

[349] P. P., p. 245.
[350] Cf. p. 246 : " And now it comes to mind, I will tell you a story, etc. . . ."
[351] For the kiss of peace in church, see P. P., p. 205.
[352] A liberty which throws light on this personal confession of Bunyan : " When I have seen good men salute those women they have visited or that have visited them, I have at times made my objection against them . . . I have told them, it is not a comely sight." G. A., par. 315.
[353] P. 239.
[354] P. 280.
[355] P. 229.
[356] P. 249.

His language is warm, brisk and to the point. " He was a man that had the root of the matter in him," [357] he says, and in a few words has defined the dominant quality of Mr. Fearing: that essential sincerity of a deeply-rooted faith. " We have met with notable rubs already," [358] he admits to Mr. Contrite, and by using this word ' rubs ' which signifies the small accidents of life he unwittingly reveals the humility of the strong. And finally certain forms of speech came to him naturally which even then must have been starting to age: " I was with him most an end ".[359]

Honest has concrete solidity, and Bunyan had the audacity to make his pilgrim himself point this out to us: " Not Honesty in the abstract, but Honest is my name." [360]

Honest's impact on us can serve as a contrast to Ignorance who always remains remote in spite of his psychological verisimilitude. Ignorance does not allow us to forget that he is a ' character ', whereas Honest is a friendly presence—of whom Fielding or Trollope might have been proud.[361]

V. *The Pilgrim's Progress* as a Work of Art [362]

SO all the pilgrims have passed in front of us like actors in an authentic drama.

The best among them are struggling, however imperfectly, to realise a dream of perfection, and the joy that they finally achieve

---

[357] *P. P.*, p. 231.   [358] P. 256.

[359] P. 231 : " Most an end " signifies " almost continually ". The *New English Dictionary* gives several examples of this turn of phrase between 1570–1587 and 1691.   [360] P. 229.

[361] John Livingston Lowes, art. *cit.*

[362] This section presents a bird's-eye view, but the whole of this long chapter contains remarks about the literary value of the *Pilgrim*. See for example : symbolism, p. 146; dramatic interest, pp. 150, 160; vocabulary and rhythm, p. 157; love of nature, pp. 149, 184; humour, pp. 189, 191; the quality of some ingenuous episodes, pp. 147, 148; creative imagination, pp. 173–184; indirect vision, p. 158; retrospection, pp. 148, 162; interior landscape, pp. 152, 162; the bourgeois novel, pp. 164–165, 191; the emblem, pp. 179–180; improbabilities, pp. 149; inconsistency of certain portraits, pp. 200, 201; absence of becoming in the characters, p. 162.

is not the mere exaltation of exertion and steep ascents, but the outcome of a certainty—the certainty that at the top of the mountain lies the Holy City. So from this point of view *The Pilgrim's Progress* might seem a Christian version of the myth of Sisyphus in which hope gives meaning to effort.

The worst among them provide a spectacle of pitiable humanity. They run around talking, lying and betraying each other. They make entertaining comedy . . . but where is the allegory?

Should not an allegory personify abstractions? Show us virtues and vices by means of the automatic gestures of transparent bodies? As these cross the stage we should be able to recognise each immediately and name him correctly—until we fall asleep.

But no intelligent reader has ever fallen asleep over *The Pilgrim's Progress*. And who could fasten an allegorical label on all the pilgrims? Greed, Lust, Faith, Charity . . . each of Bunyan's characters in fact represents a little more, and a little less, than these capital-lettered names imply in their abstraction.

The point is that all the pilgrims are real men—villagers on whom their neighbours have bestowed nicknames, as Coleridge has said so well.[363] First-rate actors in a comedy of manners that has an undertone of gravity, they have too much flesh and blood to be merely allegorical; but they give that vitality and clarity to the work for which it is traditionally praised.

It is fair praise and yet from another point of view absurd praise. To bestow such lofty appreciation on what is not allegorical in Bunyan's allegory is surely to pronounce it excellent for the very reason that it is weak.[364]

We are hardly exaggerating. If there existed a technician in allegory stupid enough to judge *The Pilgrim's Progress* solely by the rigid rules of the art, he would certainly declare it defective. But genius is not the slave of rules and Bunyan's story is a superb allegory in spite of everything.

To begin with it is allegorical in its wide sweep. Having based his

[363] S. T. Coleridge: consult *Miscellaneous Criticism* (ed. by Ths. Middleton Raysor, London, 1936), p. 31.
[364] Cf. Herbert Eveleth Greene, *The Allegory as Employed by Spenser, Bunyan and Swift* (P.M.L.A., IV, 1889), pp. 146 *et seq.* and particularly p. 162. This essay is excellent.

story on a universally accepted symbol—pilgrimage as an image of life—Bunyan creates a powerful initial delusion. This he prolongs by means of the union of the familiar with the unfamiliar which never fails to beguile us and close our eyes to the smaller improbabilities.

He takes us—and with what movement—into that land of mirages where reality is peopled with the divinities of dream and the marvellous lies open to creatures of flesh and blood. The first scene of the dream reveals the vitality of the rhythm, the marriage of Heaven with Earth, and the universality of the symbols.

" As I walk'd through the wilderness of this world, I lighted on a certain place, where was a Den; and I laid me down in that place to sleep: and as I slept I dreamed a dream. I dreamed, and behold I saw a man cloathed with rags standing in a certain place, with his face from his own house, a Book in his hand, and a great burden upon his back. I looked, and saw him open the Book, and read therein; and as he read, he wept and trembled: and not being able longer to contain, he brake out with a lamentable cry; saying, what shall I do ? "

Here there are three phrases in which the statements are co-ordinated and pile up without slowing down the cadence.[365] The imperfect form of the verb, which we might have expected (" As I was walking "), is rejected in favour of the aorist. This is because the sleeping man must obey the impetuous rhythm of the dream. His pilgrim's pace becomes his own. As the intoxicating movement gains on him, he strides forward into his dream and loses both himself and us there. He shows himself only so as to withdraw. After the first phrase, he disappears.

The Anglo-Saxon vocabulary of the passage quoted, with its mainly monosyllabic words, with the pure clear vowels borne along by the serried consonants, is admirably expressive of urgency. And since Bunyan describes things in their bare essential lines, he does not burden himself with adjectives. The verbs expressive of action, " I walk'd . . . I lighted . . . I slept . . . I dreamed " follow each other at short intervals so as better to sustain the force of the start. His very sleep takes on the appearance of deliberate action by the use of the verb " lay " followed by the personal complement—" I laid

---

[365] We owe some useful suggestions to J. B. Grier, *Studies in the English of Bunyan* (Philadelphia, 1872).

me down "—when a return to the verb "lie"—("I lay down ")—would have given a completely different lilt to the phrase.

Rapid co-ordination, as we were saying, is the means by which Bunyan creates an instantaneous synthesis of all the actions, similar to that which the eye receives when it first looks at a person. He obtains the effect of unity that a picture gives when seen from a distance. And owing to the intensity of the vision the man whom he paints will throw his shadow over the whole narrative; the preliminary details—the ragged clothes, the face turned towards the horizon, the book—all these will still be with us when we have reached the heart of the story.

The student of Bunyan will be continually amazed by his instinctive art. Neither Balzac nor Flaubert could have done better though they knew the value and strength of these opening pictures, and the current of energy that can be accumulated initially so that it spreads to the furthest end of the book.[366]

We were talking about generally recognised symbols. "The man in rags," as the historian, George Macaulay Trevelyan, has noted, had been a familiar figure in Protestant England since the time of Wycliffe.[367] He was a national symbol. But with a burden on his back he becomes a universal symbol.[368] Like him, we all have a heavy burden to bear. In walking beside Bunyan's pilgrim we walk beside ourselves. The sensation of movement gains on us too; and this is perhaps why *The Pilgrim's Progress* conveys so well the idea of space.

If space and horizons and free air are to be conjured up before us, landmarks on a road such as a gate, a slough, a cross and a palace are not enough. No, a feeling of muscular exertion must be induced in the reader by the movement of the prose.

It is then that the narrative and the landscape—Christian's joy and the hill, his languor and the path, his peace and the high mountain

[366] On the technique of the novel it is profitable to consult Percy Lubbock, *The Craft of Fiction* (1st ed., 1921), to whom we owe more than one valuable suggestion.

[367] G. M. Trevelyan, art. on Bunyan in *Clio, a Muse, and other Essays* (ed. 1930), p. 52.

[368] Mr. Gandhi took *The Pilgrim's Progress* as a text-book (in 1925) with his students at Sabarmati. R. Winboult Harding, *John Bunyan, his Life and Times* (London, 1928), p. 89.

—blend into the "almost unique harmony" so much admired by John Livingston Lowes; [369] and, as in modern science, the alchemies of art set a whole chain of reactions in motion, and we see the simple characters acquiring the relief of three dimensions.[370] And here Dickens again comes to mind.[371] The people in *The Pilgrim's Progress* (Christian and Faithful being the most obvious exceptions) are nearly all "flat characters" as E. M. Forster would say, and yet they are capable of swelling out, of becoming round, of giving an impression of human depth like those in *Pickwick Papers*.[372] Bunyan knew how to awake his reader's imagination. His slightest flick of the brush is more suggestive than another man's full stroke.

These effects of drawing, perspective and movement probably defy exhaustive analysis. But the *tempo* of the work is an important factor in this art of suggestion and also precision of vocabulary, the sense of the syntactical possibilities of language, the acuteness of vision revealed in the single line which sometimes sums up a character. Dimension and movement. . . . Indeed *The Pilgrim's Progress* is very far from the 'character books' to which it owes so much; it is much nearer to the novel.

In England as in France at that time the vogue for 'Characters' was raging, and Molière's Madelon was not the only person to be "furiously for portraits".[373] Bunyan tried his hand at this art as at the art of emblems and for the same reason: to teach.

The didactic value common to both these literary forms was commented on by Sir Thomas Overbury as early as 1614. Do not forget, he said in effect, that character comes from 'kharassein' which signifies 'to engrave', to make a deep impression. The 'character' is 'a short emblem'; though brief, it contains much.[374]

---

[369] J. Livingston Lowes, art. *cit.*, p. 27.

[370] We owe to John Livingston Lowes (art. *cit.*) some valuable suggestions for this analysis. [371] See *supra*, p. 207.

[372] E. M. Forster, *Aspect of the Novel* (1st. ed., 1927, ed. used, 7th, 1945), pp. 93 *et seq.* See in particular his excellent pages on Dickens: ". . . at any moment we may look at Mr. Pickwick edgeways and find him no thicker than a gramophone record. But we never get the sideway view. Mr. Pickwick is far too adroit and well trained. He always has the air of weighing something, and when he is put into the cupboard of the young ladies' school he seems as heavy as Falstaff in the buck-basket at Windsor." P. 98.

[373] *Précieuses Ridicules*, sc. 10.

[374] Sir Thomas Overbury, 'What a character is', *Miscellaneous Works*

However, unlike Sir Thomas, we do not think that Bunyan had any ambition to be witty. If he gave his characters certain oddities and eccentricities such as various English portrait-painters were aiming at,[375] it was to a certain extent in spite of himself. In fact our author attributes nothing to his pilgrims that is not really in them. He desires to be true. If he is mistaken about them it is in good faith. That is why the "brisk lad" Ignorance is sympathetic: he stands out as authentically himself across the prejudices of his painter.

When at his best, Bunyan the artist imposed on Bunyan the man the detachment necessary for lucidity. So there are no caricatures in his book. The satire is restrained. Even in the portrait of By-ends the irony is overlaid by a humour without bitterness.

That Bunyan saw and painted with justice, in spite of his religious passion and didactic will, shows that he must have had a singularly wide and strong humanity. He could not help sometimes laughing at the peculiarities that enraged him, and his anger is often involuntarily tempered with merriment. Whence the feeling of measure and amplitude which perhaps makes up the better part of his genius.

There are no grounds in *The Pilgrim's Progress* either for Butler's attacks or for the shafts of Joseph Hall and Sir Thomas Overbury,[376] and while the portraits in the 'character books' were packed tight as in a museum without ever coming into contact with each other, in *The Pilgrim's Progress* the characters cross and re-cross each other's paths, exchange ideas, and have atmosphere and perspective. Yes, Bunyan was already a novelist.

In *The Pilgrim's Progress* he wrote two novels—two dissimilar novels: a novel of character or action in the first part, and a novel of manners in the second. For the countless differences that we have noted between the two parts can all be summed up in that distinction.

(ed. by Edw. F. Rimbault, London, 1856), p. 168. See Elbert N. S. Thompson, *Literary Bypaths of the Renaissance* (Yale Univ. Press, 1923), which contains an excellent essay on the 'character books'. Consult too David Nichol Smith's essay prefacing his anthology, *Characters from the Histories and Memoirs of the Seventeenth Century* (Oxford, Clarendon Press, 1918).

[375] See, for example, Sir Thomas Overbury, *op. cit.*, p. 169: "To square out a character by our English levell, it is a picture (reall or personall) quaintly drawne, in various colours, all of them heightened by one shadowing."

[376] Sometimes, however, Bunyan allows himself facile plays on words: "He came to an ill end with his By-ends," p. 253.

The first offers a dramatic unity which is lacking in the second. It is essentially the spiritual biography of one man. Compared with him all the other characters are secondary. Apart from their own interest they are there primarily to enrich the character of Christian (even by showing up his faults) and to reveal him by contact with themselves.

The dramatic tension of the book is the tension of the hero's life, and its conclusion, far from being a literary artifice, is a supreme experience, the crowning of that life.

By contrast, as we have said, there is no tension in the second part of *The Pilgrim's Progress*. No urgency, no development of the creature in his necessity. Our interest is stimulated only by the number and variety of the companions on the road. In following them we forget time because for them time does not exist. Christian's life, on the other hand, expresses duration, if not in the ageing of his body, at least in the flowering of his soul.

The first part of *The Pilgrim's Progress* prefigures the dramatic novel in which time reveals the man; the second foreshadows those novels in which the characters live, it would seem, only so as to assert themselves as moral types—as in Dickens' overcrowded canvasses, for example.

As we pointed out when analysing the pilgrims' personalities, the style of the dialogue is vivacious, pointed and above all precise, and from these it derives its psychological value. We were looking at it from the point of view of the literary critic, but here is the opinion of a master of the theatre, George Bernard Shaw, speaking professionally: " Only a trained dramatic speaker can appreciate the terse manageableness and effectiveness of this speech . . . The sentences go straight to their mark; and their concluding phrases soar like the sunrise, or swing and drop like a hammer, just as the actor wants them." [377]

Countless examples come to mind: the conversation between Apollyon and Christian, between By-ends and his friends, the loquacity of Talkative and the tittle-tattle of Mrs. Inconsiderate. However, the dialogue does not always have this force. Indeed it sometimes assumes the aspect of a catechism class in which one little question serves as a pretext for the learned teacher to set forth his convictions.[378]

[377] G. B. Shaw, *Dramatic Opinions and Essays* (2 vols., London, 1907), ' Better than Shakespeare ', II, 143.
[378] For instance, pp. 126–129, in which Christian questions Hopeful about his conversion.

Happily Bunyan is so pressed upon by images that he seldom has the leisure to be boring. In the scenes as well as in the narrative there is a flow of charming proverbs and sound provincial expressions: " They be fine feathers that make a fine bird.[379]. . . His house is as empty of religion as the white of an egg is of savour.[380] . . . Will a man give a penny to fill his belly with hay?[381] . . . Christian snibbeth his fellow: Thou talkest like one upon whose head is the shell to this very day.[382] . . . Their king is at their whistle.[383] . . . Away with such fantastical fools from the town, a good riddance, for my part, I say of her.[384] . . . When he came at the Hill Difficulty, he made no stick at that.[385] . . . I promise you, said he, you have gone a good stitch.[386] . . . They were all in a pelting heat. . . ."[387] And always the same simplicity, the same naturalness. Bunyan is far from dipping his pen in strange ink, coining " strange inkhorn terms ", as Thomas Wilson [388]—the old apostle of the simple style—puts it. His words, polished by use, give to the

[379] *P. P.*, p. 37. [380] P. 73. [381] P. 118.
[382] P. 117. [383] P. 120. [384] P. 171.
[385] P. 233. [386] P. 254. [387] P. 200.

[388] Thomas Wilson, *Arte of Rhetorique*, 1560, ed. by G. H. Mair (Clarendon Press, 1909), p. 162. In fact Thomas Wilson was not the first to use this expression; it first made its appearance in 1543 (according to the *New English Dictionary*).

See too Roger Ascham : " For good and choice meates be no more requisite for healthie bodies than proper and apte wordes be for good matters, and also plaine and sensible utterance for the best and depest reasons : in which two pointes standeth perfite eloquence, one of the fairest and rarest giftes that God doth give to Man." *The Scholemaster*, 2nd book, *English Works* (Cambridge Engl. Classics), p. 265.

There have always been good people to commend simplicity of expression and force of vocabulary long before the Royal Society aimed at doing so. Everyone knows the celebrated passage of Sprat, the Society's first historian, in which he urges the necessity of a bare style, compact, and almost mathematical in its precision. These pages of Thomas Sprat can be found in *Critical Essays of the Seventeenth Century*, edited by J. E. Spingarn (2 vols.; Clarendon Press, Oxford, 1908), II, pp. 112–119 and especially pp. 117–118.

Consult : *The Cambridge History of English Literature*, vol. VIII, chap. 16, ' The essay and the beginning of modern prose'.

Joan Bennett, ' An Aspect of the Evolution of Seventeenth Century Prose ', *Review of English Studies* (1941), vol. XVII, pp. 218 *et seq.*

Hugh Macdonald, ' Another Aspect of Seventeenth Century Prose ', *Review of English Studies* (1943), vol. XIX, pp. 33 *et seq.*

language of his celestial pilgrims a flavour of time and a taste of the earth. They are at once expressive and modest. One forgets them in the instant of grasping them. Bunyan's style does not rise up like a screen between the reader and the story that is being told. *The Pilgrim's Progress* enables one to see how right Coleridge was when he said: "Works of imagination should be written in a very plain language; the more purely imaginative they are the more necessary it is to be plain." [389] From this point of view Bunyan's allegory could serve as a model to countless novelists to whom he could also teach the art of weaving the conversation into the story, which George Saintsbury [390] admired so much.

There is no hiatus between the narrative and the dialogue. True, the tonality and the cadence change, but our author seems always to be guided by a sure instinct of possible combinations of sound and rhythm. In conversation the pauses are more numerous, the syntax more abrupt,[391] the phrase adapts itself to the inflections of the voice and it sometimes seems that it relies a little on diction to acquire full clarity. In the narrative the current is more regular and more musical, but it too has the character of oral style.

In Bunyan the writer was born out of the orator; he was formed in the Elstow square, in barns and in fields, in the centre of the attentive circle of the faithful. Such an influence is not easily forgotten, and Bunyan listened to his phrase rather than saw it, if he saw it at all. Probably this is why it was so easy for him to move from a narrative to a dramatic scene and then back again to carry the narrative yet farther. It is always the same man who is talking, now on his own behalf and now on behalf of others. The narrator transforms himself into an actor and then the actor withdraws and the narrator reappears.

[389] S. T. Coleridge, 'Table Talk', in *Miscellaneous Criticism* (ed. by Ths. Middleton Raysor, London, 1936), p. 406.

[390] George Saintsbury, *A History of English Prose Rhythm* (London, 1922), pp. 88, 127, 129.

[391] " Then I stepped to him that pluckt him out, and said, Sir, wherefore, since over this place is the way from the City of Destruction to yonder Gate, is it that this place is not mended, that poor travellers might go thither with more security ? " *P. P.*, p. 17.

" So he said that he would show me a better way, and short, not so attended with difficulties, as the way, Sir, that you set me . . ." P. 22.

But once at least Bunyan does better still: he interlaces two stories and leads them along side by side. It is thus that the story of Little-faith is inserted into the principal narrative and that the two stories go forward simultaneously; [392] while relating Little-faith's adventures, Christian is making his own way towards the fulfilment of his destiny. And we have the impression that he lengthens his step and hastens his pace at the very moment when he quickens the rhythm of the story he is telling and has a fairly brisk exchange of words with Hopeful who is too sturdy a pilgrim to understand Little-faith's weaknesses. [393] In all these pages dialogue and narrative knot and unknot themselves with a curious virtuosity. And in the centre Christian dominates always, keeping the unity of the work intact.

But this brisk and forceful style has not a sufficiently extended register. There is more amplitude in the best moments of the sermons. As Bunyan aged, his style acquired greater softness and suppleness, but he lost a little of the breath which inspired *Sighs from Hell*, for example. [394]

There is freshness on every page, a natural dignity even in the most homely observations, subdued music in many descriptive passages, tremor in the moments of emotion—there is all that in *The Pilgrim's Progress*; but we miss the powerful harmonies of the bass and, at the other end of the scale, the free fantasy in the high notes expressive of the joys of Paradise.

But, after all, style cannot do more than reproduce a man's own thoughts and dreams, and Bunyan's could not possess a flight of freedom and fantasy that his imagination knew nothing of. [395]

However, the inadequacies and faults of *The Pilgrim's Progress*

[392] *P. P.*, pp. 115-121.

[393] And there is more. By the very manner of relating Little-faith's story, and by the compassion he shows for him, Christian reveals if not a new aspect of his nature, at least a deepening of his human sympathies. We feel that he has altered, aged, gained in broadness of spirit.

[394] John Livingston Lowes has expressed an opposite opinion that we have pondered at length, not only out of a spontaneous movement of respect for Coleridge's notable exegete, but also through the demands of that modesty that a critic of a foreign literature should always have. See, in particular, p. 40 of the quoted article: 'Bunyan's language is an instrument of many stops.' The author draws his examples, true enough, from the dialogues; and at any rate we are in agreement with him on this point.

[395] See *supra*, p. 182.

seem minute compared with its qualities. We have pointed out one or two of these and might well have indicated many more. Everything we could have said would have been true, yes, but it sometimes happens that what is true does not constitute the whole truth.

The truth is that *The Pilgrim's Progress* is one of the rare works which give man his measure—his weaknesses, his imperfections, his meannesses, but also his will, his courage and his thirst for the absolute. Bunyan does not confine himself to one extremity but he touches both at the same time, and in that lies the best testimony to his genius.

4

The Life and Death of Mr. Badman, 1680

Do not these things belong to our age ?   And is it not the
alamode in all countries among the greatest gallants ?
BENJAMIN KEACH (*Lay-preacher in Bunyan's time*)

MR. BADMAN was born of Bunyan's delight in contrast. He
wanted to confront the Christian with the Atheist, the road to
Paradise with the road to Hell.[1]

His model for Christian was largely himself; for Badman he looked
to his neighbours and acquaintance.

In 1671 the Baptist Church at Bedford had been compelled to
excommunicate Richard Deane for being " ungoldly " and " dishonest ".[2]   Two years later it was John Rush's turn, who had been
dragged from the *Swan* by three men after a bout astonishing even for a
drunkard.[3]   In 1677 sanctions had been imposed against Edward
Dent for not paying his debts,[4] and subsequently against William
Man for " committing fornication and uncleannesse with severall ",[5]
against John Stanton for beating his wife,[6] and against John Wildman
for calumniating the minister Bunyan.[7]

[1] *Badman*, preface, p. 590.
[2] " Lived a loose and ungodly life accompanied with defrauding in his
calling." *Church-book*, f. 45.
[3] " Was above the ordenary rate of drunkerds for he could not be carried
home from the Swan to his own house without the help of no less than three
persons, who when they had brought him home could not present him as one
a live to his familie, he was so dead drunke." *Church-book*, f. 53.
[4] *Ibid.*, f. 66.   [5] *Ibid.*   [6] *Ibid.*, f. 68.
[7] *Ibid.*, f. 68. This was the Church's curious formula of excommunication:
" We did then and ther cast him [Wildman] out of the church and deliver
him up to Satan for the destruction of the flesh, and that his Spirit may be
saved in the day of the Lord Jesus." *Ibid.*, f. 66.

These are a few of the people who served as models for our author's Badman. When Bunyan gave him the vices of pride, debauchery, lust, contempt for the Gospels, the habit of swearing, lying, drunkenness, sloth and tyranny [8] it was not (as James Blanton Wharey thought) [9] because they constituted Arthur Dent's list of " the nine manifest signs of damnation ".[10] Though we know that Dent's influence over Bunyan was strong, the condemnation of these sins was traditional and the author of *Badman* could not have failed to hear them often mentioned.[11] Moreover in this book he was recalling less what he had read than what he had seen and was seeing every day around him. He made no secret of his debt to the scandalous reports of his time in general and of Bedford in particular. Everything I relate, he wrote, has been " acted upon the stage of this world, even many times before mine eyes ".[12] " I have as little as may be gone out of the road of mine own observation of things." [13] He says, too,

[8] Arthur Dent, *op. cit.*, p. 32.

[9] J. B. Wharey, ' Bunyan's Mr. Badman ', in *Modern Language Notes*, Feb., 1921.

[10] Arthur Dent, *op. cit.*, p. 31.

[11] See, for example, among Bunyan's contemporaries : William Ames, *De Conscientia et eius iure vel casibus, Libri quinque* (Amsterdam, 1630), and, especially, *liber quintus, De officiis Hominis erga proximum*, pp. 188 *et seq.* Concerning Ames, the historian Richard Tawney writes : " The most influential work on social ethics written in the first half of the 17th century from the Puritan standpoint was Ames' *De Conscientia*, a manual of Christian conduct which was intended to supply the brethren with the practical guidance which had been offered in the Middle Ages by such works as *Dives et Pauper*," *op. cit.* (ed. of 1943), p. 216. W. Ames' study led us to consult, on a particular point—that of usury—a more intransigeant Puritan tract, *Usury is Injury* by Nath. Holmes (London, 1640).

Read, too, Thomas Dekker, *The Seven Deadly Sinnes of London* (1606) (Cambridge Univ. Press, 1905).

Consult the enormous in-folio ed. (1,143 pages) of Richard Baxter's *Christian Directory* (London, 1673), in which personal duties are discussed at length : " The first part is largest, because I thought that the heart must be kept with greatest diligence and that if the tree be good the fruit will be good." (Advertisement.)

A study of Bunyan's " rival " B. Keach is capable of making us understand our author's thought better—in particular in connection with *Badman*. *The Progress of Sin or the Travels of Ungodliness* (1684). We have used the ed. of 1707 (4th ed.).

[12] *Badman*, III. Preface.

[13] *Ibid.*

that he could have given many names but that he desired to render vice loathsome rather than hit out at individual people.

A penetrating observer of the lives of scoundrels, Bunyan also had an intimate knowledge of their souls. The key to Badman's character in fact lay in Bunyan's own adolescence, and he might well have found it there, and discovered the principle according to which certain failings grow and thrive; his borrowings could have been so illuminated from his own experience that they made up a living being, but in fact he has merely pieced together a character on to whom all the sins could be grafted without having roots. " One massy body of sins," as he himself wrote.[14]

" One massy body of sins." Badman could not be better described, but at the same time there could be no more apt or pithy criticism of the art that constructed him. For we have in him a painstaking accumulation, as it were, not a natural birth and growth.

" Vile bodies must not be depicted from on high," Mauriac once wrote. " They must be stronger than their creator if they are to live. He must not lead them, rather they must pull him." [15] And this holds good for all imaginary creatures endowed with intense reality, and not only for base humanity. The novelist must listen to them and follow where they lead. He must not interfere in their exploits nor impose arbitrary rules on their behaviour. But Bunyan knew nothing of these artist's scruples, these exigencies of the craft: all he wanted to do was to teach. He would not have been able to conceive of the modern novelist's ambition " to compete with the national register ", as Balzac aptly put it. It was in spite of himself, as we have said, that he succeeded in creating so many unforgettable characters in *The Pilgrim's Progress*. Bunyan possessed all the qualities necessary for giving fictional beings life—all he had to do was to let himself go, allow the theologian to give way to the Old Adam of the artistic temperament. Edifying though it may be, *The Pilgrim's Progress* nevertheless marks a victory for this Old Adam. It is quite the reverse with *The Life and Death of Mr. Badman*.

And yet what an abundance of observations there are in this book! What knowledge of life even along those crooked alleys which are the haunt of rascals! And it can hardly be said that Bunyan depicts

[14] *Badman*, III, 646.
[15] François Mauriac, *Le Roman* (Paris, 1928), p. 79.

from "on high". In order to observe the "wicked" he puts himself on their level. Sin does not frighten him. He looks it in the face so as to strike it in the face. He sets up in front of himself this personage, in whom all the vices are incarnate, and hits out at him like Christian at Apollyon or Great-heart at the giants.

Badman is a 'character' in La Bruyère's sense. He is the sinner, we might almost say sin. And indeed for the Puritan sin is a being, "our being", as Luther said.[16] If it can so be put, sin is a word with no plural but whose singular is legion. To talk of 'sins' is merely a convenient way of distinguishing between the different manifestations of an interior principle unique to man, the diverse aspects of one creature. In the same way Badman is not a living individual but a multiform entity. He is a generic portrait in which the accumulation of detail freezes the features and turns the gestures to stone. In the course of the story he stretches and sprawls rather than becomes. In following him we do not watch a man live so much as learn a good deal about the customs of the time. We are offered a series of little pictures,[17] but they are juxtaposed rather than interwoven; no warm organic current passes from one to the other so as to establish a bond of continuity in depth.

The reader must not expect to find a great romantic figure in the book, but a ruthless picture of the vices of the Restoration, and his awakened curiosity will lend Bunyan's long story such life as it has; it will pick out the aspects of a squalid life which, if transferred to the nineteenth century, would have tempted Zola. For our part, we shall follow Badman's career with a keen eye on all the details illustrative of the manners of the time.

★

He was the child of honest parents, carefully brought up and given an example of virtue, and yet he shows signs of corruption right from his childhood. His first awakening holds the germ of his whole life or, as Bunyan puts it, "his very beginning was

[16] Quoted by Imbart de la Tour, 'Luther', *Revue des Deux Mondes*, 15 Sept., 1912.

[17] Bunyan reveals his whole artistic ambition in these words: "I have drawn him forth in his features and actions from his childhood to his grey hairs. Here therefore, thou hast him lively set forth as in cuts." (P. 591.) He wrote a book that might have tempted a puritan and popular Hogarth—and the first ed. of the work appeared with five wood-engravings.

CHRISTIAN ENTERS THE WICKET GATE

Drawing by Henry C. Selous for the 1844 edition

BYWAY TO
HELL

After a design by David
Scott, etched after his
death by his brother
W. B. Scott and appear-
ing in the edition pub-
lished by Fullerton &
Co. in 1865

CHRISTIAN LEAVES HOME
Drawing by Edward Ardizzone, 1947 edition (Faber and Faber)

THE MAN CLOTHED WITH RAGS
By Thomas Dalziel, Ward Lock edition, 1866

ominous ".[18] He was among the reprobate. An implacable pre-destination had to lead him from one impurity to the next.

Bunyan made no use of his own experience, of his knowledge that the soul is not simple, that good and evil are all mixed up together. The minister imposed silence on the writer. Dogmatic belief wiped out the knowledge of the heart, and Badman was built up according to a wholly exterior logic and a pessimistic view of man based on the Bible.

Bunyan starts out by showing what his imitator, Benjamin Keach, called " the journeys of Tyrant Sin " into the realms of childhood.[19] So Badman begins with lying [20] and goes on to roam gardens, orchards and even farmyards, stealing.[21] Then he robs his own father whose death he desires.[22] His reason for swearing seems to be some sort of perverted pride and a desire to ape the great: " To swear is gentleman-like." [23] Church is detestable to him and Sunday bores him. Like the erstwhile John Bunyan he prefers " abominable books " to the Bible; but whereas Bunyan merely wished to further the flights of his imagination, Badman seeks to excite his senses.[24] He reads salacious stories rather than tales of chivalry at the house of the master to whom he is apprenticed.

This worthy man's virtuous example is lost on Badman who gets drunk and then steals to pay for his orgies.[25] Sometimes he sells goods belonging to his master and sometimes deflects certain articles to his own profit.[26] But girls and brothels soon exhaust his resources. The horrors of syphilis, which Bunyan describes with a bitter pen,[27] by no means daunt Badman and his cronies from their debaucheries.

[18] *Badman*, III, 596.

[19] B. Keach, *The Progress of Sin* (ed. of 1707), p. 68.

[20] P. 597.

[21] P. 598. Cf. *Grace Abounding*, pars 4 and 9 : " . . . laid myself open even to the stroke of those laws, which bring some to disgrace and open shame before the Face of the World ".

[22] P. 599.   [23] P. 601.

[24] " . . . Would get all the bad and abominable books that he could, as beastly romances, and books full of ribaldry, even such as immediately tended to set all fleshly lusts on fire." P. 607.

[25] Neither has bad example any importance for a reprobate : " Example is not the root, but rather the temptation unto wickedness. The root is sin within." Pp. 596–597.

[26] P. 610.   [27] P. 612.

Finally he wearies of living in an honest household and with a master with whom he gets on " as fire and water do ".[28] Badman runs away. A new master who is himself an ingrained scoundrel takes him in; but if he is glad to have an apprentice prepared to cheat his clients, he has no desire to be swindled himself. So Badman has to leave. At this point he turns his steps towards his father's house, which excellent man receives him with great tenderness. He opens both his heart and purse to the prodigal son. Two hundred pounds enable Badman to " set up " for himself and to lead a gay life, until, again penniless, he has to turn his thoughts to marrying a girl with a substantial dowry.

There happens to be one in the district, but she is so good and religious that Badman hardly seems the man to win her. Nevertheless he goes about it, and as he is no fool,[29] and also tall, good-looking and well-dressed, he has quite a few trumps in his hypocritical hand. To pretend is not difficult for a rogue when the catch is big. He does this so well that the girl marries him; and from that moment Badman returns to his whores and comes home drunk. He answers his gentle wife's reproaches with oaths. " Then she was whore, and bitch, and jade! and it was well if she missed his fingers and heels. Sometimes also he would bring his punks home to his house and woe be to his wife when they were gone if she did not entertain them. . . ."[30]

If the luckless woman wants to go to a religious service he forbids it, and when she insists he threatens to become an " informer ".[31] Thereafter this new opportunity of debasing himself and earning money is too tempting to be resisted. From the threat Badman passes to the act. He climbs trees, lurks in meadows, so as to take Baptist " meeters " by surprise.[32]

In business he plays the same successful game as he played with his wife, cajoling everyone, so as to make profits.[33] And besides his shop he has other ways of becoming rich. Neighbours who

---

[28] *Badman*, p. 614. [29] P. 619. [30] Pp. 620–621.
[31] P. 624. [32] P. 625.
[33] P. 626. Compare Arthur Dent : " I do certainly know some shop-keepers which (to utter their bad wares and to blind the eyes of the simple) do trade in lying all the day long : from sun to sun, from the opening of the shop and windowes to the shutting of the same." *Op. cit.*, p. 155.

see him leaving home on horseback at night and returning " dirty and weary " in the morning, wonder what shady enterprise he is engaged on. Yes, Badman is a highwayman.[34] He is, as Bunyan warned us, " one massy body of sins ". All the vices are within him in seventeenth-century costume.

At this time when commerce was expanding and capitalism pushing ever deeper roots, Badman discovers the swindler's trick of " breaking " —which Thomas Dekker called " Politick bankruptisme ".[35] Our crook starts a business, " drives a very great trade by selling things for less than they cost him, to get him custom wherewith to blind his creditors' eyes ". He asks them for further credit which they grant. Then he makes important purchases, conceals part of his merchandise and then suddenly stops all payment. Thereupon he sends " mournful and sugared " letters to his creditors, promises to pay them as much as he can, perhaps half-a-crown in the pound. The creditors protest and are forthwith offered five shillings which the fear of losing all makes them accept. The trick has worked. The bankrupt can lift his head and go off the richer by some thousands of pounds.[36]

Bunyan takes his time over depicting these goings-on so as to awaken consciences, for fraudulent bankruptcy was the fashion of the day. The bankrupt conceals linen, jewels, silver and merchandise. And this way of getting rich was " as common as four eggs a penny " [37] as Bunyan nicely puts it, bringing us, in one brief comparison, a whiff of the period.[38]

But our cunning rascal has more than one trick up his sleeve. He has a special measure for his purchases and another for his sales; and if his client evinces some doubt as to his honesty, Badman's employees vouch for his good faith. Find fault with such a man! And nothing would be gained by going to verify his weights for they are exact: it is the scales that are at fault!

[34] *Badman*, p. 628.
[35] Thomas Dekker : " For after he hath gotten into his hands so much of other mens good or money as will fill him to the upper deck, away he sayles with it, and politickly runnes himselfe on ground to make the world beleeve he had sufferd shipwrack." *Op. cit.*, p. 23.
[36] *Badman*, p. 628.　　　　　　　　[37] P. 632.
[38] Concerning Puritan principles in matters of commerce, cf. *infra*, Bunyan's Social Thought.

Deception as to quality, deception as to price, exaction of the
payment of bills twice over—these are a few of Badman's methods. [39]
"Nor is it my business", Bunyan says, "to rake to the bottom
of that dunghill." [40]   Yet he takes his prong and investigates, so as
to uncover the corruption of the ways of commerce.   He denounces
pawnbrokers and he denounces retailers who starve the people by
reselling piecemeal and at scandalous prices the food they have bought
wholesale. [41]   Bunyan's opinion of these "hucksters" thus coincides
with that of Thomas Fuller as expressed in his *Worthies* : "A great
famine was caused by huckstering husbandmen, those knaves in
grain." [42]

Badman, puffed up with pride, considers himself a sage among
sages, and equal to the best; [43] he is barely courteous to men of his
own rank and insolent to his inferiors.   At this point Bunyan abandons his 'hero' while he brushes in the 'character' of proud people
in general, who give themselves away by the way they hold their
heads—"Heart-pride is discovered by a stretched-out neck and by
mincing as they go." [44]   Neck, foot, tongue, all betray their presumption.   Bunyan piles up Biblical quotations [45] and strikes out
at this puppet he has fabricated and set up before himself.   He outlaws
pearls, gold and all expensive raiment; curls on the forehead, bare
shoulders and breasts.   "Why are they for going with their bull's
foretops, with their naked shoulders, and paps hanging out like a cow's
bag ? " [46]   His fierce indignation was served by a sharp tongue for
which Arthur Dent had provided the model. [47]   Who said that the

---

[39] *Badman*, p. 637.   [40] P. 638.   [41] P. 638.

[42] Thomas Fuller, *Worthies of England*, quoted by G. Offor, III, 638,
note 1.

[43] *Badman*, p. 642.

[44] P. 643.   His master Arthur Dent also sketched a charming portrait of
the proud : "They think they touch the clouds with their heads and that the
earth doth not bear them . . . they do contemptuously overlook thee as a
lyon should overlook a mouse, a king a beggar." *Op. cit.*, p. 39.

[45] P. 643.

[46] P. 645.

[47] Arthur Dent : "For when they have spent the good part of the day
in tricking and trimming, pricking and pinning, pranking and pouncing,
girding and lacing and braving up themselves in most exquisite manner,
then out they come into the streets with their pedlers shops upon their back
and carry their crests very high. . . ." *Op. cit.*, p. 40.

Puritans dressed in sombre clothes? Bunyan denounces even the
" godly " for their elaborate attire.[48]

On reverting to Badman after this digression on pride it is to
add to the mass of his sins. A liar, thief and lecher, Badman is now
as atheist as could be, or as people thought it possible to be, at the end of
the seventeenth century. " Instead of honouring God, and of giving
glory to him for any of his mercies, or under any of his good providences towards him . . . he would ascribe the glory to other
causes." [49] He throws doubt on the authenticity of the Bible:
" How do you know them to be the works of God ? " [50] And the
reader will remember that in the past Bunyan talked like that.[51]
But whereas these thoughts had torn at the tinker's heart, Badman
throws them out mechanically. Cynicism has replaced honest
doubt; facetious scepticism and denigration have ousted painful
scruples. Whereas it had made Bunyan indignant to see someone
who professed religion behaving badly, Badman gloats over the
scandal caused. " Hang them rogues, there is not a barrel better
herring of all the holy brotherhood of them ! " [52]

But at this juncture our man breaks his leg and his atheism fades
like a poor dye.[53] He prays, and Bunyan is highly amused in watching him. " He said, O God, and, O Lord, help me. But whether
it was that his sin might be pardoned, and his soul saved, or whether
to be rid of his pain, I will not positively determine, though I fear it
was but for the last. . . ." [54]

Fear makes him tremble and, with a pleasing exaggeration in the
manner of Rabelais or Molière, Bunyan shows us the patient's bed
shaking with his emotion.[55] Beneath the sustained comic note
we hear the ring of yet lighter humour when the domestic tyrant
becomes soft and coaxing. The ridiculed wife becomes " his good
wife, his godly wife, his honest wife, his duck and dear, and all ".[56]
He implores her to pray that hell may be spared him. He listens to
her, sighs, receives the ministers against whom he has railed, converses with them agreeably. The whole town talks of this big

---

[48] " I have seen many myself, and those church-members too, so decked
and bedaubed with their fangles and toys. . . ." *Badman*, p. 644.
[49] P. 646.   [50] P. 646.   [51] *G. A.*, par. 96.
[52] *Badman*, p. 647.   [53] P. 648.   [54] P. 648.
[55] P. 649.   [56] P. 650.

change, the little gossiping town which leaves its mark throughout Bunyan's book. Then the doctor brings Badman's conversion to an end. Such fears, he says, come from distemper, come from the " sick party " not being able to sleep—" for that the vapours disturbed the brain ". Rest, he advises, and " those frenzies " will leave you.[57] In this way, writes our author in a marginal note, " ignorant doctors kill souls while they cure bodies ". Bunyan's old quarrel against ignorant " physicians " who pose as unbelievers !

Our villain recovers. It is his wife who dies, unable to endure the sight of her husband resuming his debauched life. Badman does not mourn her at all nor does he want another wife. After all, he has his whores. " Who would keep a cow of their own ", he asks, " that can have a quart of milk for a penny ? "[58] However he is reckoning without the wiles of a harlot who makes him drunk to obtain a promise of marriage. Such is the irony of chance. Badman has found a creature viler than himself, for " to be plain ", writes Bunyan, " she was a very whore ".[59] She receives her lovers at home or else meets them in the ale-house. Her foul language is no less rich than her husband's. She gives oath for oath and blow for blow. The couple live thus for fifteen years at the end of which, having spent all their money in orgies—" sinned all away "[60]—they separate. Gouty, syphilitic and finally consumptive, Badman soon dies, and does so as tranquilly as if he has never committed a single sin; " as quietly as a lamb ".[61]

People have seen in Badman's end a proof of Bunyan's psychological realism, in contrast, for example, to Defoe's moralising sentimentality as it appears in the preface to *Moll Flanders*: " There is not a wicked action in any part of it, but is first and last rendered unhappy and unfortunate; there is not a superlative villain brought upon the stage, but either he is brought to an unhappy end, or brought to be a penitent; there is not an ill thing mentioned but it is condemned, even in the relation, nor a virtuous, just thing but it carries its praise along with it."[62] For our part we would say that Bunyan's realism

[57] *Badman*, p. 651. [58] P. 654. [59] P. 654. [60] P. 655. [61] P. 659.
[62] Defoe, *Moll Flanders, Works* (George Bell, London, 1887), vol. III, preface, xi. However we can contrast Bunyan even more profitably with Richardson, as Q. D. Leavis does : " Bunyan had observed the life around him as closely as Defoe, and he was free from the necessity which made Defoe a journalist. His observation is truer and his morality juster (that is to

coincides with his preconceived idea of his character. It was necessary that the reprobate should go to the utmost limit of his destiny. If Bunyan did not trace the pattern of an edifying conversion it was certainly not through his scruples as a psychologist nor through artistic delicacy. He could not have conceived of Badman making good. Even if he had conceived of it he couldn't have allowed it. The creature is not allowed to make a single free action—it is the writer's will that governs. By an act unconsciously imitative of the arbitrary decrees of his God, Bunyan had predestined his character before he was so much as born in the pages of his manuscript.

No, the realism lies always in the picturesque detail of this life, not in the line of its development. Exact precision in depicting manners, but gratuitous logic in the personal psychology. A peppering of truths on the one hand, total absence of truth on the other. Badman is the triumph of that derisory realism which asks nothing from the gust of poetry; it is the realism that would reduce sculpture to mere casting from nature, as Eugène Delacroix more or less said.[63] However, we do not wish to overwhelm Bunyan with reproaches for not having achieved what it was never his purpose to achieve; but he is big enough to do without the laurels that are sometimes thrust on him, without the homage of a traditional admiration devoid of all significance.[64]

★

When we summarise Badman's life it moves swiftly and holds the attention; but in the book it is drawn out by such lengthy digressions

---

say, wiser) than Richardson's, his version of the pattern of life is more satisfying than Richardson's, proceeding from a finer mind. In consequence he is a better novelist, and whereas Richardson's interest for the reader of Dostoievsky and Henry James is almost entirely historical, Bunyan's is intrinsic." *Fiction and the Reading Public* (London, 1932), p. 99.

[63] *Journal d'Eugène Delacroix* (ed. by Paul Flat, Plon, Paris), vol. III, p. 379. "What would be a realist art in sculpture, for example? Mere casts from nature would always be better than the most perfect imitation the hand of man could make."

[64] Cf. Edmund Gosse : "It is absolutely original as an attempt at realistic fiction. . . . It is intensely interesting, and as a story, epoch-making." *A History of Eighteenth Century Literature* (London, 1889), p. 85. That is the type of pious exaggeration. Anyway Gosse did not know Bunyan at all well. For a terse yet wise judgment see Bonamy Dobrée's introduction to the 'World's Classics' ed. of *Badman* (1929).

that from time to time we lose track of it.   The moralist lets slip no opportunity to instruct us.   If an incident in Badman's career reminds him of serviceable anecdotes he at once recounts them.   He has gleaned them from popular anthologies such as Clark's *Looking-glass for Sinners* or Beard's *Theatre of God's Judgments*, or he has been told them by word of mouth.   And he feels no reserve about acknowledging his borrowings.[65]   He is less concerned to prove his literary originality than to present old stories in new garb and give them the tone that will awaken consciences.

So Bunyan conceived his book in the form of a conversation. Perhaps he had in mind the *Plaineman's Pathway to Heaven*, but the art of dialogue was so familiar to our author that it is hardly necessary to look for models.   Arthur Dent had made use of four interlocutors,[66] whereas Bunyan makes do with Wiseman and Attentive.

The first prefers holding forth to listening to his friend's remarks, while the second prefers listening to talking.   Rare godsend for a *raconteur* to have an insatiable audience!   Could you not, Attentive repeatedly urges, could you not illustrate your meaning with some example?[67]   And that is all the encouragement Wiseman needs to pour out his anecdotes.

Bunyan intended this exchange of opinion to be living.   I have told my story in dialogue, he writes, so " that I might with more ease to myself and pleasure to the reader, perform the work ".[68]   We nevertheless suspect our author of having himself had misgivings as to his success, and of having sometimes felt the weight of monotony in spite of his perseverance.   We have ingenuous proof of this when Attentive's serene forehead suddenly puckers:

Attentive: But pray, do it with as much brevity as you can.
Wiseman: Why, are you weary of my relating of things?
Attentive: No: but it pleases me to hear a great deal in a few words.
Wiseman: I profess myself not an artist that way. . . .[69]

[65] *Badman*, p. 614, for instance, or p. 649 : " I have read in Mr. Clark's *Looking-glass for Sinners*, etc. . . ."
[66] " Theologus, a divine; Philagathus, an honest man; Asunetus, an ignorant man; Antilegon, a caviller." *Op. cit.*
[67] " Can you not give some example of God's judgments upon liars? etc. . . ." *Badman*, p. 598.   [68] P. 590.   [69] P. 633.

There is monotony in the development, monotony in the automatic reactions, monotony in the exclamations with which Attentive punctuates the recital—unless these are intended to cover up the poverty of Attentive's critical faculty. Wiseman makes him aware of this when, to his friend's reiterated phrase: " Well, this Badman was a sad wretch," he answers, " Thus you have often said before." [70] In spite of his apostle's fervour, Bunyan must sometimes have found his task lacking in "ease", to let such avowals slip out in a moment of humour!

If dialogue is to have didactic value it should be carried forward briskly and the clash of personalities should cause the sparks to fly that enlighten our thoughts. But Attentive and Wiseman are as alike as two brothers and understand each other so well that the one could have voiced the opinion just expressed by the other. [71] Bunyan almost forgets that Attentive is not supposed to know Badman. Carried away by the pace of the story he puts into Attentive's mouth words that his companion should have uttered; it is thus that Attentive begins to describe Badman's behaviour on Sundays until Bunyan suddenly notices his error. He could have scrapped the inopportune tirade and started over again in better order, but that would have been a waste of time. [72] So he merely makes his character say: " I take the liberty to speak thus of Mr. Badman, upon a confidence of what you, Sir, have said of him is true." [73] This is such a blatant correction of carelessness that it draws attention to the mistake!

[70] *Badman*, p. 637.

[71] Bunyan's error may be found in the majority of the political and religious tracts of the period. In her study, *The Dialogue in English Literature* (New York, 1911), Elizabeth Merril quotes an interesting passage from *Characteristics* in which Shaftesbury criticises the method : " 'Tis by their names only that these characters are figur'd. Tho they bear different titles and are set up to maintain contrary points, they are found, at the bottom, to be all of the same side ; and, nothwithstanding their seeming variance, to co-operate in the most officious manner with the author, towards the display of his own proper wit, and the establishment of his private opinions and maxims. They are indeed his very legitimate and obsequious puppets ; as like real men in voice, action and manners, as those wooden or wire engines of the lower stage." P. 86.

[72] And a Puritan is accountable before God for his time. Defoe says : " Time is no more to be unemploy'd than it is to be ill employ'd." *The Complete English Tradesman* (2nd ed., London, 1727), p. 50. Cf. Arthur Dent : " God doth allow none to live idly : but all, great and small, are to be employed one way or other." *Op. cit.*, p. 172. [73] P. 601.

But what does all this matter to our author! Teach, go ahead, lay siege to consciences and then take them by storm—those are his aims. He wants to think of a story that will attract and hold his reader; but he will not let this concession to human frailty hold him up on account of technical niceties.

His will to teach explains furthermore the large number of anecdotes that interrupt the sequence of the principal narrative. Just as in his sermons he accumulates quotations from the Bible as proofs, so in his story he piles up a variety of facts which are his proofs in the moral order. Here as in his sermons we find the same absence of critical faculty, the same inability to select and, above all, the same persistent procedure of a man who, both by temperament and experience, believes in the value of repetition.

But the stories are not all without interest nor are they badly told. It is well known how much Robert Browning [74] liked the one about Old Tod who one day interrupted the sessions so as to make accusations against himself. The judge saw a man enter " clothed in a green suit, with his leathern girdle in his hand, his bosom open, and all on a Dung sweat ". " My lord, he said, here is the veriest rogue that breathes upon the face of the earth. I have been a thief from a child. When I was but a little one, I gave myself to rob orchards . . . and I have continued a thief ever since." [75]

Indeed it is a good story. But where we are struck by the dramatic power of remorse and by a case of conscience that appeals to our sympathy and curiosity, Bunyan simply measured the length of Tod's list of misdeeds. He had no desire to look into his soul—either to analyse the cause of his tardy scruples, or to study the growing strength of a habit formed with a child's first theft. He saw no psychological problem, only an example to be quoted to endorse his advice: " It is pat to our purpose." [76]

" Our purpose." We always have to come back to Bunyan's didactic intentions. *The Life and Death of Mr. Badman* is a treatise on practical morality, but, so as not to frighten a feather-headed public, he had to dress himself up as a story-teller. His costume had neither

---

[74] Robert Browning, ' Ned Bratts ' in *Dramatic Idylls*, 1st series. Browning describes Tod and his wife in this line which he puts in Tod's mouth : " Worst couple, rogue and quean, unhanged search near and far ! "

[75] *Badman*, p. 599. [76] P. 600.

the gay colours nor pleasing appearance of the one Addison and Steele were to put on in the following century, and yet the one heralded the other. The faces, emerging from it, were equally grave. Bunyan had not the same views about life and the world as the authors of the *Spectator*, and yet all these men had a recognisable family resemblance. They had the same concern for practical questions, for a morality that should open out over the earth even if its life-giving breezes should come from heaven.

Bunyan's determination to write a didactic work will lead us later on to give *Badman* its place in relation to some of his other works—*Christian Behaviour* and *A Few Sighs from Hell*—and to the currents of moral thought in his time. It is as testimony to social history that the book is interesting. It is inseparable from the period in which it was born. It throws light on the history of the Puritan seventeenth century, and the more so for the modern reader who already knows something about it. Hence its value is historical; the value of *The Pilgrim's Progress* is intrinsic.

People familiar with the problems peculiar to the Commonwealth and the Restoration learn much from the detail in the *Pilgrim's* back-cloth and their knowledge is enriched by that work. Yes, but the *Pilgrim* provides meaning and interest for the reader of all time, even if he knows nothing about history. And to attach a great deal of importance to historical detail when a pilgrimage is being made by someone of Christian's dramatic tension and fervour is a kind of mis-construction. The *Pilgrim* is a work of the creative imagination, *Badman* the product of minute observation. In this book Bunyan has not recreated society; he has merely given painstaking examples of its spirit and its manners.[77]

[77] I must here record my debt for everything concerning questions of 'structure' in the imaginative works to Edwin Muir, whose critical intelligence makes itself plain in his valuable study on the novel, *The Structure of the Novel* (London, 1928).

5

The Holy War, 1682

What in me is dark
Illumine, what is low raise and support,
That to the height of this great argument
I may assert eternal Providence
And justify the ways of God to Men.

MILTON

BETWEEN 1680 and 1682 Bunyan published nothing, but worked at his most deeply meditated book, *The Holy War*. But the very ambitiousness of his design was responsible for its partial failure; he was going against the spontaneity of his genius. He, who was never happier than when his pen was running away with him, when he was being carried away by the passion of his overmastering vitality, actually spent two whole years re-hashing for the populace, and in prose, the epic that Milton had told to an élite in the most majestic poetry. *The Holy War* is a heavy work. The admiration of Macaulay and G. B. Harrison—who thought this book the greatest English allegory judged as a work of art [1]—is all the more surprising because insufficiently backed up by reasons. These two critics made only a rapid survey of the subject and did not shed on the work a light strong enough to show up beauties we might overlook. And we cannot eulogise mere arrangement of detail, as John Brown does in the course of an admittedly fuller study. If that kind of ability were a literary quality, the first place in literature would go to the detective story. Surely it is better for us frankly to admit that we cannot ourselves subscribe to all this praise.

It is obvious that Richard Bernard's *Isle of Man* was in Bunyan's

---

[1] G. B. Harrison, *John Bunyan, a Study in Personality* (London, 1928).

240

mind while he was writing his *Holy War*.[2] This popular book was published in 1627 and had reached its sixteenth edition in 1681, when Bunyan's work was in progress. In his excellent study of our author's sources, James Blanton Wharey pointed out the main resemblances between the two allegories.

There is the same central idea in both: the conflict of the forces of good and evil in the human soul. The scene of Richard Bernard's drama is Soul's-town situated in Manshire. Bunyan, seeking after a more comprehensive generalisation, took Mansoul for his theatre of war, a city lying in the Continent of Universe.

[2] Other sources have been suggested. Richard Heath ('The Archetype of the Holy War', *Contemporary Review*, 1897) held that Bunyan had borrowed his material from Anabaptist tradition and that Mansoul was Münster. A fragile thesis. The relations between the German Anabaptists of the 16th century and the English Baptists of the 17th century were too distant and too slight.

On these historical questions consult for example: Champlin Burrage, *The Early English Dissenters in the Light of Recent Research* (2 vols., Cambridge, 1912); C. E. Whiting, *Studies in English Puritanism from the Restoration to the Revolution 1660–1688* (London, 1931); W. T. Whitley, *A History of English Baptists* (London, 1932); F. Palmer, 'Les Anabaptistes,' *Revue de Metaphysique et de Morale*, special number on the Reformation, 1918.

Ernest Troeltsch shares R. Heath's opinion but brings no proofs to bear. " In his *Holy War* no less a person than Bunyan had before his eyes the idea of Münster, while his *Pilgrim's Progress* is connected with the story of Tobias in the Wanderings of Hendrik Niclaes." English translation under the title : *The Social Teaching of the Christian Churches* (2 vols., London, 1931) of his book *Die Soziallehren der Christlichen Kirchen und Gruppen* (1911). This phrase is an example of groundless affirmation in a serious work that we admire a great deal. We come back to solid proofs and arguments with G. R. Owst (*Literature and Pulpit in Medieval England*, Cambridge, 1933) (cf. Chap. ii, Scripture and Allegory), who points out how certain images of medieval rhetoric were carried right into the 17th century by popular tradition of sacred eloquence. Bunyan owes much to Richard Bernard, but his debt to contemporary sermons is by no means negligible. This whole chapter, as, indeed, Owst's whole book, deserves to be read. We will quote one passage of importance to us here : " . . . This use of the figure of the ' Castle of Mansoul ' in English preaching can actually be traced back to a sermon of the so-called *Lambeth Homilies* compiled approximately at the end of the 12th century.

" According to Bromyard the foundation of the fortress is Faith ; its outer wall is Charity, its lofty keep is Hope ; its inner ramparts the other virtues ; its gates, the five senses ; its hidden postern, the thoughts of the heart ; its janitor, the Will ; its castellan, or constable, the Reason." P. 80.

The centre of interest in Richard Bernard is an inn called the *Heart*; in Bunyan a palace which a marginal note tells us is the heart. Five doors give access to the inn, called Hearing, Sight, Taste, Smell and Touch; five gates lead into Mansoul called Eargate, Eye-gate, Mouth-gate, Nose-gate and Feel-gate.

There are obvious resemblances between people's names. Bernard has a Wilful-Will and Bunyan a Lord Will-be-will. Enlightened Understanding is the First Constable on the Isle, and my Lord Understanding the Mayor of Mansoul. Conscience is Judge of the Isle and the Recorder of Mansoul.

But, as always, Bunyan was not at the mercy of his memory. Rather than hinder his imagination, his memories give it a firmer flight; so much so that the points of contact between the work under creation and the one momentarily recalled are merely similarities of structure and verbal analogies.[3] The spirit is altogether different. Apostle and psychologist, Bunyan improved on what he borrowed in the interests of his own self-expression and so as to convert his contemporaries. From fragments of cast-off clothing he created a new garment; we might have said new finery, had the art been greater and the form more beautiful.

*

Self-expression for Bunyan meant to re-live his own conversion yet again. The scattered allusions in his sermons were followed by a total confession in *Grace Abounding*; the suggestions surrounding Christian, by *The Holy War*. From detailed sketches to sweeping frescoes, from an intimate private narrative to a generalisation of

---

[3] It is astonishing to see the calm assurance with which critics sometimes affirm that Bunyan had read such and such a book. It is thus that Edmund Arbuthnott Knox (*John Bunyan in Relation to his Times*, London, 1928, p. 107) writes that our author borrows from *Paradise Lost* the council of the fallen angels and Satan's flight towards earth. It is certainly possible that Bunyan could have had Milton's poem in his hands, but no proofs could be based on such vague resemblances. It is more fitting to know that Benjamin Keach, Bunyan's constant rival, had written a Miltonian poem which the humble people of Bedford read rather than *Paradise Lost*; cf. *The Glorious Lover*, a divine poem upon the adorable mystery of sinners redemption, by B. K., author of *War with the Devil* (3rd. ed., London, 1685). Chap. 7 describes the council of the fallen angels (p. 74) in which Apollyon, Beelzebub, Satan and Lucifer all want war. As in Milton, Satan undertakes the journey to the Earth alone (p. 77).

personal experience, from the pilgrimage of a single man to the struggles of a populous city that is watched by the whole universe— what a proud exaltation of self! But at the same time how significant the enlargement is! To know one person's soul is to guess at each man's.

Thus conversion constitutes the principal theme of the new work, but others are introduced in counterpoint. As in a fugue, now one voice and now another holds our attention; but Bunyan's knowledge of harmony was not sure enough to enable our ear to appreciate each new theme as it comes. *The Holy War* is too overloaded to satisfy the aesthetic sense.

In this work we are intended to read: a symbolic story of the fall and the resurrection of man, an account of the events of Bunyan's time, and, if we are familiar with the belief in the millennium which the seventeenth-century sects had, a prefiguration of the New Jerusalem.

Four themes are thus interwoven which should rightly correspond with each other and finally melt into a single chant; but as it is each is struggling to assure its own victory, and where harmony should reign we have confusion.

★

Mansoul is in Universe. " Well watered, richly adorned with hills and valleys," it is " very fruitful, well peopled and has a very sweet air "; and Bunyan did not see it in the light of a dream, but visited it, he says, in the course of his travels.[4] Hence his epic begins in the manner of many celebrated stories, for example *Gulliver's Travels*, which derives a thousand precise details from a fancied reality.

In Mansoul the people are not all alike. Language, mode and way of religion vary " tis said " like the planets.[5] However the author soon learns the essentials of the languages of the different regions and makes the manners and customs his own. The life pleases him and Mansoul would have become his adopted country " had not my Master sent for me home to his House there to do business for him, and to over-see business done ".[6] The opening of the book is one of its few beauties. In this phrase Bunyan sums up his whole life. No details. He is surveying his past from on high so as to understand its

[4] *Holy War*, ed. *cit.*, p. 7.   [5] P. 7.   [6] P. 7.

direction and impulse. And with one simple and noble curve, the allegory encompasses a whole life dedicated to Christ.

Mansoul was built by a certain King Shaddai for his own pleasure. In its centre there rises a stately palace—" for strength a castle, for pleasantness a paradise ", and " copious " enough to contain the world but where Shaddai wishes to rule alone.[7] The City itself is surrounded by walls so strong that no outside force can break them down without the consent of the inhabitants. " A house ", Péguy was to say later, " will never perish except from within."[8] This is Bunyan's thought. At the beginning, then, beauty and harmony reign in Mansoul.

But elsewhere there lives the giant Diabolus, " a great and mighty prince, and yet poor and beggarly ".[9] The phrase is pregnant with a promise that is not to be fulfilled. It encourages us to expect a grandiose picture of the devil, a Satan whose beggarliness comes from his own knowledge of his fall; yet, though Bunyan does not deny Diabolus a free intelligence nor deform his devils along the lines of medieval imagination, he is nevertheless incapable of rising to Milton's moving conception of angels still glowing with divine reflections and carrying in their breasts the incurable and anguished longing for the paradise lost. " Majestic, though in ruin." [10]

To be revenged on Shaddai, Diabolus decides to make an assault on Mansoul. He summons a council and no voice is raised in favour of peace.[11] So the devils make themselves invisible and set out for Ear-gate. Diabolus approaches the fortified wall by himself, sounds a trumpet and addresses a discourse to the chiefs of Mansoul

[7] *Holy War*, p. 8.

[8] Charles Péguy, *L'Argent*, chap. I (N.R.F.)

[9] *Holy War*, p. 9.

[10] *Paradise Lost*, II, 299.

[11] In this Bunyan's epic resembles that of Benjamin Keach (*op. cit.*), in which Apollyon, Beelzebub, Lucifer are all in favour of war (" Shake off your fears," " My sentence is for war," " Come shew your valour, I'll command the van," p. 76), while Milton makes Belial and Mammon advise peace :

" Thus Belial, with words clothed in reason's garb,
    Counselled ignoble ease and peaceful sloth." (II, 226–227.)

" . . . all things invite
    To peaceful counsels. . . ." (II, 278–279).

which we would appreciate more if we did not remember the simplicity of the Bible story. Bunyan can never escape from this comparison. His fluent and subtle paraphrase offers a painful contrast to the economical and stark story in the Book of Genesis. And we must be generous enough to forget one grotesque metaphor: " At this the town of Mansoul began to prick up its ears." [12]

While Diabolus is talking, a fury, Tisiphone (for Bunyan's hell combines in one and the same horrific vision the monsters of pagan fable and the fallen angels of the Bible) slays Captain Resistance, the most valiant of the townsmen. Without him the will of the inhabitants collapses. Mansoul, " wholly left naked of courage ",[13] gives way to the temptation of surrender, and Diabolus marches in, warmly applauded by a changeable and soulless people.[14]

Installed in the fortress of Heart, the devil sets about reshuffling the magistrates. Like Charles II, he sacks the men who resisted him and installs his own followers.[15] The Biblical theme disappears at this point, and contemporary history breaks into the story. For in 1681, while Bunyan was working on *The Holy War*, Charles was embarking on his warfare with his people. He dissolved his Fourth Parliament and, if he called a Fifth, it survived for a week only. But its dissolution was an expedient; we must get to the root of the trouble, and this lay in the choice of the burgesses. The corporations chose the burgesses and hence the King resolved to secure control of the corporations.[16]

In Bedford, for example, in the spring of 1681, Miles Wale and Andrew Freebody, both chamberlains of the town, were suspended from their functions for not having taken the Sacrament at church within twelve months of their election.[17] In December the Recorder, Robert Audley, was nearly dismissed at the request of the Earl of Aylesbury; but he went to the King himself, reminded him of his loyalty to his father's cause, and stated boldly that he had never frequented a conventicle in his life, but might do so some day as conventiclers preached so much better than Churchmen.[18] The

[12] *Holy War*, p. 14.   [13] P. 16.   [14] P. 17.
[15] Consult, for example, David Ogg, *England in the Reign of Charles II* (1934), vol. I, pp. 198–199.
[16] Concerning all this see John Brown, *op. cit.*, p. 327.
[17] *Ibid.*, p. 328.   [18] *Ibid.*, p. 328.

King left him in his place and did not resume his warfare against
the Bedford Corporation until 1683, and he concluded it in 1684, two
years after the publication of *The Holy War*. This did not matter:
from the opening phases of the conflict Bunyan could guess what the
outcome was to be,[19] and could cull scenes for the work in hand.
For example the eulogy of Mr. Recorder Conscience can be interpreted as homage to Robert Audley, Recorder of Bedford. " He
was a man of courage and faithfulness, to speak truth at every occasion;
and he had a tongue as bravely hung as he had an head filled with
judgment. Now this man Diabolus could by no means abide;
because he could not by all wiles, trials, stratagems and devices make
him wholly his own." [20]

He could not make him his own, no, but he succeeded nevertheless
in degrading him by luring him into debauchery. Time and again
Mr. Recorder tries to pick himself up, and he roars and thunders
against vice, but no one takes him seriously. He annoys my Lord
Will-be-will, a man of high birth, courageous and resolute, but
whose pride leads him to commit treason. This nobleman rallies to
Diabolus because he does not want to be in a position of obedience,
but prefers honours and privileges.

With him Lord Lustings and Mr. Forget-good also defect and
become respectively Mayor and Judge. Then the small fry of the
bourgeoisie : " For who doth not perceive, but when those that sit
aloft are vile and corrupt themselves, they corrupt the whole region
and country where they are ? " [21] Thus the following become
officers, governors and magistrates : Mr. Incredulity, Mr. Haughty,
Mr. Swearing, Mr. Whoring, Mr. Pitiless, Mr. Drunkenness and Mr.
Atheism.

At this point the allegory has a double meaning. Sharp and
clear, a stylised sketch of Restoration manners detaches itself, heightened by a streak of humour : " And let this serve to give a taste to
them that love to hear tell of what is done beyond their knowledge,
afar off in other countries." [22] But across this sketch can be dis-
cerned the story of a soul whose will is degraded and whose conscience
is asleep. The author wants to express at one and the same time
the drama of a single man and the drama of a whole generation—

---

[19] Bunyan knew, furthermore, what was going on in other towns.
[20] *Holy War*, p. 19. [21] P. 25. [22] P. 25.

and he is not unsuccessful when the symbols of both one and the other happen to coincide.

King Shaddai hears of the surrender of his town. A messenger gives him a detailed account of the work accomplished by Diabolus, and in this summary, quite lacking in art, Bunyan can once again take his bearings and make in his book one of those massive joints which he judges necessary. There follows the grief of King Shaddai and the grief of his son—although both had foreseen the defeat of Mansoul [23] and wanted to lose it so as the better to regain it.[24] Emmanuel offers himself to fight Diabolus and reconquer the City.

But the devil knows all about the royal intentions. He keeps a keener watch over the town than ever and demands of the inhabitants a new oath of allegiance which they all accept. " As if it had been a sprat in the mouth of a whale, they swallowed it without chewing." [25]

One of Diabolus' henchmen, Mr. Filth, spreads throughout the country " writings whereby he granted and gave licence to all to do whatever their lustful appetites prompted; no man was to let, hinder or control them ".[26] To invite Mansoul to wallow in sin was surely a means of alienating King Shaddai. But the astute devil does not stop there. He announces to the inhabitants the imminent arrival of Emmanuel and falsifies the purpose of his coming. The prince is coming to destroy them " root and branch ", he says.[27] For this devil has as sharp a tongue as Bunyan's contemporaries! He provides his followers with helmet, breastplate, sword and shield —ancient weapons but endeared to the tinker by romantic tradition. They lend themselves to satire under cover of the allegory, and a marginal note made by Bunyan in this connection is revealing: " It is a symbol for our time . . ." (Apocalypse, IX, 9). The helmet, Diabolus explains, represents the hope of salvation whatever kind of life one leads; the breastplate is a hard heart that is not afraid of the judgment and can never give way to compassion; [28] the shield is unbelief.[29]

Meanwhile Shaddai's army, with banners flying in the wind and led by four Captains—" rough-hewn men ",[30] " stout generals " [31]—

---

[23] *Holy War*, p. 28.   [24] P. 29.   [25] P. 31.
[26] P. 31.   [27] P. 33.   [28] P. 34.
[29] P. 35.   [30] P. 37.   [31] P. 36.

arrives, 40,000 strong, in front of the town. Throughout their march his men have lived at the King's expense without robbing or ill-treating anyone, as disciplined as Cromwell's soldiers.[32] Before opening fire the captains try to recall Mansoul to loyalty. These speeches resemble the dialogue of a soul at war with itself, yet they are so stiffened by the logic of oratorical statement and rhetoric that they are incapable of following the leaping, tormented progress of the self's language with self. Some inner flame nevertheless manages to give a glow to one or two of the passages cast in a Biblical style: " For he is the former of all things, and if he touches the mountains, they smoke. Nor will the gate of the King's clemency stand always open; for the day that shall burn like an oven is before him, yea, it hasteth greatly, it slumbereth not." [33]

The battle between Shaddai and Mansoul is at first indecisive so as to follow the ebb and flow of the inner conflicts that Bunyan himself had undergone. For a whole summer blows are exchanged without any apparent result. And yet within the City a change is taking place. With the incessant sounding of the alert, fear is making its inroads, as in a soul where the conscience is awakening. Winter comes, unprecedentedly mournful. " That Winter was to the town of Mansoul a Winter by itself." [34] In vain Mr. Anything has recourse to all his artifices, the town feels new thoughts surging within it.

Anything . . . a name that is a whole conception of life! But this person lives only by virtue of our recollection of his forebears, By-ends in *The Pilgrim's Progress*, or the glorious Latitudinarian in *The Defence of the Doctrine of Justification*—for there is no clear-cut outline nor any of the incisive observations that paint a soul. And in this lack alone we can measure all that *The Holy War* loses in interest through not depicting really visual or vital people.

Mansoul, thoroughly upset, engages in conversations with Shaddai's captains. The town would recognise their King's authority if their Lord Mayor, Forget-good, could be left them, if it could be guaranteed

[32] According to contemporary evidence quoted by Sir Charles Firth : " No man swears but he pays twelvepence; if he be drunk he is set in the stocks or worse. How happy were it if all the forces were thus disciplined." *Oliver Cromwell and the Rule of the Puritans in England*, p. 92.
[33] *Holy War*, p. 46. [34] P. 53.

248

that none of Diabolus's servants would be ill-treated, and if the satanic rights and privileges were respected.   Here again the progress of the story is dictated by Bunyan's personal memories, and now it is the theme of conversion that has almost ousted the others—the fear of a soul which hears God's voice and desires to respond without, however, renouncing the delights of the world.   " Thus, I said unto God, depart from me for I desire not the Knowledge of thy ways." [35]

But how much more vital was the song of *Grace Abounding*! In the present work it is inserted into too vast a symphony and so loses in emotional vigour.   The orchestration, which should amplify it, deprives it of the persuasive fervour that one soul's frank confession should offer to another soul.   In reading *Grace Abounding* we followed the debate between faith and reason with ever-renewed interest, whereas Mr. Incredulity's arguments, though following the same rationalist dialectic, leave us cold. [36]

At the same time we must not overlook the felicitous choice of allegorical vocabulary.   Whereas the Diabolonians appeal to reason alone, Shaddai's subjects had in the past consulted Mr. Understanding, their Mayor.   By this simple opposition of words, the author shows how bleak the philosophy of rationalism seems to him; for reason is but one of the properties of that Understanding which can and should embrace the irrational truths as well as the rational ones.

Meanwhile the town, just like a man, revolts.   The revolt which breaks out is in the image of the confusion of the spirit, [37] so it is not without surprise that we notice Bunyan's face brightening with a smile in spite of everything.   The explanation is that the allegorical transposition leads him to describe material combat, and we know how much he enjoys brisk hand-to-hand " broils ". " And it made me laugh to see how old Mr. Prejudice was kicked and tumbled about in the dirt . . . [38] and his crown soundly cracked to boot! " [39]   As for Mr. Anything, if he only has a broken leg— though " he that did it wished it had been his neck "—he nevertheless provides an entertaining spectacle! [40]

---

[35] *G. A.*, par. 10.   [36] Cf. *Holy War*, p. 57.

[37] " And with that every man began to tell his own tale, so that nothing could be heard distinctly."   P. 61.

[38] *Holy War*, p. 61.   [39] P. 62.   [40] P. 62.

That is what is good in the tradition of the popular story and Bunyan's laugh resounds clear and young. But these skirmishes seem puerile in an epic and cannot translate the grievous dualism of the heart.[41] Moreover the merriment is out of harmony with the true state of a spirit on the road to conversion. In such a case, the new man does not gleefully triumph over the old. Hence the allegory falsifies the meaning of the battle in which a divided soul is always engaged. This "old man", this Myself which is overcome little by little, cannot be represented by the same symbol as a flesh-and-blood enemy such as Mr. Prejudice or Mr. Anything. The passion of a soul victorious over itself is not of the same quality as the passion of a partisan who is crushing an adversary; one is pure while the other is covered with dross. And if they have not the same *timbre*, how can they be reconciled in the counterpoint? Bunyan had not enough artistic sensibility to perceive the mistake he was committing, and it must also have escaped his biographers and critics, for they have not pointed it out.

Stripped of convincing spiritual significance, the battles of Mansoul recall more aptly the conflicts of the time. Diabolus imprisons Lord Understanding and Mr. Conscience as Charles II imprisoned the Puritans. And the devil—as ironical as the English monarch—asks why, if Shaddai is powerful, are his subjects enslaved? "None in the universe so unhappy as they." [42]

The forces of evil increase, but their triumph is ephemeral: Emmanuel's army is on the march. The description becomes more animated, pulsating with the lilt of trumpets and the flapping of banners, scintillating and golden in the reflection of hope. For here was Bunyan's consolation, and that of all those who believed in the millennium. For them, in fact, Emmanuel was Jesus as Governor of the world.[43] Was not Emmanuel the name of the King under whom Isaiah predicted the fulfilment of the millennium? [44] If Bunyan had too much good sense to share the revolutionary illuminism of the fanatics known in history as "Fifth Monarchy men", he never-

[41] Whereas Christian's single combat with the monster Apollyon expressed this private conflict admirably.

[42] *Holy War*, p. 64.

[43] As always, York Tindall gives many and interesting references to contemporary works, *op. cit.*, chap. vi, p. 150.

[44] Isaiah, vii, 14; cf. York Tindall, *op. cit.*, p. 150.

theless believed in the Fifth Monarchy [45] like most of the Baptists of the period.

Mansoul opposes the redemption offered by Prince Emmanuel out of respect for the laws and customs of the city. " We are bound by the law and the custom of this place." In putting this avowal on the lips of corrupt men, Bunyan shows his contempt for social conformity, and lets us guess at a political attitude that we shall study further on.

Then Diabolus himself speaks and tries the effects of his dialectic on Emmanuel. [46] Very clever, and ready to accept a compromise if necessary, [47] Diabolus has the appearance and the soul of a humanity without greatness. Perhaps this conception of the diabolical is good psychology: are not men simply mediocre cads rather than criminals on a big scale ? But the epic demands something loftier, and here again Diabolus offers a pitiable contrast to Milton's Satan.

The ruse fails. The compromises are rejected. Emmanuel, victorious, penetrates into the city and the townspeople await the sentences of justice in fear and trembling. Several times they implore his mercy and the successive messengers who are sent to approach him —Wouldlive, Gooddeed and Weteyes—recall yet again the episodes of conversion. Humility fills their hearts and one of them cries out, like Bunyan in the past: " I see dust in mine own tears, and filthiness in the bottom of my prayers." [48] When they are finally pardoned, they abandon themselves to joy. The bells ring, the people sing and the royal troops execute some impeccable manoeuvres in the manner of Cromwell's army. [49]

---

[45] Cf. Robert Barclay: " The idea of the near approach of a ' Fifth Monarchy ' was most widely spread, and this must not be identified with the opinions of the few crazy enthusiasts called ' Fifth Monarchy men '," *op. cit.*, p. 182, note. It seems moreover probable that at the time of the Venner revolt the ' Fifth Monarchy men ' had quite a following among the Baptists; cf. W. T. Whitley, *A History of British Baptists* (London, 2nd ed., 1932), p. 109.

Bunyan's friend, Henry Jessey, was a ' Fifth Monarchy man '. Observe that in his *Differences in Judgment about Water Baptism*, II, 617, Bunyan considers his meeting with H. Jessey to be ' providential '.

On all this question read York Tindall, *op. cit.*, chap. vi, ' The Holy City '.

[46] *Holy War*, p. 72. [47] P. 84. [48] P. 101.

[49] " They marched, they counter-marched; they opened to the right and left; they divided and sub-divided, then closed, they wheeled, made good

Then the Prince clothes the citizens in white garments, a ceremony pregnant with significance (as the marginal reference that Bunyan gives [50] would remind us if it were necessary), for those readers in whom there burned the hope of the Holy City!

After the merry-making, Emmanuel prepares for future work: he puts honest and enlightened men in positions of command. If Mr. Understanding becomes Mayor again, and Mr. Knowledge is made Recorder, it is because Bunyan wants to express his respect for the intelligence and affirm, yet once again, that ignorance cannot serve as an excuse.

Finally a good number of Diabolonians are judged and crucified.[51] The charter is renewed. And as Emmanuel believes that the people should have teachers, he gives them two. The first is Shaddai's Lord Chief Secretary, and the interpreter of his will: Spirit. The second, a simple citizen, is no other than our old friend Mr. Conscience to whom falls " the teaching of moral virtues and civil and natural duties ".[52] Apart from these two masters in thought, Mansoul will have other men to direct it, and the Captains of Shaddai's army are pastors as well as soldiers. Finally the tranquillity of order can reign in Mansoul, for everyone has a place in which he can work in obedience and joy.[53]

The book should close on this vision of a regenerated world; it would gain in compactness. But Bunyan had not yet expressed his whole thought and did not want to cut short the learned interlacings of his allegorical themes, even though the continuation of the story after Emmanuel's triumph—which we had hoped definitive—can only be full of improbabilities.

Why was Diabolus not crucified with the rank and file of his servants ? Why be so hard on the subordinates and spare the chief ? Why was Mr. Incredulity allowed to escape ? Is it possible that Emmanuel was unable to arrest all the Diabolonians within Man-

---

their front and rear with their right and left-wings, and twenty things more, with that aptness, and then were all as they were again, that they took, yea, ravished the hearts that were in Mansoul to behold it." P. 3.

[50] Apocalypse, XIX, 8. It was on this book that belief in the millennium was founded ; cf. H. Knollys, *An Exposition of the Whole Book of Revelation* (1689).

Henry Danvers, *Theopolis, or the City of God, New Jerusalem* (1672).
[51] *Holy War*, p. 135. [52] P. 141. [53] P. 150.

soul ? As J. A. Froude puts it so well, Bunyan is merely propounding yet again and with added complications the mystery which he set out to explain.[54] We should really say the triple mystery: the historical and supernatural mystery of Christ's Incarnation and the Redemption, the mystery of the conversion of an individual soul, and finally the mystery of the apocalyptic hope in a Second Coming of the Saviour.

But Bunyan could not conclude his book on a note of peace and a vision of Paradise, when every day and all round him he saw English " Diabolonians " pursuing their nefarious practices under the leadership of Diabolus-Charles II. He could not allow himself such a happy ending when, in spite of his doctrine of election, he knew and felt conversion to be always incomplete. Finally, like all the millennarians, he believed that evil forces would still persist during the millennium itself,[55] and that during the last phase of the Fifth Monarchy there would be a new fall, Gog and Magog descending on the New Jerusalem. " Indeed after this New Jerusalem hath had her golden day in this world I say, just towards the ending thereof, she will yet once again be beset with raging Gog and Magog." [56]

The artisan of Mansoul's fall is a certain Carnal-security, son of Presumption and Fearless. Here Bunyan is illustrating one of his strongest convictions: namely that for a Christian, the absence of all tension is a danger.

Carnal-security incites the inhabitants of Mansoul to forsake Emmanuel, who thereupon withdraws from the city.[57] But Godly-fear manages to warn Mr. Conscience, and the repentant citizens lead the advocate of the easy life to the stake.[58]

An appeal is made to Emmanuel to return, but he does not answer. Encouraged, the Diabolonians write to their master to come and recapture the town. The townspeople determine to fight the devil's army, alone if necessary; however, once the battle has started,

---

[54] J. A. Froude, op. cit., p. 119.

[55] Cf. Holy City, III, read p. 448, all the right-hand column, and in particular : " I am not yet convinced that the highest church-state that ever was, or ever will be in this world, could possibly be so, all of them, the elect of God, but that there would get in among them some that had not saving grace ; the same also I believe touching the state of this Jerusalem."

[56] New Jerusalem, III, 447.

[57] Cf. Holy War, pp. 150 and 153.   [58] P. 157.

Emmanuel comes with help. He comes and he conquers. Meanwhile the Bloodmen, among whom Bunyan puts the Pope, do not consider themselves to be beaten. They return to sow the seeds of doubt in souls, but they are finally arrested and executed.

In a last speech Emmanuel explains his work, promises that Mansoul will one day become a celestial city,[59] and concludes with these words: " I will put upon you none other burden; but that which ye have already, hold fast till I come." [60]

The apocalyptic theme has finally effaced all the others. A song of hope, indeed of certainty, surely gave the initiated all the justification they needed for suffering and fighting.

★

As a personal document, and as historical evidence, *The Holy War* is not without importance; and, if it is too long-drawn-out and overweighted and obscure to add very much to Bunyan's literary glory, its perusal reveals, perhaps better than any other of his works, the scope, strength and delicacy of his spirit. One cannot help admiring so much knowledge, so much ability in the art of overlaying the meaning, in a simple brazier or tinker—a craftsman so humble that Richard Baxter aligns him with beggars and other illiterate down-and-outs.[61] *The Holy War* shows above all, as we have never failed to point out, that its author was aware of the complexity of mental life and that he knew how to remain balanced even when judging his enemies. There is something lofty about Mr. Whoring in spite of his swaggering,[62] and Mr. Haughty is so worthy that even the judges have to acknowledge it.[63] My Lord Will-be-will is heroic in battle.[64] And so the psychology of his people is enriched by the impartiality of his judgments.

[59] *Holy War*, p. 248.

[60] Apocalypse, II, 24–25.

[61] Richard Baxter : " If any would raise an army to extirpate knowledge and religion, the tinkers and sowgaters and crate-carryers and beggars and bargemen and all the rabble that cannot reade, nor ever use the Bible. . . ." *The Poor Husbandman*, ed. Powicke (Manchester Univ. Press, 1926), p. 24.

[62] *Holy War*, p. 122.

[63] Mr. Haughty's language is firm and brisk like his soul : " Gentlemen, I have always been a man of courage and valour, and have not used, when under the greatest clouds, to sneak or hang down the head like a bulrush." P. 131.

[64] " . . . The valour of the Lord Will-be-will, etc. . . ." P. 51.

As always with Bunyan, there is also much that is picturesque—oddities that are malicious and naïve at the same time, amusing effects based on the beliefs of our author and his contemporaries. Seeing the universe according to Ptolemy's conceptions, Bunyan tells us that the joy of Emmanuel's soldiers rose so high in the heavens that it "caused them that dwell in the highest orbs to open their windows, put out their heads" to see where the tumult was coming from.[65]

The dialogue is sometimes as alive as in the best parts of *The Pilgrim's Progress*, teeming with good old expressions: "Mr. Godly-fear, are you not well? You seem to be ill of body or mind, or both. I have a cordial of Mr. Forget-good's making, the which, sire, if you will take a dram of, I hope it may make you bonny and blith, and so make you more fit for us, feasting companions."[66]

He makes his words leap and trip to express joy: "But who can think what a turn, what a change, what an alteration, this hint of things do make in the countenance of the town of Mansoul."[67] And we have a clear impression, here, that the pleonasms are brought about in a deliberate way just for the pleasure of the trochaic rhythm: "What a turn, what a change, what an alteration." Sometimes there are flowing balanced periods with a fine classical amplitude not to be found in *The Pilgrim's Progress*: "And though through thy subtlety, and also the subtlety of the Diabolonians within, we have sustained much loss, and also plunged ourselves into much perplexity, yet, give up ourselves, lay down our arms, and yield to so horrid a tyrant as thou, we shall not; die upon the place we choose rather to do."[68] This is an orator's sentence, throwing the ball with a gesture the calculated vigour of which delights him. The beginning is a little slow, several words of more than one syllable are lined up in force; then briskly the cadence alters on the central pivot (yet), the Anglo-Saxon monosyllables pile up, the infinitives mount in a pyramid until they reach the imperious auxiliary verb "shall". Certainly Bunyan understood the magic of words and rhythms.

His vocabulary retains the richness of concrete suggestion which we have admired ever since *Grace Abounding*. Bunyan does not vaguely

---

[65] *Holy War*, p. 93. The fact that Bunyan takes Ptolemy's astronomy for granted does not mean, as some people have concluded, that he had read Milton. Those ideas were current at the time.

[66] P. 154.　　　　[67] P. 109.　　　　[68] P. 201.

refer to a work being "in hand" but "upon the wheel". ". . . Those bold and hellish contrivances that were upon the wheel." [69] It is a villager's imagery; he is thinking of his comrades among the rural craftsmen, of the potter, the spinner, perhaps both at once.

So *The Holy War* has its beauties, but they are few and far between and within too heavy a framework. The work has not the youth, the vitality, the breath of *The Pilgrim's Progress*, and our whole criticism of it may be summed up in one sentence by Edward Dowden who said that *The Holy War* was "an allegory rather manufactured than inspired".[70]

[69] *Holy War*, p. 182.
[70] Edward Dowden, *op. cit.*, article 'Bunyan', p. 236.

PART III

BUNYAN'S THOUGHT

1

Bunyan's Religious Thought

Faith in Christ and holiness of life, without respect to
this or that circumstance, or opinion in outward and
circumstantiall things.   JOHN GIFFORD

THERE was no hiatus between Bunyan's thought and his life.
We, who have watched him living, already know the ideas that
guided him.   And yet the spectacle of his soul laboriously seeking
to capture the truth both in private conflict and from his experience
of men—this twisting, panting progress—has befogged us.   At the
end of the race we feel the need to look back and take a bird's-eye
view of the road that has been covered.   And then the zig-zag line
straightens out; for, as Emerson said,[1] the authentic act of one day
explains the authentic acts of the day before and the day after.   A
life's unity is less the fruit of a coherent dialectic than the reward for
daily sincerity; and with an ardent person who makes conscience a
light and each duty a truth, the unity of thought finally becomes fused
with the unity of life.   At any rate the time has come to pick out the
resultant of all the spiritual forces.

Bunyan's thought was the flower of his longings.   He thirsted
for deliverance and dreamt of a paradise of innocence, order, peace
and unity, and so he gradually worked out a religious, moral, social
and political thought in which he made all borrowed elements his
own.   Born of the needs of his heart, his thought seems to have been
a passion of his whole being, as with Luther, whose *Commentary on*
the Epistle to the Galatians brought him so much comfort.[2]

But familiarity with Bunyan's thought does not only enable us
the better to judge his powerful personality, it helps us to probe the

[1] Emerson, ' Essay on Self-Reliance ', in *Essays* (Everyman), p. 38.
[2] *G. A.*, pars. 129–131.

259

ideas of the rural and working population to which he belonged. Bunyan's religious and moral convictions were the same as those of thousands and thousands of ' little ' men; more vigorous, perhaps, and better knit together, but fundamentally similar. The tinker understood, assimilated and preached more or less what numberless other peasants and artisans learnt and remembered. He was a child of the people, and thus expressed them in expressing himself. His work is a contribution to social history, as modern historians recognise by always giving a place to the author of *Mr. Badman*.

Bunyan's ideas on the behaviour both of the individual and society proceeded from his religious convictions. His faith shone in the centre of his thought as it shone at the heart of his life. For him, as for Carlyle's medieval monk,[3] religion was his daily bread.

The Gospel he preached was essentially a Gospel of consolation. He had known despair and thus wished to save others from knowing it. He believed in the small number of the elect and yet we have known him address souls as if all could finally be saved. In the fervour of his appeal he seemed to promise heaven to all fighters able to make the climb—" to wrestle for heaven ".[4] In his best moments, when the love in his soul dictated what he said, he could have made Lefèvre d'Etaples' words his own: " Yes, but God does not refuse his grace to those who do their utmost." [5] Hence his heart contradicted his mind [6] without his mind realising it. And the song of hope which almost always contrived to smother the voice of logic reechoes loud and clear in *The Pilgrim's Progress*.

True, Despair was a cruel giant who kept men gasping in his dungeons, but the prisoners managed to escape and find the path leading to the Delectable Mountains. Was there ever a nimbler pilgrim than Hopeful ? The monster Apollyon did not venture to

---

[3] Carlyle, *Past and Present*, Bk. II, chap. xv, p. 113 (Everyman).

[4] *The Strait Gate*, I, 369.

[5] Imbart de la Tour, *L'Evangélisme*, p. 147.

[6] This contradiction is also to be found in Calvin who, in a fine moment, wrote : " *Car ceux qui, par foy, communiquent vrayment en Jésus Christ se peuvent bien asseurer qu'ils appartiennent à l'élection éternelle de Dieu et qu'ils sont ses enfants . . . voilà Dieu qui s'abaisse à nous ; il nous montre de quoy en son fils ; come s'il disoit : Me voicy, contemplez moi, et cognoissez comment je vous ay adoptés pour mes enfants.*" Henri Bois, art. cit., *Revue Métaphys. et Morale,* special number on the Reformation, 1918.

confront him at first, and, at the end of the pilgrimage, the river of Death which each man had to cross held no fears for him. He probably believed more strongly than all the others in the invisible kingdom whose splendour is hidden from the eyes of the world.[7]

But there was no need to be a visionary to march steadily towards the heights. Neither women nor children ran any risk if accompanied by a sure guide. Even Feeble-mind and Much-afraid acquitted themselves well in the end. Everyone, Ready-to-halt included, pushed ahead. Indeed the road does not seem so very narrow in the light of the second part of *The Pilgrim's Progress*. God is love. For him, to cease to love would be to cease to be.[8] All shall be well. That is the message that we take away with us from the dreamer's allegory.

Yet if it seems to us that the Puritan preacher echoed Juliana of Norwich and repeated her " all shall be well ",[9] we are immediately struck by a paradox. For Bunyan was also the author of *Reprobation Asserted*.[10] We have already seen him twisting St. John's remarks about " all that the Father giveth me shall come to me " to prove that " all " does not mean " all ".[11] We remember terrifying passages [12] where hope is refused even to the sincere believer. Bunyan even goes so far as to say that we can repent, humil-

---

[7] *The Strait Gate*, I, 375.

[8] Cf. *supra*, p. 82.

[9] *Sixteen Revelations of Divine Love Shewed to Mother Juliana of Norwich*, 1373 (Kegan Paul, London, 1920), 13th revelation, chap. xxxi. " I may make all thing well; and I can make all thing well; and I shall make all thing well; and I will make all thing well; and thou shalt see thyself that all manner of thing shall be well." P. 74.

[10] John Brown did not believe that this work was by Bunyan. He based his opinion on consideration of style : " It neither begins nor ends in Bunyan's characteristic fashion, nor is there in it a single touch to remind us of his own peculiar vein. Let him write on what subject he may, he writes not long before he melts with tenderness or glows with fire." *Op. cit.*, pp. 244–245.

Mr. G. B. Harrison however remarked that this same hard and logical style is to be found elsewhere in Bunyan's works, for instance *Questions About the Nature and Perpetuity of the Seventh-day Sabbath*. *Op. cit.*, pp. 125–126.

We are of G. B. Harrison's opinion. Let us recall that Charles Doe included this book in the catalogue of his friend's works.

[11] Cf. *supra* : the sermons, 2nd part, chap. I, section II.

[12] *Strait Gate*, pp. 384–385.

iate ourselves, possess the faith of Christ, await his salvation, weep
and pray every day, and yet be damned.

This paradox, this dialectical tension quite unsuspected by the
reader who only knows *The Pilgrim's Progress*, sometimes gives
Bunyan's work the thrill of drama. But now, having shown that he
could involve himself in contradictions with the facility of unaware-
ness, we must point out that he was equally capable of spanning the
gulf between the demands of his doctrinal determinism and those of
his compassion. At such times he attempted the impossible and
strove to resolve the contradiction. He wanted at least to postpone
the evil hour so as to give the unlucky ones the joys of brotherhood
with the elect. In the New Jerusalem of his dreams the Church
would make an ample harvest of sinners.[13] He seemed to see the
" Scriptures " marching " with open arms towards the latter end of the
world, even as if they would grasp and compass about almost all people
then upon the face of the whole earth with the grace and mercy of
God ".[14] The kings shall cease their fornications with Babylon and
flock to the City. The Jews shall be converted.[15] Even the reprobates will be admitted into the New Jerusalem if they lead a holy life.

True, the Revelation of St. John the Divine foretells that only
" they who are written in the Lamb's Book of Life " [16] will be able
to enter, and it is unlikely that the damned could be in this book.
But Bunyan was equally cunning in mercy as in harshness and was
not to be put out by this objection. Distinction should be made, he
says,[17] between the Book of God's eternal grace where the elect are
recorded for ever, and the Book of Life in which " the Lord Jesus
hath all recorded that are visible saints by calling ", and who follow
" the rules and bounds of visible church-communion ". In this way
the reprobates will know great joys in the bosom of the Church in
spite of everything. For if the dawn of the world was a paradise, its
dusk will also be a paradise.[18] The tree of life—that is to say
Christ [19]—will spread its freshness over its mere servants as over its
beloved sons. God's throne shall be in the City and all shall con-

---

[13] *Holy City*, III, p. 443.
[14] *Ibid.*, p. 443, see too *Of Antichrist and his Ruin*, p. 54.
[15] *Ibid.*, p. 447.
[16] *Ibid.*, p. 449; cf. Apocalypse, XXI, 27.   [17] *Ibid.*, p. 449.
[18] *Ibid.*, p. 454.   [19] *Ibid.*, p. 453.

template His face.[20] "Golden World." [21] The eternal sun of a green spring: "it will be then always summer, always sunshine, always pleasant, green, fruitful and beautiful to the sons of God." [22] "Holiness, goodness, and truth shall then, with great boldness, countenance, and reverence, walk upon the face of all the earth." [23]

In this way Bunyan's longings were exalted and appeased in the dream, he was humiliated but proud, persecuted but already triumphant [24] and uniting vengeance with pardon. He could not bring himself to refuse repentance to kings and nobles.[25] He had not the heart to chase from the City the "servants" whom God had not called. But he did not go as far as his longings. He did not raise the "servants" to the dignity of "sons". Though admitted into the New Jerusalem they were not saved for ever.[26] As soon as he thought about it, Bunyan was convinced of predestination. It was in spite of his rational and unbreakable convictions, almost in spite of himself, that he so often wiped away people's tears and gave them hope.

And it is not surprising that consoling words came easily to him, nor that he could spread light, so to say, with both hands. He had always dreamed of the sun, of warmth and peace—the images reiterated in *Grace Abounding*: women talking joyfully,[27] chatting on a mountain bathed in sunbeams; [28] sparkling texts [29] and as if starred with spangles; [30] texts with a "sweet glance" [31]—all those images which sprang spontaneously from his pen reveal his true sensibility and an undercurrent of power. They are key-images.

★

Yet this Christianity, while consoling man, in no way debilitates him. There was no mawkishness about Bunyan. The gentleness of Jesus, His "wonderful innocent smile" [32] of which Christian speaks, never effaces His divine majesty. Bunyan devoted many works to the love of God but he also drew up a *Treatise on the Fear of God*. Christian's Master leads His disciple along a hard road having, initially, demanded his abandonment of home, wife and children.

---

[20] *Holy City*, III, p. 458.   [21] *Ibid.*, p. 459.
[22] *Ibid.*, p. 459.   [23] *Ibid.*, p. 459.
[24] See *Of Antichrist and his Ruin*, p. 65.   [25] *Ibid.*, p. 74.
[26] *Holy City*, III, p. 450.   [27] *G. A.*, par. 38.
[28] *G. A.*, par. 53.   [29] *G. A.*, par. 121.
[30] *G. A.*, par. 235.   [31] *G. A.*, par. 113.   [32] *P. P.*, p. 177.

Not every man is called to follow in Christian's footsteps; and his author would be the first to agree with this; [33] and yet there is no doubt that he considered renunciations of this kind to be sometimes imperative and indeed almost natural in their necessity. If we diluted and sweetened Bunyan's message [34] we would falsify the meaning of his work and forget the lesson of his life. He had not hesitated to abandon his own wife and children, even his dear little blind daughter, rather than betray his faith. Christian is Bunyan *minus* the anguish described in *Grace Abounding*—a lack we may regret; but the heroic vigour of the two men is the same.

Help is ceaselessly offered to the weak—to Christiana, Mercy and Much-afraid and to the other pilgrims; and yet they all had to tear themselves away from the calm of their homes to embark on the pilgrimage, and they all exposed themselves to danger. Finally, if God is love he is also justice. He knows how to forgive, though he does not hesitate to punish.

Hence his elect also have a duty to show severity when occasion demands. Bunyan directed the little Bedford community with a firm hand. He believed it was necessary sometimes to be angry, and, though an apostle of toleration, he freely acknowledged that intolerance was sometimes a sacred obligation. The war waged against the agents of Satan was a " holy war ". When the City of Mansoul was reconquered by Emmanuel's armies it was given a theocratic and military government. [35] Whoever abandoned himself to " carnal security " deserved punishment, and still more whoever allowed himself to fall into scepticism. [36]

After reading this allegory we cannot help doubting whether Bunyan, if in charge of the destinies of a nation, would have applied the principles of toleration he often defended. Against the Papists the fight seemed to him legitimate: indeed a wall of prejudice and tragic memories stood between the Non-conformist sects and Rome, between Bunyan and the " modern Babylon ". There had been

[33] Cf. *infra*, p. 278.

[34] Cf. H. Grierson, *op. cit.* : " Christian's abandonment of his wife and children has nothing in common with Gautama's or Count Tolstoi's flight from home. It means no more than that he has to take his own way in the Christian life he has resolved to live." P. 199.

[35] Cf. *supra*, *The Holy War*.

[36] *The Holy War*, pp. 156–157, and also p. 227.

" Bloody Mary ", the massacre of St. Bartholomew, the threat of the Armada, and the gun-powder plot had been only three-quarters of a century earlier. Whence the fear and hatred of Catholicism throughout the whole of Great Britain. Even a hundred years after Bunyan's death Wesley was still to have nightmares in which he saw the Catholic invaders coming to torture him.[37]

But nothing could better illustrate the feelings of Protestant England towards Catholicism at that time than a letter from the enthusiastic pacifist and heroic conscientious objector, George Fox, advising the officers of the army to make war against Rome and Spain.[38]

We may also think that his love of unity would have drawn Bunyan into other religious persecutions. True, in the seventeenth century the spirit of toleration began to raise its voice—in the *Agreement of the People* (1647), in Milton's *Areopagitica* (1644), in the *Discourse on the Liberty of Prophesying* by Jeremy Taylor (1646), and Locke's *Letter concerning Toleration* (1689 to 1692). But there were countless men who never achieved this detachment. A strong faith readily denounced as impious the respect for beliefs foreign to it. In 1645 the Ecclesiastical Synod gathered at the College of Sion declared that toleration was at the root of all bitterness.[39] Thomas Edwards published his catalogue of heresies so that the reader might " discerne . . the monstrousnesse of the much effected toleration " [40] and some London ministers declared that they " detested " and " abhorred " it.[41]

We may remember too how Bossuet hit out at Basnage with indignant irony for having written: " We live peaceably when we live under Protestant domination." M. de Meaux [42] replied to this: " Let us say, then, happy is the country where the heretic sleeps as well as the orthodox, where vipers are cherished like doves and innocent animals, where those who compound poisons enjoy the same peace as those who prepare remedies: who would not admire the

[37] Agnès de la Gorce, *op. cit.*, p. 297.
[38] Robert Barclay, *op. cit.*, 137–138.
[39] Cf. Ch. Firth, *Oliver Cromwell and the Rule of the Puritans*, p. 172.
[40] Ths. Edwards, *Gangraena* (2nd. ed., 1646) (James Cranford).
[41] Ch. Firth, *op. cit.*, pp. 152–153.
[42] *Défense de l'Histoire des Variations contre la réponse de M. Basnage, 1re discours, oeuvres complètes* (Vivès, Paris, 1863), vol. XV, p. 492.

clemency of these Reformed States? The Old Law bid us chase the blasphemer from the camp and may all cast stones at him."

Bunyan, author of *The Holy War*, had the same respect for the just harshness of the Old Law.

He extolled suffering and demonstrated its necessity. Spiritual suffering marks the awakening of the sinner and is the preliminary step towards conversion. This is what his personal experience had taught him and our study of his life has enabled us to follow the progress of his thought in this respect. As for physical pain, it is an ordeal that God sends us for our good. "God has appointed who shall suffer. Suffering comes not by chance or by the will of man, but by the will and appointment of God." [43] Our flesh swarms over us like a weed; without harsh winters it would soon stifle the spirit.[44] Blessed is persecution which wrenches our houses, lands, money and liberty from us! When everything is withdrawn from us there remains only our soul. "All is gone but the soul."[45] This denudation is the condition of our development, and Bunyan recalls Jesus's words according to St. John: "I am the true vine, and my Father is the husbandman. Every branch in me that beareth not fruit he taketh away." [46]

Such is the advice which the man who passed twelve years in gaol gave to the afflicted. But he brought them the promise of immediate reward too: the martyr's prison is more beautiful than a palace.[47] As God draws near to His persecuted creature, He reveals the splendours of the eternal Kingdom to his soul's eye.[48]

As we see, there is nothing original in this teaching of suffering, except perhaps the warmth of his conviction and, as always, the fervour of his appeal.

★

This Christianity, while being so efficacious for this conduct of life, renews and expresses itself in a cult of the greatest simplicity. There were few sacraments and rites in the Church. As we have seen [49] its members looked on baptism by water as a mere symbol, an external aid brought to the sinner; for true baptism made its mark

[43] *Strait Gate*, I, 723. [44] *Ibid.*, 694.
[45] *Ibid*, 697. [46] *Ibid.*, 725, and St. John xv, 1–2.
[47] *Ibid*, 700. [48] *Ibid.*, 699.
[49] Cf. *supra*, 2nd part, chap. I.

invisibly in the soul and was revealed to the outside world only by the radiance of faith. When they came together for the mystical supper, the faithful expressed their love, veneration and gratitude with hymns.[50] They expounded the Scriptures tirelessly so as to probe their whole meaning. Faith was a divine grace, but it could not do without human intelligence—that is what Bunyan's allegorical figures expressed. Was not the Lord Mayor of the town of Mansoul called Understanding? And did he not assume that he would be the first person to be deposed by the triumphant Diabolus? And even when suspended from office did he not try to enlighten the citizens and urge them to revolt against the devil? When Emmanuel returned to Mansoul he installed Understanding in a well-defended tower and ordered him to read the Apocalypse daily to find a ruling for his actions.[51] So we see that the intelligence plays a necessary, though limited, part: it should help man to understand God's revelation, but should go no further than that, because the intelligence is fallible and reason can be mistaken.[52] Bunyan did not agree with his contemporary John Smith, who said that to follow reason was to follow God.[53] No, the Holy Spirit must pierce the intelligence, penetrate into it and enlighten it; [54] and then it can expound in a language accessible to all men the silent confidences that God has made to the creature he has chosen as his " instrument ". Bunyan commented on and paraphrased St. Paul at length: " If I

[50] *P. P.*, pp. 45–46.
Cf. Richard Baxter: " Understand and stand to thy baptismal vow and see that thy belief, love and practice of known Christianity according to our Creed, Lord's Prayer and Decalogue, in love to God, thy soul and thy neighbour, in godliness, charity, justice, sobriety, be serious and sincere, and then thou art certainly of that catholic church which Christ is the head of and will save." *In Search from the English Schismatic* (1681), quoted by J. M. Lloyd Thomas in his introduction to Baxter's autobiography (Everyman), XXI, XXII; and in the *Autobiography* : " The creed, the Lord's Prayer and the Ten Commandments do find me now the most acceptable and plentiful matter for all my meditations. They are to me as my daily bread and drink." P. 107.
[51] *Holy War*, p. 157.
[52] *Law and Grace*, I, 510, where Bunyan speaks of " beguiled reason ".
[53] Cf. Basil Willey, *The Seventeenth Century Background* (1934), p. 72.
[54] *I Will Pray with the Spirit* : " An understanding well enlightened is of admirable use," I, 633, and, on the same page, " He that hath his understanding opened by the Spirit needs not to be taught of other men's prayers."

pray in an unknown tongue, my spirit prayeth, but my understanding, and also the understanding of others, is unfruitful."[55] The understanding has an essential task—to translate God's message into human language. If religion were not enriched by enlightened understanding it could even bring dangers. Bunyan remembered that he would never have escaped from despair nor become conscious of the exact nature of his sin if he had not reflected.[56]

The study of his life can lead us to an entirely different opinion about Bunyan's faith, to look on it as a triumph of sensibility and irrational impulse. Bunyan believed because he had terrifying or, alternatively, consoling visions, because, to use John Smith's words, he had the " sensation " of God.[57] But it is interesting to note that he desired to have a lucid faith, and to understand the most obscure parts of the Bible: it was his secret hope one day to see the whole Bible enlightened by a new grace of God and on behalf of reason. In this way Bunyan helps us to grasp how Puritanism,[58] having left its rigorous post-Reformation dogmatism behind, yielded, from the seventeenth century onwards, to its instinct for free examination and to the influences of Cartesian philosophy in order to try to rationalise religion after the manner of the erudite neo-Platonists of Cambridge, of Whichcote or John Smith with whom we were contrasting Bunyan just now. Bunyan was a long way from these university men but we can see clearly the path which led from the one to the others.

In this stripped Church, but which seemed to him immense, and in the meditation on the word of God, all Christians should be at their ease. And in the New Jerusalem [59] there would be no distinction between Papists and Quakers, Episcopalians and Presbyterians, Independents and Anabaptists—they would all be brothers following the same road under the same light. Bunyan did really dream of a

[55] *I Will Pray*, I, 632.

[56] *Ibid.*, 634.

[57] John Smith : " Were I indeed to define Divinity I should rather call it a divine life than a divine science ; it being something rather to be understood by a Spiritual sensation than by any verbal description." 'A Discourse Concerning the True Way or Method of Attaining to Divine Knowledge ', I, p. 2, *Select Discourses* (London, 1660).

[58] Cf. Basil Willey, *op. cit.*, p. 135.

[59] *Holy City*, III, pp. 419, 437.

universal Church. The lessons of his master, John Gifford,[60] and perhaps of the worthy author of *The Practice of Piety*, Lewis Bayly,[61] had borne fruit in him.

However necessary might seem to him the assembly of the faithful and the communion of souls in public worship, which fosters a collective fervour and enables the weak to draw inspiration from the strong, Bunyan found the true flowering of his religious life in personal prayer. He was convinced that no forms of prayer found in prayer-books could raise man's heart and mind to God.[62] He knew nothing about the force of habit and was insensitive to the ever-new grace of traditional prayer. He never discovered the peace that lies in the repetition of words only apparently worn with use, nor guessed that in those inevitable moments when God seems to withdraw from man, the familiar prayer strengthens the will and marks a fresh stage on the road.

And it is true that he would have despised this peace. Only the depths and the heights were real to him. Whence his hatred of all formalism, and his irony: " But here now the wise men of our days are so well skilled as that they have both the manner and matter of their prayers at their fingers-ends ; setting such a prayer for such a day, and that twenty years before it comes . . . They can tell you, also, when you shall kneel, when you shall stand. . . ." [63] He adds that the Apostles were not so wise.

When somebody pointed out to him that it was Christ who taught us the Our Father, Bunyan answered: [64] Yes, but now " He is not here in his person to teach us." Let us now be attentive to His spirit and not to the words of men who seek " repute and applause for their eloquent terms and seek more to tickle the ears and heads of their hearers." [65]

[60] Read in the fac-simile edition of the archives of the Bedford church (Dent, 1928), ff. 2–4, the admirable letter that John Gifford left for his friends. Here are some extracts : " Concerning separation from the church about baptism, laying on of hands, anointing with oil, psalms, or any externals, I charge every one of you respectively, as you will give an account of it to our Lord Jesus Christ, who shall judge both quick and dead at his coming, that none of you be found guilty of this great evil." And again : " When you are met as a church there's neither rich nor poor, bond nor free, in Christ Jesus."

[61] We recall Bayly's aim : " I have endeavoured to extract out of the chaos of endless controversies the old practice of true piety ", The Epistle Dedicatory, *op. cit.* (ed. of 1842), XXXIII.

[62] *I Will Pray*, I, 634.   [63] *Ibid.*, 628.   [64] *Ibid.*, 635.   [65] *Ibid.*, 637.

True prayer is always personal and spontaneous, the sincere outpouring of a soul. It is the heart laying itself bare before God: " an unbosoming of man's self ".[66]

It is a dialogue of the creature with his creator, the longing for God to which Bunyan alludes when he quotes Psalm 42: " As the hart panteth after the water brooks, so panteth my soul after thee, O God. My soul thirsteth for God, for the living God." [67]

The entire man is thus absorbed in prayer [68] which leaps up with the violence of a jet of blood: " As blood is forced out of the flesh."[69]

Prayer is a humble and total submission of oneself to the will of God. " Prayer doth submit to the will of God." [70]   Bunyan prayed like all the great believers, like Pascal at just about the same time: " Give to me, take from me, but conform my will to yours . . . Lord, I know that I only know one thing, that it is good to follow you." [71]

Such a prayer is often nothing but a long and inexpressible sigh.[72] Ejaculatory and bathed with tears, it can never be taught even to the youngest. The father must simply tell his son " what a cursed creature he is ", [73] that God's wrath is spreading above him. Then the tears will flow from the children's eyes and it will be as natural for them to groan " as it is for a sucking child to cry for the breast ", Bunyan wrote, using an image [74] which, though familiar, is a little out of place in the context.

But there is a higher form of prayer in which man no longer unbosoms himself, nor listens to himself, but forgets himself and creates a void within himself so that God can come down and speak. The prayer is then a sort of dialogue: the Spirit chooses the soul of His creature and converses with Himself there, and asks Himself what is suitable for this creature He is inhabiting. For, as Bunyan says with St. Paul, " we know not what we should pray for as we ought ".[75]

When we read from the tinker's pen that through prayer the empty soul is filled; [76] and again that there can be no prayer so long

---

[66] I Will Pray, I, 625.

[67] Ibid., 624.

[68] Ibid., 624. " Engaged in prayer."

[69] Ibid., 624.

[70] Ibid., 627.

[71] Prayer for the good use of Sickness, pars. XIII and XIV.

[72] I Will Pray, I, 631.

[73] Ibid., 635.

[74] Ibid., 636.

[75] Ibid., 627.

[76] Ibid., 623. " The soul though empty is filled."

as the Spirit has not entered into the heart,[77] we can measure the similarity of religious experience in the most diverse kinds of Christians. To remain within the century let us content ourselves with quoting Bérulle: " Man . . . needful of God, capable of God, and filled with God if he so wishes." [78]

In his *Discourse on Prayer*, which Bunyan wrote at the beginning of his captivity, we touch the heights of his religious thought. In this work he forgets Calvin and Luther and all his masters and describes his personal emotions and feelings; and it is then that he takes his place among the greatest figures of Christianity.

[77] *I Will Pray*, I, 631. " When the Spirit gets into the heart, then there is prayer indeed, and not till then."
[78] Quoted by Ch. du Bos, *Approximations* (6th series), article on Bérulle.

2
Bunyan's Moral Thought

BUNYAN'S moral thought was narrowly linked to his faith. As with Luther and Calvin, his ethics were the fruit of his religion. Though first rejected from the Christian life, works were reinstated and finally played an essential part in it. Not an original doctrine, then, but one capable of fostering personal vigour and impetus, and above all such a keen joy in rediscovering the Decalogue that it seemed altogether new.

Before his conversion Bunyan had been unable to feel satisfied with works; he felt them to be insufficient in the eyes of divine justice.[1] But as soon as he moved into the realm of grace and knew himself to be saved in spite of the insignificance of his good actions, he felt a daily joy in moral rectitude and gathered happiness every day in the field of duty. Having handed over the care of his eternal destiny to God [2] he could follow the road " so dangerous for the soul " when " God is not in charge " [3]—the road marked out by the Ten Commandments.

Here we see Luther's strong influence, which is usually only touched on and not given its due prominence by Bunyan's critics, with the exception of the always perceptive Coleridge.[4] Yet our author made no secret of the indelible impression made on him by the

---

[1] Cf. *supra*, 1st part, chap. 2, and *The Doctrine of Law and Grace, Works*, I, 493 *et seq.*

[2] *Seasonable Counsel*, p. 703 : " Thou must also leave all the concerns of thy soul and of thy being an inheritor of the next world wholly to the care of God."

[3] *Ibid.*, p. 703.

[4] Coleridge : " Bunyan may have been one [a Calvinist] but I have met with nothing in his writings (except his anti-peadobaptism, to which too he assigns no saving importance) that is not much more characteristically Lutheran." *Literary Remains* (London, 1838), vol. III, p. 398.

Commentary on the Epistle to the Galatians.[5]   Doubtless he had already come across some of Luther's ideas elsewhere, but a direct contact with his work and with the intimate confidences that here and there give it such warmth [6] must have engraved the master's thought more deeply on Bunyan.

Who could make Bunyan feel the necessity of personal asceticism and moral action better than Luther?   For " a Christian is not he who is without sin but he to whom God does not impute sin ".[7] The saints are not without vice; they still retain " the dregs of their natural corruption ".[8]   Whence the tension of the being, and the urgent necessity to master physical nature so that she may be in harmony with the inward man.   Whence, too, the necessity of the Law, and the recourse to the Ten Commandments which had formerly been rejected.[9]

Bunyan remembered this lesson all the better as he turned his eyes more keenly on to himself and could measure what was lacking in his spiritual growth; [10] then, carried away by moral faculties of a rare vigour, he savoured, naturally and spontaneously, a solemn delectation in obeying the law which his conversion transfigured. " Now also that fiery law, that it [his soul] could not once endure, nor could not once delight in, I say, now it can delight in it after the

---

[5] *G. A.*, par. 129.

[6] See for example p. 336 (ed. *cit.*), " When I was a monk, etc. . . ."
We presume that Bunyan had read one of the complete translations of Luther's book.   The first appeared in England in 1575, and various editions were published in the course of the 16th and 17th centuries (cf. British Museum catalogue—Bible (Galatians)).   In 1642 there came from Henry Atkinson's press in London a summary which would certainly have interested Bunyan if he knew of it, for it contained the translation of the Latin quotations in *The Practice of Piety*, one of the two books that his first wife introduced to him.   However we do not think that par. 129 of *G. A.* alludes to this slender little work.   Luther's essential ideas are certainly there, but the force, the glow, the soul of the complete text are lacking.   That this mediocre summary should have been the book which Bunyan found so striking is unbelievable.

[7] *Commentary on the Epistle to the Galatians* (ed. *cit.*), p. 72.

[8] *Ibid.*, p. 102.

[9] Consult Robert Will, *La Liberté chrétienne, étude sur le principe de la piété chez Luther* (Strasbourg, 1922).

[10] " I know not anything that ever I did in my life but it had a flaw, or wrinkle or spot, or some such thing in it.   Mine eyes have seen vileness in the best of my doings," *Works*, I, 175.

inward man; now this law is its delight, it would always be walking in it." [11]

But he did not think of this creaturely felicity as the reflection of the joys awakened in God by the spectacle of human goodwill. [12] No, it did not come from divine radiance mirrored in the individual soul, but rather from who knows what new gift bestowed by the Lord. " I tell thee, Christian, be but rich in good works and thou shalt have more than salvation; thy salvation thou hast freely by grace through Christ, without works, but now being justified and saved . . . thou shalt be rewarded for every work that proves good." [13]

Not that the thought of this reward was the motive for Bunyan's moral actions. If man is, by nature, " rather a hearer than a doer ",[14] this was certainly not the case with the tinker. He needed action. With him peace matured in action because therein lay the evidence that his faith was alive.[15] Rather than meditation, he preferred practical achievement, the soul of religion.[16]

Furthermore, however convinced he may have been that faith alone can save us, he perceived an immediate danger in Luther's doctrine— namely antinomianism. After all he had had a " Ranter " among his friends. He knew the excesses to which an intelligence can abandon itself when ignorant of the nature of salvation and the human condition: and a soul when it does not realise that " we are children and yet sinners: we are accepted and yet we do not give satisfaction ".[17]

He strove therefore to throw light both on the consequences of the Redemption and on the residue of nature which still stains purified man. Certainly, he says, " there is no law to come in against the sinner that believes in Jesus Christ ; for he is not under that . . ." [18] Despite their sins, " all those that are under this second covenant are in a wonderful safe condition "; [19] not because the elect cannot live

---

[11] *Law and Grace*, I, 548.
[12] Cf. Calvin : *" Il ne se peut faire que Dieu n'ayme pas les biens qu'il leur a conferez par son Esprit,"* Inst. III, XVII, 5.
[13] *Christian Behaviour*, p. 572.
[14] *Ibid.*, III, 570.
[15] *Ibid.*, p. 572. " Faith without works is dead."
[16] " The soul of religion is the practick part," *P. P.*, p. 74.
[17] *Luther* (ed. Clemen, Bonn), I, 241 ; quoted by R. Will, *op. cit.*, p. 293.
[18] *Law and Grace*, I, 538.   [19] *Ibid.*, I, 552.

without committing sin—admitted though this be [20]—but because, as the convenant is not concluded with them, they cannot break it.[21] You must believe in this truth with passion so that your anxieties may wither and die; and when Bunyan says " you " we must understand " I ", or rather " I and you ", for the surplus of the consolation which he showers over himself rebounds over others.

At all events the regenerated Christian must not think that he has full leisure in which to sin—" sin and sin again ".[22] God would punish him. There is retribution for evil as well as for good. Following the teaching of Luther and Calvin, Bunyan failed as they did to back it up with convincing rigorous logic. The sceptic can always repeat his diabolical objection: " How can God punish me since I am of the elect and so saved from all eternity ? " And Bunyan followed a happier inspiration when he appealed to sentiment, to the reasons of the heart of which the mind knows nothing: he who lives in Jesus Christ does not dream, simply does not dream of sinning for pleasure.[23]

Finally, if he does not have to justify himself before God, the converted Christian must justify himself before men by his works.[24] In particular Bunyan must demonstrate that a consoling faith does not lead to " looseness of life ",[25] and, if need be, he must fix rules for daily action. So he wrote a clear and practical treatise on Christian morality for the use of the poor. Like Baxter and Defoe he considered that there were not enough of such works in families [26] at a moment when they were particularly needed. Morality, already become debased during the last years of the Protectorate, had sunk still lower since the Restoration. It was not an abstract disquisition on works in general that was needed, but a sort of pocket manual.[27]

[20] *Law and Grace*, I, 552, " For who lives and sins not ? " and Prov. XXIV, 16.
[21] *Ibid.*, 553.
[22] *Christian Behaviour*, II, 554.
[23] *Ibid.*, II, 554.
[24] *Ibid.*, II, 549.
[25] *Ibid.*
[26] Cf. Richard Baxter, *Christian Directory* (London, 1673). Defoe, *The Family Instructor* (London, 1751).
[27] Bunyan's manual is much briefer and more practical than Baxter's enormous treatise and Defoe's book. There is a modern abridged edition of the *Christian Directory*. Highly interesting for those who are only interested in the history of social and economic thought, it is inadequate for anyone wanting to make a deep study of Puritan morality : *Chapters from a Christian Directory*, Selected by Jeannette Tawney (London, 1925).

Bunyan drew on his experience as husband, father and preacher, and his treatise contains precise advice on personal, social and family morality. The author takes his reader by the hand and leads him with a friendly but firm grasp. The life towards which he is leading him is solemn and difficult.

If Bunyan did not go so far as to consider work to be religion, at least he held that the Christian expresses himself and fulfils himself in his work. It is necessary to be "fruitful": this word occurs time and time again in his work, and is one of those "keys" to the character of which we were talking elsewhere. Once his conversion was established, if not completed, Bunyan showed no desire to lose himself in contemplation. We rather sense in him, as in almost all Puritans, the will to do his share in the construction of the kingdom of God, or at least, as the Pilgrim Fathers said, to be the stepping-stones that others will be able to use so as to accomplish that task.[28]

For people who talk and do not do—for Talkative and the other inhabitants of Prating-Row—he had only contempt. And in his enthusiasm for action, Bunyan was actually led to express an idea which is surely heresy for a Puritan: "Let us assure ourselves that at the day of Doom men shall be judged according to their fruits. It will not be said then: *Did you believe?* but, be you *Doers* or *Talkers* only? . . . The end of the world is compared to our Harvest, and you know men at Harvest regard nothing but Fruit."[29]

Without knowing it Bunyan did more here than restore a place to works as being the fruit of faith—he undermined the whole structure of predestination. That dogma was forgotten in the interests of practical morality and immediate demands. If a man tended towards laziness (was "rather a hearer than a doer") should he not be pushed into work? Did not idleness give birth to every corruption? Badman was first an idler.[30] Instead of staying in his shop he frequented the ale-house, glutted himself with beer and food and then went after girls. "Great nourishment and grosse food is the shop of lust."[31]

Hence the Puritan preached work and austerity at one and the

---

[28] Nathaniel Morton: ". . . although they should be but as stepping-stones unto others for the performance of so great a work," *New England's Memorial* (1669) (Everyman), p. 10.

[29] *P. P.*, pp. 74-75.   [30] *Badman*, III, 681.

[31] Arthur Dent, *op. cit.*, p. 63.

same time. All the satisfactions of the flesh led to moral and material ruin. " Who seek to please the flesh, themselves undo." [32] Most certainly man's end was happiness—Bunyan always carried within him the vision of the Delectable Mountains, of Paradise, of light and music—but the immediate aim of human life was endeavour—the self's endeavour with self, for we must always raise ourselves up, but also endeavour with regard to the good of others. The desire for personal perfection should open on to a dream of social perfection —the conquest of self leading to the conquest of the world.

But this is not the moment to make a survey of the whole of Bunyan's ethical development and the whole purport of Puritan morality. First we must discuss the nature of the duties of the individual towards himself and try to give an exact picture of Bunyan's type of virile severity. [33]

His expression sometimes outstripped his thought, and this might lead the unwary to see in him an ingrained pessimism. It is this isolation of formulas that has falsified the meaning of Puritanism. " The world hateth thee if thou be a Christian; the men of this world hate thee ; the things of this world are snares for thee, even thy bed and table, thy wife and husband, yea, thy most lawful enjoyments." [34] So said Bunyan in *The Strait Gate*. But read *The Pilgrim's Progress* and you will also hear laughter. Read *Christian Behaviour* and you will find advice which shows a reasonable confidence in the world. We have only to look at *The Imitation of Christ*, for example, to understand what a true distrust of the world can be like, and so measure Bunyan's relative optimism.

The life that he proposed is marked less by rigorous asceticism than by a gravity that is prepared to become heroic if necessary. Certain renunciations seemed to him demoniacal. We need only remember his hostility to the Quakers: " Now they must wear no hatbands; now they must live with bread and water; now they must give heed to seducing spirits, and doctrines of devils, which bids them abstain from marriage, and commands them to abstain from meats, which God hath created to be received with thanksgiving." [35] The quotation corrects the passage that we have already taken from *The Strait Gate* and gives an idea of the moral climate of all Bunyan's work.

[32] *P. P.*, p. 104.　　　　[33] *P. P.*, p. 81, " Quit yourselves like men."
[34] *Strait Gate*, I, 370.　　　　[35] *Gospel Truths*, II, 153.

Richard Baxter also gave a prominent place to these personal duties of the Christian because, he said, if the tree is good the fruits will be good too.[36]   And he treats these personal duties separately, distinguishing them from family duties, duties towards the Church, and duties towards our fellow-men and political leaders.[37]   Bunyan did not make these precise classifications but integrated our personal duties with those towards others.

It is to be noted that his first counsel is given to man as head of the family.   He looked on the family as the primary unit of Christian society.   To loosen family bonds was to open the door to disorder: Badman was more attached to his companions than to his father and mother [38] and felt no qualms about rejoicing in their coming death.[39]

The fact is that the Puritans inherited from medieval Catholicism [40] —which in its turn had inherited from the primitive Church—a patriarchal conception of society in which the natural authority of the head of the family was made sweet and gentle by the love he bore for his own and which they bore for him.

For Bunyan did not hold that the average man was called, like Christian, to leave his home in search of higher duties.   A great spiritual destiny could be worked out within the family circle—" a work to do for God " [41]—and a horizon, though near, could have its own particular light.

John Geree [42] boldly says that the father should make a church of his family, and Bunyan illustrated this by his work and his life. " In his family ", wrote his biographer and friend, " he kept up a very strict discipline in prayer and exhortations." [43]

And since a Christian family could only be founded by a marriage between believers, it was fitting that future husbands and wives

---

[36] R. Baxter, *Christian Directory* (1673), Advertisements.

[37] *Ibid.*, " 1. Christian ethicks (or private duties), 2. Christian aeconomicks (or family duties), 3. Christian ecclesiasticks (or church duties), 4. Christian politicks (or duties to our rulers and neighbours)." This is the list of contents of the work.

[38] *Badman*, III, 599.   [39] *Ibid.*

[40] Let us point out, once and for all, that many Anglicans profess the same personal and social ethic.

[41] *Christian Behaviour*, II, p. 555.

[42] *Op. cit.*, p. 5.   [43] Cf. *Works*, I, 64.

should show suitable prudence. Young girls in particular should not hesitate to ask their elders for advice so that they might not be taken in by an atheist like Badman.[44]

In such a home the father should comport himself as a model of moral rectitude and piety.[45] As the spiritual shepherd of his children he should provide for their material upkeep as well. He should be neither prodigal nor miserly, but strive to assure his family a decent way of life.[46]

Bunyan instructed and corrected his own son in a language composed of gentleness and simplicity.[47] Here he was not the pupil of any master. His ideas on education were the fruit of his own experience and that gives them their value. And they show lucid intelligence and great wisdom. He held so strongly by these ideas that he used them as a foil in *Badman* [48] as well as expounding them in *Christian Behaviour*. He urged the father to be patient always and to be exceptionally calm if he had to have recourse to the birch.[49] He should not mix his reproaches and threats with an indulgent laugh, for this only troubles and hardens the child. To speak little, with gravity and relevance, should be the golden rule for the educator.[50]

This paternal gentleness must have been very necessary to temper the terrifying religion that Bunyan, as we have seen, proposed to teach to small children. But here too we should distinguish between the theoretical statement and the practical application. The hard

---

[44] *Badman*, III, 622. Compare Defoe's *The Family Instructor*, vols. XV and XVI, *Works* (ed. Oxford, 1841). A man who has married a bad woman repents bitterly. His house seems to him " a temple of the devil " (vol. XVI, p. 13). " I have the money and the woman but not the wife; she is no wife to me," p. 14.

[45] *Christian Behaviour*, II, p. 556.

[46] *Ibid.*, II, p. 557, and compare anonymous biography, *Works*, I, 64, " He always had sufficient to live decently and creditably."

[47] *Christian Behaviour*, II, p. 558.

[48] *Badman*, III, p. 617.

[49] *Christian Behaviour*, II, p. 558. Compare Defoe : the rich tradesman, very worthy, very honest, falls into rages and whips his children uncontrolledly, vol. XVI, pp. 178–180.

[50] Compare biography, *Works*, I, 64, where it is said of Bunyan : ". . . not given to loquacity or much discourse in company unless some urgent occasion required it."

theologian who considered children to be " cursed " [51] was the same
man who spoke of his little blind child and of all his family with such
exquisite tenderness; the same man who showed such a lively love
of children in the family descriptions in *The Pilgrim's Progress*;
and finally the same man who was affectionately accused by one of his
friends of being an over-indulgent father.[52]

If we want to see the true countenance of Puritanism, we should
not only listen to what the ' saints ' said, but we should look at their
lives.   And if real life sometimes gives a harsh illustration of their
doctrines, it can equally well happen that it corrects and subtly
modifies them.

Finally, in his manual on morality Bunyan also defined the rôle
of the woman.   To begin with she must never have the first place.
" The man that suffereth his wife to take his place, hath already transgressed the order of God." [53]   However, once this principle was
established, Bunyan felt free to recall with insistence that the wife
should not be the slave of the man but his companion in the yoke.[54]
After him she should have the ordering of everything.   In his
absence the supreme authority should fall on her.[55]   The home
should be the pivot of her whole activity.   She should express and
fulfil herself through her home.   And she certainly does not lack tasks.
Christiana could hardly have said, like Mrs. Timorous, that she " had
little to do this morning! " [56]   In the life of a good wife there should
be no time for gossip or empty vanities.[57]

The woman should share with her husband the duty of edifying the
servants by the holiness of her life.   The tinker thought no differently
on this point from the more instructed Puritans such as Baxter and
Ames.   " *Omnes hujusmodi superiores, debent studere ut eminenti*

---

[51] " Besides little children die, but that they could not, were they not of
God counted sinners; for death is the wages of sin." *Instructions for the
Ignorant, Works*, II, p. 677.

[52] " For he was both a loving and tender husband and an indulgent father,
perhaps somewhat to a fault." *A New and Authentic Account of the Life and
Death of Mr. John Bunyan*, late minister of the Gospel at Bedford, written
by a friend to the cause of true religion, p. 28.

[53] *An Exposition on the Ten First Chapters of Genesis*, II, p. 438.

[54] *Christian Behaviour*, II, 561.

[55] *Ibid.*, II, 561.

[56] *P. P.*, p. 170.

[57] *Christian Behaviour*, II, 561.

quodam exemplo, in bene vivendo suis inferioribus praeire possint." [58]
And masters cannot edify their servants better than by giving them a
just wage and, in Bunyan's magnificent words, " the same bread of
God " as is given to the children of the household.[59]

This respect for the human person, this sense of the dignity of
the poor, this love of equity, were to be the main ingredients of Bunyan's social thought, which was the final flowering of his moral thought.

[58] Ames, *De Conscientia* (Amsterdam, 1630), p. 227.
[59] *Christian Behaviour*, II, 559.

3

Bunyan's Political and Social Thought

We are all one body.

ST. PAUL

BUNYAN'S social thought is manifest in his treatises as well as in his stories. From one end of his work to the other there re-echoes a protest against the selfishness of the rich. The protest is basically the same throughout though it varies in form—more violent at first, more moderate at the end; at first all mixed up with personal rancour and later, when this has been vented, steeped in human sympathy. For the obscure and wandering preacher had been replaced by ' the bishop ', and the indigent tinker [1] by a man capable of assuring his family a decent livelihood. [2]

In his early works Bunyan was at times irritated when reminded of his humble birth, [3] and at times he drew attention to it himself; [4] so beneath a humility which imagined itself to be sincere and wholehearted we can discern wounded pride.

A Few Sighs from Hell, in particular, reveals an intense class-consciousness. He reproaches the privileged of this world for despising the poor. He cannot tolerate that a rich man should pass

---

[1] Cf. *G. A.*, par. 15, " as poor as poor might be."

[2] " He always had sufficient to live decently and creditably." Anonymous biography, see *Works* (Offor), I, 64. See his will of 1685 in John Brown, *op. cit.*, pp. 350–351.

[3] Cf. *G. A.*, par. 2.
A Few Sighs from Hell, III, 674, and *supra* his controversies with W. Fowler and Paul, Kiffin and Danvers. Note too his wife's remark to the judges : " Because he is a tinker, and a poor man therefore he is despised, and cannot have justice." *Relation of the Imprisonment of Mr. John Bunyan*, p. 426.   [4] *G. A.*, par. 2.

on the other side of the road so as to avoid a poor one,[5] nor that a rich man should look at a poor one as if he wanted to devour him,[6] nor that he should refuse to remain under the same roof as a poor man.[7] Like Baxter he thought that Christians were in duty bound to know each other so as to understand and love each other.[8]

Whence did the rich get their pride? Did they not know of Christ's predilection for the poor?[9] Were they not aware that their possessions constituted a danger to their souls?[10] Did they not realise that their much vaunted education could not possibly replace the "experimental" knowledge of God which alone counted?[11]

Bunyan raised a still more indignant cry against their cruelty. He attacked property-owners who drove out poor farmers or pulled down their cottages[12]—the more so when they were simultaneously building commodious quarters for their hounds.[13] For Bunyan noted, with the same bitterness as George Fox, that "the ungodly world do love their dogs better than the children of God".[14]

And he promised them the wrath of heaven. "There is a time coming, O ye surly dogged persecutors of the saints, that they shall slight you as much as ever you slighted them . . . and in your greatest need and extremity they shall not pity you.[15] . . . The righteous shall rejoice when he seeth the vengeance, he shall wash his feet in the blood of the wicked."[16]

[5] *A Few Sighs*, III, 677.   [6] *Ibid.*, III, 676.   [7] *Ibid.*, III, 677.
[8] Richard Baxter, *Last Treatise*, ed. by F. J. Powicke (Manchester Univ. Press, 1926), p. 41.
Compare these ideas with the contrary advice issued in the Middle Ages by N. Bozon in G. R. Owst, *Literature and Pulpit in Medieval England* (Cambridge, 1933). "Bozon actually advises the poor to shun the rich in this life . . . and so definitely encourages the attitude of suspicion and estrangement," p. 299, footnote. Concerning Bozon consult Paul Mayer, *Les contes moralisateurs de Nicholas Bozon.*
[9] *A Few Sighs*, p. 675.
[10] *Ibid.*, "Rich men are most liable to the Devil's temptations," p. 676. "A man of wealth and a child of the Devil may make but one person," p. 675.   [11] *Ibid.*, p. 673. Cf. too pp. 695 and 716.
[12] *Ibid.*, p. 676.   [13] *Ibid.*, p. 677.
[14] *Ibid.* Cf. George Fox, "Ye are so rich, fat and swolen with wealth that ye esteem far lesse of plaine men, then you do of your horses or doggs which ye feed and pamper." *Englands Troublers Troubled* (1648). Quotation made by York Tindall, *op. cit.*, p. 254, note 76.
[15] *A Few Sighs*, p. 687.   [16] *Ibid.*, p. 705, and Psalm LVIII, 10.

The extreme violence of his tone was caused by the utter poverty of the countryside. Bunyan's protest was that of a witness who suffered through sympathy, like that of his contemporary Richard Baxter.

Our author wrote the above in 1658. In 1691, two months before his death, Baxter made similar accusations in an admirable speech which remained in manuscript form until 1926 when F. J. Powicke published it. This work amplifies Bunyan's and throws more light on the " hell " of the poor—who " toyled like beasts, endangered for want of necessary warmth, and distracted with cares to pay their rents ".[17] Even an ascetic like Baxter, so indifferent to food, trembled with disgust when describing the meals of those poverty-stricken men—" some of them are glad of a piece of hangd bacon once a week, and some few that can kill a Bull eate now and then a bit of hangd biefe, enough to try the stomack of an ostrige ".[18]

This evil was not new. Ever since the communal agricultural system of the Middle Ages had been little by little eaten into by modern capitalism, the poverty of small farmers had never ceased to increase.[19] These men's main complaint was that the rich had suppressed the right of pasture, enclosed their personal lands and even bits of the common meadow-land.[20] Deprived of pasturage the wretched peasants could not rear cattle or even assure the tillage of their parcel of land—much less pay the rent. Poverty clamped down on them and made them vagabonds and robbers.[21] The countryside was abandoned. "Where have been a great many householders and inhabitants, there is now but a shepherd and his dog,"

---

[17] Baxter, op. cit., p. 20.
Cf. Arthur Dent, " They are even weary of their lives. These poor silly creatures are faine to drudge and toile all the year long, in Winter and Summer, in frost and snow, in heat and cold, to provide their rents that they may be able to pay their cruell landlord at his day. . . . The poor children cry for bread," op. cit., p. 187.   [18] Baxter, op. cit., p. 25.

[19] Cf. Richard Tawney : " Capitalism, as an economic system, resting on the organisation of legally free wage-earners, for the purpose of pecuniary profit, by the owner of capital or his agents and setting its stamp on every aspect of society, is a modern phenomenon." Foreword to the English ed. of Max Weber : Gesammelte Aufsatze zur Religions soziologie (1920), The Protestant Ethic of Capitalism (London, 1930).

[20] E. Lipson, The Economic History of England, vol. I, chap. 4. ' The Agrarian Revolution '; see, especially, pp. 116 and 120.

[21] Thomas More, Utopia, Bk. I, pp. 23 et seq. (Everyman).

said Latimer in a sermon,[22] and others, including Bernard Gilpin and William Tyndale, protested in vain. " God gave the earth to men to inhabit, and not unto sheep and wild deer," [23] said Tyndale, and Gilpin: "Never were there so many gentlemen and so little gentleness! " [24] " These enclosures be the causes why rich men eat up poor men, as beasts eat grass " [25] a satirist of the time remarked, and in a celebrated passage of his *Utopia*, Sir Thomas More gave his opinion barely tempered with humour. Sheep, he wrote, so gentle and undemanding as to pasture, " have become devourers of men . . . they unpeople villages and towns. . . ." [26]

Bunyan's treatise published in 1658 takes on a burning actuality when we think of the petition sent to Parliament a year later by various Bedfordshire freeholders.[27] After the Civil War the condition of the small proprietors was more critical than before by reason of the heavier taxation, as Gerrard Winstanley, John Barker and Thomas Star pointed out to the Commons.[28]

And the lot of the simple agricultural workers was harder still. When Bunyan wanted to find a really strong image for describing poverty he inevitably said: " He became poorer than they that go with flail and rake." [29]

---

[22] Latimer, *Sermons* (Parker Soc. Pub.), I, 100, quoted by E. Lipson, *op. cit.*, I, p. 142.
[23] All these quotations are from E. Lipson, *op. cit.* W. Tyndale, *Doctrinal Treatises* (Parker Soc. Pub.), 202, Lipson, I, p. 142.
[24] Bernard Gilpin, Lipson, I, p. 141.
[25] Lipson, I, p. 142 from Stubs in *Ballads* from MSS., I, 32.
[26] Thomas More, *Utopia*, Bk. I, p. 23 (Everyman).
[27] *To the Parliament. . . . The Humble Representation and Desires of Divers Freeholders and Others Well Affected to the Commonwealth of England, Inhabiting Within the County of Bedford*, London, 1659.
[28] "You have taken their money in taxes, and freequarters from them, whereby they are made worse able to live than before the wars." *An Appeal to the House of Commons, etc.*, by Gerrard Winstanley, John Barker and Thomas Star, *in the Name of All the Poor Oppressed in the Land of England* (London, 1649), p. 5.
Taxation was one of the concerns of the ' Levellers '. Lilburne and his friends suggested the aboliton of all indirect taxes in favour of one tax " by an equal rate in the pound upon every reall and personnall estate in the nation." Art. xix, p. 6. *An Agreement of the Free People of England Tendered as a Peace-Offering to this Distressed Nation*, 1649.
[29] *A Few Sighs*, III, 705

In fact, although for seven months out of the twelve—from March to September—these workers toiled from five in the morning till seven at night (in accordance with the prescriptions of an Act of 1653),[30] they earned only 8d. a day, which was a weekly wage of about 4s.[31] And if we realise that 10s. per week was, in the opinion of Judge Matthew Hale,[32] the minimum on which a family of six could be housed, clothed and fed, we can get some idea of the poverty of the worker during such time as the mother and children were not able to make a contribution. "Neither contemporary nor modern economists can explain how they lived," writes David Ogg.[33] As the Dissenters counted many of the poor among their number [34] and as some among them—for instance John Lilburne—evinced a political radicalism which in 1647 was epitomised in "The Agreement of the People ",[35] and as two years later twenty men led by Everrard

---

[30] See Lipson, *op. cit.*, II, 394.

[31] Of course this wage varied according to district; moreover it was perpetually being increased in the course of the seventeenth century, as Thorold Rogers tells us in *A History of Agriculture and Prices* (Clarendon Press, Oxford, 1866–1902), IV, 525, V, 673.

Bunyan says that 8d. a day was the average wage of a day-labourer; but J. Cook, a well-known jurist, stated that in 1648 the wage was only 6d. "Most day-labourers in matters of husbandry earn but 6d. a day, who being 6 or 7 in family, what will 3s. a week do to maintain them? It will but half buy bread for they have little else to eat." *Unum Necessarium or the Poore Mans Case* by John Cook of Graies Inn, Barrester (1648), p. 5.

[32] Cf. E. Lipson, "Chief Justice Hale, whose *Discourse Touching Provisions for the Poor* was published in 1683, though written earlier, asserted that a man and wife with four children could not maintain themselves in meat, drink, clothing and house rent under 10 shillings per week ", *op. cit.*, vol. II, p. 392.

To bring home the inadequacy of this wage, David Ogg points out that it was less than the "dole " granted to the down-and-outs. Cf. David Ogg, *op. cit.*, vol. I, p. 85.   [33] David Ogg, *op. cit.*, vol. I, p. 85.

[34] E. D. Bebb, however, draws attention to the fact that the Dissenting movement also included representatives of the greater and lesser nobility : "In an account of conventicles in London, of 1664, it is reported that the Countesses of Valentia, Peterborough and Anglesey, and ' others of quality ' were present at a Dissenters' meeting, a former justice of the peace offering prayer." *Nonconformity and Social and Economic Life, 1660–1800* (London, 1935), p. 48.

[35] Cf. G. P. Gooch, *English Democratic Ideas in the Seventeenth Century*, 2nd ed. with notes and appendices by H. J. Laski (Cambridge, 1927). "The Agreement of the People sets forth the political philosophy of the Levellers or radicals both without and within the army," p. 128.

and Winstanley tried to install themselves on a Surrey hill, it was not unnatural that the rich began to identify these sects with the Revolution.

Already in Queen Elizabeth's reign Richard Hooker had suggested that the Puritan reformers were seeking to gain the favour of the common people [36] by their criticism of the privileged. And in a Parliamentary speech of 1641 Edmund Waller had said:

I look upon Episcopacy as a counterscarp, or out-work; which, if it be taken by this assault of the people, and, withal, this mystery once revealed, *that we must deny them nothing when they ask it thus in troops*, we may, in the next place, have as hard a task to defend our property, as we have lately had to recover it from the Prerogative. If, by multiplying hands and petitions, they prevail for an equality in things ecclesiastical, the next demand perhaps may be *Lex Agraria*, the like equality in things temporal.[37]

The fears expressed by Waller were so widespread that Baxter had to deny being a ' Leveller ' so that his appeal to the rich might be more sympathetically heard.[38]

This roughly brushed-in historical background is necessary if we are to understand *A Few Sighs*. But we shall now examine aspects of Bunyan's social thought as expressed in various other works.

He devoted more space to the tradesman than to the landed pro-

[36] " The Common Sort." *A Preface to Them that Seek (as they term it) the Reformation of the Law and Orders Ecclesiastical in the Church of England* (ed. Everyman, p. 97). Hooker makes an interesting quotation in a footnote of which this is an extract : " A certain writer for reformation . . . writeth of noblemen and gentlemen . . . Whereof came, saith he, this division of such personages from others seeing all men came of one man and one woman ? Was it for their lusty hawking and hunting ? for their nimble dicing and cunning carding ? for their singing and dancing ? for their open bragging and swearing ? for their false fleering and flattering ? for their subtle killing and stealing ? for their cruel polling and filling ? . . ."

[37] The Parliamentary debate centred round a petition signed by 15,000 Londoners for the total abolition of the episcopacy. Cf. *D. N. B.*, vol. XX, 581. Concerning Waller's speech consult, too : Ch. Firth, *Cromwell*, p. 55, and G. P. Gooch, *op. cit.*, p. 175. These references refer to the speech but do not quote it. It is given verbatim in Samuel Johnson, *Lives of the Most Eminent English Poets*, ' Waller '.

[38] Richard Baxter, *Last Treatise*, p. 52.

prietor and this is not without its significance. Just about when Bunyan was writing *Badman* the minister Richard Steele published his edifying work entitled *The Tradesman's Calling*; [39] and the comment made by Richard Tawney concerning this ecclesiastic might well be applied in a certain measure to our author: "No one who was writing a treatise on economic ethics to-day would address himself primarily to the independent shopkeeper, as the figure most representative of the business community, and Steele's book throws a flood of light on the problems and outlook of the bourgeoisie in an age before the centre of economic gravity had shifted from the substantial tradesman to the exporting merchant, the industrial capitalist and the financier." [40]

Bunyan protested against commercial lying and fraud. He did not consider it right either to boost or unjustly depreciate merchandise. [41] He condemned bankruptcy, usury and in particular the monopoly of goods which in his opinion was the most odious form of it. [42] Pawn-shops seemed to him to be an exploitation of poverty under the guise of charity. [43]

He urged that the conscience should throw its light over every transaction. [44] In business both buyer and seller should fix their eyes on the glory of God. [45]

Bunyan's message was the same as that of his master, Arthur Dent, and his rival Benjamin Keach, [46] and the same as Baxter's and Ames'.

Arthur Dent also relegated to eternal malediction those cruel proprietors who were the "caterpillars and cormorants of the earth", [47] those "bloodsuckers" [48] of the people who "grinde the faces of the poore" and devour them. [49]

---

[39] Richard Steele, *The Tradesman's Calling*, being a discourse concerning the nature, necessity, choice, etc. . . . of a calling in general (London, 1684). We would like to emphasise that the similarity only exists up to a point; Bunyan and Steele are different, cf. *infra*, pp. 294–295.

[40] Richard Tawney, *Religion and the Rise of Capitalism* (ed. of 1943), p. 244. [41] *Christian Behaviour*, II, 566.

[42] *Badman*, III, 638. [43] *Ibid.*, 638. [44] *Ibid.*, 638.

[45] *Ibid.*, 640. "In all a man does he should have an eye to the glory of God."

[46] B. Keach, *The Progress of Sin* (1684) (4th ed., London, 1707), pp. 139 et seq. [47] A. Dent, *op. cit.*, p. 180.

[48] *Ibid.*, 190. [49] *Ibid.*, 180.

Ames exhorted everyone to behave according to the laws of charity: " *Spectanda semper et observanda regula aequitatis et charitatis.*" [50] For all of them—Dent, Ames, Baxter and Bunyan—social morality was merely an extension of personal morality. The whole of life should be in tune with the lessons of the Bible.[51]

No quibble was to be tolerated, no distinction recognised as valid between economic necessities and the demands of love for one's neighbour. And if we were to remind Baxter that everybody cannot be a saint, he would make the simple rejoinder: " Therefore all shall not be saved: for heaven is a place for none but saints." [52]

Like Baxter, Bunyan brought out clearly the link between personal morality, individual asceticism and social charity. For it is in order to flatter the flesh and vanity, to subsidise the expenses of a luxurious household, that the rich oppress Lazarus.[53] As Bromyard said in the Middle Ages, if the wolf has killed more sheep than he needs for his own personal sustenance, it is simply because he has other people in mind.[54]

Baxter formulated Puritan morality with a precision lacking in Bunyan. Very often what is implicit in our author was salient in *The Christian Directory* or *The Poor Husbandman's Advocate* (Baxter's " Last Treatise ").

So we see that the fundamental beliefs of the Puritans, by which man is merely the steward of his possessions, dictated the whole of Bunyan's ethic while itself remaining implicit, whereas Baxter brought it into the limelight. The rich, he wrote, " thinke they may please themselves with *their owne* as they list. As if they knew not that there is no *Absolute Property but God's.* . . . No man hath any other propriety than that of a Trusted Servant, or Steward, or a child in minority, who is at his father's will. You have a sub-propriety which, *in foro humano*, may be pleaded against all that would dispossess you. . . . We are no Levellers. . . . But you shall answer for all, even the uttermost farthing, to him that entrusted you." [55]

---

[50] Wil. Ames, *op. cit.*, p. 290.   [51] *A Few Sighs*, pp. 720, 721.
[52] Richard Baxter, *Last Treatise*, p. 47.
[53] *Ibid*, p. 36 and *Badman*, " For all that a man has over and above what serves for his present necessity and supply serves only to feed the lusts of the eye," III, 641.
[54] Bromyard, *s.v.* " Acquisitio mala," quotation in G. Owst, *Literature and Pulpit in Medieval England*, p. 321.
[55] Richard Baxter, *Last Treatise*, p. 36.

Since the Father has a care for all his children, and more, since his predilection goes to the poor, the rich steward has the imperative duty to help the poor. In business it is not a matter of making profits but of being obedient to God's will. It is much better to lose than to sin.[56]

Like Ames, Baxter probably tolerated lending money with interest, in this following the example of Calvin,[57] but he did not allow usury in the bad sense of the word, and one can say of him as has been said of Calvin, that he " dealt with usury, as the apothecary doth with poison ".[58] Bunyan lacks precision on this burning subject, but a perusal of *Badman* gives the impression that he was stricter than Baxter or Ames.[59] Perhaps he had never had occasion to meet one of those professional lenders with interest who were beginning to penetrate even the countryside.[60] If his personal experience had enabled him to observe shameful cases of usury, we are inclined to think that he would have reacted like Nathaniel Holmes [61] or the Puritan lawyer, Cook, who had come to regret " Papist times ". [62]

The fact is that—some over-subtle canonists excepted—people had treated the usurer with great severity before the Reformation. And Bunyan, Holmes and Cook borrowed most of their social ideas from the tradition of medieval Catholicism. If we need conviction on this point we have only to turn to G. R. Owst's analyses and quotations in his studies on English literature in the Middle Ages. From the Dominican John Bromyard or the Franciscan Nicholas

[56] Richard Baxter, *Christian Directory* (1673), p. 120.

[57] Consult Henri Hauser, *A propos des idées économiques de Calvin* in *Mélanges d'Histoire offerts à Henri Pirenne*, 2 vols. (Brussels, 1926), vol. I, p. 3. Calvin would have liked there to be two words, one for honest lending with interest : " usura ", " per se honestum " and another for the " foenus ", " odiosum ".

[58] Quoted by Tawney in his remarkable introduction to Thomas Wilson's *Discourse upon Usury* (1572) (London, 1925), p. 118.

[59] Richard Baxter, *Christian Directory*, pp. 125 *et seq.* Ames, *op. cit.*, pp. 287–288.

[60] R. Tawney, Intro., *cit.*, p. 88.

[61] N. Holmes, *Usury is Injury* (London, 1640), a vigorous attack on Ames' theories.

[62] J. Cook, *Unum Necessarium or the Poore Mans Case*, by John Cook, of Graies Inne, Barrester (1648), " For in times of Popery, it was an odious thing and a usurer as much detested as one that had the French pocks or a leprosie," p. 49. Concerning J. Cook, cf. *D. N. B.*, IV, 995–996.

Bozon, from Master Wimbledon or Master Rypon, to Bunyan, the distance of four centuries seems negligible when we examine the substance of their sermons.

Let us compare the passage from *Sighs from Hell* quoted at the beginning of this chapter [63] with the following words of Nicholas Bozon: "Go to now, ye rich men, weep and howl for your miseries that shall come upon you . . ."; [64] and with Bromyard's scene from the Day of Judgment in which the poor pass judgment with admirable fire and fury on the rich, each one flinging out phrases which begin with the accusation: "We have hungered. . . . We have thirsted and been naked. . . . We were made infirm. . . . We were without shelter. . . . And those robbers yonder gave not our own goods to us when we were in want . . . but to their hounds and horses and apes. . . ." [65]

And now let us compare Langland and Bunyan, *The Pilgrim's Progress* with *The Vision of Piers Plowman*, Madam Bubble with Lady Meed, Badman with Coveting, and the poor peasant of Bedfordshire with Piers himself, since both led the same frugal life.

> ' 'I haue no peny,' quod Peres ' poletes forto bigge,
> Ne neyther gees ne grys, but two grene cheses,
> A fewe cruddes and creem, and an hauer cake,
> And two loues of benes and bran, ybake for my fauntis.' [66]

Lady Meed possesses the county of Coveting and coasts all around such as Usury and Avarice.[67] She corrupts the Judge and condemns the poor man.[68]

Coveting lies, cheats about weight,[69] lends without compassion, showing as much pity to the poor as a pedlar shows to the cat whose skin he wants:

> ' I haue as moche pite of pore men as pedlere hath of cattes,
> That wolde kille hem, yf he cacche hem myzte for coucitise of here skynnes.' [70]

---

[63] Cf. *supra*, p. 283.

[64] Nicolas Bozon, MS. Caius Coll. Camb. 334, fol. 155, quoted by G. R. Owst, *op. cit.*, p. 298.

[65] S. P. Bromyard, *s.v.* Furtum, see G. R. Owst, *op. cit.*, pp. 301–302.

[66] Langland, *Piers Plowman*, C passus VI, 282–285.

[67] *Ibid.*, B passus II, 85–86.

[68] *Ibid.*, B passus III, 157, and C passus IV, 214–215.

[69] *Ibid.*, A passus V, 217–218. [70] *Ibid.*, B passus V, 257–258.

His thought is riveted on his wares instead of God's grace.[71]
He is a monster, and the whore who sells her body will go to Heaven
sooner than the usurer.[72]

Langland no more admits man's right to absolute ownership than do
Bunyan and Baxter, and he recalls that God withdrew his riches and
his reason from Solomon when the latter ceased to make good use of
them and to behave himself well.

> For God gaf to Salomon grace upon erthe
> Rychesse and reson whyle he ryht lyuede,
> And as sone as god seih he suwed nought hus wille,
> He reuede hym of hys richesse and of hus ryht mynde.[73]

So Richard Tawney is right when he says that " if the Reformation
was a revolution, it was a revolution which left almost intact the
traditional scheme of social thought ".[74]   Canon law, he continues,
was nationalised, not abolished.[75]   The Established Church refused
to break all links with the past.   Thomas Wilson, Secretary of
State, refused to admit that all that the Popes had written should be
condemned " as though no good lawe coulde bee made by them ".[76]
" Naye, I will saye playnely, that there are some suche lawes made
by the Popes as be righte godly, saye others what they list." [77]

But during the seventeenth century the tradition dried up and
was in danger of being swept right away by a new civilisation in which
commerce and finance gained in importance every day.   And it
was because they were aware of this threat that Dent and Bunyan and
Holmes put such passion into the exposition and defence of their
economic ideas.   Actually the word ' economic ' does not really apply
here.   For thorough-going Calvinists there were only ethical and
religious problems.   The whole of life was conceived in terms of
duty, or, as the " old Puritan ", John Geree, said, religion commits
us to duty.[78]   Bunyan was no less exacting; religion was the whole of
life: " Many Christians live and do in this world, as if religion were
but a by-business, and this world the one thing necessary; when indeed
all the things of this world are but things by the by; and religion only
the one thing needful." [79]

[71] Langland, *Piers Plowman*, C passus VII, 284–285.
[72] *Ibid.*, C passus VII, 306–307.   [73] *Ibid.*, C passus IV, 326–329.
[74] *Op. cit.*, p. 154.   [75] *Op. cit.*, p. 159.
[76] *Op. cit.* (ed. Tawney, 1925), p. 281.   [77] *Ibid.*
[78] John Geree, *op. cit.*, p. 5.   [79] *Christian Behaviour*, II, 557.

From St. Thomas to Baxter, from the Franciscan and Dominican friars to Bunyan, there was the same affirmation of a universe in which faith floods its light over everything, and of a civilisation in which the spiritual is sovereign.

But these Puritans were crying in the desert. Already their contemporary, Richard Steele, was explaining to the small tradesman that there were men whose religious zeal was unreasonable.[80] Whereas Bunyan had rejected every material advantage for himself and his family,[81] Steele considered this attitude to be absurd.[82] Forty years after the publication of *Badman*, Defoe was warning tradesmen against an excessive piety that was harmful to business.[83] The slightest lie on the tradesman's part made Bunyan indignant, but Defoe considered it necessary—regrettable, yes, but excusable,[84] and he gave chapter 19 of his manual, *The Complete English Tradesman*, this significant title: " Of honesty and veracity in Dealing. In what cases a little latitude seems allowable to a tradesman. . . ."[85] Latitude!—that word so abhorrent to our tinker who saw in it the justification for every shameful compromise.

The rigid morality of Bunyan and Baxter was thus insidiously undermined by the casuist. " The duties of life which are either spiritual or secular," wrote Defoe, " must not interfere with or jostle one another out of its place."[86] And so we have the principle of a double morality presented to us—that of Sunday and that of the working day.[87] And others, bolder even than Defoe, lost no time in making use of the consequences of this new vision of things. Under guise of economic necessity they justified forms of oppression which would have horrified the author of *Robinson Crusoe*.

The contrast between Bunyan on the one hand and Steele or Defoe

---

[80] Richard Steele, *op. cit.*, p. 85. " But there is a preposterous zeal in some tradesmen. . . . But the diligent man considers that God in his great wisdom appointed the six days for work and a seventh for rest."

[81] See *supra*, p. 69.

[82] " May not a man aim at riches by his calling, that he may have ease in his old age. . . . You may design to get an estate, but not merely for your own sake, but chiefly for God's sake. . . ." *Op. cit.*, p. 204.

[83] Defoe, 'The Complete English Tradesman,' in *The Novels and Miscellaneous Works of Daniel Defoe*, London, 1841, vol. xvii, p. 34.

[84] *Ibid.*, pp. 179–180.   [85] *Ibid.*, p. 177.

[86] *Ibid.*, p. 33.   [87] See note 80, *supra*.

on the other can be partly explained by their very different ways of life.

Bunyan, who was brought up in a hamlet and spent his life in a very small town,[88] retained a longing for rural civilisation where there were vast pasture grounds, where sales were made direct from producer to consumer, and where the "pretium justum" of the scholastics was still—and might always have been—generally respected.

In *The Life and Death of Mr. Badman* there is a passage in which the author takes us and plunges us into the atmosphere of the English country of his time, enabling us to see its influence upon his thought:

"There is a poor body that dwells, we will suppose, so many miles from the market; and this man wants a bushel of grist, a pound of butter, or a cheese for himself, his wife, and poor children; but dwelling so far from the market,[89] if he goes thither, he shall lose his day's work, which will be 8d or 1od damage to him, and that is something to a poor man. So he goeth to one of his masters or dames for what he wanteth, and asks them to help him with such a thing; yes, say they, you may have it; but withal they will give him a gripe, perhaps make him pay as much more for it at home, as they can get when they have carried it five miles to a market, yea, and that too for the refuse of their commodity . . . Now this is a kind of extortion, it is a making a prey of the necessity of the poor, it is a grinding of their faces, a buying and selling of them." [90]

Honest bartering was, at bottom, what Bunyan desired. For pedlars and all other middlemen such as Badman he had a thoroughly medieval distrust. For people to live by a simple exchange of goods,

---

[88] And how we understand this nostalgia when we read the following lines by J. L. Hammond and Barbara Hammond : "The most important social fact about this system is that it provided opportunities for the humblest and poorest labourer to rise in the village. The farm servant could save his wages and begin his married life by hiring a cottage which carried rights of common, and gradually buy or hire strips of land." *The Village Labourer, 1760–1832* (1st ed., 1911), ed. used 4th, 1927, p. 9. See the recollection of past times in Richard Baxter, *Last Treatise*, p. 21.

[89] Cf. Lord Ernle : " Each village was at once isolated and self-sufficing. Communication was difficult ", in *English Farming Past and Present* (3rd ed., London, 1922), p. 132. And " Markets were, in many parts of England, not only difficult of access but few in number ", p. 133.

[90] *Badman*, III, 637.

CHRISTIAN AND EVANGELIST

Wood engraving by Blair Hughes-Stanton, Cresset Press limited edition, 1928

GIANT DESPAIR

From a lithographed illustration by Clarke Hutton from the S.C.M. Press
edition, 1947

without having had the trouble and sweat of producing them, seemed
to him immoral and dangerous to the soul. As Henri de Ghent
said " *Summe periculosa est venditionis et emptionis negotiatio* "; [91]
and our author abundantly illustrates this "periculum" in *The Pilgrim's Progress, The Life and Death of Mr. Badman* and *The Holy
War.*

It was in a market-town that By-ends and his friends were taught
by their master, Mr. Gripe-man. At Vanity, a flourishing commercial metropolis, Beelzebub was sovereign. And to take possession of Mansoul, Lucifer proposed to corrupt it by business, to fatten
it and make it rich. [92]

Distrust of wealth and commerce, we were saying; but it would
be more correct to say downright horror. Whoever wanted to add to
his earthly possessions was a muck-rake whose eyes were fixed on " the
straws, the small sticks and dust " [93]—all the derisory booty that he
preferred to a heavenly crown. At the sight of such a spectacle
Christiana could not withhold her tears, and she realised sorrowfully
that there was only one man in ten thousand who ever besought
God *not* to give him wealth. " Give me not riches." [94] That
prayer, said the Interpreter, has now become " rusty ".[95]

Hence Bunyan was a kind of anachronism in his century, but to
grasp the full tardiness of his thought in economic and social questions
we should contrast him not only with his contemporaries, such as
Steele and Defoe, but with a forerunner like Calvin. Calvin had
the originality frankly to accept the fact of modern economics and to
recognise the necessity and appreciable benefits of lending with interest.
He saw what was specious in the arguments of the scholastics, borrowed

---

[91] Henri de Ghent : *Aurea quodlibeta*, p. 42 b, quoted by E. Schreiber,
Die volkswirthschaftlichen Anschauungen der Scholastik seit Thomas v. Aquin
(1913), p. 135, and by R. Tawney, *Religion and the Rise of Capitalism*, p. 33.
[92] *Holy War*, "You know Mansoul is a market-town, a town that delights
in commerce; what therefore if some of our Diabolonians shall feign themselves far-country men, and shall go out and bring to the market of Mansoul
some of our wares to sell—and what matter at what rates they sell their
wares, though it be but for half the worth?—Now let those that thus shall
trade in their market be those that are witty and true to us, and I will lay
my crown to pawn, it will do." P. 217.
" Let Mansoul be taken up in much business, and let them grow full and
rich, and this is the way to get ground of them." P. 217.
[93] *P. P.*, p. 184.   [94] *P. P.*, p. 185.   [95] *P. P.*, p. 185.

demned unreservedly all forms of individual and social oppression.
Yet at the same time Bunyan was conservative, as sincere Christianity often is: because nothing can exist in the world that God
does not wish to conserve for ends that He alone can know.

So we should be committing a grave error if we imagined from
reading *Sighs from Hell* that Bunyan desired a radical reform of
civil power, and that his repeated protestations of loyalty to the
sovereign were nothing more than hypocritical time-serving.[109]

Apart from the direct influences that Bunyan perhaps underwent
(for instance from a loved book such as Luther's *Commentary on the
Epistle to the Galatians*—Luther, who had such respect for
authority),[110] his deepest currents of thought and feeling must inevitably have led him towards a conservative standpoint.

To begin with he had a horror of anarchy. In the Valley of the
Shadow of Death no individual detail seems to him more horrifying
than the general impression : " In a word it is every whit dreadful,
being utterly without Order." [111] Bunyan was not revealing here

---

[109] Cf. especially *Seasonable Counsel* (1684), II, 709. Richard Tawney, to
whom we ourselves owe so great a debt, is mistaken when he writes that Bunyan was an " innate Republican ". *Religion and the Rise of Capitalism*, p.
201. Compare with Bunyan, Baxter's *Last Treatise* (p. 53), in which he
distinguishes sharply between " commonwealth " and " democracy ";
of the first of these terms he writes : " it is the ' genus ' to monarchy and
aristocracy also " and he could have added " theocracy ". See his *Holy
Commonwealth* (1659), theses 24, 46 and 192 which we have quoted. Let us
add here thesis 74 : " Of all the three ordinary forms of government, democracy is to most people, and usually the worst." Interesting too is thesis
204 where as a true Calvinist he asks that a great difference be made between
the good and the bad, and also thesis 214 in which he discusses the vices
which should disqualify people from being electors.

[110] Cf. Luther, *A Commentary on St. Paul's Epistle to the Galatians* (London,
1940).
" In civil policy obedience to the law must be severely required," chap. II,
p. 62. " The first use of the law is to bridle wickedness. Therefore God
hath ordained magistrates, parents, ministers, bonds, and all civil ordinances
that if they do no more, yet, at least, they may bind the devil's hands, that
he rage not in his bond-slaves after his own lust," chap. III, p. 189. E.
Ehrhardt quotes this passage which we have not referred to : " *Saepe a me
audistis, quod ordinationes politicae et economicae sint divinae, quin, Deus ipse
ordinavit et apportavit eas ut solem lunam et alias creaturas.*" " *Le Sens de la
revolution religieuse et morale accomplie par Luther,*" *Revue de Métaphysique
et de Morale* (1918), no. *cit.* [111] *P. P.*, p. 59.

an ordinary intellectual conviction, he was confessing the essential demands of his nature.

Our author felt that all true reform was first and foremost the reform of the individual, and that every citizen's primary duty was to attempt such a personal change: " Every Christian man is made a king by Christ. But then, his dominion as such doth reach no further than to himself. . . . His office is to govern, and bridle, and keep under, himself . . . to bring his body into subjection to the will of God." [112]

Finally Bunyan was optimistic. He believed in the ultimate triumph of God, and this inclined him to a resigned expectation.[113] Moreover—and in this he was nearer to medieval Catholicism than to his beloved Luther—he saw the evolution of the universe as a constant progress: " I observe, that in the creation of the world, God goeth gradually on, from things less, to things more abundantly glorious. . . . First he bringeth forth a confused chaos, then he demands matter to appear distinct, then the earth bringeth forth trees, and herbs, and grass; after that beasts . . . and last of all, Let us make man. . . . This wonderful piece of the workmanship of God." [114]

Bunyan gives his enthusiasm full vent, in beautiful and worthy language: " God [shows] respect to this excellent creature, in that he first provideth for him, before he giveth him his being; He bringeth him not to an empty house, but to one well-furnished with all kind of necessaries, having beautified the heaven and the earth with glory." [115]

However pessimistic Bunyan was when looking at the individual, there always persisted in him a radiant hope in the progress of the world. Over the fishes of the sea and the beasts of the earth, over the birds that fly and the creatures that creep on the earth, over all

---

[112] *Seasonable Counsel*, II, 706.
[113] With Luther resignation came from pessimism. In an unjust world peace was a by-product of justice. Princes were scoundrels necessary for keeping a silly population in check. " *Nous logeons dans une hôtellerie où le Diable est aubergiste et où toutes les mauvaises passions sont servantes.*" We can only say that the nature of the house is to be thus, and submit to being tortured. Cf. Ch. Andler, " *L'esprit conservateur et l'esprit révolutionnaire dans le luthéranisme,*" *Revue de Métaphysique et de Morale*, no. *cit.*
[114] *An Exposition on the Ten First Chapters of Genesis*, II, 422.
[115] *Ibid.*, 422.

things visible and invisible—men, angels and demons, in Heaven, on earth and under the earth—Christ is King.[116]   And the day will come when his name will be adored from one extremity of the globe to the other, and " all shall become the kingdoms of our Lord, and of his Christ ". [117]

Like the early Christians, Bunyan lived in a state of waiting. And, after all, even injustices and persecutions are insignificant beside conviction concerning the end of the world.   And so the same man could rail against the cruel follies of the great and yet judge them tolerable in the perspective of history.   That is a contradiction which the greatness of man's heart can easily comprehend.

That faith in the Millennium should have pushed Venner and a few other people to insurrection proves nothing against the pacifism of the majority of those who believed in it.   Bunyan, as one of his friends said, was " none of those light fanatic spirits that our age abounds withal " [118] and as a start he was careful not to prophesy dates like John Rogers and John Canne whose writings seem to us typical of the illuminism of the period.[119]   My Lord, wrote John Canne to Cromwell, this is now the question: what is to follow ? [120]

Contrast this self-assured impatience with the tinker's serene conviction: " Antichrist shall be brought to ruin gradually; [121] that is, by degrees.   The time of her fall is not certainly known by the saints." [122]   Oh certainly the time was drawing near, for there were signs, in particular the sign of the ephemeral triumph of the " beast " [123] and the persecution of the children of God.[124]   But this nearness was altogether relative to one who saw the eternity of the divine Kingdom in terms of the grains of sand by the sea or the drops of water in the ocean.[125]

---

[116] *An Exposition on the Ten First Chapters of Genesis*, II, 423.

[117] *Ibid.*, 423.   [118] *A Few Sighs*, III, preface signed J. G., p. 672.

[119] Consult too Louise Fargo Brown, *The Political Activities of the Baptists and Fifth Monarchy Men in England during the Interregnum.   Prize essay of the Historical Association* (U.S.A.), 1911.   (Oxford Univ. Press, 1912.) This is an important study.

[120] John Canne, *A Voice from the Temple to the Higher Powers* (London, 1653), see too *The Time of the End* (1657) which is preceded by *An Epistolary Perambulation or a Word to Everyone round the world*, by John Rogers.

[121] *Of Antichrist and his Ruin*, Works, II, 55.

[122] *Ibid.*, p. 58.   [123] *Ibid.*, p. 65.

[124] *Ibid.*, p. 65.   [125] Cf. *A Few Sighs*, III, 683.

We must suffer, we must endure. This is the constant theme of his counsels to his afflicted brethren.[126] This resignation in faith casts its rays over his whole thought and gives it a remarkable unity. Let us repeat: with him everything held together, suffering purifies us, puts us on the road to Christ and is a sign of God's predilection for us. Hence our pain is our victory. "Saints are not said to be overcome, when they are imprisoned, banished and killed for their faithful testimony: No, by these things *they overcome*." [127] Similarly John Geree took the Cross as his "banner" (sic), prayer and tears as his weapons, and he entered the fray crying *Vincit qui patitur*.[128]

Who can fathom God's designs ? Sometimes good people have been the cause of the Church's misfortunes, and bad people the instruments of her greatness.[129] One must be wary, too, of accusing kings, for they see through the eyes of their advisers and act according to the counsels they are given.[130] Just as the Anglican Church, though mistaken, is not Antichrist, so Protestant kings, though blind, must not be confused with the kings of "Babylon".[131] Snatched by God from the doomed City, they will one day destroy it.[132] " Let the King have verily a place in your heart," Bunyan concludes, " and with heart and mouth give God thanks for him." [133] We see that the tinker was appropriating the ancient belief in despotism as the *causa remota* chosen by the Eternal One for the realisation of his designs.[134]

All magistrates are " God's ministers ".[135] In 1652 the London Baptists had voiced the same doctrine in their "Confession of Faith".[136]

---

[126] *Seasonable Counsel or Advice to Sufferers* (1684). Compare Bunyan's attitude with that of the right wing of the ' Fifth Monarchy ' men. Cf. Louise Fargo Brown : " The principles of the moderate wing were well set forth by William Aspinwall in the Summer of 1656. While waiting for the Fifth Monarchy, he says, it is right for the Saints to obey the Fourth and even hold office under it, however corrupt it may be. The Fifth Monarchy men are the best and truest friends unto government. Only they take themselves bound in conscience to rebuke sin." *Op. cit.*, p. 104.

[127] *Of Antichrist and his Ruin*, II, 65.

[128] John Geree, *op. cit.*, p. 6.　　　　[129] *Of Antichrist*, p. 45.

[130] *Ibid.*, p. 45.　　[131] *Ibid.*, p. 61.　　[132] *Ibid.*, p. 72.　　[133] *Ibid.*, p. 74.

[134] Cf. E. Troeltsch, *op. cit.*, vol. I, p. 291.

[135] *Seasonable Counsel*, II, 705.

[136] " A civill magistracy is an ordinance of God," p. 11 of *A Confession of Faith of the Several Congregations or Churches of Christ in London, which are Commonly (though Unjustly) Called Anabaptists*, 4th impression, 1652.

That these pacific protests did not prevent some of his co-religionists —Henry Danvers, for example [137]—from preaching the call to arms, proves nothing against Bunyan's sincerity and that of the majority of Baptists.

When we read his work in the light of his life we can have no doubt as to his loyalty. His attitude in prison, the words he said to Cobb, are in agreement with his writings.[138] Like all Puritans, he judged it better to obey God than man,[139] but his resistance to civil power, however proud and strong, was a spiritual protest accompanied by submission to the punishment imposed. There was neither temerity nor cowardice. Bunyan did not seek out suffering any more than he ran away from it.[140]

Thus Bunyan's thought was in line with Protestant thought here. For even Calvin tempered the right to resist.[141]

Our author undoubtedly looked on himself as a guide for the people, a guide whose task was to edify his neighbour, convert him and hence win the only durable victory. " Christians are like the several flowers in a garden, that have upon each of them the dew of heaven, while being shaken with the wind, they let fall their dew at each other's roots, whereby they are jointly nourished and become nourishers of one another." [142]

To spread the word of God in this way, by each remaining at his post and fulfilling his own function, was the surest way of establishing a holy community; and this thought was so dear to Bunyan that he expressed it several times using almost identical imagery: " When Christians stand every one in their places, and do the work of their relations, then they are like the flowers in the garden, that stand and grow where the gardener hath planted them, and then they shall both

---

[137] Cf. Louise Fargo Brown, *op. cit.*, p. 100.

[138] Cf. *supra*, Intro.

[139] John Geree, *op. cit.*, p. 4. The Puritans make constant allusion to Peter's and John's words : " Whether it be right in the sight of God to hearken unto you more than unto God, judge ye." Acts, IV, 19.

[140] Cf. *Seasonable Counsel*, p. 694.

[141] Cf. E. Troeltsch, *op. cit.*, II, 612, 630.

[142] *Christian Behaviour*, II, 570. Bunyan recalls the Bible : " My doctrine shall drop as the rain, my speech shall distil as the dew, as the small rain upon the tender herb, and as the showers upon the grass." Deut. xxxii, 2.

honour the garden in which they are planted, and the gardener that hath so disposed of them." [143]

In *The Pilgrim's Progress* the Interpreter takes Christiana into his garden and says : "Behold the flowers are divers in Stature, in Quality, and Colour, and Smell, and Virtue . . . also where the Gardener has set them, there they stand, and quarrel not one with another." [144]

It is a beautiful comparison which exactly conveys Bunyan's need for peace and order, and yet suggests a static conception of the world which was quite foreign to him. In order to express his faith in the progress of the universe, the march of creation towards perfection,[145] and his dream of a spacious social architecture, he would have done better to have taken up his metaphor about " the house " which God is ceaselessly organising, embellishing and enlarging, in accordance with his eternal designs.[146]

We wonder whether his frequent allusions to the harmony of a garden sprang spontaneously from him as a villager, whether they were suggested by the Bible [147] or whether he was remembering a traditional metaphor of medieval sermons. The image is certainly in the spirit of medieval Catholic thought and thus betrays Bunyan a little.[148] And yet whatever his unconscious debt to the pre-

[143] *Christian Behaviour*, II, 550.
[144] *P. P.*, p. 187.
[145] *An Exposition on the Ten First Chapters of Genesis*, II, 422.
[146] *Ibid.*
[147] See note 142 preceding page.
[148] G. R. Owst, whose opinion we sought on the subject of Bunyan's image of a garden, has reinforced our personal opinion with his expert authority. "The comparison with a garden and with flowers that you quote," he writes to us, " seems to me so familiar and so natural, whatever the period or whoever the author, that for myself I would hesitate to attribute its origins—with any certainty, that is—to the influence of an earlier literature. . . . At the same time it is very true that the image of a garden and its various plants was often used by the theologians and homily-writers of the Middle Ages to illustrate the Church, or religion, particularly the latter, in the sense of the ideal monastic community in which all the virtues flower."
The medieval preacher was very fond of the vineyard imagery and its three orders of husbandmen (St. Matthew xx, 1–14). Cf. *Literature and Pulpit in Medieval England*, pp. 549–551. Master Wimbledon considered priests, knights and labourers to be necessary—the priests " to kut away the void braunches of sinnes ", the knights " to maintaine Goddis law . . . and to

Reformation religious tradition in England, Bunyan was a Protestant. And though the Puritan might still see the world as "a cosmos of vocations" [149] this word meant something other than in the Middle Ages. Ernest Troeltsch, in some beautiful passages, has shown the difference between the Catholic "officium" or "ministerium" and Calvin's idea of the "vocatio"—the "calling" of the "saints".[150]

The passive obedience of the believer was replaced by the desire for active collaboration (while each remaining in his place and station) with the divine work on earth. Christian morality no longer exercised itself *in vocatione* but *per vocationem*. Individuality expressed itself in its very respect for the community. The good servant no longer thought of his master, but of God's designs for himself and the world.[151] St. Paul's words to the Colossians take on a new accent: " And whatsoever ye do, do it heartily, as to the Lord."

In one sense the "saint" had only one task here below—to get well out of it, as the Methodist preacher, John Nelson, said.[152] But this single task implied thousands of others, and the first necessity was to devote oneself to the public good for which man is born.

When Bunyan was in prison, and thought himself to be on the eve of his execution,[153] he wrote feverishly to his Bedford brethren to bring them help for the last time: "Though there I shall rest from my labours and be in paradise . . . yet it is not there, but here, I must do you good." [154]

---

kepe the londe from enemies of other londes. . . And to labourers it falleth to travail bodelich and with their sore swete geten out of the earth bodilich lifelode for hem and other partes ".

And all have the duty to love each other. " For whan the even is come, that is the end of this world, than everye man shall take reward, good or evill, after that he hath travailed here." *Sermon at St. Paul's Cross*, 1388, quoted by G. R. Owst, pages indicated.

[149] Cf. Troeltsch, *op. cit.*, I, 293.

[150] *Ibid.*, I, 293, and II, 609, 610.

[151] Cf. *Christian Behaviour*, p. 564.

[152] " I have no business in it [the world] but to get well out of it," quoted by E. D. Bebb, *Nonconformity and Social Economic Life, 1660–1680* (1935), p. 98.

[153] " Thus have I, in few words, written to you, before I die," *Christian Behaviour*, p. 574.

[154] *Ibid.*, p. 574.

Conclusion

IN his *Bibliotheca Mysticorum*, published in Amsterdam in 1708, Pierre Poiret wrote: " Bunian, Ioan, Anglus egregius." But nowadays Bunyan's mysticism is frequently denied, in words of which Sir Herbert Grierson's are a typical example: " Nor was Bunyan in any manner or measure a mystic. He was an intensely practical English peasant." [1] This is a curious juxtaposition of terms—as if the mystical life had ever undermined the practical sense of the men and women who led it! No one would deny the spirit of enterprise, the gift for organisation, nor the clear-sightedness of a Teresa of Avila or an Ignatius Loyola. The literary critics who fix on this psychological test by-pass the heart of the matter; they cannot so much as guess at its breadth or character.

They should try rather to determine the nature of Bunyan's spiritual experiences. Did he ever know the state proper to mysticism —ecstasy, the absorption of the individual in the Godhead ? And mysticism has its degrees, of which the supreme one is when the presence of God is felt without visions, without words, but by a revelation the nature of which is rather like music or a dark clarity. Pseudo-Dionysius speaks of the " supernatural radiance of divine darkness " and Tauler of a " darkness " that is " light ".[2]

Ecstasies such as these are not recorded in Bunyan's autobiography, and we could hardly look on the oral and visual hallucinations described therein as mystical phenomena.[3] Indeed the greatest

---

[1] Sir H. Grierson, *Cross-currents in English Literature of the Seventeenth Century—or the World, the Flesh and the Spirit, their Actions and Reactions* (London, 1929), p. 198.   [2] J. Maréchal, *op. cit.*, vol. I, p. 148.
[3] R. P. Aug. Poulain, S. J., *Des graces d'Oraison*, chaps. 20 and 21. We have used the English translation, *The Graces of Interior Prayer, a Treatise on Mystical Theology* (London, 1910). Notice especially chap. 21, p. 322 : " Practically, in the case of those who have not attained to high sanctity, we can admit that at least three quarters of their revelations are illusions. I am led to believe that illusion is easier in the case of interior locutions (intellectual or imaginative) than with imaginative visions. They are much more nearly allied to the ordinary operations of the human mind in which ideas and phrases arise perpetually."

mystics have never attached importance to "external and physical visions".[4]   And as they have experienced genuine divine revelation, it is easy for them to recognise counterfeits.   Saint Teresa, for example, was sometimes the victim of nervous disorders, but she was never taken in by them.[5]

Nevertheless it does seem that Bunyan did sometimes have an intuition of the presence of God.   We are thinking particularly of the experience described in paragraph 174 of *Grace Abounding*— the experience which at first he kept to himself.   He alludes to it finally with a kind of modesty, trying to harm it as little as possible in translating it into the approximations of language.   "That sudden rushing of wind was as if an Angel had come upon me . . . it commanded a great calm in my Soul."   True, it is a long, long way from that calm to the supreme "union" in which, as Silesius says, "*die Einheit hat die Anderheit verschluckt*".[6]   With Bunyan there was no illumination in the total silence of the soul—Biblical texts at once started "falling" upon it; but it is indubitable that he looked on this experience as something apart, as miraculous in the sensation and peace it brought to the soul rather than in the content of the words heard.   Certainly this must be considered a minor mystical phenomenon.

The truth is that Bunyan was possessed of the spirit and natural disposition of the mystic, but these could not expand because his religious convictions stultified their growth.   Protestantism, by har-

---

[4] See Aug. Poulain, *op. cit.*, chap. *cit.*

See too J. Maréchal, *op. cit.*, I, 198.   "*Aussi bien les visions, de quelque nature qu'elles soient, et on en dira autant de tout le merveilleux 'somatique', n'expriment point l'essence du mysticisme ; elles n'en sont que des épisodes voyants, secondaires et souvent discutables.   Elles peuvent aider la vie mystique par le réconfort ou le stimulant qu'elles apportent ; mais les plus éminents de leurs bénéficiaires sont unanimes à répéter avec saint Paul : 'Aemulamini charismata meliora '.*"

[5] Let us recall a phrase of St. Teresa on this subject; it has a general validity and is not confined to the context : "Our wretchedness is such that our soul, that poor little prisoner, participates in the infirmities of the body."   *Life*, chap. 11, p. 41, in the abridged ed., *Les Mystiques espagnols, Sainte Thérèse, Saint Jean de la Croix*, in the collection "Cent Chefs-d'Oeuvre étrangers".

[6] Quoted by F. Heiler, *La Prière* (Paris, 1931), p. 288.   Our debt towards this lovely book is considerable.

nessing faith to the Scriptures, usually puts a check on the introversive movement of the soul and deflects religious feeling into other channels. The individual, aware that he has no rôle of his own in justification but that the drama is played out quite outside him, lays the main emphasis on the sacred texts whence he draws his convictions; he inclines his flight towards external ends.

Bunyan had his hours of mute contemplation but, on the whole, his life became one impassioned dialogue between his soul and a God whose voice came from without.[7] This God, now father, now judge, now affectionate, now severe, enjoyed being petitioned and importuned. He smiled at His creature's wilfulness, answered him, encouraged him and, affectionately imperious, urged him on to further labours. And so Bunyan's road went from obstacle to obstacle, and on each, as he passed, he left one of the doubts and difficulties that at first had laid him low. The pilgrim's way was a way of health and joy. Christian quitted the city where he could not breathe and set out towards ever vaster and brighter horizons. His pilgrimage was his growth.

But the allegory is a dyptich in which each panel is necessary for the understanding of the other. Christian gives place to Great-heart, or rather let us boldly say that Christian becomes Great-heart. When characters are incarnations of their author's spirit we should see, not a substitution, but a metamorphosis.

Thus the man who set out alone and fought solitary battles finished his journey in numerous company; the man who strayed in the slough of despond ended up by leading others. The man in rags, plaintive and vulnerable, became successively the ferocious adversary of Apollyon and the Knight in invisible armour.

But he gained no less in cheerful friendliness than in steadfastness and assurance. The world he had renounced was restored to him and he found himself happy in the midst of his family.

But was Bunyan's triumph so complete in the spiritual order? Who could think so? There is all the distance of an artist's dream between the allegory and personal reality.[8] Great-heart incarnates, for the whole of twenty-four hours of every day, and as if it were a

[7] See in F. Heiler, *op. cit.*, the characteristics of prophetic piety.
[8] Evidence for this is given in his treatise. Cf. *supra*, "Bunyan, Controvertialist and Preacher".

definitive good, the harmony of soul that his author knew only in isolated moments. Bunyan never attained that static joy, that calm water in which summer dips a corner of the sky, but a tranquillity in which hope was ruffled by unrest.

But he learned to know the movements and rhythm of his soul and hence each setback was followed by the certainty of a new departure. In the concentration of his effort he remained master of himself. His "principal talent", his will, managed sooner or later to rule all the others.

At the beginning of his life a thousand duties pressed upon him over which he established no hierarchy; whence that feverish confusion into which broke new and unreasonable injunctions which he had to obey. Morality imposed itself upon him from without.

His conversion, inasmuch as it was the assurance that he, John Bunyan, was elected and saved from all eternity, lifted his main fear from his soul and made of ethics a natural growth, a good-will, simple, strong and sincere but heedless of possible failure. Thenceforward his whole life proceeded from a single deep movement which always managed to absorb the secondary currents.

Robert White has left us a portrait of that Bunyan, and it is not so very different from Great-heart as we imagine him.

In the portrait the face is full, the mouth firm and well-modelled and with a delicate sensuality. The large nose is sensual too, but the eyes are dreamy even though he is smiling. This man is serene when faced with reality. He is a virile Englishman, solidly built, his head set well on his shoulders, in fact indistinguishable from a thousand others. Though he has lived within the vision of the invisible Kingdom, he nevertheless looks what he is—a good father of a family. Like Kierkegaard's " knight of faith " he can express " the sublime flight in the daily round ".[9]

And his friends saw him very much as we see him in the portrait. Charles Doe wrote: " He was tall of stature, strong-boned, though not corpulent, somewhat of a ruddy face, with sparkling eyes, wearing his hair on his upper lip, after the old British fashion; his hair reddish, but in his latter days, time had sprinkled it with grey; his nose well set, but not declining or bending, and his mouth moderate large; his forehead something high." [10]

[9] S. Kierkegaard, *Crainte et tremblement* (Paris, 1925), p. 58.
[10] *Works*, I, pp. 64–65.

CONCLUSION

Robert White shows us a forehead that is wide too and this helps to give the face its calm energy and dignity. It is not the face of an ascetic but of a soldier for whom the world should be a universe of heroes. The English have always seen him as the personification of pure and virile strength which they like to think is characteristic of their national genius.

At any rate Bunyan incarnates the Puritan spirit at its best and most durable: its gravity, its solemn approach to life, its taste for endeavour. And probably all this is the better expressed in his work in that he wrote when the historic moment of the Puritans was over.

Throughout the Restoration and especially at such times as foreign invasions threatened,[11] the whole population recalled the reign of the " saints " and particularly of their admirable leader. " It is strange," notes Pepys on July 12, 1667, " how everybody do now-a-days reflect upon Oliver, and commend him." And on September 4, 1668: " The business of abusing the Puritans begins to grow stale and of no use, they being the people that at last will be found the wisest."

Puritanism had made such a deep mark on the soul of the nation that its stamp was never to be effaced. Well on in the eighteenth century, when free thinking seemed to have taken firm root, the provinces still retained their piety and refused to listen to rationalist ministers.[12] The faith, preserved intact, was only awaiting the eloquence of Whitfield and Wesley.

Hence Bunyan's work gained in power, richness and harmony by being born in the days of Puritanism's oppression and sorrow and not in the exaltation of its ephemeral political triumph. By its late birth it had the advantage of the author's wide human experience and of a closer contact with the people. Puritanism would probably not have become aware of itself if its self-expression had taken place in the fever of action. It was in recollection that it was able to produce as mediator a man in whom memory was the soul of thought.

[11] Elie Halévy, 'La naissance du méthodisme en Angleterre', *Revue de Paris* (1906).
[12] *Ibid.*

A HISTORICAL OUTLINE OF THE PURITAN MOVE-MENT FROM QUEEN ELIZABETH'S REIGN TO BUNYAN'S BIRTH

EVER since 1564 a movement of protest against the Elizabethan compromise had been making itself felt.[1] It was crystallised in 1571 under the impetus of Thomas Cartwright, Lady Margaret Professor of Divinity at Cambridge. Cartwright had been a student in Geneva, and he rose up against the power of the bishops, against the sign of the cross at baptism, against surplices, the exchange of wedding-rings—in short, against the whole legacy of the Catholic Church to the Anglican. All these grievances were tabulated in the Millenary Petition presented to James I on his arrival in England in 1603, a petition that represents the authentic Puritanism of the time.[2]

Nevertheless the Puritans were still loyal to the Church they wanted to reform,[3] on account of their reverence for order and

[1] Daniel Neal: " In the year 1564 . . . when those that refused were first called puritans, a name of reproach derived from the Cathari or Puritani of the 3rd century after Christ, but proper enough to express their desires of a more pure form of worship and discipline in the church." *Op. cit.*, Preface, vol. I, p. v.

[2] Here is a brief extract : " In the church service. That the cross in baptism, interrogatories ministered to infants, confirmation as superfluous may be taken away . . . The cappe and surplice not urged . . . The long formes of service abridged. Church song and musick moderated to better edifying. That the Lordes Day be not prophaned : that rest upon holy days be not so strictly urged . . . No popish opinion to be any more taught or defended : nor ministers charged to teach upon people to bowe at the name of Jesus."

[3] Some extremists, however, left the national Church. The insignificance of their number serves only to bring out Puritan loyalism. The question has often been dealt with. See, for example, M. Knappen's excellent work, *Tudor Puritanism* (Chicago, 1939), chap. 15, ' Separatism '.

their respect for royal authority.[4] When the Armada threatened to bring its fleet almost to the coasts of the fatherland, it was fitting that Englishmen should stand together and not be divided.

Cartwright himself said that non-conformity was unjustifiable.[5]

The exalted patriotism expressed with lyrical fervour by Shakespeare's John of Gaunt did not silence all the critics, but it removed their violence and bitterness. In their prisons the Puritans prayed for the Queen who was persecuting them. History has kept alive the memory of John Stubbe, who, with his right hand chopped off with a butcher's knife, preferred to lose the other rather than be suspected of a failure of loyalty.

The Stuarts were less clever than Elizabeth, and little by little they extinguished that love. They made the dissensions and struggles that were to tear the country for nearly a century inevitable. Of a sect, as Macaulay puts it, they created a faction.[6]

When James I arrived in his new kingdom in 1603 he was quite determined not to tolerate the clerical tutelage to which he had had to submit as James VI of Scotland. The dead queen had once advised him not to show tolerance towards " a sect of perilous consequence such as would have no kings but a presbytery ".[7] To the demands of the Millenary Petition he gave a categorical refusal. And at the Hampton Court Conference he declared: " A Scottish Presbytery agreeth as well with a monarchy as God with the devil. Then Jack and Tom and Will and Dick shall meet, and at their pleasures censure me and my council. . . . No bishop, no king! " [8]

Those days in January, 1604, at Hampton Court, marked a turning-point for Anglicanism and the Puritan movement.

Elizabeth's prelates, like Thomas Cranmer before them, had con-

[4] Let us append what M. Knappen calls : " the lingering medieval horror of sects and the ill-repute of the continental anabaptists." *Op. cit.*, p. 303.

[5] See W. A. Shaw, ' Elizabethan Presbyterianism ', in *Eng. Hist. Review*, Oct., 1888. See too G. P. Gooch, *English Democratic Ideas in the Seventeenth Century*, ed. of 1927 (Cambridge), p. 35.

[6] T. B. Macaulay, *History of England* (ed. of 1852, 4 vols.), I, 60, and Sir Charles Firth, *Oliver Cromwell and the Rule of the Puritans in England*, ed. of 1933, p. 18.

[7] *The Letters of Queen Elizabeth*, ed. by G. B. Harrison (London, 1935), p. 203, letter of July 6, 1590.

[8] Hampton Court Conference, Jan. 14, 16, 18, 1604.

served the episcopacy for reasons of convenience, without really judging it to be necessary.[9]   James' bishops considered it to be essential to the good, and even to the existence, of a Christian society. William Laud, who became Bishop of London in the year of Bunyan's birth, inclined the Anglican Church towards the doctrines of Arminius and an Erastian discipline.   He preached passive obedience to the Crown, while another prelate, Lancelot Andrewes, publicly declared the monarch to be inspired by the Holy Ghost.[10]

The gulf which separated the Puritans from the princes of the national Church became alarmingly wide.   It was no longer a breach caused by fairly superficial divergences of opinion on matters of ceremonial and vestments;   no, it was now being made by essential differences of dogmatic opinion.

On the one side there were those who believed in free-will and the possible redemption of whomsoever believed in Christ; on the other those who believed in the dogma of predestination and the salvation of the " children of God " only.   To the latter Laud's ritualism seemed a return to Catholicism.   The very heart and soul of religion, said Cromwell, were in danger of being eaten away.[11] Susceptibilities became sharper: " a bow was not an expression of reverence, but a confession of idolatry; a surplice, not a few yards of white linen, but a rag of Rome ".[12]   More and more Puritans left the national Church to establish churches of their own.   The Presbyterian current had been born of Calvinism; now the Congregationalist current began to emerge.

As the Puritans were in a minority, the very logic of their situation [13] drove them to attack the political power that denied them their

---

[9] On these well-known facts and on the opinion of a bishop such as Jewel, for example, see any history of England ; we suggest T. B. Macaulay, *op. cit.*, vol. I, p. 74 *et seq.*, or S. R. Gardiner, *op. cit.*, vol. III, p. 243.

[10] Compare Richard Baxter (1668) : " But whoever be the sect-masters, it is notorious that the prelates (though not they only) are the sect-makers ", *op. cit.*, pp. 2, 3,

[11] It was in 1658 that Cromwell pronounced these strong words : " To innovate upon us in matter of religion, and so to innovate as to eat out the core and power and heart and life of all religion, by bringing on us a company of poisonous popish ceremonies." Cf. C. H. Firth, *Oliver Cromwell and the Rule of the Puritans in England* (ed. of 1933), p. 36.

[12] C. H. Firth, *ibid.*, p. 26.

[13] As Harold Laski puts it, quoted by Helena M. Chew in a very interesting

right to existence; and, by one of history's great ironies, those men whose religious beliefs should have led them to be champions of an aristocratic and authoritarian government—for were not the elect the chosen few who should curb the reprobates?—those men became the artisans of democracy.

It is doubtless exaggerated to say [14] that every Puritan is *ipso facto* a republican, but it is undeniable that in certain circumstances Calvinism makes way for a republic. Once it was borne in on them that political liberty was necessary to religious liberty, and that religious liberty was necessary to human liberty, the Puritans strove to obtain that first essential liberty. Hence the political conflicts redoubled the religious conflicts; and hatred, at first directed towards ceremonial and vestments, forthwith spread to people—to the bishops in particular and thence to their head, the King.

The meaning of the word " Puritan " stands out so sharply in this rapid sketch that it is surprising how often it is misunderstood. Puritanism and Presbyterianism should not be contrasted so as to make the former synonymous with Congregationalism. Presbyterianism and Congregationalism are merely two different aspects of Puritanism and like the two arms of one river. The Presbyterian does not conceive the organisation of the Church in the same way as the Independent or the Baptist, but all have in common a basic doctrine concerning God and man which unites them whatever they may think about it.

Bunyan was born at the very moment when the conflict was becoming more violent between the Puritans and their enemies,

---

study of James I published in *The Social and Political Ideas of Some Great Thinkers of the Sixteenth and Seventeenth Centuries* (ed. by F. J. C. Hearnshaw, London, 1926). This article enables us rapidly to pursue the evolution of the doctrine of Gelasius and of the ideas concerning the separation of the spiritual and temporal jurisdictions. Helena Chew reminds us that a proclamation of independence with regard to ecclesiastical authority ended by becoming an affirmation of the superiority of that very authority. On the one side Jesuits such as Bellarmine, while denying the Pope the right to intervene directly in temporal affairs, recognised his duty to act once the salvation of souls was at stake. On the other side the Calvinist Churches demanded the right to subordinate the political to the spiritual in case of conflict between the two of them. James I, then, had to defend himself on both sides. See his *Apologie for the Oath of Allegiance*, 2nd ed., 1609.

[14] As Richard Tawney does, *Religion and the Rise of Capitalism* (London, 1926), ed. of 1943, p. 208.

between the defenders of Parliamentary rights and the partisans of royal absolutism. In 1628, the Duke of Buckingham, that ill-starred favourite bequeathed by James to his son Charles, was assassinated. By the Petition of Rights a Parliament, in which Cromwell sat, rose up against—among other abuses—the illegal levy of taxes and imprisonment without trial. So, from 1629, Charles did without Parliament. He placed his confidence in two men who further incited the people's anger: William Laud, because he tried to impose uniformity of practice, and the supreme authority of the King, in religious matters, and Strafford because he upheld the King's autocracy in the field of politics.

WHEN WAS *THE PILGRIM'S PROGRESS* WRITTEN?

ON page 166 *et seq.* we examined the most substantial hypothesis. But there is another put forward in 1927 by one of Bunyan's best critics, G. O. Griffith.[1]

Like Southey,[2] John Brown,[3] and all Bunyan's serious readers, G. O. Griffith is of the opinion that *The Heavenly Footman* resembles *The Pilgrim's Progress* more closely than does *The Strait Gate*.

But if it is to be proved that the *Pilgrim* grew directly out of the *Footman* it must be established that the two works were written at more or less the same time.

1. *What, then, was the date of* The Heavenly Footman?

Only one fact is certain: it was written after *The Law of Grace*, that is to say after 1659, since in it Bunyan recommends the perusal of that book.[4]

Having made this point, we are tempted, by reason of an indication in the book itself, to place it in the year 1660. For Bunyan writes that he has professed the faith for a little while only: " I have observed that little time which I have been a professor." [5]

But, as our psychological study of *Grace Abounding* demonstrated, our author's sense of time was very vague. Indeed Mr. Daniel

---

[1] *John Bunyan*, London, 1927, pp. 221–226.

[2] The ed. of the *Pilgrim* preceded by the *Life of Bunyan*; the 1881 ed., p. 84.

[3] It is in the 4th ed. of his biography that John Brown admits that *The Heavenly Footman* might well be the source, or the pretext of the *Pilgrim*. Our attention was drawn to this edition by the indefatigable searcher, Frank Mott Harrison. Cf. *John Bunyan, a Record of Recent Research*, typescript copy in the Library at Bedford, p. 71.

[4] *Heavenly Footman*, p. 273. " But I have treated more largely on this in my book of the two covenants."

[5] P. 272.

Gibson points out another example of this inexactitude when he draws our attention to two contradictory statements.[6]

(a) In the *Brief Relation of my Imprisonment* Bunyan refers to himself as having been, in 1660, a converted Christian of long standing.[7]

(b) In *The Heavenly Footman*, published, as we have just seen, in that same year 1660 at the very earliest, Bunyan describes himself as being but a neophyte.

Apart from its psychological interest, this comparison between the *Brief Relation* of 1672 and *The Heavenly Footman* prompts us to fix a second boundary.

As surely as *The Heavenly Footman* was written after 1659, it was written before 1672. For, if in 1672 Bunyan could describe himself in the *Brief Relation* as having been, in 1660, a long-standing member of the Bedford church, he would surely not have described himself as a Christian of short standing in a second book written in the same year, 1672. Hence 1672 marks a boundary.

But, by reason of this very statement in *The Heavenly Footman* which we have already quoted: " I have observed, that little time which I have been a professor " we think that the work saw light much earlier. However unreliable Bunyan was in his perception of duration of time, he could not have written this phrase in the years immediately preceding 1672, when he felt he could see so clearly into his past.

In our opinion the work was written shortly after 1666. After rather than before, for, while Bunyan published no fewer than nine books from 1660 to 1666, he published nothing from 1667 to 1671. It is reasonable to suppose that at that time he was writing the tracts that were published after his death,[8] the ones that he judged it better not to give the public himself for reasons unknown to us.

[6] Daniel Gibson, ' On the Genesis of the Pilgrim's Progress ', *Modern Philology*, 1935, vol. XXXII, p. 368.

[7] " Having made profession of the glorious Gospel of Christ a long time . . . I was apprehended at a meeting of good people in the country," p. 390.

[8] In 1689, *The Acceptable Sacrifice*; in 1692, *An Exposition on the Ten First Chapters of Genesis, Justification by Imputed Righteousness, Paul's Departure and Crown, Israel's Hope Encouraged, The Desires of the Righteous Granted, The Saint's Privilege and Profit, Christ a Complete Saviour, The Saints' Knowledge of Christ's Love, The House of the Forest of Lebanon, Of Anti-Christ and his Ruin.* In 1698, at last, *The Heavenly Footman.*

APPENDICES

2. *When was the* Pilgrim *written?*

If the *Footman* was written round about 1667, then the *Pilgrim* must have been written earlier than is generally supposed, if it grew out of the treatise. And this is precisely G. O. Griffith's opinion.

According to him the *Pilgrim* was written before 1672. Bunyan showed it to his friends and, on the advice of some of them, put it on one side to take it up again during his second imprisonment.

The reader will find on p. 168 of our study the psychological reasons which forbid us to accept this hypothesis; we cannot conceive of Bunyan having that patience in view of the tone of his *Apology*.

3. *Addendum* (1950)

Since the appearance of the French edition of my book, Miss Joyce Godber, by presenting a new hypothesis as to the date of Bunyan's second imprisonment, has made possible a new hypothesis as to the date of the composition of *The Pilgrim's Progress*. This hypothesis has been put forward by Miss Vera Brittain in a life of Bunyan so carefully documented that one can only regret its " romantic " form.

As all Bunyan's previous biographers, Miss Vera Brittain admits that the break in *The Pilgrim's Progress*, marked by the well-known ' So I awoke from my dream ', corresponds to an interruption in the writing of the work: the last third having been written at another period than the earlier section. Only, whereas, according to John Brown, the early section had been written by the time of the second imprisonment, the rest being finished at home, Vera Brittain believes that the allegory begun during the first imprisonment was afterwards abandoned, not to be taken up again until the second imprisonment.

Let us examine the arguments. If Bunyan was not re-imprisoned in the county gaol until December, 1676, the work which he had interrupted in order to devote himself entirely to *The Pilgrim's Progress* could not have been *The Strait Gate*, which was definitely published during the year 1676. But, according to Miss Vera Brittain, *The Pilgrim's Progress* grew out of an earlier work, *A Confession of my Faith, and a Reason of my Practice* (1672). Therefore it could only have been commenced during the first imprisonment, and put aside for several years, it was not returned to till 1676–1677, when Bunyan was once more in prison.

Moreover, continues Miss Brittain, since Bunyan was not released until July 1677, he could not possibly have had the time to write the remaining third of the book before December 22, on which date the book was entered at Stationers' Hall.

The only conclusion of Miss Brittain that seems to me sound—and even then it would be necessary to admit that Bunyan was certainly not arrested the second time before the end of 1676, that is to say, we must change Miss Godber's hypothesis into a certainty—is that *The Strait Gate* is not the seed from which grew *The Pilgrim's Progress*.

But Miss Brittain has not firmly established the relationship between *A Confession of my Faith* and *The Pilgrim's Progress*. Furthermore, her assertions: (1) that Bunyan could not have written the last third of *The Pilgrim's Progress* in five months of liberty, and, (2) that he interrupted his work for four years, seem to me unacceptable.

This vigorous book, in which one feels the pressure of creative force and creative joy, and the need to press forward as quickly as possible to the end of the road that lies ahead, this book could not possibly have been laid aside for four years. On the contrary, even Bunyan's pastoral duties could not have prevented him from writing in five months (July to December, 1677) the last section of this book which had so powerful a hold on him.

Certainly it is true that Bunyan enjoyed correcting the book after publication, and expanding it, but these retouchings do not prove, as Vera Brittain thinks, that Bunyan was satisfied to write his book slowly. But I have touched here on a question of the psychology of artistic creation which lies outside the scope of this note.

[See *In the Steps of John Bunyan*, by Vera Brittain, Rich and Cowan (London, 1950), pp. 15–33.]

NOTES ABOUT THE FIRST EDITION OF *THE PILGRIM'S PROGRESS*

EXCELLENT editions of the first edition of *The Pilgrim's Progress* [1] are now available to everyone and Bunyan's admirers can peruse this text at their leisure.

The spelling is often faulty, there are numerous turns of phrase which bespeak the oral style, and the grammar is irregular. [2] And, most interesting of all, the story differs a little from the one we read in all our modern versions.

Thus Christian sets out without seeing his wife and children again. The whole passage opening with " In this plight therefore he went home " as far as " I saw also that he looked this way and that way " is lacking, and with it, some degree of warmth and friendliness.

Christian does not come across Worldly-Wiseman until the second edition; nor does he encounter Evangelist a second time, nor confess his first errors to Good-will (p. 27 in the Venables–Peacock edition), nor speak of his wife and children with Charity.

Evangelist does not come to prepare Christian and Faithful for the persecutions at Vanity Fair (pp. 80–82); and if By-ends is there (p. 138 Elliot Stock edition) his portrait is incomplete since he is not given the opportunity of conversing with his friends Hold-the-world, Money-love and Save-all. This passage of high comedy does not make its appearance until the third edition.

No mention is made of the monument of Lot's wife, nor of Giant Despair's wife, nor of the trumpets of the King (p. 145 Venables–Peacock edition).

There is an excellent study of the various editions in James Blanton Wharey's notes, the Clarendon Press edition, 1928.

[1] (*a*) Edition published by Elliot Stock, 1895. (*b*) Edition of Noel Douglas, 1928.
[2] Consult John Brown, *op. cit.*, pp. 265–266.

PORTRAITS OF BUNYAN

1. The best portrait of Bunyan is Robert White's, a painter whose distinctive talent, according to Horace Walpole, lay precisely in his clever portraiture.[1] It is a pencil study (Crocherode Collection, British Museum) and Robert White first used it for his engraving of the sleeping man which served as frontispiece for the third edition of *The Pilgrim's Progress* (1679), and afterwards for the portrait which decorates the first edition of *The Holy War* (1682).

2. The National Portrait Gallery possesses a portrait done in oils by the painter Thomas Sadler, and it represents Bunyan at the age of fifty-six (1685). It was used in 1767 by Simpson, the engraver (in-folio edition of the works published by Johnston); towards 1780 by Richard Houston (a monochrome engraving, published by Carington Bowles); and in 1783 by T. E. Haid, and finally by Spilsbury.

3. The first in-folio edition of the works—1692—is illustrated by an engraving on copper by Sturt, after a "living" portrait done, Charles Doe assures us, by one of Bunyan's friends: "from an original paint, done to the life, by his very good friend, a limner" (cf. G. Offor, III, 767). Of this painter we know nothing, and the canvas, if it still exists, is at the time of writing unknown.

For more details on these questions see James Blanton Wharey, the Clarendon Press, 1928, edition of *The Pilgrim's Progress*, note A., pp. 329 *et seq.*

[1] Horace Walpole, *Anecdotes of Painting.*

BIBLIOGRAPHY

I GENERAL WORKS

Cambridge History of English Literature (art. " Bunyan ", vol. VI).
Cambridge Bibliography of English Literature (1940) (esp. Vol. II, 1660–1800).
Dictionary of National Biography.
Histoire de la Littérature anglaise, by H. Taine.
Histoire de la Littérature anglaise, by Emile Legouis and Louis Cazamian (Hachette).

II BIBLIOGRAPHICAL SOURCES

Anderson, J. P.   Bibliography of Bunyan's works and critical and biographical studies in Edmund Venables, *Life of John Bunyan*, London, 1888.
Brown, John   *John Bunyan, his Life, Times and Works*, London, 1885.
Harrison, Frank Mott   *Bibliography of the Works of John Bunyan*, Bibliographical Society, 1932.
   A Handlist of Editions of the First Part of the Pilgrim's Progress, Hove, 1941.
   " Notes on the Early Editions of *Grace Abounding*," *The Baptist Quarterly*, 1943, vol. XI.
Tindall, York   *John Bunyan, Mechanick Preacher*, New York, 1934.
Wharey, J. Blanton   *The Pilgrim's Progress* (bibliography of the first editions), Oxford, 1928.

III BUNYAN'S WORKS

All the references given refer to the complete edition of the *Works*, in 3 volumes, edited by George Offor, London and Edinburgh, 1862.
1. But the references to *Grace Abounding* and *The Pilgrim's Progress* are taken from the edition of Edmund Venables, revised and corrected by Mabel Peacock, Clarendon Press, Oxford, 1925.
2. The references to *The Holy War* and *The Heavenly Footman* are taken from the edition of Mabel Peacock, Clarendon Press, Oxford, 1892.

APOCRYPHAL WORKS QUOTED

T. S. (Thomas Sherman)   *The Second Part of the Pilgrim's Progress from this Present World of Wickedness and Misery to an Eternity of Holiness and Felicity*, 2nd ed., London, 1684.

Anonymous *The Pilgrim's Progress from this World to that which is to Come—The Third Part—Delivered under the Similitude of a Dream, to which is added the Life and Death of John Bunyan, Author of the First and Second Part, this Compleating the Whole Progress*, London, 1693.

IV   THE MORAL, RELIGIOUS AND POLITICAL BACKGROUND

A.   *Works from the XVI to the XVIII century*

Ames, William   *De Conscientia et eius iure vel casibus*, Amsterdam, 1630.

Bacon, Nathaniel   *A Relation of the Fearful Estate of Francis Spira in the year 1548, Compiled by Nathaniel Bacon, Esq.*, London, 1653.

Baxter, Richard   *A Holy Commonwealth*, London, 1659.

   A Christian Directory or a Summ of Practical Theologie and Cases of Conscience, London, 1673.

   The Reverend Richard Baxter's Last Treatise (1691), edited by Frederick J. Powicke with an introduction by George Unwin, Manchester, 1926.

   The Autobiography of Richard Baxter, edited by J. M. Lloyd Thomas, London, 1925, and Everyman edition.

Bayly, Lewis   *The Practice of Piety, Directing a Christian How to Walk that he May Please God*, edited by Grace Webster, London, 1842.

Beaumont, Agnes   *The Narrative of the Persecution of Agnes Beaumont in 1674*, edited by G. B. Harrison, London, 1929.

Bunyan Meeting   *The Church-Book of Bunyan Meeting*, 1650–1820 facsimile presented by G. B. Harrison, London, 1928.

Burrough, Edward   *Truth (the Strongest of All) Witnessed Forth in the Spirit of Truth, Against all Deceit*, London, 1657.

Canne, John   *A Voice from the Temple to the Higher Powers*, London, 1653.
   The Time of the End, 1657.

Collier, Jeremy   *Of Usury, Essays upon Several Subjects*, Part III, London, 1705.

Cook, John   *Unum necessarium, or the Poore Mans Case* : being an expedient to make provision for all poore people in the kingdome, London, 1648.

Crook, John   *A Short History of the Life of John Crook*, containing some of his spiritual travels and breathings after God in his young and tender years ; also an account of various temptations wherewith he was exercised and the means by which he came to the knowledge of the truth, posthumous publication, London, 1706.

Danvers, Henry   *Theopolis, or the City of God, New Jerusalem* (a commentary on chapters 20 and 21 of the Apocalypse), London, 1672.

   A Treatise of Baptism, with a brief Answer to Mr. Bunyan About Communion with Persons Unbaptized, London, 1673.

BIBLIOGRAPHY

Defoe, Daniel *The Complete English Tradesman*, vol. XVII, *Works* edited by Walter Scott, Oxford, 1841.
  The Family Instructor, vols. XV and XVI.

Dekker, Thomas *The Seven Deadly Sinnes of London* (1606), Cambridge, 1905.

Dent, Arthur *The Plaine-mans Pathway to Heaven wherein Every Man May Clearly See Whether he Shall be Saved or Damned*, 21st edition, London, 1631.

Edwards, Thomas *Gangraena or a Catalogue and Discovery of Many of the Errours, Heresies, Blasphemies and Pernicious Practices of the Sectaries of this time*, 2nd edition, London, 1646.

Evans, Arise *An Eccho of the Voice From Heaven or a Narration of the Life and Manner of the Special Calling and Visions of Arise Evans*, London, 1652.

Fiennes, Celia *Through England on a Side-saddle in the Time of William and Mary*, London, 1888.

Fowler, Edward *The Design of Christianity* (1671), 4th edition, London, 1760.
  Dirt Wip't Off or a Manifest Discovery of the Gross Ignorance, Erroneousness and Most Unchristian and Wicked Spirit of one John Bunyan, Lay-preacher in Bedford, London, 1672.

Fox, George *Journal*, 2 vols., Leeds, 1836.

Geree, John *The Character of an Old English Puritan or Nonconformist*, London, 1640.

Hobbes, Thomas *Leviathan*, Everyman edition.

Holmes, Nathaniel *Usury is Injury*, cleared in an examination of its best apologie alleaged by a country minister, out of Doctor Ames, in his cases of conscience, as a party and patron of that apologie, London, 1640.

Hooker, Richard *The Laws of Ecclesiastical Polity*, 2 vols., Everyman edition.

How, Samuel *The Sufficiencie of the Spirit's Teaching Without Human Learning* (1st edition, 1639, Holland), edition used, London, 1835.

Howard, John *State of the Prisons in England and Wales*, Everyman edition.

Hutchinson, Lucy *Memoirs of Colonel Hutchinson*, Everyman edition.

Keach, Benjamin *The Glorious Lover, a Divine Poem Upon the Adorable Mystery of Sinners Redemption*, 3rd edition, London, 1685.
  The Progress of Sin or the Travels of Ungodliness (1684), 4th edition, London, 1707.

Knollys, Hanserd *An Exposition of the Whole Book of Revelation*, London, 1689.

L'Estrange, Roger *Considerations and Proposals in Order to the Regulation of the Press* together with diverse instances of treasonous and seditious pamphlets proving the necessity thereof, London, 1663.

Lilburne, John *An Agreement of the Free People of England Tendered as a Peace-offering to this Distressed Nation* by Lieutenant Colonel John Lilburne, Master William Walwyn, Master Thomas Prince and Master Richard Overton, Prisoners in the Tower of London, May the first, 1649.

More, Sir Thomas *Utopia*, Everyman edition.

Morton, Nathaniel *New England's Memorial* (1669), Everyman edition.

Perkins, William *Works*, Cambridge, 1609 : esp. *The Arte of Prophecying*, vol. II.

Rogers, John *An Epistolary Perambulation or a Word to Everyone Round the World*, serving as preface to *The Time of the End*; see John Canne.

Smith, John *Select Discourses*, London, 1660.

South, Robert *Sermons*, vol. I, London, 1737.

Steele, Richard *The Tradesman's Calling Being a Discourse Concerning the Nature, Necessity, Choice, etc., of a Calling in General.* London, 1684.

Stubbes, Philip *Anatomie of Abuses* (1583), editor F. J. Furnivall, New Shakespeare Society, London, 1876.

Trapnel, Anna *A Legacy for Saints*; being several experiences of the dealings of God with Anna Trapnel in, and after her conversion (written some years since with her own hand), London, 1654.

Wesley, John *The Journal* (edited by Nehemiah Curnock), 8 vols., London, 1912.

   Sermons, 1st series, vol. VI of the complete works, 5th edition, London, 1860.

Wilson, Thomas *A Discourse Upon Usury*, by way of dialogue and orations, for the better variety and more delight of all those that shall read this treatise (1572), edited by R. H. Tawney, London, 1925.

Winstanley, Gerrard *An Appeal to the House of Commons, desiring their Answer*: whether the common people shall have the quiet enjoyment of the commons and waste land; or whether they shall be under the will of Lords of manors still, by Gerrard Winstanley, John Barker and Thomas Star, London, 1649.

B. Historical Studies and Modern Biographies

Barclay, Robert *The Inner Life of the Religious Societies of the Commonwealth*, 3rd edition, London, 1879.

Bebb, E. B. *Nonconformity and Social and Economic Life 1660–1800*, London, 1935.

Brittain, Vera *In the Steps of John Bunyan*, London, 1950.

Brown, Louise Fargo *The Political Activities of the Baptists and Fifth Monarchy Men in England During the Interregnum*, Oxford, 1912.

Bryant, Arthur *The England of Charles II*, London, 1934.

BIBLIOGRAPHY

Burrage, Champlin *The Early Dissenters in the Light of Recent Research* (1550–1641), 2 vols., Cambridge, 1912.

Carlyle, Thomas *Oliver Cromwell's Letters and Speeches*, with elucidations by Thomas Carlyle, 3 vols., Everyman edition.

Coulton, G. G. "The High Ancestry of Puritanism", *Ten Medieval Studies*, Cambridge, 1930.

Crouch, Joseph *Puritanism and Art, an Inquiry Into a Popular Fallacy*, London, 1910.

Ernle, Lord (E. R. Prothero) *English Farming Past and Present*, 3rd edition, London, 1922.

Firth, Sir Charles *Oliver Cromwell and the Rule of the Puritans in England* (1909), London, edition of 1933.

   Cromwell's Army, the History of the English Soldier from 1642 to 1660, 2nd edition, London, 1912.

Flynn, J. S. *The Influence of Puritanism on the Political and Religious Thought of the English*, London, 1920.

Gardiner, S. R. *History of England, 1603–1642*, 10 vols., London, 1883–1884.

Gooch, G. P. *English Democratic Ideas in the Seventeenth Century*, edition revised by H. J. Laski, Cambridge, 1927.

Green, J. R. *A Short History of the English People*, London, edition of 1889 and Everyman edition (2 vols.).

Hague, Dyson *The Life and Work of John Wycliffe*, revised and corrected edition, London, 1935.

Halevy, Elie "La naissance du méthodisme en Angleterre", *Revue de Paris*, 1906.

Hammond, J. L., and Barbara *The Village Labourer, 1760–1832, a Study in the Government of England before the Reform Bill*, London, edition of 1927.

Hauser, Henri "A propos des idées économiques de Calvin", vol. I of *Mélanges d'histoire offerts à Henri Pirenne*, 2 vols., Brussels, 1926.

Knappen, M. M. *Tudor Puritanism, a Chapter in the History of Idealism*, Chicago, 1939.

La Gorce, Agnes de *John Wesley, maître d'un peuple (1703–1791)*, Paris, 1940.

Lipson, E. *The Economic History of England*, 3 vols., 5th edition, 1929.

Macaulay, T. B. *History of England*, 4 vols., London, 1852, and Everyman edition.

Miller, Perry, and Johnson, Ths. H. *The Puritans*, New York, 1938.

Milsand, M. J. "The Quakers", *Revue des Deux Mondes*, 1850.

Neal, Daniel *The History of the Puritans, or Protestant Nonconformists, from the Reformation in 1517 to the Revolution in 1688*, 3 vols., London, 1837.

Ogg, David *England in the Reign of Charles II*, 2 vols., Oxford, 1934.

Palmer, F. "Les Anabaptistes", *Revue de Métaphysique et de Morale*, special number on the Reformation, 1918.

Pearson, Scott *Thomas Cartwright and Elizabethan Puritanism*, Cambridge, 1925.

Powicke, F. J. *A Life of Richard Baxter (1615–1691)*, London, 1924.

Schneider, Herbert Wallace *The Puritan Mind*, London, 1931.

Scholes, Percy E. *The Puritans and Music in England and New England*, Oxford, 1934.

Sée, Henri "Dans quelle mesure puritains et juifs ont-ils contribué aux progrès du capitalisme modern ", *Revue Historique* (1927), vol. 155.

Shaw, W. A. " Elizabethan Presbyterianism ", *English Historical Review*, October, 1888.

Tawney, R. H. *Religion and the Rise of Capitalism* (1926), London, edition of 1943.

Trevelyan, G. M. *England under the Stuarts*, 10th edition, 1922.

Troeltsch, E. *The Social Teaching of the Christian Churches*, English translation, 2 vols., London, 1931.

Trotter, Eleanor *Seventeenth Century Life in the Country Parish*, Cambridge, 1919.

Tulloch, John *Rational Theology and Christian Philosophy in England in the Seventeenth Century*, 2 vols., London, 1874.

Vattier, Victor *John Wycliff, sa vie, ses oeuvres, sa doctrine*, Paris, 1886.

Weber, Max *The Protestant Ethic and the Spirit of Capitalism*, English translation, London, 1930.

Whiting, C. E. *Studies in English Puritanism from the Restoration to the Revolution*, London, 1931.

Whitley, W. T. *A History of English Baptists*, 2nd edition, revised and corrected, London, 1932.

Workman, Herbert B. *John Wyclif, a Study of the English Medieval Church*, 2 vols., Oxford, 1926.

V   THE LITERARY BACKGROUND [1]

A. Poems, Stories and Essays

Bevis of Hampton *Sir Bevis of Hamtoun*, a metrical romance, now first edited from the Auchinleck MS. (by W. B. D. D. Turnbull), Glasgow, 1838.
The History of the Famous and Renowned Knight Sir Bevis of Hampton, London, 1662.

Browne, Sir Thomas *Religio Medici*, Everyman edition.

---

[1] Consult too " The Moral, Religious and Political Background ".

BIBLIOGRAPHY

Butler, Samuel *Characters and Passages from Note-books*, edited by Alfred Milnes, London, 1881.
> *Hudibras*, edited by Alfred Milnes, London, 1881.

De Deguileville, G. *The Pilgrimage of the Life of Man, Englished by John Lydgate A.D. 1426, from the French of Guillaume de Deguileville*, edited by F. F. Furnivall, with introduction, notes, glossary, and indexes by Katharine B. Locock. Roxburghe Club, London, 1905.

Defoe, Daniel *Moll Flanders*, vol. III, Complete Works, London, 1887.

Fuller, Thomas *Selections*, edited by E. K. Broadus, Oxford, 1928.

Johnson, Richard *The Seven Champions of Christendom*, 2 vols., London, 1755, and also edited by F. J. Harvey Darton, London, 1913.

Langland, William *Piers the Plowman*, edited by W. Skeat, 2 vols., Oxford, 1886.

Milton, John *Poetical Works*, Globe edition.

Overbury, Sir Thomas *The Miscellaneous Works in Prose and Verse*, edited by Edw. F. Rimbault, London, 1856.

Quarles, Francis *Emblemes*, London, 1639.

Sprat, Thomas "The History of the Royal Society of London " in J. E. Spingarn, *Critical Essays of the Seventeenth Century*, vol. II, Oxford, 1908.

Walton, Izaak *The Compleat Angler* (as it was originally published), London, 1876.

Wilson, Thomas *Arte of Rhetorique* (1560), edited by G. H. Mair, Oxford, 1909.

B. Literary Studies

Bennett, Joan "An Aspect of the Evolution of Seventeenth Century Prose ", *Review of English Studies*, vol. XVII, 1941.

Bone, G. D. "Tindale and the English Language ", *The Works of William Tindale*, by J. L. Greenslade, London, 1938.

Brown, John *Puritan Preaching in England*, London, 1900.

Bush, Douglas *English Literature in the Earlier Seventeenth Century*, Oxford, 1945.

Dottin, Paul *Daniel De Foe et ses romans*, Paris, 1924.

Dowden, Edward *Puritan and Anglican*, London, 1900.

Freeman, Rosemary *English Emblem Books*, London, 1948.

Grierson, H. J. C. *Cross Currents in English Literature in the Seventeenth Century—or the World, the Flesh and the Spirit, their Actions and Reactions*, London, 1929.

Jusserand, J. J. *L'épopée mystique de William Langland*, Paris, 1893.

Leavis, Q. D. *Fiction and the Reading Public*, London, 1932.

Lewis, C. S. *The Allegory of Love, a Study in Medieval Tradition*, revised and corrected edition, Oxford, 1946.

Macdonald, Hugh "Another Aspect of Seventeenth Century Prose", *Review of English Studies*, vol. XIX, 1943.

Masson, David *The Three Devils, Luther's, Milton's and Goethe's*, London, 1874.

The Life of John Milton, 6 vols., London, 1877.

Merril, Elizabeth *The Dialogue in English Literature*, New York, 1911.

Mitchell, W. Fraser *English Pulpit Oratory from Andrewes to Tillotson, a Study of its Literary Aspects*, London, 1932.

Owst, G. R. *Preaching in Medieval England, an Introduction to Sermon MSS of the Period, 1350–1450*, Cambridge, 1926.

Literature and Pulpit in Medieval England, Cambridge, 1933.

Ressler, Kathleen *Jeremy Collier's Essays, Seventeenth Century Studies*, edited by Robert Shafter, 2nd series, Princeton University Press, 1937.

Saintsbury, George *A History of English Prose Rhythm*, London, 1922.

Smith, David Nichol Essay on the " character ", *Characters from the Histories and Memoirs of the Seventeenth Century*, Oxford, 1918.

Spurgeon, Caroline *Mysticism in English Literature*, Cambridge, 1913.

Thompson, Elbert N. S. *Literary Bypaths of the Renaissance*, Yale University Press, 1923.

Willey, Basil *The Seventeenth Century Background*, London, 1934.

VI   STUDIES ON RELIGIOUS MYSTICISM AND PSYCHOLOGY

Works of a Religious Character.[1]

Aegerter, E. *Madame Guyon, une aventurière mystique*, Paris, 1941.

Augustine, Saint *Confessions*.

Brémond, Henri *John Henry Newman*, Paris, edition of 1932.

Delacroix, Henri *Essai sur le mysticisme spéculatif en Allemagne au XIVe siècle*, Paris, 1899.

La religion et la foi, Paris, 1922.

Guitton, Jean *Le temps et l'éternité chez Plotin et saint Augustin*, Paris, 1933.

Portrait de Monsieur Pouget, Paris, 1941.

Heiler, F. *La prière*, French translation, Paris, 1931.

Hügel, Frederick von *The Mystical Element of Religion as Studied in Saint Catherine of Genoa and her Friends*, 2 vols., 2nd edition, London, 1909.

James, William *L'expérience religieuse*, Paris, 1906.

Juliana of Norwich *Sixteen Revelations of Divine Love Shewed to Mother Juliana of Norwich*, 1373, London, 1920.

Kierkegaard, Sören *Crainte et tremblement*, Paris, 1935.

---

[1] Consult " Religious Background ".

BIBLIOGRAPHY

Leuba, James H. *Psychologie du mysticisme religieux*, translated by Lucien Herr, Paris, 1925.

Mainage, Th. *Introduction à la psychologie des convertis*, Paris, 1913.

Maréchal, Joseph, S. J. *Etude sur la psychologie des mystiques*, 2 vols., Paris, 1937–1938.

Messiaen, Pierre "Soeur Elizabeth de la Trinité", *Bulletin Joseph Lotte*, January, 1940.

Poulain, Aug., S. J. *The Graces of Interior Prayer (Des grâces d'oraison) a Treatise on Mystical Theology*, London, 1910.

Pratt, James Bissett *The Religious Consciousness*, New York, 1921.

Sabatier, Paul *Vie de saint François d'Assise*, 2nd edition, Paris, 1894.

Starbuck, E. Diller *The Psychology of Religion*, London, 1899.

Underhill, Evelyn *Mysticism, a Study in the Nature and the Development of Man's Spiritual Consciousness*, London, 12th edition revised and corrected, 1930.

Wahl, Jean *Etudes Kierkegaardiennes*, Paris, 1938.

Luther and Calvin

Andler, Ch. "L'esprit conservateur et l'esprit révolutionnaire dans le luthéranisme", *Revue de Métaphysique et de Morale*, special number on the Reformation, 1918.

Bois, H. "La prédestination d'après Calvin", *Revue de Métaphysique et de Morale*, special number on the Reformation, 1918.

Buisson, F. "Note additionnelle sur la Réforme française", *Revue de Métaphysique et de Morale*, special number on the Reformation, 1918.

Calvin, J. *Institution de la religion chrétienne*, original text of 1541, reprinted under the direction of Abel Lefranc, Paris, 1911.

Chevalier, J. "Les deux réformes : le luthéranisme en Allemagne, le calvinisme dans les pays de langue anglaise", special number quoted of the *Revue de Métaphysique et de Morale*.

Ehrardt, E. "Le sens de la révolution religieuse et morale accomplie par Luther", special number quoted of the *Revue de Métaphysique et de Morale*.

Febvre, Lucien *Un destin : Martin Luther*, Paris, 1928.

Kuhn, Felix *Luther, sa vie et ses oeuvres*, 3 vols., Paris, 1883–1884.

La Tour, Imbart de *Les Origines de la Réforme*, vol. III, *L'Evangélisme 1521–38*, Paris, 1914; vol. IV, *Calvin et l'institution chrétienne*, Paris, 1935.

Luther, Martin *A Commentary on St. Paul's Epistle to the Galatians*, London, 1940.

Will, Robert *La liberté chrétienne—étude sur le principe de la piété chez Luther*, Paris, 1922.

VII BIOGRAPHICAL AND CRITICAL STUDIES ON BUNYAN [1]

A New and Authentic Account of the Life and Death of Mr. John Bunyan, late minister of the Gospel at Bedford, written by a friend to the cause of true religion. London, printed for Alex Hogg, at the King's arms (No. 16), Paternoster Row.

Bain, J. A. Kerr *The People of the Pilgrimage, an Expository Study of the Pilgrim's Progress as a Book of Character*, 2 vols., Edinburgh, 1887–1888.

Blois, A. Kennedy de *John Bunyan; the Man*, Philadelphia, 1928.

Brown, John *John Bunyan, his Life, Times and Works*, London, 1885, and edited with marginal notes and addenda by Frank Mott Harrison, London, 1928.

Coleridge, S. T. *Literary Remains*, vol. III, London, 1838.

Doe, Charles *The Struggler*, given in the third volume of Offor's edition of Bunyan's complete works.

Firth, Sir Charles *John Bunyan*, The English Association leaflet No. 19, October, 1911; to be found also in *Essays Historical and Literary*, Oxford, 1938.

Froude, J. A. *John Bunyan*, London, 1880.

Grier, J. B. *Studies in the English of Bunyan*, Philadelphia, 1872.

Griffith, Gwilym O. *John Bunyan*, London, 1937.

Harding, Winboult R. *John Bunyan, his Life and Times*, London, 1928.

Harper, Ch. H. *The Bunyan Country, Landmarks of the Pilgrim's Progress*, London, 1928.

Harrison, Frank Mott *Some Illustrators of the Pilgrim's Progress* (part one), *John Bunyan* reprinted by the Oxford University Press, from the transactions of the Bibliographical Society, *The Library*, December, 1936.

Nathaniel Ponder, the Publisher of the Pilgrim's Progress, from *The Library*, December, 1934.

John Bunyan, a Record of Recent Research (1940). MS. Bedford Library.

Harrison, G. B. *John Bunyan, a Study in Personality*, London, 1928.

Kelman, John *The Road, a Study of John Bunyan's Pilgrim's Progress*, 2 vols., London, 1917.

Knox, E. A. *John Bunyan in Relation to his Times*, London, 1928.

Lindsay, Jack *John Bunyan, Maker of Myths*, London, 1937.

Lowes, John Livingston " The Pilgrim's Progress, Study in Immortality ", *Of Reading Books*, London, 1930.

Macaulay, T. B. Essays on Bunyan, vol. V and vol. VII of *Complete Works* London, 1866.

Pacheu, Jules *De Dante à Verlaine*, Paris, 1912.

---

[1] The books and articles that we have quoted constitute only a very small part of the biographical and critical literature devoted to Bunyan.

BIBLIOGRAPHY

Porter, Arthur *The Inside of Bunyan's Dream, the Pilgrim's Progress for the Man of To-day*, Chicago and London, 1927.

Shaw, G. B.[1] " Better than Shakespeare ", *Dramatic Opinions and Essays*, vol. I, London, 1907.

Southey, R. *Life of Bunyan* in his edition of *The Pilgrim's Progress* (1830), edition used, London, 1881.

Stevenson, R. L. *Bagster's Pilgrim's Progress*, vol. XXII of the Swanston edition of the Works, London, 1912.

Tindall, W. York *John Bunyan, Mechanick Preacher*, New York, 1934.

Trevelyan, G. M. Essay on Bunyan, *Clio, a Muse and Other Essays*, new edition, London, 1930.

Wharey, James Blanton *A Study of the Sources of Bunyan's Allegories, with Special Reference to Deguileville's Pilgrimage of Man*, Baltimore, 1904.

White, W. H. *John Bunyan, by the author of Mark Rutherford*, 1933 edition.

Whyte, Alexander *Bunyan Characters*, 4 vols., Edinburgh, 1893.

Willcocks, M. P. *Bunyan Calling, a Voice from the Seventeenth Century*, London 1943.

VIII   ARTICLES AND REVIEWS QUOTED

Draper, John W. " John Bunyan's Mr. Ignorance ", *Modern Language Review*, vol. 22, 1927.

Firth, C. H. " Bunyan's *Holy War* ", *The Journal of English Studies*, I, January, 1913.

Gibson, Daniel " On the Genesis of *The Pilgrim's Progress* ", *Modern Philology*, vol. 32, 1935.

Godber, Joyce " The Imprisonments of John Bunyan ", *Transact. of the Congreg. Hist. Society*, xvi, No. 1, Apr., 1949.

Golder, Harold " John Bunyan's Hypocrisy ", *North American Review*, vol. 223, 1926.

" Bunyan's Valley of the Shadow ", *Modern Philology*, vol. 27, 1929.

" Bunyan and Spenser ", *Publication of the Modern Language Association*, vol. 45, 1930.

" Bunyan's Giant Despair ", *Journal of English and Germanic Philology*, vol. 30, 1931.

Greene, H. E. " The Allegory as Employed by Spenser, Bunyan and Swift ", *Publications of the Modern Language Association*, vol. 4, 1889.

Hussey Maurice " Bunyan's Mr. Ignorance ", *Modern Language Review*, vol. xliv, No. 4, Oct., 1949.

Noyes, Alfred " Bunyan, a Revaluation ", *The Bookman*, October, 1928.

---

[1] G. B. Shaw makes frequent allusion to Bunyan in his prefaces, esp. that to *Man and Superman*.

Sharrock, Roger "Bunyan and the English Emblem Writers", *R.E.S.*, vol. **xxi**, No. 82, Apr., 1945.

Smyth, Mary W. "Puritan Bunyan and Catholic Dante", *The Nineteenth Century*, vol. 104, August, 1928.

Wharey, James Blanton "Bunyan's *Mr. Badman*", *Modern Language Notes*, February, 1921.

INDEX

INDEX

Dent, Arthur, 24, 44, 53, 71 (*notes*), 117, 206 (*note*), 210, 226, 230 (*note*), 232, 236, 237 (*note*), 276 (*note*), 284 (*note*), 288–9, 292

Design of Christianity, 99–102

Desires of the Righteous Granted, 316 (*note*)

Despair, *see* Giant Despair

D'Etaples, Lefèvre, 260

Diabolus, 244–7, 250–3, 267

Dickens, Charles, 218, 220

Differences in Judgment about Water Baptism, 105, 251 (*note*)

Diffidence, Mrs., 152

Dirt Wip't Off, 24, 101, 103 (*notes*)

Discontent, 198–9

Discourse on Liberty of Prophesying, 265

Discourse on Prayer, 271

Discretion, 148

Dissenters, beliefs of, 37; persecution of, 6–7, 12, 198; social motives of, 45–7, 286 (*see also* Puritans)

Dobrée, Bonamy, 235 (*note*)

Doctrine of the Law and of Grace, 5, 18 (*note*), 20 (*note*), 27 (*note*), 29 (*note*), 58 (*note*), 76–7 (*notes*), 79 (*note*), 109–13 (*notes*), 120 (*note*), 122 (*note*), 267 (*note*), 272 (*note*), 274–5 (*notes*), 315

Dod, John, 112 (*note*)

Doe, Charles, 11, 32 (*note*), 124, 308, 320

Dowden, Edward, 91, 207 (*note*), 256

Draper, John W., 212

Du Bos, Charles, 27 (*note*), 133, 176 (*note*), 271 (*note*)

Ebal and Gerizim, 10 (*note*)

Ecclesiastical Synod, 265

Edward, Jonathan, 33 (*note*)

Edwards, Thomas, 60 (*note*), 123, 265

Election, doctrine of, 60, 62, 80, 262, 275

Eliot, George, 191

Elizabeth, Queen, 296 (*note*), 311

Elizabeth of the Trinity, 45 (*note*), 78

Elstow, 1, 2 (*note*), 3–4, 25, 31–3, 57, 60, 63, 73, 90, 147, 186–7

Emblems, 179–80, 218

Emerson, R. W., 259

Emmanuel, Prince, 247, 250–5, 267

Enlightened Understanding, 242

Ernle, Lord, 294 (*note*)

Essay on Man, 212

Eston, John, 35

Evangelist, 142–4, 319

Evans, Arise, 23, 123 (*note*)

Everrard, 286

Exposition on the Ten First Chapters of Genesis, 280, 299, 300, 303, 316 (*notes*)

Faint-heart, 154, 187

Faithful, 76, 132, 150–1, 160, 190, 197–200, 206–7, 211, 218, 319

Fearing, Mr., 185, 213–4

Febvre, Lucien, 22, 55, 89 (*notes*)

Feeble-mind, 165, 213, 261

Few Sighs from Hell, A, 2 (*note*), 5, 29 (*note*), 36–7 (*notes*), 56 (*note*), 77, 89 (*note*), 116–8, 122, 181 (*note*), 223, 239, 282, 287, 291, 298, 300 (*note*)

Fielding, Henry, 214

Fiennes, Celia, 186

Fifth Monarchy, 250–1, 253, 301 (*note*)

Filon, Augustin, 145 (*note*)

Filth, Mr., 247

Finney, Charles G., 66

Firth, Sir Charles, 3, 43, 151, 163, 170, 172, 184, 188 (*note*), 192 (*note*), 248 (*note*), 311–2 (*notes*)

Five-mile Act, 5–6

Flatterer, 155

Flaubert, Gustave, 217

Forget-good, Mr., 246, 248, 255

Formalist, 146, 167

Forster, E. M., 218

Fowler, Edward, 24 (*note*), 99–103, 189, 212

Fox, George, 95 (*note*), 97, 123, 138, 185 (*note*), 265, 283

Foxe, John, 24

Franklin, Benjamin, 297

Free Discussion between two Intimate Friends, 100

Freeman, Rosemary, 179 (*note*)

Froude, J. A., 3 (*note*), 9, 20, 75, 158 (*note*), 253

Fuller, Thomas, 192, 232

Gaius, Innkeeper, 164

Gangraena, 60, 123, 265 (*notes*)

Gardiner, S. R., 38, 51 (*note*), 312 (*note*)

Geree, John, 107 (*note*), 278, 292, 301, 302 (*note*)

Ghandi, Mahatma, 217 (*note*)

Ghent, Henri de, 295

Giant Despair, 152–3, 183, 260

Gibson, Daniel, 315–6

Gifford, John, 4, 22, 35, 64, 83, 104, 200, 269

Gilpin, Bernard, 285

Godber, Joyce, 6 (*note*), 13 (*note*), 317–8

Godly-fear, 253, 255

Goethe, 145 (*note*), 176

Golder, Harold, 24, 164 (*note*), 170, 172–5, 183 (*note*)

Gooch, G. P., 46, 286–7, 311 (*notes*)

INDEX

Good Will, 144, 159

Gosse, Sir Edmund, 49, 235 (*notes*)

Grace Abounding, 17–30, 131–40; additions to, 19, 25; and Bunyan's psychological knowledge, 154; and Bunyan's spiritual life, 10, 52, 63, 65, 74, 81 (*note*), 83, 106 (*note*), 108 (*note*), 122 (*note*), 129, 173 (*note*), 175 (*note*), 213 (*note*), 242, 306, 315; as a work of art, 28; biographical value of, 1–4, 17–31, 203; compared with *Holy War*, 249; compared with *P.P.*, 155, 160, 177, 197, 201, 264; controversial opinions upon, 20–4; poetry and truth in, 129, 131–40; purpose of, 131; style of, 110, 134, 139, 255, 263

Great-heart, 160–1, 164, 189, 191–3, 202–3, 212, 307–8

Greatness of the Soul, 77, 79, 127 (*notes*)

Green, J. R., 3, 33 (*notes*), 193

Greene, Herbert Eveleth, 146

Gresham, Richard, 296 (*note*)

Grewe, John, 35

Grier, J. B., 216 (*note*)

Grierson, Sir Herbert, 50 (*note*), 305

Griffith, G. O., 31 (*note*), 315, 317

Grim, Giant, 189

Gripe-man, Mr., 209, 295

Grotius, Hugo, 33

Guilt, 154, 187

Guitton, Jean, 18, 21, 36 (*notes*)

Gulliver's Travels, 243

Hague, Dyson, 124 (*note*)

Hale, Sir Matthew, 8, 286

Hall, Christopher, 41 (*note*), 57

Hall, Joseph, 219

Hammond, J. L. and B., 294 (*note*)

Hampton Court Conference, 311

Hardy, Thomas, 164

Harper, Charles G., 186 (*note*)

Harrington, Anthony, 35

Harrison, F. Mott, 1–3, 17, 19, 165–6, 191–2, 315 (*notes*)

Harrison, General, 39

Harrison, Professor G. B., 53, 90 (*note*), 240

Hate-good, Lord, 7, 188

Haughty, Mr., 246, 254

Hauser, Henri, 290, 296 (*notes*)

Hawthorne, Nathaniel, 143

Hearne, Thomas, 24

Heath, Richard, 241 (*note*)

Heaven, Bunyan's idea of, 89–90

Heavenly Footman, 83–7 (*notes*), 125, 167, 177–80, 315–7

Heiler, F., 306–7 (*notes*)

Hell, Bunyan's idea of, 89, 116–8

Help, 143

Hill, N., 171 (*note*)

Hobbes, Thomas, 24 (*note*), 101, 102 (*note*), 189

Hold-the-world, 209, 319

Holmes, Nathaniel, 226 (*note*), 290, 292

Holy City, The, 10, 180

Holy Commonwealth, 37, 298 (*notes*)

Holy War, The, 240–56; allegorical characters in, 35, 54, 267; compared with *P.P.*, 180 (*note*), 255–6; contemporary allusions in, 37, 245–6, 250–1, 295; ending of, 252–3; interwoven themes of, 243, 253; merits of, 240, 254–5; sources of, 170, 241–2; theme of conversion in, 243, 249, 251

Honest, Father, 164, 203, 212–4

Hooker, Richard, 36, 287

Hopeful, 150–7, 160, 169, 190, 195–7, 200–1, 211, 223, 260

House of the Forest of Lebanon, 316 (*note*)

Howe, Samuel, 123

Hudibras, 23, 44, 120, 181 (*note*)

Hügel, F. von, 27, 31, 42, 61 (*notes*)

Hugo, Victor, 118

Hussey, Maurice, 209–10 (*note*)

Hutchinson, Colonel, 52

Hypocrisy, 146

Ignorance, 154, 157, 167–8, 196, 204, 209–12, 214

Imitation of Christ, The, 277

Inconsiderate, Mrs., 220

Incredulity, Mr., 246, 249, 252

Interpreter, The, 145, 160, 179, 191, 198, 208, 303

Ireton, Henry, 39

Isle of Man, The, 170, 240

Israel's Hope Encouraged, 316 (*note*)

I Will Pray with the Spirit, 10, 43 (*note*), 60 (*note*), 109 (*note*), 267–71 (*notes*)

James (*P.P.*), 165

James I, 311–4

James II, 12 (*note*), 13

James, William, 47, 57, 65–6, 80 (*notes*)

Jefferies, Lord, 188

Jerusalem Sinner Saved, 28, 29 (*note*), 55 (*note*), 58 (*note*), 119 (*note*), 126 (*note*), 128 (*note*)

Jessey, Henry, 24 (*note*), 32, 251 (*note*)

Jewel, Bishop, 312 (*note*)

Johnson, Richard, 172–3 (*notes*), 177

Johnson, Samuel, 145 (*note*), 176, 287 (*note*)

Johnson, Thomas H., 37–9, 45, 118 (*notes*)

Jonson, Ben, 187–8

INDEX

No Way to Heaven, 58, 109 (*notes*)
Noyes, Alfred, 79 (*note*), 161

Obstinate, 205, 207
Offor, George, 32, 54, 58, 99 (*notes*), 103, 170
Ogg, David, 286
O'Hara, Lt.-Col. Charles, 3
Old Tod, 238
Origen, 24 (*note*)
Overbury, Sir Thomas, 2 (*note*), 181 (*note*), 218-9
Owst, G. R., 112-3, 171 (*note*), 173 (*note*), 241 (*note*), 283 (*note*), 290, 303 (*note*)

Pagan, Giant, 150, 163
Paracelsus, 154
Parker, Samuel, 101 (*note*)
Parry, William, 9 (*note*)
Pascal, Blaise, 64, 109, 125, 270
Paul, Thomas, 105
Paul's Departure and Crown, 316 (*note*)
Peaceable Principles and True, 105
Peacham, 180
Pearson, Scott, 36 (*note*)
Péguy, Charles, 52, 118, 244
Pepys, Samuel, 309
Perkins, William, 22, 51, 108 (*note*), 115 (*note*), 123 (*note*), 183 (*note*)
Perpetuity of Seventh Day Sabbath, Questions about, 114, 261 (*notes*)
Petition of Rights, 314
Philips, Edward, 180
Piers Plowman, 291
Piety, 148
Pilgrim's Progress, The, 141-224; as a work of art, 214-24; background of, 184-94, 239; Biblical influence upon, 33, 138, 173-4, 182; biographical interest of, 54, 102, 155; borrowings in, 170-4, 178-9, 182; characters of, 194-214 (*see also individual names*); compared with *Piers Plowman*, 291; date of, 13 (*note*), 167, 169, 315-8; first edition of, 319; how written and published, 166-72; kinship of, with tales of chivalry, 174-5; making of, 172-84; 'marvellous' elements in, 172-7, 184; plot and symbolism of, 141-66, 176, 216, 303; realism in, 184-214, 295; style of, 133, 138, 155-6, 255-6; wide popularity of, 13, 169
Pilgrim's Progress, Second Part, 13, 158-166, 176, 189, 220, 261; second part by 'T. S.', 156 (*note*), 169; third part, 165
Plaine-Man's Pathway to Heaven, 44, 236

Plato, 122
Playfere, 107 (*note*)
Playford, John, 50 (*note*)
Pliable, 142-3, 204, 207
Poems by Bunyan, 10
Poiret, Pierre, 305
Polemical Works of Bunyan, 94-105
Ponder, Nathaniel, 165-6 (*notes*)
Poor Husbandman's Advocate, 254 (*note*), 289
Pope, Giant, 150, 163
Porter, Arthur, 144, 145 (*note*), 152, 200 (*note*)
Poulain, R. P. A., 305-6 (*notes*)
Powell, Vavasor, 124
Powicke, F. J., 97, 113 (*notes*)
Practice of Piety, 44, 269, 273 (*note*)
Pratt, James Bissett, 17 (*note*), 31, 83, 177
Predestination, belief in, 35, 60, 263, 276
Prejudice, Mr., 249-50
Presumption, 146, 161
Prison Meditations, 10, 77, 81 (*notes*)
Profitable Meditations, 10 (*note*)
Progress of Sin, The, 226 (*note*)
Prudence, 148, 192
Prynne, William, 50 (*note*), 189
Ptolemy, 255
Puritanism, historical outline of, 310-4; in Bunyan's time, 34-9, 45, 50-1, 84, 88, 191-3, 268, 276-7, 280, 309
Puritans, and Charles II, 12; and James II, 13; attitude and beliefs of, 25-6, 35-9, 51, 91-2, 117, 289, 309, 312; culture and amusements of, 50-1, 191-3; dress of, 39, 233; in Bedfordshire, 34-5; political and social aims of, 3, 45-7, 313; rule of, ends, 5-6, 12
Pym, John, 37

Quakers, autobiographical tradition of, 132; Bunyan's opposition to, 5, 94-9, 153, 277; persecution of, 12
Quarles, Francis, 180, 204 (*note*)

Rabelais, François, 233
Ransome, Arthur, 148 (*note*)
Ranters, 25, 52 (*note*), 60 (*note*), 95 (*note*), 97-8, 274
Ready-to-halt, 165, 192, 204, 261
Relation of the Imprisonment of Mr. J. Bunyan, 6-9 (*notes*), 75, 107 (*note*), 282 (*note*), 316
Reprobation Asserted, 261
Resistance, Captain, 245
Resster, Kathleen, 296 (*note*)
Resurrection of the Dead, 99

338

INDEX